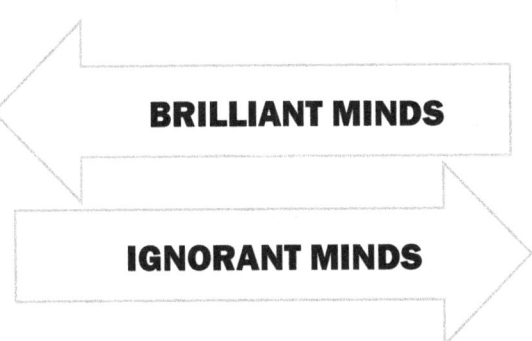

One Man's Journey

Through Racism

and Self-Discovery

VERNON M. O'GARRA

i

BRILLIANT MINDS, IGNORANT MINDS

One Man's Journey Through Racism and Self-Discovery

Dedication

To:

Dr. Alford H. Ottley

To my mentor, advisor, and big brother, who saw potential in his little cousin and fanned the spark into a flame. Thank you for teaching me the value of critical thinking and the power of the pen.

Contents

Preface

'Brilliant Minds, Ignorant Minds.' What does this statement mean? If you are a Black American or a person of color, talk to one of your White American friends or co-workers, maybe even your boss or CEO, about race. While they might be exceptionally skilled and knowledgeable in their profession, ask them a race question. You will likely discover their lack of awareness regarding the daily struggles faced by Black Americans.

Living in predominantly White neighborhoods, they are often unaware of how deeply race is ingrained in the fabric of American society.

The vast majority of White families in the community where I grew up were homeowners, own multiple cars, have substantial bank accounts, and have plenty of disposable income. They earn six-figure salaries, send their children to elite schools, and take two or three lavish vacations yearly. They have maximized their White privilege, and life is good for them.

Growing up in the suburbs of New York City, these are the White people I've known all my life. While not all White people are wealthy, they are generally faring much better than Black Americans and other people of the global majority.

They could care less about the underclass, and why should they? They have their one Black friend or co-worker. They know who Martin

Luther King was and who Barack Obama, Michael Jordan, and Michael Jackson are. "We're not racist," they will say, "We love Black people."

To that, I say, what about your racist family members and friends? You love them, too, and you've been around them your whole life. You've heard them talk poorly about Blacks as regularly as talking about the weather, and you've said and done nothing about it. The Police Officers, School Board officials, the Town Councilman, the Local Business Association members, and the Librarians have done it occasionally. Most Caucasians know who the racist people are in their respective lives and communities.

Still, they dare not disassociate themselves or speak out against them. They would never tell their kids that their great-great-granddaddy owned slaves and that their families became wealthy using the free labor of the enslaved.

What White people, in general, don't understand is that by not speaking up against racism, they become complicit. They seek to enjoy the benefits of their White privilege and the system of racial oppression, which they do on a daily basis. Consider how voting rights have been systematically dismantled.

Through tactics like gerrymandering, strict voter ID laws, and purging voter rolls, efforts have been made to suppress the voices of marginalized communities.

These measures disproportionately affect Black Americans and other people of color, undermining their political power and perpetuating racial inequities. The erosion of voting rights serves as a stark example of how systemic racism continues to operate, often with little opposition from those who benefit from the status quo.

Brilliant White minds have actively perpetuated racism and the legacy of Jim Crow, maintaining their impact since its inception. Simultaneously, the indifference of Ignorant minds ignores these societal injustices, providing fertile ground for systemic racism to thrive. This pervasive mindset extends into policy-making circles in the United States, shaping laws and regulations. White ignorance is not always unintentional or innocent; it can be deliberate and carefully crafted. This ignorance can manifest in the form of biased laws and rules that perpetuate discrimination against Black people, immigrants, and people of color. The quote from renowned Professor of Philosophy Charles W. Mills highlights the idea of active and aggressive ignorance that actively maintains and perpetuates systemic injustices. It emphasizes that this ignorance is not limited to the uneducated but can also be found at the highest levels of society, masquerading as knowledge. These words reflect the daily reality of African Americans. American Racism persists because White Americans fail to acknowledge the potential contributions Black Americans offer across various fields beyond sports and entertainment. Despite our expertise in politics, agriculture, education, economics, banking, and manufacturing, the ruling class often ignores our contributions. This cycle of ignorance perpetuates racist and unfair practices, persisting for decades.

As an African American man holding Bachelor's and Master's degrees in Business Administration and Healthcare Administration, respectively, I am qualified for numerous management and administrative roles within the healthcare sector. However, despite my expertise, I consistently face obstacles in advancing my career. I firmly believe that racial discrimination is the root cause of my professional stagnation.

In 2013, I filed a racial discrimination complaint against my employer, the Municipal Hospital System. Throughout my employment at this institution, I observed promotions to management positions were predominantly given to women and White men. My complaint was submitted to the NYS Division of Human Rights, which found probable cause that unlawful discrimination had occurred. My employer settled the first case by offering me a cash settlement, accompanied by a threat to drag out the case for several years if I refused.

Despite this settlement, by 2015, my situation had not improved. I remained in a low-paying clerical position for the entirety of my twelve-year career at Municipal Hospital. Consequently, I filed a second discrimination complaint against my employer, which forced me to endure the entire process again under more strenuous conditions. What I've found in my journey is that one of the major pitfalls for African American men in corporate America is Title VII legislation. This legislation identifies women as "protected class" individuals.

Through my research, I've found that this classification is used to help those holding the assigned "protected class" status gain much quicker access to the workforce and can matriculate up the corporate ladder into management significantly faster and in much greater numbers than African American men. In short, by assigning that status to women and others, people like myself, Black men, are getting overlooked by employers looking to meet their quota of "diversity" hires.

For example, under this law, African American women fulfill both race and gender criteria, which dramatically limits career opportunities for African American men. In the eyes of the law, African American men are deliberately excluded from "protected class" status, and it gives racist employers a free pass to pass us over. This law specifically creates challenges and barriers for African American men, which other groups don't have to deal with. We are victims of flawed legislation. In the end, when employers can't see past our race, they lean on following a law designed to hurt instead of help.

"Black men with the same skills as White men are only half as likely to rise from supervisor to manager," provided the Black men even get to a supervisory level occupation. (Cox, 2004). Their findings also "suggest that race and gender are not separate sources of discrimination but compound each other in limiting access to power and promotion. Elliot and Smith found that superiors (primarily women and white men) are much more likely to fill positions of power with subordinates of the same race and sex as themselves. This tendency toward in-group favoritism is stronger in filling higher-level managerial positions than in filling lower-level supervisory positions." (Cox, 2004).

Ironically, this same legislation permits employers to ignore and surreptitiously discriminate against African American men and other minority males with impunity. When you examine the makeup of corporate leadership and board of director structures of the average company in corporate America today, the absence of minority males is blatantly obvious. Research indicates that inside numerous companies across this nation, minority males, especially African Americans, are subjected to a human resource system that occupationally sorts us into sectors of the labor force that pay the least amount of money.

Housekeeping, transportation, security, food service, mail room, and civil servants are all essential jobs. However, they are occupations that pay low wages and restrict advancement opportunities (more so than other occupations) to move into management.

Conversely, high-paid salaried Executives, Administrators, and Directors are primarily women and Caucasian males who do not view Black men as equals. If diversity programs (DEI) diversity, equity, and inclusion were correctly administered, highly educated African American men would be allowed to realize the same career success as Caucasian men and women from all ethnic groups. The leadership structure where I was employed has turned a blind eye and a deaf ear toward the racial injustices that qualified and highly skilled minority males suffer inside the workplace.

When corporate leadership sits idly by and maintains a status-quo attitude, they are complicit in the discriminatory treatment that African Americans and other minority men must endure every day. It is an insult to the very idea of diversity when certain members of the workforce don't have access to the same opportunities as everyone else. Managing diversity, equity, and inclusion is more than simply promoting women. Diversity involves recognizing the value that qualified minority men can bring to the table.

There is a troubling racial climate that is prevalent in our society and inside the Municipal Health System where I am employed. I am committed to addressing this problem. That is my reason for fighting this injustice.

Human Resource professionals must do more to combat discrimination and promote inclusiveness. How long can we continue to bury our heads in the sand about the treatment of qualified African American men with aspirations of career advancement into management and leadership positions? We deserve the same opportunities as everyone else in the workforce. The thing about employment discrimination is that it can be hidden and swept under the rug. African American men can be very covertly excluded from high-salaried management positions, and complaints of discrimination can be challenging to prove.

This book is about one man's journey through legalized workplace discrimination, racism, and self-discovery. How he eventually sees how racism shapes his life and his legacy, and his struggles with how racism affects African Americans and is specifically aimed at Black men. His story explores how he has to fight every day of his life to deal with its insidious effects. The dynamics between Black men and women inside the corporate workplace are observed. The effects of diversity, equity, and inclusion initiatives and how these initiatives exclude African American men are observed. The psychological impact of racism on African American men and their relationships is observed.

This is the story of how these racial circumstances led to a discrimination lawsuit and the court's decision, a battery of attorneys, and limitless legal resources against one lonely Black Man.

The story and characters are based on several events drawn from various sources, including published materials and interviews. Although this story is based on actual events, certain long-standing institutions, agencies, and public offices are mentioned, but the characters involved are wholly imaginary. Any resemblance to persons, living or dead, is entirely coincidental.

1

Born Into Racism

1955, Emmett Till, Rosa Parks, and the Civil Rights Movement

I'm only a few months old, but I can feel my mother's tears landing gently on my face as she weeps for Mamie Till, mother of Emmett Till, who decided to leave her son's casket open so the world could see the horror of what had happened to her son.

"When she arrived at the train station to pick up her only son's remains, Mamie was outraged to see his ear severed, his teeth missing, and his eye hanging out of the socket. In an act that would change the world, Mamie Till-Mobley requested an open casket at his funeral and instructed the mortician not to touch the boy's face. Fifty thousand people are reported to have gone to Till's funeral. With permission from his mother, JET magazine ran photos of his body in the coffin in the article "Nation Horrified by Murder of Kidnapped Chicago Youth." Mamie Till-Mobley wanted people across America to see what two White men in Mississippi did to her son." (Jet Magazine, 1955), (Team Ebony, 2022).

My mom cried for him, but she also cried because she knew what lay ahead in life for her young Black son, who was born into racism in the United States. By the time I was twelve years old, my mother had told my brother and me how horrified she and our dad were to read the original Jet Magazine article with the photos of Emmett Till.

Later in life, my dad told me how the Brown v. Board of Education Landmark Supreme Court case affected his decision to leave NYC and move to Huntington, Long Island, to raise a family. "I wanted you and your brother to have an opportunity to get a good education," he would say. He told me that the courts ruled that racial segregation of children in public schools was unconstitutional, and that opened the door for our "Colored" children to get as good of an education as the White kids. My brother and I had no idea what Dad meant at the time, but we would soon realize his words had much meaning.

Before I was a year old, Rosa Parks was arrested in Montgomery, Alabama, for refusing to surrender her seat on a bus to a White passenger. The incident sparked the Montgomery Bus Boycott, led by Martin Luther King, Jr., which brought a renewed urgency to the civil rights struggle. Wow! Martin Luther King and the Civil Rights struggle in America, Malcolm X and the Muslim (Nation of Islam) movement, The Little Rock Nine, and lunch counter sit-ins that lead to the evolution of the Civil Rights protests of the sixties.

Unfortunately, I was just an infant. Still, my parents would provide my brother and me with a wealth of stories and history lessons about everything that was going on in the country during our childhood.

My brother and I quickly realized that growing up in the Lucille household (My mother Lucille's house) would turn into homeschooling at the Black History School of Higher Learning. By the time I reached fifth grade, my parents had ordered the Britannica Encyclopedia

Collection. My mother declared, "You and your brother are going to read every volume of these books." I looked at her in amazement, thinking, *there's no way I can read all these books.*

Both of my parents were athletes. My dad was a semi-pro baseball player who played with some of the old Negro League baseball players, and my mom played tennis with Althea Gibson. This love for sports was passed down to my brother and I, who played sports growing up.

The Civil Rights Act (CRA) of 1960 was signed into law by President Dwight D. Eisenhower on May 6, 1960. The Act established federal inspection of local voter registration rolls and introduced penalties for anyone who obstructed a citizen's attempt to register to vote or cast a ballot.

My mom took us to the grand opening of the Huntington Station Library. The local press was there, and my brother and I were in the Newsday Newspaper the next day.

Fifty-seven years later, I was at the same library writing this very book. I got up for a break to use the restroom, and the janitor, who was cleaning the bathroom, told me to go up to the second floor. I went up there to find the floor had been completely remodeled. It was my first time going up there. There was a wall of photos set up for Black History Month, and to my shock and amazement, there was a photo of my brother and I attending the grand opening of the Huntington Station Library. Unbelievable. I find myself wondering if this is some kind of good omen or something. Our names were not on the photo. I wondered how they got that picture.

Later, my brother told me to send the library the original newspaper clipping with our names on it. The only problem was that the original photo and newspaper article were in a storage locker with many of my family's personal effects. It would take me forever to find them.

But that entire day motivated me to stay focused while writing this book. I really needed a boost to keep going through the process. A few months had passed since I'd written consistently, and reading all this through again now had given me a new perspective.

Traveling with my dad

Throughout my childhood, my dad was an avid driver. He loved his automobiles (Pontiacs), and he loved to drive. Growing up, my dad took us on many trips across the United States.

We would travel to Montreal, Canada, to the EXPO 67 World's Fair. We also visited St. Louis, Missouri, for my cousin's wedding and a host of other places. There was no GPS in those days, so my dad bought all the latest Road Atlas Maps. As soon as a new map was available, my dad purchased it and studied it intensely.

On one of the many road trips, we went to Erie, PA, to visit my godfather, Hayes Houston. He was also one of my dad's army buddies, and I loved visiting him because he was a great guy. Plus, we had many cousins and family friends in Erie who were (basically) the same age as my brother, Billy, and me. During one particular trip, we went out to eat at a Chinese food place. It was my first introduction to Egg Foo Young, something I would come to love as I got older. Listening to my dad and

Uncle Hayes (what I called him) talk, I also got my first taste of how the government could screw us over whenever they wanted to.

"How's Detroit Duke and Slim?" Dad asked Uncle Hayes. "Remember how much fun we used to have in the Black Bottom?"

Uncle Hayes responded, "Ahhh... forget about all that. They demolished the entire town."

"What do you mean, Uncle Hayes? What are you talking about?"

"The U.S. Government demolished the whole place," Uncle Hayes repeated.

My dad paused, the almost forgotten memory coming back to him in his eyes. "Oh yeah," he said. "That Eisenhower Highway Act thing, that's right. All the best Black towns in the country were destroyed. Oh well, I guess we won't be taking that trip to Detroit."

I was too young to understand what my Dad and Uncle Hayes were talking about. As I got older, I learned about The Highway Act of 1956. The brilliant minds of the times that designed this new highway legislation would use this Federal Act to destroy once thriving and flourishing African American urban centers and business districts throughout the United States. The spirit of this initiative was to aid interstate commerce and improve travel throughout the country.

What ended up happening was the (complete) destruction of many Black townships and neighborhoods where residents sometimes got only pennies on a dollar for their properties. Many Black residents received no assistance at all with their relocation costs. Burgeoning communities in Houston, Dallas, Detroit, Chicago, New Orleans, Buffalo, Miami, and Virginia all succumbed to the new "Urban Renewal" program under the guise of what the government called the slum clearance objective. These wonderful Black communities were turned into parking lots and highways because, under this initiative, President Eisenhower allowed each state to build highway systems that were designed to extinguish Black townships and business districts.

It was tragic and terrible, and a part of our life, and my first introduction to it was through a random conversation between my Dad and godfather, who I called Uncle Hayes.

1963 – News of the world through a child's eyes

It's 1963, I was eight years old. The country seemed to turn extremely violent towards Black people. I was inquisitive and always asked questions about what was happening in society. One day, I overheard my parents talking at the kitchen table, and it was not a happy conversation, as sometimes they weren't. Civil Rights leader Medgar Evers was murdered, and my parents were very upset about it. My parents were saying how President Kennedy was speaking out against racism and how the KKK murdered Medgar Evers and would never be prosecuted. My dad said the Ku Klux Klan could kill Black men in Mississippi and get away scot-free. My Mom also told us that Medgar Evers led boycotts and voter registration drives. It wasn't only Martin. Medgar did a lot for his people to fight against segregation.

"What does segregation mean?" I asked.

"Well," Mom told me, "You know how Blacks and Whites go to school together in your school? In Mississippi, there were *'Whites Only Schools'* and *'Blacks Only Schools.'* That's Segregation. It means separation based on race."

That was a new concept for me as a kid. The street we lived on was mixed. There were White families on either side of us and Black families across the street. There were about eight Black and White kids, girls and boys, all around the same age, and we played together every single day. Sometimes, we fought each other, but mostly, we played. We also understood what racism and hate meant.

Every night, I watched the news with my Mom or Dad, and it seemed like something terrible was always happening to Black people. I remember looking up at my Mom and telling her I didn't want to go to summer camp or YMCA anymore. Those White kids tortured me every day. Calling me racist slurs like Nigger, Coon, or Black Sambo. In response, my Mom politely asked,

"Did any of those White boys put their hands on you?"

"Nope," I said, "Just a lot of talk."

"Well then, you will definitely be at camp tomorrow because you and your brother have to show those White kids that you are better than they are."

I didn't understand it at the time, but as the years passed, it became clear to me what my mother was telling me and what point she was trying to make.

The March on Washington happened on August 28th, 1963. Martin Luther King's famous "I Have a Dream" speech was epic. My Mom kept us home from school and had us watch King's speech on television. Shortly after, she purchased it on vinyl and would play it on a turntable (old school).

A month later, on September 15th, a bomb blast at the Sixteenth Street Baptist Church in Birmingham, Alabama, killed four African American girls during church services. At least fourteen others were injured in the explosion. To my young mind, it seemed like all hell was breaking loose. Civil unrest was erupting in major cities around the country. In Birmingham, Alabama, police used vicious dogs and fire hoses to attack anyone (primarily Black folks) who was involved in civil rights demonstrators.

My parents were great at making sure my brother and I had fun growing up and didn't get depressed with all the racial unrest in the nation. My parents, aunts, uncles, and cousins made sure we were always aware of what was happening.

There was a loud bang on our front door one night during TV time. I got up to go to the door, and my Dad told me, "Boy, get away from that door. I'll answer it." My Dad carefully opened the door, but no one was there—only a burlap sack. My Dad looked into the sack to find a dead raccoon.

"What the hell is this!" he exclaimed. Upon looking into the sack, he found a dead raccoon inside. "They're calling us Coons. Let me get rid of this." My Mom said, "Wait, Harold. Please don't throw it away. Bunny knows how to cook Coon. We'll bring it to her."

The next day, we rode over to my mother's friend Bunny's house, and my Dad gave her the sack. She looked at the raccoon, thanked my parents, and told them that she would cook that coon to perfection. I looked at Ms. Bunny like, *do my ears deceive me? You're really going to cook that raccoon??* On the drive home, my Mom and Dad laughed and cracked jokes about the raccoon. Ms. Bunny reminded me of 'Granny' on The Beverly Hillbillies. Granny knew how to cook "coon". We always knew how to turn lemons into lemonade or raccoon in a tasty meal. That's a part of the Black experience, how we can turn scraps into goldmines.

Cousin Tootsie

The year ended with John F. Kennedy's assassination. His death was way too much for an eight-year-old kid to comprehend. Still, my parents drilled it into our young minds regularly. Shortly after President Kennedy's assassination, my cousin "Tootsie" appeared on Dick Clark's "American Bandstand."

My cousin Cassandra (Tootsie) was like our big sister. Tootsie would watch, feed, and discipline us when our parents were not around. Sometimes, she let us get away with mischief and nonsense so long as we didn't get into too much trouble. Tootsie was a teenager, and as teenage girls can be, she'd get pissed if her watching us got in the way of her going to a party or hanging out with her friends, but she'd do it anyway. I always like to think that it was because even though she was older, she was a kid just like us. We were on the same team.

Tootsie lived in the Bronx with my grandmother, aunt, and my aunt's son, Ronald. Her mother passed when she was little, and her father, my uncle, gave up custody of her to my grandmother. Family could be that way, sometimes fractured by the troubles of the world. But like a Black family, we took care of our own. My grandmother stepped up and cared for her like she was her own.

My family lived in Long Island, but despite the distance between us, we were one big happy family. Now, Tootsie loved to dance and was good at it. She knew all the latest dance steps and sometimes practiced them with her classmates in the apartment. She was the one who kept us up to date on all the latest trends.

The older Tootsie got, the more plugged in with the New York Party scene. When the Dick Clark American Bandstand Show came to New York, she knew right where to go for auditions. I don't doubt that Tootsie was the best dancer there, either. And it showed because even though she was a "Negro" (as we were called back then), she was selected as one of the first Black people to appear on American Bandstand.

The day Tootsie was on television, our entire family surrounded the television set, and we were all screaming for her! *That's my cousin right there! She's on national television!* I rode on that high for weeks after, telling anybody I could that my cousin was on the biggest dance show in the nation.

After High School, Tootsie enlisted in the U.S. Military. We were proud of her. She'd show up all clean-cut in her fatigues during her annual visit, looking sharp as a tack. And when she was gone, she wrote to us now and then, and we looked forward to reading every letter.

But time passed, and we lost touch as the years rolled by. It happens with family sometimes, and by that point, she was an adult in her own life.

In one of her letters, Tootsie told us she was stationed at an Army Base in Virginia. We started planning a family road trip to see her, but she was shipped out just like that.

We got word that she was killed in an accident. She was operating a military vehicle at the time. I remember thinking that it wasn't fair. Tootsie was still young, with a whole life left ahead of her. And how long had it been since we'd seen her? How could she be just…*gone?*

I still hold Tootsie in my heart to this day. The young girl who taught me to dance and looked the other way when I did little things that might get me into big trouble. Who looked out for her little cousins and kept us fed and safe. Tootsie was a big part of my life; I will never forget her. R.I.P.

1964 – Peg Leg Bates Country Club and the Swimming Pool Incident

In the Summer of 1964, my parents took us to a resort in the Catskill Mountains in New York. We stayed at the Peg Leg Bates Country Club. Bates was the first Black resort owner in Ulster County, New York, in the Catskill Mountains.

All my parents' friends were there, and we were having a blast. I remember there was a beautiful swimming pool that we were not allowed to swim in without our parents present. I distinctly remember my Dad telling my brother and me to "stay out of the pool" as he walked off with my Mom. It was a hot summer day, and that pool looked so tempting (to us) as we stood there with the sun beating down on our skin. Finally, my brother couldn't wait any longer. He walked over to the deep end of the pool and climbed up onto the diving board. I screamed at him, "What do you think you're doing? You heard what Daddy said! Get off that diving board!!"

"I can swim, don't worry," Billy yelled back. "I will just take a quick dip."

Before I knew it, Billy jumped into the pool. I stood there, shocked and frozen, as it happened right in front of me. He hit the water with a splash, then sank like a brick straight to the bottom of the pool. A few seconds passed before he came back up again, arms flailing, water splashing everywhere. Then he sank right back down again.

I panicked and started screaming *help, help, help*!!! "My brother can't swim! Help, help!!!" Luckily, the lifeguard appeared out of nowhere with a twenty-foot pole. He didn't even jump in the pool to save my brother Billy. He just stuck the pole into the water for my brother to grab and dragged him to the side of the pool. I ran around to the edge of the pool, where he was to pull him out. He was coughing and spitting up water. "What the hell is wrong with you?" I screamed. "Don't you know I can't swim? You almost drowned, you dummy."

My Dad returned to the pool to see my brother soaking wet and crying uncontrollably. As he consoled him, I gave my Dad the rundown of what happened. Billy jumped in and almost drowned, and the lifeguard had to come and save him. We were a mess!

If I had to sum up my brother Billy's personality in a story, that's the one I always tell. That's my brother, a knucklehead who never listens and does his own thing. This attitude was born into his DNA and would follow him into adulthood.

Just Enough for The City

I was nine years old when my Dad came home from work early, upset and irritable, with a fire lit under him. My family had been experiencing more violence around the neighborhood in the city lately, and the effect of that had finally come to a head. My grandmother had been knocked down in the street coming back from the grocery store. The incident was just the final straw in a rash of violence all around.

My Dad told us, "My mother, sister, and little nephew are not safe in the city by themselves. I'm going to bring them out to Long Island to stay with us for a week or so until this violence dies down". When I asked what happened, he started telling us about a Black student who was shot and killed by police in front of his friends and about a dozen other witnesses. About 300 students from a nearby school spilled out into the streets and began rioting. This incident set off six consecutive nights of civil unrest that affected the Bronx, Brooklyn, and Harlem areas. At the time, my grandmother lived in the South Bronx, right in the middle of all the strife. The decision was made, and my Mom said we had to pick up Grandma that night. She gathered us together, packed a dinner bag to munch on, and we hit the road, headed to the Bronx, New York.

This is what life was like in the sixties (1960s), the major differences between Whites and Blacks in America. Many of the White kids I grew up with in the neighborhood regularly called us niggers or some other racial slur, not so much because it was racist but more as a way of teasing and insulting us. We would fight them, curse them back, and the next day, we would be playing again like best friends. Racial disharmony was a part of our existence and even our language. That kind of thing was like any other day for me as a child.

For example, if there was one place where I got the most racial slurs hurled at me, it was the local YMCA. My Mom enrolled me in a swimming class one summer. I imagine this was because of my brother almost drowning earlier that summer at the Peg Leg Bates Country Club. Swimming class was a real drag, mainly because of how brutal the White kids were to me. "Little Black Sambo, your dick looks like a burnt-up hotdog! Go back to Africa!" I'd have to listen to shit like that at every practice. That was a very long and agonizing four weeks. Despite the efforts of the White kids to discourage me, I ended up completing the class, and I learned how to swim.

A few months later, Malcolm X was assassinated. Our parents sat my brother and me down and told us the story about his life. Although we were too young to understand everything about him, as the years passed, we realized Malcolm X was a great man and one of the most influential leaders in African American history.

The Talk

By the time I was twelve years old, I was beginning to understand the world around me. That was around the time my Dad sat me down one day to have *"The Talk."* No, not that talk. This was the talk that every Black father had to give to his Black children so that they knew how to be safe in this world.

He started by asking me what I knew about the police. I tell him this story:

"I was walking home one evening after my basketball game at the rec center, and these two cops pulled up beside me in their squad car.

"Hey, come over here," one said as he leaned out the window. I walked over to them, and he looked me up and down and asked, "Where are you going? Do you live around here?"

"Yes, I do," I responded. "I'm on my way home."

"Are you sure?" the cop asked.

"Yes, I'm sure."

"Did you go to school today?"

"Yes, I went to school today," I responded.

"What's your name?"

"My name is Miles…"

"Miles What?" The cop asked, looking me over as if I might be hiding something. I didn't know why they were stopping me or what these questions were about, but I had a distinct air of fear around me as he narrowed skeptical eyes at me.

I swallowed hard and responded with my name. "Miles Livingston."

I don't know what I expected to happen next, but whatever it was they were looking for, I didn't have it, and that seemed pretty clear to them for one reason or another because the cop ended up saying, "Alright, you better get home now and stay out of trouble."

And that was it. They drove off, leaving me puzzled by the entire encounter. That was the first time I had ever been questioned by the cops, and I didn't even know why."

When I was done telling my Dad the story, he nodded as if in approval. Then he told me always to obey the police. "They can take your life in a heartbeat over nothing. They hate Blacks and have no respect for us. Avoid altercations with the police at all costs. It's a no-win situation. Do you understand me, son?"

"Yes, Daddy, I understand."

Whenever the topic of police came up with friends at school, my cousins, or any of my peers, we all shared similar stories with our parents or uncles about how to avoid situations with cops. The bottom line was that the police are extremely dangerous and should be avoided if at all possible because, for us, it could mean the difference between life and death.

...And a Happy New Year

Racial turmoil aside, my Mom was busy making the season bright come the holidays. It was snowing, and I felt like any other kid. Playing in the snow, messing around with my friends, taking advantage of snow days.

I distinctly remember Mom humming and singing to herself in the kitchen a few days after Christmas when the snow had freshly fallen outside and was glittery from the bright sunlight in a clear blue sky. I couldn't wait to get out in the snow, track it all up with my boots, and make snowballs to throw at my brother.

My Mom seemed to be in a good mood during the holidays anyway, but that year felt special somehow. I remember walking into the house after enjoying a fine winter day and stepping into a glorious cloud of warm and inviting smells. Mom had been cooking all day.

"Hey Ma'," I asked her as I entered the kitchen. "What's going on? Why are you cooking all this food, and why is the tablecloth on the table?"

"Your Aunts are coming over," she said. "I want you and your brother to get yourselves cleaned up, and I need you to go to the market and pick up some items for me." I hadn't even gotten my coat off when she handed me a shopping list and some money. I took it without complaining. My aunts coming meant we were about to have a big dinner and family time, which we always looked forward to.

"Make sure you count your change!" Mom called after me as I bolted out of the house.

To my Mother's joy, I practically ran to the store. On the way, I ran into my friends Debra and Freddy, and they came along with me.

"Hey Miles, The Supremes are going to be on television tonight," Debra exclaimed.

"Really?"

"YES!" Freddy practically screamed. "On the Ed Sullivan Show."

"Oh, Wow!" That's when it occurred to me that *that* was why my Aunts were coming over, and my Mom was making a big dinner! Debra told me that The Supremes were going to be the first Black singing group to ever be on television. It wasn't just big news. It was an event.

Later that night, my aunts and my cousins came over. It's eight o'clock, showtime. The Supremes came on, and they rocked the house. Wow, my family is so happy to see them perform. My Mom is dancing around and singing along. It's truly a historic night.

Less than a month later, Sidney Poitier won the 1964 Academy Award for Best Actor for his performance in the film, "Lilies of the Field." He was the first African American man to win a Best Actor Oscar. My parents were so happy for him that you'd think he was a personal friend or a member of our family. My Dad took us to the drive-in theatre over the summer to see the movie; I remember it well. My parents dressed us up in our pajamas, and all the kids would play in the drive-in theatre playground until the movie started. Then, our parents would let us stretch out in the back of the station wagons, which were like today's SUVs in comparison, and we'd watch the movie. Most of us kids would fall asleep before the movie ended, so all the parents had to do was drive home and put us right into bed. That's how we rolled back in the day.

1967 – The first Black Supreme Court Justice, Race Riots in Detroit, and My New Shoes

In July of 1967, there were two major events in America. Thurgood Marshall became the first African American to become a United States Supreme Court Justice. A week later, Detroit erupted in civil unrest for five days. Forty-three people were killed, more than a thousand were injured, and seven thousand were arrested. Of the two events, I ended up doing a book report a year later, which covered the events of the racial unrest, using a book entitled "Nightmare in Detroit."

At some point during all this, I asked my parents for a pair of Converse Chuck Taylor basketball sneakers, but they refused to buy them for me. Back then, it was as if the kids of today wanted a pair of $300 Jordans. Instead of the Converse, my Mom brings me a pair of John's Bargain Store Skip sneakers.

"Mom!" I exclaimed, mortified that she would bring those in the house instead of my Chuck Taylor Converse. "I can't wear skips to school! It's embarrassing."

She said," Look, boy, you'll wear those sneakers I bought and like it!"

What Mom didn't understand was that I attended a school with what I viewed as a wild bunch of ghetto kids and country-ass niggers as my classmates. At the time, I was just a young, skinny kid. The last thing I wanted was to get caught wearing Skips or what we used to call cheap sneakers. Back then, if you weren't wearing Converse, Pro-Keds, or

Adidas, you were wearing Skips, and believe me, you did not want to be caught out there in Skips.

The next school day, I put on my cousin's "hand-me-down" sneakers, which I'd been wearing before, instead of the new shoes my Mother brought home. Those shoes had holes in both soles, and the sides were striped, but at least they were Converse. As soon as I walked out of my room with those sneakers on, my Mom looked at my feet and said, "Take those shoes off and put on the new ones I just bought for you."

"Aww, Mom, do I have to???"

"Yes, you have to. Now go and put them on."

Reluctantly, I go to my room and put them on. There was no point in arguing, and in the back of my mind, I knew I was in for a rough day, wearing brand-new Skips instead of my old ratty Converse.

I managed to make it to the bus stop without being seen in those shoes. When I was waiting for the school bus, one of my loudmouth friends walked up and said, "Hey, Miles, what kind of sneakers are those? I never seen them before."

I tried to play it off and say, "Oh, these are the new 'Coach Cons.' They just came out."

He looked at my feet, his nose turned up skeptically. "They don't look like Coach Cons to me."

That was just the beginning of a long day that started from the moment I got on the bus all the way until school was over and I was on my way home. I'd been teased and poked fun over those shoes all day. I felt like throwing those things off a bridge and just going barefoot.

While I was riding the bus home, a group of rough-neck bullies attacked me. They held me down and took off my sneakers, then threw them out the window of the bus. It seemed like I'd gotten my wish. After I got off the bus, I realized I would have to walk back to the spot where they threw out my sneakers and then walk home. As I had envisioned, it was a terrible day, and my friends teased me for a long time.

The Summer of '67 and the Fall of a King in '68

The following year, I had a newspaper route around the summertime. I had been saving up my pennies, so when school finally ended for the summer, I found myself with a few dollars in my pocket. On top of that, my parents decided that my brother and I could spend the summer in Brooklyn, NY, with our cousins. Me and Billy were ecstatic with joy! Finally, we had a chance to get out of Huntington and be with our cousins in an All-Black community. It was heaven for us.

By the time we ended up with our cousins in Brooklyn, the Circus had come to town. We missed it a month earlier in Long Island, but now that the Circus was in Brooklyn at the same time I was, I couldn't wait to go. What was better than that was that I had my own money this time! During the first few days in Brooklyn, I was bugging my cousins to take us. It was all I could think about.

It wasn't until my cousin reluctantly told me we couldn't go. It was about a day or so into my campaign to get us to the circus.

"Why not?" I asked him.

"That Circus is in the wrong part of town."

"The wrong part of town," as it turned out, was the part of Brooklyn that Black people weren't allowed to go to, Sheepshead Bay. It wasn't like official segregation or anything. However, if we were caught on that side of town, we ran the risk of facing violence or even being run out of the neighborhood by the White residents.

"They don't come into our neighborhood," my cousin told me, "and we don't go into theirs." That was all that needed to be said about it. I was extremely disappointed, but by then, I understood the racial climate of the times.

It was still an amazing summer. I witnessed a shootout, rode on the back bumper of a NYC bus, and "watched" a bunch of my friends ride up and down on a housing project elevator. One thing I loved doing was going to the playground to watch the girls jump double-dutch. It was amazing to me how skilled these girls were when jumping rope. I could watch them for hours. Sometimes, the simple things in life give you the most pleasure. This was crazy stuff for a kid from Long Island.

At the same time, across the river in New Jersey, there was a race riot going on. But they weren't the only ones. Riots were happening in other cities, like Detroit, and they seemed to be lasting for days and days. The News was shocking to me, and as I was entering my teen years, I was beginning to have an understanding of one thing – Blacks were not welcome in America.

By the end of the summer and the beginning of school, we all vowed not to say the pledge of allegiance anymore. Every Black kid I knew swore that from then on, at every assembly, sporting event, and morning pledge, we would all stay seated in defiance against what was happening to Black people all over the country. My brother and I were too young to understand the gravity of what was happening around us, but we knew everything was happening because of the color of our skin. It all ended up coming to a head on April 4, 1968, when Dr. Martin Luther King, Jr. was assassinated in Memphis, Tennessee. The entire country blew up. To add to the budding unrest on the East Coast, one hundred twenty-five cities in twenty-nine states experienced mass rioting. By April 11th, forty-six people were killed, and thirty-five thousand were injured in these confrontations. By June, JFK's little brother Robert was killed in L.A., and the world seemed like it had cracked open at the seams.

Our parents kept us home from school during the coming week of unrest. To keep us busy, they enrolled us in various activities designed to get us to interact better with the White kids in the neighborhood. Still, throughout all that was happening, my parents believed in Dr. King's hope for unity among the races. As a result, my brother and I were signed up for the church choir, and various activities at the YMCA, including Little League baseball, and Summer camp. It was a nice idea. I just wish someone had told the white kids that.

We were routinely called racial slurs, and we spent our days in arguments and fistfights against racist white kids. During that time, Thurgood Marshall was appointed as the first Black Supreme Court

Justice, and Shirley Chisholm was the first Black woman elected to Congress. Olympians Tommie Smith and John Carlos, who won gold and bronze medals, protested while playing the U.S. national anthem at the 1968 games in Mexico City by holding up clenched fists, the symbol for Black Power. It seemed like we were all battling against racial injustice in our own ways, with our fists, through the law, or by showing solidarity.

The show of support from John Carlos and Tommie Smith had a direct effect on me at the time. I remember going to the convenience store with my cousin and getting that poster for my bedroom wall. I hung it proudly, right next to my poster of Angela Davis.

That summer, James Brown released his epic hit - *"SAY IT LOUD, I'M BLACK, AND I'M PROUD."* When the school year began, all of us Black students had an air of confidence and self-worth as we walked the halls of our respective high schools. That record validated our feeling of Black Pride.

Keeping on Track

Huntington Middle School instituted a "Tracking System" when I was a kid. The system placed students on a track based on their test scores, from one to four. In short, track one was for the most intelligent students, and track four was for the students presumably with lower intelligence. In a move that wasn't a surprise, most Black boys were placed into track four. It was one of the first times I ever heard my Mother admonish and browbeat my teacher. It made me feel proud to be her son. When she found out that I would be put into track four, she told my guidance counselor, in no uncertain terms, that I would *not* be separated from the rest of the students. "They should all be in class together and be able to learn from each other. You are discriminating against these Black students, and I am taking my son out of this school. I will be filing a complaint with the principal."

My mother didn't stand alone. She and all the other Black parents banded together and, in protest, kept many of the Black male students home until the policy was changed. It didn't take long. The experience was a sign of solidarity for the Black students, and we felt proud that our parents supported us.

Before long, I was in high school and already stretching my athletic legs. I made my junior high school freshman basketball team in my freshman year. I was good at basketball by this point, and it felt like I'd been training my entire life for this moment. This was my chance to be on an organized, structured school basketball team where I could get the opportunity to showcase my skills. I couldn't wait.

Before making my high school basketball debut, I was selected for the boys' choir. I was scheduled for an audition by my teacher, so I went and performed a solo to the best of my ability. At the time, I thought nothing of it. By the time I made the basketball team, I had forgotten about my audition for the boys' choir.

Two weeks later, a letter from my school came to the house. My Mom opened the letter. To our surprise, I was selected to sing at the annual sing-off competition in Catskills, New York. My Mother was so happy and proud. She grabbed me and planted a big kiss on my face, which I promptly wiped off.

"May I see that letter?" I asked. She gave it to me, and I looked it over in disbelief. I had completely forgotten all about the choir.

"Mom, I can't go on this trip."

"Why not?"

"I made the freshman basketball team, and the first game of the season is on the same day. So, I won't be able to go."

My Mother lost it. All the joy she'd had just a second ago was gone and replaced with rage. "Don't even think about not going on this trip," she yelled, "YOU'RE GOING!!!"

"But Mom, I can't go. The first game of the basketball season is on the same day, and I made the team."

"You play that stupid basketball all day, every day," she said. "You can do that anytime. This choir trip is important. You're the only Black student selected, and you will most certainly go on this trip to the Concord Hotel in upstate New York to represent your school and your race."

And just like that, I had to miss the first game of the season. From my Mother's point of view, this was far more important than a basketball game. While I didn't see it that way, I'd have been a fool to defy my Mother. Out of all the kids selected to represent our school, there was one other kid and me on the team. Like my Mother said, I was the only Black kid. I had to represent. On my first day of practice, the coach told me the guidance office told him we would miss the opening game. I begrudgingly attended the choir trip, and my school won the best choir award. My Mother was ecstatic and with joy. I would hear Mom telling her sisters and girlfriends about the award I won, and I was the only Black student selected to sing in the choir. My Dad could see that I was depressed and tried to cheer me up. "Your Mother is very proud of you, Miles." You should feel proud of yourself. They chose you to be a member of the choir, and that's a great accomplishment. As it turned out, my class choir won the singing competition. We all received these choir ribbons, and my Mom was so happy she showered me with more unwanted kisses.

Meanwhile, the basketball season began and progressed, and I was sitting on the bench. I could destroy all the White boys on this basketball roster, but I rarely got to play. With only ten games to the season, I thought the coach would never put me in.

Eventually, my time came in the ninth game. Surprisingly, the coach was not at the game. He had family commitments and elevated the team point guard, Bobby, to player-coach. As it turned out, the opposing team had a future professional NBA player, Toby Knight, on their team. He would eventually go pro and play for the New York Knicks. At the time, though, he was the local basketball phenom, considered the best basketball player in the state. In the first half of the game, I was riding the bench, watching as Toby and the opposing team destroyed us.

In the second half of the game, Bobby, our point guard, finally said, "Hey, Miles, go in." I did, and as soon as I got the ball, I pulled up from twenty feet and drained a jumper. Then I hit three more jumpers in a row. I'm hot!!! I'm instant offense off the bench. As time ran down, I got the ball one last time, rose up again for another jumper, and got fouled. I made one of two free throws and finished the game with a team-high nine points. The next day, the coach approached me during practice and said, "I heard you had a good game. I will start you in the final game of the season. Be ready."

"Yes, Coach."

The day of the season's last game also fell on the morning of my Mom's planned trip to Barbados in the West Indies. It was a big deal because Mom's parents were both born in Barbados, and she had never been. Mom was excited to take her first trip to her parents' homeland. The entire family woke up at three in the morning to drive my Mother to the airport. Once we said our goodbyes and returned home, I asked my Dad to wake me up at seven so I would not be late for homeroom. It was important because missing homeroom meant I couldn't start in the last game of the season. Dad agreed, but he ended up oversleeping. By the time I got to school, it was too late. I missed homeroom—just my luck. Coach, of course, benched me for cutting school.

I missed the first game of the season and the last game of the season!

Little did I know then, but those circumstances would ultimately define the end of my public school basketball career.

1970 – My Cousin's Wedding

My cousin, Al, got married in the summer of 1970, and my parents allowed me to travel to St. Louis, Missouri. My older cousin Diane – Al's sister- and I boarded a flight, and I was excited, nervous, and a little jittery. That was my first official plane ride. It wasn't a great first experience; it was a bumpy and turbulent flight, but we arrived safely in St. Louis. Wow, I could see the St. Louis Arch from the plane. It was the Midwest, a different world I was flying into. We arrived in St. Louis, and Al picked us up from the airport. From there, we drove across the Missouri River to East St. Louis. On the way, we must have passed by a dozen barbecue places along the way. I guess they love their barbecue.

I met Al's fiancé, Sharmelle, and her parents when we returned to their house. She was beautiful, super friendly, and had a great personality. They let us stay in their beautiful five-bedroom house until the wedding. We were treated like family by Al's soon-to-be bride and in-laws. It is one of the better childhood memories I still have. In any event, I was excited to see my cousin, Al, and meet his new fiancé. I had the honor of joining them for the wedding dinner that night and the rehearsal the following day.

My parents and little brother drove to St. Louis from New York with the rest of the family for the wedding. My Dad used an 8mm movie projector to videotape the entire wedding. We all had a fantastic time, capped off with a nice, scenic cross-country drive back to New York.

A week after we got home, my Dad developed the 8mm film, and a week later, he came home with the wedding films. We had a movie night and decided to watch it together. My Dad set up the projector in the living room for us to gather around. When the video started, we watched my cousin's wedding, engaging in fond memories with one another. When it got to the part where the groomsmen walked the bridesmaids down the aisle, Dad said, "Hey, Miles, you're walking funny. Is something wrong?"

"No, Dad. What do you mean?"

"You're walking with a slight limp on your left side."

When the film ended, my Dad pointed out another shot of me walking towards the bride and groom. He stopped the video and rewound it. "Watch closely," he said, "you are walking with a limp."

I watched the video of myself and said, "I don't notice anything. That's just how I walk, Dad."

He turned to my Mom and said, "Hey, Cutie" (That was his nickname for her). "What do you see?"

Mom looked at the video a few more times. Finally, Mom said, "I didn't see it at first, but now that you mention it, I see Miles limping a little bit."

I still don't see it. My parents talked back and forth about it, but I didn't think too much of it after that.

Fast forward to the beginning of the school year; sure enough, my parents were right. Something was going on with my hips. I tried out for the football team, and to my surprise, I couldn't run. *What's wrong with me*, I wondered. I was always one of the fastest kids in my class. After stumbling through the tryouts, the coach pulled me aside and told me, "You are banned from practicing with this team until you return with a doctor's note. Do you understand me?"

"Yes, Coach."

"All right then. Hit the showers."

Bilateral Hip Surgery

If I'm being honest, there were signs of a problem long before my Dad noticed the problem with my gait in my cousin's wedding video. I was always in pain after playing basketball, but I ignored it. After all, who isn't sore after working out? After the football tryouts, it wasn't something I could ignore any longer.

My Dad took me to an orthopedic surgeon for an evaluation, where I was diagnosed with Slipped Capital Femoral Epiphysis (SCFE). This hip condition occurs in teens and pre-teens who are still growing. For reasons that are not well understood, the ball at the head of the femur (thighbone) slips off the neck of the bone in a backward direction.

During that first visit, the doctor said, "Mr. Livingston, I want Miles in a wheelchair because I don't want any more weight on those hips. He could experience a hip dislocation at any moment that would complicate his surgery."

My Dad asked, "Is his condition that serious?"

"Yes, it is," the doctor responded. "I have arranged a bed at the hospital for your son. They are expecting him. Please take him to the hospital right now, and I will meet with you and your wife in a couple of hours."

The nurse entered the examination room with a wheelchair and told me to get in. Still hardheaded and thinking it was not all that bad, I told her I didn't need the chair. I can walk just fine. My Dad stepped in and said, "You heard the doctor. No more weight on your hips. Now, get into that wheelchair."

I did as I was told but didn't want to go. During the ride over to the hospital, I begged Dad to take me home. "Dad, this doctor is a quack. Are you going to let him give me an operation?"

My Dad chuckled, "Look," he said, "I've known all along that something was wrong with your hips. Remember the wedding films? You told me that you had pain after you played ball, right? We must let this doctor fix you. Trust me, you'll feel much better after your hip surgery." I reluctantly agreed, but I was scared to death.

It was a two-year ordeal of surgery, pain, physical therapy, homeschooling, model boats, model car building, and wheelchair basketball. Recovering from surgery leaves a lot of time on your hands. When I finally got home after a month-long hospital stay, I found that my Mom had redesigned the living room for me because I couldn't climb the stairs. I wasn't thrilled about that, but what could I do? The doctor specifically told us that I couldn't put any weight on my hips. Being in the living room made it easy for me in the long run.

One day, my Mom came home with this huge box. "Open it up," she said. I opened the box, and it was a model of an ancient sailing ship, complete with sails, string, and, like, a thousand parts. "Thanks, Mom," I said, "but this will take me forever to build."

"Well, son, you'll have plenty of time to work on it. You'll be home for a long time."

As daunting as it seemed, it turned out to be a great gift for me, now being a young teenage kid who was frustrated and confined to a wheelchair. Back then, things like computers and video games were not yet in existence. Fun for me translated into going outside to hang out with my friends, and now that was off the table. It took me about four months to build and paint the ship. I amazed myself by the time I finished. My Mom knew I could build model cars, but those I could build relatively quickly. She knew an ancient sailing ship with a thousand parts would take me a long time and fill my days. It was like therapy for me. The focus I had to have to put together all the tiny details of the ship took my mind off my troubles and made the days go by a little quicker. The finished product was beautiful and amazing. When I was done, she placed it on the dining room shelf underneath a Mother's Day bean picture I had created for her a few years earlier.

The story behind that bean picture is a special one for me. When I was in fifth grade, my teacher decided that the students in her class would make bean pictures for our Mothers for Mother's Day. She introduced the class to a similar paint-by-numbers project, only with different colored beans and peas. Everyone picked out a picture from a stencil book. The stencils were placed onto an overhead projector that projected an image onto a canvas. Each student would have to carefully trace the image onto a canvas and make a notation of the colors.

This project was right up my alley because my cousin had gotten me into building model cars, which took patience and a steady hand. By this time, I'd been doing that on my own for a while, so when I got this project, I felt like a surgeon. I was meticulous when tracing the image of my Rooster stencil, creating the perfect color scheme, and making the tail feathers as vibrant as possible with the colored beans. It was the best bean picture in my class. When I presented it to my Mom on Mother's Day, she framed it and hung it prominently on the wall in the dining room.

It was my first real work of art, and my Mother was very proud of it. All of her friends and even family members were impressed. They couldn't believe her ten-year-old son had made that bean picture artwork. Our next-door neighbor hired me to make one for her (A bald eagle that came out better than the rooster I made for my Mother). I did it for a few other neighbors, friends, and family, but it was too time-consuming for a ten-year-old boy with bigger dreams and ambitions.

The great thing about those pictures was that, as the years rolled by and I grew into an adult, those bean pictures withstood the test of time. Twenty years later, my Mom still displayed her picture, and my neighbor, who had moved into a new house and remarried, still displayed her bean picture.

First-hand Black History

My Black History education also flourished during this time. I learned all about the Black Panthers, Bobby Seale, Huey P. Newton, Stokely Carmichael, H. Rap Brown, Angela Davis, Jesse Jackson, Muhammad Ali, and many others who had fought and were still fighting for racial equality. What a time to be alive. I felt a real connection to the people who were Black as if I were also fighting for the rights of all Black people along with them.

By the summer, I had healed enough to spend time with family out of state. I ended up in Tallahassee, Florida, with my cousin Al (Who we called Freddy), a Florida A&M University professor. Staying with my cousin was ideal because (through him) I had full access to the university athletic facility. He also managed to get me a part-time job at Publix Supermarket and a motor scooter to run around the city. This one day at work, I was on shopping cart duty, and I gave a shopping cart to a middle-aged White couple as they got out of their vehicle to enter the supermarket. They took the cart from me but exchanged it for a different one at the store entrance. Watching them, I realize they did that because a Black boy (me) gave them that particular shopping cart. I stood transfixed in disbelief as I watched this racist White couple return the shopping cart and grab another one. I'd heard stories like that before, but up until that point, I'd never witnessed them. It's a memory I will carry to my grave.

After a week in Tallahassee, one day, my cousin (Al) came home around lunchtime and found me sleeping. He woke me up and said, "What are you still doing in bed?"

"I'm tired," I said, rubbing the sleep out of my eyes. He looked me straight in the eye and responded, "Didn't you just have surgery on those hips? You have full access to a state-of-the-art athletic facility! And you're in bed sleeping. Didn't you tell me you wanted to rehab your hips so you could play basketball? Hey Miles, you better focus and get your shit together. I didn't bring you down here to be lazy and sleep all day. You've got a motor scooter to get around, you have a job to keep a little money in your pocket, and you have the time to work those hips back to full strength." After that tongue-lashing, he stormed out of the apartment and slammed the door behind him.

His talk set the tone for the next seven weeks of my life. I made sure I was in the FAM-U training facility at least 3-4 days per week. I was practicing basketball and strengthening my hips and legs. My favorite basketball player was Walt 'Clyde' Frazier. I patterned my game after him. The New York Knicks just won the NBA Championship, and Walt

"Clyde" Fraizer inspired me to improve my game. I was fully awake, and I realized what I needed to do.

During that summer, the American public learned about the Tuskegee syphilis experiment. After hearing about it, I asked my cousin about it. He explained to me that over the past forty years, a government medical experiment was conducted on over six hundred Black men in Tuskegee, Alabama. The government allowed men infected with syphilis to go untreated so that scientists could study the effects of the disease. Even though I was only a teenage kid, it was hard to wrap my head around what I was hearing and what my cousin was telling me. The United States Government experimented on African American men without informing them of their diagnosis or even treating them for syphilis, which put not only their lives in danger but the lives of their families as there was a real risk of transmission. I was shaken up and confused. I didn't know what to think other than that our racist government (really) hates African American men.

1972 - My Triumphant Return to High School

By the time I returned to high school, I considered myself to be one of the best basketball players in the school. I'd grown about three inches, and my hips were strong. I was in great shape and played basketball practically every day of the summer. I was ready! Of course, a handful of upperclassmen were better than me, but I was confident I could make the twelve-man roster with no problem.

Unfortunately, my 16-year-old mind was ignorant about several important factors. It was 1972. I went to an all-White school, and, most importantly, there was only room for two Black players on the team.

This was before there were any anti-discrimination laws preventing such an obviously racist decree. Still, the Black males in school weren't going to stand for it. Twelve student-athletes, including myself, demanded a meeting with the Athletic Director. We asked permission to form an all-Black squad because we had the talent to be contenders in our H.S. Division.

Of course, that was out of the question. Our reward for standing up for ourselves was that eleven of us were cut from the team entirely, along with one token White boy. All that was left for me was to play intermural and summer league basketball. Whenever I traveled away from my hometown to play, the other players couldn't believe that I had been "cut" from my High School team. By my senior year, I was good enough to start on any high school basketball team in the state.

One year later, in 1973, a highly talented group of Black student-athletes were prohibited from playing for their high school basketball team. The remaining students on the team, who were all White and quite average players, ended up finishing the season at the bottom of the division. A potential powerhouse basketball team was dismantled because of racial discrimination.

I didn't attend my high school prom. It was going to be an all-White Affair, and I wasn't in the mood for it. One of my close friends went; he was the only African American there. He told us all about it the next day. God Bless him because I couldn't do it. I never knew what all the fuss was about being in high school, prom night, or athletics until I got to college. So many of my friends recalled such happiness at their respective proms; even my brother, who was four years behind me, went to his prom night. We both went to the same high school. My brother had a crew of a dozen couples with him, and they all had fun. But for me, that was a chapter in my life that was spoiled because of a racist environment.

2

Going Off To College

It was 1973, and the world was still in turmoil. It was the beginning of my journey into the world as a college man. I was thrilled to be attending Lincoln University in Jefferson City, Missouri - an HBCU (Historically Black College or University) that words could not express. My cousin, Alford H. Ottley (Al), was an administrator at the college. He was responsible for making all the necessary arrangements for me to attend.

This was the year of the "Rumble in the Jungle," the historic boxing match between Muhammad Ali and George Foreman. There was electricity in the air for Black folks. Ali's triumph over Foreman made us feel like anything was possible. Especially a young man working his way through the college world. I got busy right away, too. I started disc jockeying for the campus radio station (KLUM) and pledged Omega Psi Phi Fraternity (Ω Dogs!), which was going well until my entire line got suspended during Hell Week. What a devastating experience.

Luckily, girls (young ladies) were everywhere. I just so happened to attend Lincoln University when the women outnumbered the men ten to one. I had no shortage of busy Saturday nights one way or another.

But I was also still looking to spread my basketball wings. A few days after I got to town, I decided to do my due diligence and play in the local park with all the neighborhood ballers to check out the competition. In that short time, they nicknamed me New York City, I imagine, because that's where I was from. My mission was to routinely school these local kids. I also met with some LU Basketballers who liked hanging out and playing in the park.

One particular day, I arrived at the neighborhood basketball court and spotted this very tall brother sporting a large afro, watching the players on the court. As I walked onto the court, a few guys pointed out that the tall guy was the Lincoln University assistant basketball coach. I kept that in mind as I chose four guys for my team and got ready to play. Knowing that somebody was there from the university, I tried my best to impress this so-called assistant coach. Now, I'm not usually a ball hog, but my teammates were struggling, and something had to be done if we were going to win this game. I took over the game and dropped four straight baskets. I hit pull-up jumpers, drove to the basket, and tipped in rebounds, and we won the game. *Next!*

Streetball was and is a culture in itself. It's a freestyle and individualistic style of play that is undisciplined and physical. When you're playing streetball, the game sometimes breaks down to every man for themselves. It becomes a battle of the fittest, and regulation rules go out of the window. It's all about who the big dog on the court is. Oftentimes, a person's ego can get the better of them. The next game started, and I took this country-ass nigger straight to the hole and scored. On my way back down the court, this fat dude named "tumble-weed" grabbed me by my arm and flung me down to the ground. That might sound like a foul to you, but it's all a part of the game in streetball. This dude felt disrespected and needed to throw his weight around on the court. Literally!

"What the fuck are you doing, man?" I bark up at him. "Oh, I see it's time to play thug ball. Okay."

That fat knucklehead laughed at me and said, "C'mon, New York. I'm not gonna let you waltz your way to the basket without fouling you."

I got up, ready to check on him, but I remembered I was being watched by the assistant basketball coach from Lincon, and I kept my cool. When I did look back, however, I noticed the assistant coach walking towards his car.

I felt like I messed up. Even though I didn't hit back with that foul, it must have looked bad. Why else would the assistant coach leave like that? After the game, I headed back to my cousin's house (I have a dorm room, but it sucks) to take a shower. I had no TV, no stereo, and no friends. And now, I might've just screwed up my chances of making the University basketball team. After my shower, I waited for my cousin to come home.

When he got home, I asked him about the assistant coach of the basketball team at the University. "Oh, yeah, Ron Alexander," he said. "What about him?"

"Some of the guys at the park told me he was there watching us play," I told him." Can you describe him?"

"Of course. He's about 6'9', big afro, dark-skinned, and slim."

My heart sinks. "Yup, that's him. He was at the park today."

According to my cousin, Alexander had a "Cup-of-Coffee" in the ABA before the league merged with the NBA. "Cup-of-Coffee" in professional sports means that a player made the team and was on the roster for a very short period. Professional basketball has ten-day contracts, Football has the practice squads, and Baseball has call-ups. Those players only play a few games, if that. Then, they are relegated back to amateur status. This usually happens when one of the regular players gets injured, and the team has an available roster spot.

"No Shit," I said. "Tell me about the head coach."

"Coach Don Corbett? He's a no-nonsense type of guy. I know him well and can set up a meeting for you."

I couldn't believe my luck. *I guess it does pay to have friends in high places.* "Thanks, please set it up."

Lincoln University had an average-sized campus, and it took about a week to meet another New Yorker. I immediately asked him about the basketball team. He told me that the LU basketball coach didn't like the New York style of playing basketball. *Oh Boy*, I think to myself, I had been working towards playing organized basketball since the ninth grade. I shuddered to think that the last four years I spent rehabbing my injury and training were now about to go to waste. I decided to stay positive. When I met Coach Corbett, I would find out for myself.

My meeting with the head basketball coach didn't go very well. He only seemed interested in my history. He started in on me, asking what high school I played for. That's when I had to let him know that I had been injured, and that led to my high school coach holding my lack of experience against me in my senior year and cutting me from the team. I tried to impress upon this coach that I was still a talented player with a tremendous upside and work ethic. I assured him that I could help his team and that I wanted to be considered a "walk-on" candidate (A walk-on is a player who becomes part of a team without being recruited or awarded a scholarship). Coaches are usually not very supportive of walk-on players because they don't know them. As a result, walk-on players (really) must impress their coaches to earn a roster spot.

This coach wasn't impressed with my passionate plea to play ball for the university, but he unofficially let me try out as a walk-on anyway. That worked out well because it allowed me to get to know all the ballers on campus. When practice officially began, two pretty good players were noticeably absent. One of these guys was better than me. He was taller and stronger, and his overall game was more polished than mine. When I asked why he wasn't on the team, I was told he had a conflict with the coach.

At the start of the second day of practice (basically all running and conditioning), the coach called me and another kid into his office. He sat us down and said, "Boys, I appreciate your efforts to join this team. However, there are no (available) spots for walk-on athletes, so thank you, and good luck."

He dismissed us, and just like that, my opportunity to play college ball at Lincoln University was over! I'd be lying if I said I wasn't disappointed about playing college basketball. Basketball was my passion, and I felt I belonged on that team. Damm, I was burnt. The fact that I was attending an HBCU was my saving grace. Being in an environment where I could be unapologetically Black was amazing.

Lincoln University exposed me to Black academic role models, like my cousin Al and others I could identify with. We all wore a proud racial identity on our respective sleeves every day. As we gained valuable knowledge inside the classroom, our confidence and self-esteem grew in the real world.

All my classmates automatically knew I went to school with Whites. It was uncanny how, after only a few minutes of conversation, my new friends immediately noticed my "New York" accent and always asked if I went to a White school. Was it that obvious? It was hilarious to me. I knew that my head was a little fucked up, having grown up and attended school with racist White kids. Of course, not all the Whites I went to school with were racist. I had a few cool White friends. But as you know, the Ignorant Minds you must deal with are always the ones you remember.

Anyway, I was in paradise now. I attended an all-Black school with beautiful, intelligent, classy young ladies. Shit! I was in seventh heaven. Most of the students attending Lincoln University were from the South and the Midwest. I was from the East Coast, and our childhood education was in stark contrast.

Many of my classmates went to segregated schools from K–12. I have always envied them because they enjoyed their high school years. There were definitely a lot of negatives for them, having grown up in places like Mississippi, Georgia, Arkansas, Oklahoma, Louisiana, and Illinois, to name a few. The racism they dealt with growing up was significantly more insidious and dangerous than mine was. My classmates shared many stories about their childhood growing up in the

South during the 60s and 70s. They lived through and experienced some of the racial turmoil my parents told me and my brother about.

I made the Dean's List my freshman year and enrolled in an African Studies class during my first semester. To my surprise, the professor was White. He was an authority on Black History. A brilliant White male mind was teaching my ignorant young mind. It took me a few weeks to wrap my head around learning Black history from a White man.

After we settled into the class and got a feel for our assignments and his teaching style, it was one of the best classes I took in college. Attending an HBCU also provided me with an opportunity to see the top entertainers in the country: Parliament-Funkadelic, The Commodores, Marvin Gaye, Ohio Players, and Earth, Wind & Fire. We partied hard at college, especially during homecoming.

One day, during my freshman year, I was walking across campus, and this unknown stranger came up to me and said, "Hey man, you look just like "Seed" are you from Chicago"?

"No, I'm not from Chicago."

"Well, you look exactly like this brother named, "Seed" from Chicago."

I'm thinking to myself, who is this guy? He doesn't know me, and I don't know him. But he's a loudmouth, and he walks off, mumbling that I remind him of some guy named "Seed."

A few days passed, and I was sitting on the Quad chatting with my classmates one day. The Quad is the quadrangle in the middle of campus, outside the student union building. A lot of students congregate there and hang out between classes and weekends. Anyway, this loud-mouthed guy walks up to me again and yells, "Seed," this is the guy who looks like Chicago, "Seed." I'm trying to ignore this guy, and my classmate says, hey, Miles, who is this guy."

"I don't even know this guy. One day, he approached me and told me I looked like a guy from Chicago named "Seed." I quickly walk away and head towards the cafeteria to get some lunch. Lo and behold, here comes Mr. Loud-mouth into the cafeteria calling me "Seed." Finally, I turn to him and say,

"Look, man, my name is Miles, not Seed."

I glanced around, and my classmate laughed and explained to his friend, "Miles is letting this guy get under his skin because he keeps calling him "Seed."

By the end of my freshman semester, all my new college friends called me "Seed." The name stuck to me like glue! The more I tried to ignore it and disassociate myself from it, the more it stuck. For the next four years, my name became "Seed."

1975 – Setting up to Fail

By 1975, the three big wins for Black people, in my opinion, were Frank Robinson becoming the first Major League Baseball manager of the Cleveland Indians, and he also played that year.

BRILLIANT MINDS, IGNORANT MINDS

Arthur Ashe's big win at Wimbledon was in his defeat of Jimmy Connors and the "Thrilla in Manilla," Muhammad Ali's latest installment in his mission statement, "I Am The Greatest." At the time, I was working in the University Placement Office through the work-study program, and my director, Ms. Thelma Brooke, recommended me for an internship with a firm in the Midwest. I attended the interview with two other African American women and felt that I had nailed the interview. I related to the interviewer and answered all the questions thrown at me. However, one of the women was chosen over me. From my perspective, there seemed to be a trend going on at our university. The recruiters who visited our university seemed to overlook Black male students for better job positions. "Perhaps the most alarming statistics are the ones demonstrating a dramatic decrease in Black male participation in the labor force. The overall labor force participation of Black men declined from 84 percent in 1940 to 67 percent in 1980." (Claude, 1986).

The University Placement Office had a recognition ceremony every semester that acknowledged the students who were placed into jobs across the country. The troubling thing about these events was that I started noticing more and more women being selected for the jobs. The Journal of Human Resources study supports the theory that EEO (Equal Employment Opportunity) laws increased the entry of women into non-traditional occupations.

"According to the empirical estimates, both Title VII of the Civil Rights Act and the federal contract compliance program increased working women's chances of being employed in a male occupation between 1967 and 1974" (Beller, 1982).

To be clear, I certainly had no qualms against these women. They were all intelligent young ladies. But I felt Black men needed to go out into the world and make a living to support their families.

"Particularly steep declines in labor force participation have been recorded for Black men ages 24 and younger and those ages 55 and older. The large departure from the labor market of Black males has contributed significantly to the erosion of wage earnings in the Black community" (Claude, 1986).

Unemployment rates were already high in our communities, and the way I saw it, if there was a trend to hire Black college-educated women instead of Black men, that was going to create problems for African Americans. "There is evidence in certain sectors that employers favor Black women over Black men as prospective employees" (Noguera, 1997). I was somewhat surprised and disappointed because I thought these recruiters had their pick of our university's best and brightest college-educated Black men. Why are they selecting women ONLY?

"As young adults, Black men have more trouble transitioning into stable full-time employment than White men do. This racial difference is particularly pronounced among men with lower levels of education. In early adulthood, even college-educated Black men earn less than White men, however" (Raley, 2015). This was what I first started to refer to as the economic castration of Black Men.

1977 - Summer of Sam and Richard Pryor

The summer before, things changed dramatically in my college life. I went home to New York for an extended summer vacation. One day, while hanging out with some of my buddies and getting high, I picked up the Newspaper. To my shock and surprise, there was a serial killer loose in New York. According to the front-page news, he'd murdered six people. All had been shot to death while sitting in their cars after partying at various nightclubs.

I read that paper in a state of shock. This happened for a year while I was in Jefferson City. And it wasn't like it is now, where you can find news from home with the click of a mouse. There was no instant access to the New York News. No internet, no Twitter or Facebook. The fact was that when you were out of town, you were really out of touch. I'd been totally cut off from world events.

Reading the article made me break out into a cold sweat. News reporters were calling him the "Son of Sam" killer. Not one of my homeboys even told me about what was happening.

All told, the "Son of Sam" shot thirteen people and killed six between July 1976 and July 1977.

They didn't catch this guy until the end of the summer. On the night of August 10, 1977, David Berkowitz was taken into custody by the New York City police homicide detectives in front of his Yonkers apartment building. He was indicted for eight shooting incidents. He confessed to all of them, initially claiming to have been obeying the orders of a demon manifested in the form of a dog belonging to his neighbor, "Sam." The entire city went wild with happiness that this maniac was off the streets.

The Richard Pryor Show aired on NBC in September 1977. It only lasted four episodes but was the funniest show on television. It was also groundbreaking as Richard Pryor was among the first comedians to produce and star in his own television show. All I knew was that the Black community was thrilled for Richard Pryor. We knew that his brand of humor was too Black and raunchy for American television, and there were plenty of bits that stirred up controversy at the time. No one was surprised when NBC pulled the plug after only a few episodes. I guess the rest of America wasn't ready for him, but we knew what we were in for. We laughed until we cried listening to Richard Pryor's records over the years. We knew what was up. I'm sure Richard made plenty of money doing live performances and making movies after his show was canceled.

Kansas City, Here I Come

In Cape Town, South Africa, there was a big protest from the students in the surrounding areas. Schools were working to try to teach students Afrikaans – the language designated by the oppressive government in South Africa. More than twenty thousand students showed up to protest against the will of an apartheid-loving government in that nation. Nelson Mandela was imprisoned, and the entire world was watching.

"It was common knowledge when 15,000 students conducted a protest march to Orlando Stadium, where they were intercepted by fully armed police who opened fire on them." "It became common practice for the police to shoot student demonstrators at will. The South African police admitted to having used 50,000 rounds of ammunition against unarmed student demonstrators in Soweto, East Rand, and the Cape

Peninsula, having killed a total of 284 and injured about 2000." (Mafeje, 1978).

The American News Media coverage of this event was epic. I sat transfixed on my couch, watching White South African police officers murder hundreds of Black school-age children. It made me sick. I got up, took a shower, and started crying uncontrollably. It was unbelievable. College kids my age, down to elementary school children, were shot to death for participating in a protest.

"Estimates of the total number of deaths varied significantly, ranging from 700 to 1,200. Only two victims were White. Many very young children." (Pohlandt-McCormick, 2000).The Ignorant minds that ran the racist apartheid regime were on full display for the whole world to see. It was hard for me to wrap my head around how the United States could sit idly by and condone such racist behavior.

At the same time, I was visiting Kansas City for the weekend. One day, I was driving around with my friends in my Mustang, and my buddy asked me to stop at the store on the way to where we were going. I pulled up in front of the store and double parked since he said he would only be a minute. Two minutes later, the cops rolled up. Lights on, WOOP, *WOOP!* I looked in my rearview mirror to see both cops getting out of the patrol car, unsnapping their gun holsters as they walked toward my car.

"Good afternoon, officer," I said as they walked up on either side of the car. I notice them looking through the windows suspiciously. "Is there a problem?"

"License and registration."

I ask the cop, "Did I do something wrong?"

He responds with, "Yeah, you're double parked."

Remembering my father's talk with me all those years ago, I asked the cop politely, "May I go into my glove compartment to get my registration?"

He nodded, and I reached into the glove box to grab my registration. I also reached into my pocket for my license.

"We're college students, officer," I told him as I gave him my information. "I came to visit Kansas City for the weekend."

He didn't respond. He just looked at my license for a second, then said, "Sit tight. Turn off your ignition and remove the keys."

I complied, and he returned to his police cruiser while the other cop stood guard on the other side. It took him about five minutes, but he eventually returned to our car.

"Do you have any drugs or weapons in the car?"

I was so shocked by the question that I stared momentarily before answering him. "No, sir," I said. "No drugs or weapons in this car."

"I want to search this car; everybody is out."

I protested, "Don't you need my permission to search my vehicle?"

"No, I don't. Get out of the car right now and open up your trunk."

We got out of the vehicle, and he pushed me down on the hood, kicking my legs apart before searching me. The other cop made my two buddies sit on the curb while all this was happening. After searching me, he directed me to open my trunk. I complied again, walked to the back of the vehicle, and opened the trunk. The officer then escorted me to the curb with my buddies and told me to sit down. Sitting there, I heard my Dad's voice telling me, *"Obey the police officer! Do everything he asks you to do and stay calm while you do it."*

The cop searched my vehicle like he was sure he was going to find something. He got down on his hands and knees, reaching under my seat, sliding his hands in between the driver's side and passenger side. Then he attacked my glove compartment, going in and taking out every shred of paper I had in there.

"NO DRUGS, NO GUNS," he barks loudly to his partner. "They're okay. Let them go."

As I walked around to the driver's side of my car to get in, the officer handed me my license and registration. I got into my car, and he leaned in my window and said, "Miles, let me give you some advice. Never double-park in front of a store with your engine running. I don't know what the hell is going on when I see that. Maybe your boy ran into the store to rob the owner, and you're the getaway driver. Who knows? Plus, you have New York plates on your car. Be careful, and have a nice day."

After they left, my other friend finally came out of the store. "I was watching from the inside of the store. What was happening?"

We told him about the cop and everything. One of my buddies said, "Hey Seed, some of what that cop said was right. You're a Black Man, and you drive this Mustang very aggressively. If I were you, I wouldn't be double parking in front of stores anymore."

The next day, we hit the road and headed back to school. I have never forgotten that experience and how it has helped shape who I am today.

1978 – The End of School and the Beginning of Adult Life

By 1978, I was all set to graduate…or so I thought. As I prepared to graduate and end my college career, I was informed that there seemed to have been a mix-up with my credits. I was standing in the registrar's office in total shock. I was told I was nine credits short of graduating.

"Shit!!! You've got to be kidding me."

"Sorry, Mr. Livingston," the woman at the counter said, "I double-checked your transcript, and you need nine credits to graduate."

I was so close, and I wanted to finish on time. I wanted to graduate with my classmates, so I decided to go to summer school and finish up. To do that, I had to ask my cousin for a loan to pay my tuition. I worked with the Missouri State Highway Department and assured him I could repay him in weekly installments. To my surprise, my cousin denied me in no uncertain terms.

"Come on, Al," I said, "I just need you to pay my tuition for the summer so I can graduate on time. The money never has to touch my hands. Just cover me for about thirty days, and I guarantee you I'll pay you back."

My cousin was what I called a real "Hard Ass." He taught me most of what I know. I have always considered him to be my mentor, my big brother, my uncle, and my surrogate Dad. It was hard to swallow that he wouldn't cover my tuition. You've got to realize that it's 1978. Summer school tuition back then was maybe five hundred dollars. I know that's a crazy statement considering how much it costs today, but this was back before the Regan presidency and before his policies changed the state of college education across the country. It was still a *lot* of money back then. Either way, I would have paid him back in about four weeks, but my cousin didn't see it that way.

I was shocked that he wouldn't loan me the money, but it was a valuable lesson. I learned that I can only depend on myself. So, that's what I did. I depended on myself, and I ended up dropping out. It wasn't that big of a thing then. Most of my classmates who weren't graduating had already dropped out, and that's because my class was the largest freshman class in school history. About twenty percent of us were still grinding it out, but there's a reason that undergrad only lasts for four years. You were supposed to do your work, graduate, and get the fuck out. The last thing I wanted to be was one of those professional students who had been in college for eight years already. You know, like John Belushi in Animal House. He was the type of guy who just partied his life away.

Well, everything happens for a reason. My reason was that it was time to leave Jefferson City, Missouri. Thankfully, I had a good job, a State job. I asked for some extra hours, and my boss granted my request.

With the extra money, I started working on repairing a few things in my life, starting with my car.

My little brother (Billy) wrecked my beautiful '66 Ford Mustang about six months earlier. I needed mufflers, tires, bodywork on the driver's side door, and a complete tune-up. It took me some time, but once I had the money, I put my car in the shop and started planning my escape. I told Cousin Al I planned on going home to New York for good.

"You don't have to do that," he said. "I'll give you the money so you can return to school."

By that point, it was too little, too late. I already made my mind up. "Don't worry about it, I'm out." And that was it.

A few weeks later, I picked up the Mustang and was ready to hit the road. On the way back to my apartment, I stopped by campus. It was the end of the semester, and only a handful of students were still on campus. I walked through the student union to look around and reminisce, and I bumped into a classmate, a girl I hung out with a few times.

"Hey girl, what's happening?" I asked. "What are you still doing here?"

"I'm going to summer school," she told me.

"Really? I was supposed to go, but things didn't work out, so I'm going home."

She smiled and said, "Home to the Big Apple Seed?"

"That's right. Hey, what are you doing later?"

"I'm not doing anything."

"Well, look, I'm in the middle of something now. Can I come back to the dorm and visit you later?"

She gave me a beautiful smile and said, "Yes."

I said goodbye to her, jumped into the Mustang, and headed to my job to pick up my final paycheck. My co-worker, a cattle farmer, surprises me with a Steer. No, he didn't show up with an actual bull in the office. You see, his family owned a cattle farm, and he'd asked his father if it was okay for him to give me one of their heads of cattle as a parting gift. This man was ready to present me with a whole *Steer* in gratitude!

I asked him, what would I do with a two-thousand-pound animal? He told me I could eat rib-eye steaks every day for the next couple of years. At this point, I'm cracking up and laughing. How would I get this bull to New York? Then I would have to find a butcher. What would it cost to slaughter and butcher a whole bull? I would need a meat locker the size of Yankee Stadium to store all that meat. I respectfully declined his offer.

I hung out with him for an hour before picking up my paycheck and signing my resignation papers. After I spent the afternoon cashing my check and closing my bank account, all the while, my mind was on home girl back at the dorm. Between the busy bank, gassing up the Mustang, and saying my goodbyes at the radio station, my day was filled with tying up loose ends.

When it was all done, I headed back to the dorm, where she was waiting for me. After a little soft music and malt liquor, we found ourselves in bed together. We make love for most of the afternoon and into the night. I think sex is probably the best thing about being young. There are no hangups or expectations. And this was the seventies, when women were coming into their own sexual liberation, and you didn't have to worry about half the things that we didn't know were right over the horizon. The troubles of the world were far behind and away from us as we lost ourselves in one another for one night. It was wonderful, and I never wanted it to end. And this woman was *beautiful*. I'd had my eye on her for a while before that night, and being able to be with her even once was a gift. When I left her dorm, I had a spring in my step and was ready to move on.

That next morning, my good buddy from Kansas City gave me some really good drugs for the drive home - Mescaline and Benzedrine. *Wow!* I was pedaling to the metal all the way home. It took me eighteen hours non-stop. My Mustang ran like a top, hauling *ass* all the way cross-country. I-70 to Pennsylvania Turnpike, then I-80 to New York City. *"Free At Last"*

Back home but not giving up

The first order of business once I was back in New York was to return to my old job in a retail store where my Dad worked. They also had a softball team that was always looking for players, so I was good to go for the summer all the way around. I have always liked playing softball, and while it wasn't basketball, it would keep me in shape for the time being. I also got to keep some money in my pocket to party and buy the things I wanted and needed. But best of all, I got to hang out with my Dad.

Once I was settled, I spent some time visiting family and friends. The Mustang was running well (the body was still slightly banged up), and it had been five long years since I left town for school. I had a lot of catching up to do.

For a little while, I spent time trying to get my bearings and connect with old friends and family. Ultimately, I returned to the educational game to complete my degree. My major was Business Administration with a minor in Broadcasting, and the first thing I had to do was determine which school I was going to attend.

Before I left Lincoln University, I sat down with the department chairman, Dr. Stamper. He did his level best to keep me from leaving school altogether. He said, "You only need nine credits. You can easily get financial aid and finish up. I would hate for you to leave school and not finish your degree."

I assured him that I would finish my degree eventually. I just needed to know what classes I needed. He gave me the Lincoln University School of Business Administration Directory of courses and called his secretary to have her pull my transcript.

Once Dr. Stamper had my transcripts in hand, he said, "Well, I've certainly seen a lot worse. You're a pretty good student, Miles. What happened to you in your sophomore year?"

I had to think about what he meant. Then I remembered my time in the fraternity before I answered, "After I pledged, I was placed on temporary academic probation."

"I see," he mused. "Well, here's what you must do to graduate. You need two core courses, which I will outline for you, and one elective." He circled the courses I needed and added, "You must attend an accredited university, and the courses you enroll in must meet our university standards and criteria. You will be what is called a non-matriculating student."

"What does that mean?"

"It means that you haven't been accepted to that university. You're only enrolled in coursework that will count towards a degree from another university. You must send me the university catalog with a complete description of the courses, and I must approve those courses before you enroll. Do you understand me, Miles?"

"Yes, sir, Dr. Stamper. I understand." We shook hands, and that concluded our meeting.

I was encouraged to know I would finish what I had started, but another goal was brewing around that time. I have always wanted to try my hand in the music business. Working as a disc jockey in school helped foster that urge. While it was a minor area of study, I already knew my elective would be a radio broadcasting course. While I was in New York, my cousin Rob had been teaching me the disc jockey business. I already started investing some money into audio equipment and records.

BRILLIANT MINDS, IGNORANT MINDS

After researching several colleges and universities, I decided to attend the New York Institute of Technology. It was a commuter college, and for me, it was about a twenty-minute drive from my house, but it was a start. I was well on my way back to getting my degree.

By the fall of that year, a few buddies of mine decided to attend the Lincoln University Homecoming event. I decided to go with them, and we all had a weekend blast. While I was there, I paid a visit to Dr. Stamper again. I presented him with the college directory from the New York Institute of Technology. He looked over my transcript to make sure I was on track. Dr. Stamper pointed out two courses I had to take to graduate. I was so excited and grateful that I rushed home and got pulled over for speeding. It wasn't as tense this time as the day I was stopped for double parking, but I took it all in stride. Oh well. I guess that's the price I had to pay for ultimate success.

3

Entering The Job Market

When I got home, I was so happy to be back in New York. New York Radio, New York Food, New York Night Life, New York Women. It was like Heaven on earth, and I was finally home. My brother joined the U.S. Army and was in Germany, so we tried to talk at least once per month, and when we couldn't, we wrote letters to each other.

My time wasn't all leisure, however. My Mom had taken to waking me up every morning at seven to get up and look for a job. "You're not going to sleep the day away in this house," she'd say. "Get up, eat your breakfast, get the Newspaper, and find a job."

So, you can imagine how happy and proud I was when I told her that I had not only landed a job with the Huntington Youth Bureau. I also re-enrolled in college at the New York Institute Of Technology. My Mom was happy but also very skeptical. Before I could commit to either of these ventures, she demanded a review of my employment papers and my college enrollment documents. My Mom was the type of woman who said talk was cheap. You better be able to verify what you say to Lucille, or else she won't believe you.

But all things considered, I was lucky. I'd only been home for a month or so, and I was already working a new job and enrolled back into school. Still, my major concern and my primary passion in life was music. I had already spent several years buying records. I even purchased some disc jockey equipment with my Dad's help. I had my eye on the prize, but my head was still in the clouds.

1981 – The MTV Generation

1981, the music game changed forever when some brilliant musical business and production minds developed MTV, or "Music Television," and launched it on August 1st, 1981. And to the surprise of nobody Black, the cable channel only features White artists. When MTV first came on the air, they very noticeably never played any Black music. Rick James and a bunch of other Black artists were pissed off. These guys and gals spent thousands of dollars on music video production, just like the White bands had. But MTV didn't want to play any videos or music by Black artists. As the story goes, the president of CBS Records had to threaten MTV to get them to play Michael Jackson's Billie Jean video, or else he would pull all the artists on the label from MTV's rotation. MTV was so racist they couldn't get out of their own way. Playing the Michael Jackson video was a watershed moment for MTV, and they did it unwillingly. The funny thing was that it took these White executives almost three years to realize that adding Black artists to their music programming was a plus for them -- a win/win. But the ignorant racist minds that were in power during that time couldn't realize that. In 1983, Michael Jackson's Billie Jean was the first video by a Black artist to be played on MTV, and it ended up being a ratings booster. The estimation that their target audience (Preppy, White, and Male) wouldn't be interested turned out to be way off.

That situation spoke volumes about the existing racial attitude and climate African Americans had to live with then and still live with today. Black music is at the heart of America's DNA and the basis for most popular music. You would think that if you owned a music television show, you wouldn't dream of discriminating against Black artists. Black music has always been a money maker. MTV's stance on Black artists was a real head-scratcher for me. The Brilliant Minds that put MTV together turned out to be Ignorant Minds. Their feeling was that the world revolves around high-net-worth White Men. That's who they wanted. That's who their sponsors wanted. Rich White Music Business and Economic Executives could only see things through their own lens.

It was in this climate that I arrived at my music engineering class. It only took two days to realize that the class was not for me. At the end of that second class, my instructor pulled me aside and invited me to a concert at a place called the" Rat-Skeller." "Hey, Miles," he says, "Let me buy you a drink tonight at the show," I told him I'd be there, but I didn't mean it.

It turned out that it became what I would call a "knucklehead" decision for me, as I decided not to go to the concert and disenrolled from the music engineering class. An ignorant-minded decision that I would regret for many, many years. The concert that I blew off turned out to be Bruce Springsteen and the E-Street Band. As I understand it, he tore the place up that night, and I would hear about it for years after.

Fast forward six or seven years later, I had developed a reputation as a top DJ. Many young underling Disc Jockeys are looking to me to produce their music. But stupid me, I dropped out of the engineering class that would have given me the skills to produce records. Ignorant Mind, for sure.

Support from Dad

The matriculation of my career included music, and that was evident from my minor in radio broadcasting in college, where one of my cousins was a mobile disc jockey. Over the years, he taught me much about the music business and becoming a DJ, and I naturally gravitated towards that.

When I turned twenty-one, my Dad sat me down for a talk. He said to me, "You're twenty-one years old now. You're a grown man. I have this life insurance policy for you that matures when you reach the age of twenty-one. We are going to take a ride today and cash out this policy."

We jumped in the car and drove into Manhattan, where he took me to the Carver Federal Bank, the only Black Bank in New York. We walked in, and my Dad immediately received the best and most respectful customer service. I felt proud to be with him as he escorted me through the turnstile and into the bank manager's area.

"This is my son, Miles," he told the bank manager, "And he turned twenty-one. We will be cashing out his life insurance policy today." The bank manager shook my hand and congratulated me for turning twenty-one. Then, he began to process some paperwork. My Dad told me I would sign all the paperwork since I was now the policy owner.

The bank manager returned with several documents and instructed me where to sign. I began signing, and it gave me a feeling of importance. Reflecting on this day, I realize how important it was for my growth and self-esteem. My proud Black father, a Black bank manager, and even a prouder Black son taking care of business. It was a monumental day in my life. After I signed the papers, the bank manager walked away and returned with five crisp brand new hundred-dollar bills. He counted them in front of me, put them inside a bank envelope, and handed them to me.

During the one-hour ride home, my Dad talked to me about fiscal responsibility and the importance of making good decisions. He asked me, "What are you going to do with your money?"

"I'm not sure. I guess I'll open a savings account and save it until I can decide."

After a few months of thinking about what I was going to do with my money, I decided to purchase a Pevey amplifier. I became so good at spinning records that I decided to commit to becoming a professional DJ. It cost me four of the five hundred dollars I had, and it ended up being an investment that served me well over the coming years.

It's a great, valuable lesson my Dad gave me. One that I will never forget. My Dad was very frugal, regimented, and disciplined. He has that army background. I believe some of those qualities rubbed off on me and my brother.

The Audition

My two best friends, Mike and Keith, encouraged me to audition for a job at this club that recently opened, The "Native New Yorker." That whole year, I had been DJ'ing in my bedroom every day for hours and hours. My cousin Rob taught me everything about the business of being a DJ, and I took it all to heart. I think I probably practiced four to five hours per day, every day. I loved music. I couldn't wait to get home and play music whenever I went out. At that time, it was my life. I even purchased two Technic turntables and a CM-Lab mixer. All I did was mix various songs over and over and over again. And usually, my friends came over to listen and hang out. We would be in my room, smoking weed, drinking, and listening to whatever mix I came up with next.

One day, my buddy Keith said, "Hey guys. Let's go to this new club tonight. There will be some pretty fine females there, and we should go and hang out." I was like, "*BET!* Let's go, I'm down." When we arrived, the club was nice, and the ladies were on point…but the DJ *sucked*! He couldn't mix to save his life. He'd let the record end, and there would be blocks of dead air between songs. The guy had no clue how to read the crowd. He's a total amateur. All night long, my buddies bugged me to ask the club manager for a job. At the time, I was too distracted. I was more interested in meeting the fine ladies around us. Besides, I was too shy to ask for a job. I mean, I was still an amateur myself. I didn't feel ready to do that kind of gig. My boys wouldn't let it go.

"Miles, you know you can mix a thousand times better than this guy," they said. "You've got to talk to the manager. He's right over there, standing by the door. Go talk to him."

Finally, I gave in. "Okay, okay. I'll talk to him."

I went to the bar and got another drink to help build up my courage. As I finished my drink, I saw my friend, Mike, gesturing at me to go over and speak to the manager. There was no sense in putting it off now.

I took a deep breath, walked over to him, and said, "I'm a DJ and would like to audition for a job at your club."

He looked at me and asked my name. I answer, "DJ Technician."

"Okay, DJ Technician, auditions are held on Wednesday nights. Come by at seven. I'll let the club owner know you're coming, and we'll evaluate your skills then." I shook his hand, thanked him, and nearly skipped back to my boys. That wasn't so bad.

At seven sharp on Wednesday night, I was there, and I was ready. I spent hours putting together a specially prepared music program for that audition. I was not going to mess this up.

The manager greeted and invited me in, saying, "Please bring in your stuff and get set up in the DJ booth." I did as I was told, grabbing my records and turntables and entering the booth. To my surprise, everything was totally messed up. Wires were all over the place, speakers were not hooked up, and the audio equipment was either disconnected or not correctly hooked up. It was a disaster. I gestured to the manager and informed him that the last person in this DJ booth had left a big mess. The only way I was going to play music for him was to connect all the components correctly. He asked me my name, and I told him. "Miles, my name is Richard. Do whatever you need to do. What are you drinking?" He brings me a drink, a screwdriver, a boxcutter, and pliers.

So there I was, troubleshooting audio equipment and performing a sound check, all before I could even audition. Thank goodness all my years of being my cousin Rob's roadie taught me how to hook up a sound system from A to Z. I was very much in my element. I took my time getting everything connected, and about an hour later, I was finally ready to audition.

I started my audition, and a few individuals who happened to be in the club got out on the dance floor and started dancing. That fueled my fire! I started mixing and displaying my skill set for the manager. I noticed another man talking to the manager. A very tall man also stopped and watched. They chatted for a few minutes, and then Richard came into the DJ booth and said, "I want to introduce you to the club owner. I'll take you to the office where we can talk."

So, I met the owner, John Blocker, and the rest was history. He offered me the job, and I was thrilled. He would later tell me he decided to hire me after I hooked up his sound system. It turned out that hooking up the sound system was all he needed to see. John was a big thinker and wanted to get into some big-time promotions. I didn't know I would play a big part in that goal.

Hey, Mr. DJ

I'm not sure when or where I'd seen or read it, but at some point, I learned that it takes ten thousand hours to master a skill. I applied that lesson by playing music and mixing records (all day) every day. I listened to the DJs on the radio, and I observed the DJs at the clubs when I went out. On weekends, I worked with my cousin Rob as his roadie whenever he had a gig. And if I wasn't working or studying, I was playing music.

VERNON M. O'GARRA

In hindsight, when I look back on my DJ career and do some number crunching, I realize that I was only twenty years old when I got serious about becoming a DJ. Before leaving college, I hosted my (own) college radio show and promoted parties on campus. By the time I was twenty-three, I moved back home and re-arranged my room into a makeshift studio. I had set up my mixer, turntables, amplifier, equalizer, and speakers. I was on that setup for approximately four to six hours per day. My parents, surprisingly, were pretty supportive. Dad made sure I knew to turn the volume low and talked about soundproofing my room. Mom had me hook up a spot-light alarm so she could contact me while I was mixing since I couldn't hear the buzzer I'd set up so she could get my attention if a phone call came in for me.

The thing about getting my attention was an issue. Let me explain. My family lived in a three-story house; my room was on the third floor. Whenever I was home, my music was blasting. I couldn't hear my parents calling me in my room whenever they needed me. So, my Mom suggested that I set up a buzzer so I could hear when she called. The only problem with a buzzer was that I couldn't hear it when my music was playing. It was 1978, and there were no cell phones. If you wanted to call the house, there was only one line for the entire family. My parents were not about to pay for their twenty-something-year-old son to have a private line in *their* house.

One day, a light bulb went off in my head after my Mom repeatedly scolded me about having to climb up the stairs to tell me to pick up the phone. For good reasons, she was sick and tired of banging on the wall to get my attention. After one trip too many, she had enough and warned me that the next time I failed to answer her, she would hang up the phone on whoever was calling. To solve the problem, I realized my Mom had one of those giant seventies globe lights in the basement. I decided to use the globe light with a buzzer that my Mom could press. I needed to figure out how to make that light blink when my mom rang it.

With a little imagination, ingenuity, and some elbow grease, I wired the light to blink whenever the buzzer rang. I went to the local Radio Shack, bought an electronic switch and a yellow spotlight to replace the bulb, then hung the light above my DJ setup. I plugged in the electronic switch and spent that afternoon running up and down the stairs, testing my spotlight alarm until I got it to work correctly. I hooked up a master switch next to my Mom's bed so she could buzz me anytime. It worked perfectly. Whenever I was playing music, I could see the light blinking when the phone was for me or if my Mom or Dad needed me.

To that end, I played my music about thirty-five hours per week, a hundred and fifty hours per month, about eighteen hundred hours per year. It wasn't the ten thousand hours that they say you needed to master a skill, but in six years, I had practiced the skill of mixing and being a DJ enough to get that much closer to mastering it. I already considered myself a master of my craft by that time. Most of the DJs I came in contact with didn't have it like me. I was head and shoulders above everybody in my area. And by the age of twenty-eight, I officially became a master by those official standards and made those ten thousand hours. *Ten Thousand Hours*. I didn't know that was the calculation at the time, but if you love what you do, it becomes part of you. So, the process was automatic for me.

One night, at the Native New Yorker Discotheque, my validation came walking up to my booth. I had just finished my set, and this guy approached me and asked, "Do you belong to a record pool?"

I didn't know what a record pool was, so I told him no. He gave me his card and told me that DJs of my caliber belong to record pools. He asked me my name. My *real* name - and I told him, Miles Livingston.

"Ok, Miles," he said, "A record pool will supply you with all the new records that are released every week. Call me on Monday, and I will schedule a time for you to meet the president of the Mojo Record Pool."

Wow! This was great news! I took his card and guaranteed him I would call on Monday.

When Monday came, I called the number on the card. Stan Dixon, President of Mojo Record Pool, set up a meeting for the next day at three in the afternoon, and I immediately agree. That next day, I traveled to his private residence in the Bronx. It was a three-story walk-up apartment house. Stan liked to let his dog run around his home. Let me tell you, that dog was funky, and so was his house. Aside from that, his living room was packed with boxes of records. I had never seen so many records. Stan had more records in his house than we had at my college radio station. Wow, I was in record heaven.

Mr. Dixon and his dog greeted me at the door and invited me in. The living room was set up like a music studio. Boxes and boxes of records were lined up all over the place. He handed me some paperwork to fill out and started the interview. "So, you're a 'DJ Technician' from Long Island?" I nod, and he smiles at me politely. "You've got a bit of a reputation for yourself, Miles. Some of the DJs in the pool heard about this guy out in Hempstead, Long Island, who had skills. So, I sent one of them to check you out and listen to you play. He was very impressed with you, so now you're in."

He told me that he was the owner/operator of Mojo Record Pool. A record pool supplies DJs with access to promotional and newly released music provided by the major record companies. As a professional DJ, it would be my job to introduce new music to my audience every week. I would have to provide feedback from my audience on feedback sheets. When I picked up my records, those sheets had to be turned in every week.

As I listened to him talk, I noticed a listing of all the top radio stations that played Hip hop, R&B, Top 40, and Pop in the paperwork he gave me. I also noticed instructions about how to begin reporting directly to the radio stations. I thought to myself, *Wow, I have arrived.*

At that time, I also began working with other promoters in the music industry, and my cousin Rob decided to come along for the ride, which was good. I needed a backup DJ whenever I had more than one gig booked. That was the beginning of my transition from DJ to Promoter to earn more income. It should have been a time of great prosperity, and in many ways, it was, but it didn't come easily. I ended up experiencing racial issues when booking acts at various venues.

I formed my own Production Company, "Nu-Demensions." As soon as I graduated college, I sat for my FCC Third Class Broadcasting Licensing exam. I passed it on the first try and enrolled in a broadcasting school that allowed broadcasting your own radio show. My radio show was called NBS Radio's "Kaleidoscope" Series. At that point, my goal was to land a job with one of the New York Radio Stations and do promotions like some other professional DJs around town.

Schooling the Amateurs

A good example was when my record pool was involved in a Record Release Party for a new recording artist at a major label. That party was planned at one of the major hot spots in New York City. The record pool president pulled me aside one day to give me the details, saying, "Miles, Mojo Record Pool will be allotted four hours in the DJ booth, and you will share your time with Tim."

"Who the hell is Tim?" I knew most of the top DJs in the record pool, but I had never heard of Tim.

I asked Stan, "Have you ever been to Club New York? They have a state-of-the-art sound and audio system. The latest mixers, equalizers, turntables, lighting, speakers, *everything*. One hundred thousand dollars worth of equipment is at the DJ's disposal. Are you *sure* Tim can handle that?

All Stan said to me was that he'd be all right. "All right???" I balked back at him. "Look, if this Tim guy looks out of his league, I will immediately kick him out of the booth. I'm not getting embarrassed by an amateur."

I dropped by Club New York a week before the record release party. Some promoters were already there handing out flyers for the party, and some of them recognized me as I walked in. It felt good to see my name advertised as the DJ for this big party coming up. The manager of the club happened to be at the entrance, so I introduced myself to him. He

74

walked me inside the club to the DJ booth, and the setup was fantastic—all the latest bells & whistles. The house DJ was there, so he took a minute and gave me the rundown about the sound system. My first thought was that *this* was the kind of shit these White boys got to play with on the regular. That being said, equipment is equipment. Either way, you must know what you're doing and how to do it. I got the feel of everything and listened to this house DJ spin. I'd say he was average at best. I hung out for an hour or so and then cut out. I'd seen everything I needed to see.

The week flew by fast; before I knew it, it was party time. The city was buzzing, and the record label had been promoting their artists and the event. My cousin Rob and my business partner, Harold, dropped me off at around ten (which was very early for me). Whenever I guest DJ'd an event, I usually didn't start spinning until after midnight or one in the morning. But tonight, I wanted to be prepared. I didn't know anything about this Tim guy, and I was representing the Mojo Record Pool and myself. As soon as I got in the DJ booth, it was no surprise that Tim was an amateur and obviously way over his head. He couldn't work the mixer and could *barely* handle the turntables. The club manager, the house DJ, and I were looking at this guy fumbling around the booth like a fish out of water. After watching him royally screw up, they both looked at me. I turned to Tim and said, "Okay. That's enough. Pack up your stuff. Let me get in there."

Tim steps back without objection. "I never worked with this kind of mixer before."

"This is a Bozak mixer. Ever used one before?"

"Nope."

"Ahh, I see. Well, watch and learn, Tim, watch and learn."

I reached into my pocket and pulled out three pages of notes about the new artists. Stan gave me all the background information about them beforehand, so I researched the rest of his stable mates on the label. I started to warm things up as the crowd started rolling in. At that time, little did I know this event would be a tremendous boost to my DJ career. I briefly welcomed everyone, introducing myself as "DJ Technician." I told the crowd about the artist who would perform that night and a little about the record company sponsoring the event. After that, there was nothing left to do but start the music.

I'm well into some of my mixes, and I noticed a line of individuals forming at the entrance to the DJ booth. The lighting technician had just arrived. He stopped and said, "Some people are waiting to speak with you."

The first person waiting introduced himself as a record industry executive, and he gave me his business card. He had two records in his hand, and he let me know that those songs were what we were promoting. He asked me if I would be so kind as to mix them into the playlist. I obliged, of course. He wrapped up by telling me he would call me on Monday. He wanted to put me on their promotional playlist.

The next person was another record label guy. He was also looking for DJs to add to his promotional distribution list. He gave me a business card. Then comes the next person.

I had to tell the lighting guy to hold off those people for a bit. I mean, I had a job to do, after all.

I got to work, and the party began to rock. After about thirty minutes, I saw the next guy, who had slipped me fifty bucks to play his record, and he left. Now, I had about four new songs to play, and I was hoping they were good. I played the first one towards the end of my first playlist set. It was a pretty nice track and kept everyone dancing. I immediately picked up the record cover and gave the audience some background information about the artist. It was heaven on earth being exposed to this type of attention for the first time. I was taking it all in stride. It was another day at the office.

It was after midnight, and my business partner, Harold, came in to let me know that my time was almost up. I was already on Cloud Nine, so I was good with it. When the house DJ came in, I decided to ask for another hour. To my surprise, he agreed. He'd been listening and watching me, so he knew I was a professional and could handle the job.

I rocked the crowd for another hour, and it was the time of my life. What a night. By the end of the event, I had about half a dozen business cards, and I planned to call everyone. I contacted all six record executives I met that Saturday night by Monday afternoon. They all took my information. Some even sent me some paperwork to fill out, which I did. About two weeks passed, and one afternoon, my Mom called to tell me a bunch of boxes had arrived for me. When I got home, four medium-sized boxes of records were waiting for me. I opened box after box after box. I couldn't believe it—brand new music from major record labels and smaller independent labels. For a DJ who spent, on average, seventy-five dollars or more on records every week, that was a blessing and a half.

The Concert Promotion World According to "TIX-Nation"

One day after work, I was reading through a publication called the Learning Annex. It was a very large organization that sponsored classes taught by various professionals in their chosen fields. I came across a piece about Tix-Nation, who just happened to be offering a class on how to become a concert promoter. My mouth dropped open. Tix-Nation was the premier promotion company in the country. If they were sponsoring a class about promotions, I had to be there.

The class cost ninety-nine dollars. I stopped everything I was doing and went straight to my bank to withdraw the money. It's 1980. I don't even think I had a debit card yet. Then, I jumped on the train and headed downtown to go directly to the Learning Annex headquarters.

By the time I arrived to sign up for his class, only ten seats were left. *Whew! Just in time.* Long story short, it was a life-changing class. If you're from New York, you know Tix-Nation, even if it wasn't by name. Who hasn't attended a Tix-Nation concert, Jones Beach Theatre, Central Park, Madison Square Garden, or PNC Arts Center? That's just in New York. I was ready to learn about the ins and outs of the business of concert promoting, the venues, the bands, other promotors, contracts, sponsorships, *everything*.

This was an excellent opportunity for me. I had the chance to hear the Tix-Nation promoters speak at this seminar. They shared so many nuggets of information and insight. Afterward, a few of us stayed behind, chatting with the presenters and asking them questions. The three fundamental pillars of promotion that I gained from that workshop were:

Number One: You must have a Venue.

Number Two: You must have a Budget.

Number Three: You must have an Artist or an Act to promote.

The most important thing I gained was what they taught us about music promotion, marketing, and life.

However, *it's not WHAT they say, it's what they DON'T say."* And what Tix-Nation didn't say was that they were one of the country's most powerful and influential promotion companies. Not that everyone in the seminar didn't know that. The point was that they didn't have to say it. The fact that they controlled a massive stable of artists who would only work exclusively for them and nobody else was common knowledge, and it spoke for them.

I left that seminar ready to conquer the world. I had financial backing from the club where I was working. The club owner had authorized ten thousand dollars to promote a show. I had the venue. Another associate of mine, Lonnell, managed the ACT Theatre, which was a forty-five-hundred-seat movie theatre. All we needed was entertainment.

My boss came up with what he thought was a marvelous idea. "Rock Bands," he said to me one day.

"*White* Rock Bands???" I gave him a puzzled look as I responded. He just laughed.

"Miles, this is Nassau County, New York. There are millions of affluent White kids in this area. We only need forty-five hundred per night. We can turn our venue into a gold mine with the right band, promotion, radio advertisement, and sponsorship."

I couldn't argue that. It sounded good to me, so I was all in.

So there I was, a young twenty-five-year-old filled with piss and vinegar, still holding on to my mission to conquer the world. The major venues were all owned by Whites who primarily only worked with other Whites. To a certain extent, I get it. I wasn't trying to rent Madison Square Garden or anything on that level. I was happy to stay in my lane. John called me early one morning. He wants me to meet him at the club at noon. When I got there, John told me that we were going for a ride over to the ACT Theatre in Hempstead. He explained that he was entertaining a business partnership with Mr. Lonnell Jackson, who runs the ACT Theatre. "I want you to listen to everything he has to say and question him so I can decide if I want to work with him," he said. "My plan is: I will handle the financing, Lonnell controls the venue, and you will book the acts."

So, we met with Lonnell. He was very detailed as he went into a presentation about the costs of operating his venue. He meticulously explained the venue capacity, ticket pricing, sound equipment, insurance costs, and staffing. As requested, I started asking Lonnell a few questions. How long have you been in business? What's your cancellation policy? What's included in the rental price? Etc., and so on.

He answered all of my questions satisfactorily. So I give John the thumbs up that he seemed like a pretty cool dude to work with.

Afterward, John and I went to lunch at the local diner. "Here's the plan," he said, "I've compiled a list of all the best college bands on Long Island."

My ears perk up. "College Bands???"

"Yeah, College Bands. *White* College Bands. We're going to book these bands at Lonnie's theatre and do the promotions on the college campuses. Miles, your job is to find the booking agent, book the act, and organize a calendar of events. I'll cover the financing you need to book the bands."

At that point, I felt ecstatic. We had to start somewhere, so why not the college scene? I couldn't believe I had been given such a high level of responsibility. I knew that I couldn't screw this up. I was focused and ready to go to work. John gave me a list of twenty bands to work with, and I hit the ground running.

I spent the following day tracking down all the talent agencies in the city. Norby Walters, Ron Delsener, William Morris, etc. As I began tracking down who was managing who, I practiced a calling script I created.

Hello. My name is Miles Livingston. I represent Native New Yorker and ACT Theatre productions. I'm interested in booking the Wailers Rock Band. Could you tell me who represents them and does their booking?

Time after time, I was told that bands were booked exclusively by the Tix-Nation Agency. Whenever I called a booking agency for a date, I was told that only Tix-Nation could book the groups. I asked about the dates they were booked and then about the dates they weren't booked. "No, no. You don't understand, Mr. Livingston. *Only Tix-Nation* can book them."

"Well, don't they want to book a gig and get paid when they have an opening in their schedule?"

"Mr. Livingston, things don't work that way. These groups you're inquiring about only work when *we* book them through Tix-Nation."

"Well, what if I want to book them?"

"If any of these bands go out on their own and book a gig, they will be dropped from our roster, and they do not want that to happen."

"Alright, what about these smaller college bands? Surely, I can book them?" "Sorry, Mr. Livingston. Tix-Nation owns all of the exclusive bookings for these bands, too."

As I went down the list of bands, and contacted the other booking agencies, the theme was the same. No outside bookings are allowed. After a week of this, I started calling the booking agencies for R&B artists like Cameo, Atlantic Starr, Lakeside, Skyy, etc. Nobody called me back.

I'll be honest: I knew that I couldn't book anybody like The Jacksons, New Edition, or Earth, Wind & Fire, but I had enough clout and financing to book these other bands. To my surprise, it was impossible. My experience was a microcosm of what the Black promoters were going through with major Black acts nationwide.

The next ninety days of my promotion, life was both agony and ecstasy. It was a backstabbing rat race of a business. When it was going good, it was great. But when it was going bad, it was terrible. Since being exposed to the Record Pool world, I had the opportunity to meet many music industry types and learn who all the top booking agency people were. They all told me that no Rock Bands would work for us, college or otherwise.

Excuse me, what do you mean? Maybe I didn't make myself clear, but I have a budget. I'm comfortable with the pricing for a two-hour show. I will provide the transportation, the food, the sound system, and all the other amenities they require. Let's do this.

It turned out it wasn't a personal thing. Every rock band in New York was contracted with "Tix-Nation" Entertainment. Taking a booking with me meant they risked being kicked off the Tix-Nation roster of bands.

Okay. So, how about this? Whatever night that the local-yokel college band is "not" booked, I would book them. It sounded like a win/win to me. I didn't encroach on Tix-Nation's world; the band would get paid for an off night, and I would have my entertainment.

Nope. Tix-Nation wouldn't do it. Even if I were a booking agent, there would still be a risk to their careers. The band hasn't worked in a month. The band needs a gig to keep going. Nope. Sorry. *Wow, so it's like that?*

VERNON M. O'GARRA

Yup, Mr. Livingston, just like that!

It was a difficult lesson to learn. Tix-Nation was so powerful that they had everything locked up. Even the local bands would rather work for crumbs just to be on a Tix-Nation promotional gig. Surely, a brilliant but greedy and ignorant mind is at work here.

So, this wasn't going to be easy. Around the same time, I stumbled across an article in Jet Magazine. The article was about the difficulties Black Promotors experience and how White promoters almost always promoted major Black acts.

"Kenneth Gamble of the Gamble and Huff producing team, who was President of the (BMA) Black Music Association" at the time, said, "It is almost impossible for Black Promoters to get the major venues." (Jet Magazine, 1979). The United Black Concert Promoters (UBCP) organization was created "To combat what members called the encroachment of White promoters into their territory, without Blacks being allowed to promote big White acts." (Jet Magazine, 1979).

You could imagine that I almost fell off my chair reading that. I considered traveling to Atlanta to speak with these brothers about the promotion business and its pitfalls. It seemed like everywhere you turned, you had to deal with racist bullshit.

While the idea of promoting White bands was a good idea, it was not going to work. I was curious how John, the club owner, would handle this situation, so I sat back and watched him work for a change. After all, he was intelligent and resourceful. I admired him from afar but dared not tell him that to his face and feed his already over-inflated ego. He was the only Black Man I knew personally who made a legitimate six-figure income. Lovely home, new car. John had it going on.

I needed a little time away, so I told John I was going to visit family for a week. He was a workaholic, so if I were going to leave, I'd better have a good excuse. I left town for Washington, D.C., Chocolate City. A lot was happening in D.C., and I had an excellent time for a few days. Back in New York, I knew how John's mind worked. He's thinking about how to put his promotion together, and I started wondering what strings he would pull to make it happen. He knew a lot of people in the business, and he had a lot of connections, just as any club owner might.

Right in the middle of all this haggling back and forth, John Lennon of the Beatles was murdered while he was standing in front of his house. Some maniac shot him, and the entire world was stunned. For my part, I took at least a half dozen Beatles albums and put together a John Lennon tribute for my audience when I worked at the club. What a tragedy.

When I returned from D.C., I headed straight to the club to see John, and he greeted me with, "What's happening, Tech?"

He called me Tech, as in "Technician," a nickname I loved. When I walked into the club that day, there was no love in his question. I could see that he was pissed.

"While you were gone," said John, "I did some digging (on my own) concerning these bands. These White bands will only work for White promoters. Ain't that a bitch?" He was hot about that, and I couldn't blame him. "Damm, man. Money is green. Don't these motherfuckers want to get paid? These White bands all work for "Tix-Nation." "They're the biggest promoters in New York."

I didn't say a word. I just listened as John ranted. "Tix-Nation has it all locked up," John went on. "Whenever they book a major show and venue, they allow all local-yokel bands to open. They booked a thirty-thousand-seat venue with a major band like The Grateful Dead, Bob Dylan, or Simon & Garfunkel. Major acts. They begin the show two hours early, and these start-up bands will sell their souls to play for them. Hell, if they're any good, at least ten thousand people will be there early to hear them. It's their chance of a lifetime. They're not going to throw all that away for a few grand. If Tix-Nation hears about them working for another promoter, they will ban them from ever playing at one of their gigs. That's how they exercise control over them."

I started doing my research. One of the articles I found was written by journalist Edward Schumacher of the New York Times. In his article entitled "Black Music Promoters Battle Whites' Control of Marketing," he says, "The audience is Black, but the promoter is nearly always White." (Schumacher, 1979).

"In the last year, Black promoters and civil rights activists, asserting that music is a Black natural resource, have been waging an increasingly bitter battle to break White control over the marketing of Black stars."

"Black promoters will hire Black florists, Black limousine companies, and Black caterers. We're going to share the wealth in our own communities. When White promoters sign Black acts, all of the ancillary business opportunities go to other White-owned businesses.

It's a dilemma for Black artists and the Black promoters." (Schumacher, 1979).

Look at it this way: We're all starving and need to eat. The starving Black artist finally makes that hit record. You've been working hard (your whole life) to break through, and finally, your time comes. When the record company recognizes you and presents the contract, what are you going to do? You sign it. That's what you do. You need that check. Your family needs that check. Now, you're locked into a contract you barely read and don't understand. Record executives have booking agents and promoters that they work with exclusively. The problem is, they are all White!

So, we Black promoters look at these Black musicians and ask them, I want to promote you! Unfortunately, the musicians are contractually obligated to their record companies, so they don't dare interfere with their cash flow. Subsequently, the Black promoters are shut out.

Rev. Al Sharpton negotiated for a piece of the '84 Jacksons Victory Tour revenues because the White promoters were in charge of everything, and the Black promoters were shut out. I was very happy about that. The Jacksons were a group that had power. They also successfully negotiated a deal for Black promoters across the county to get a piece of the pie. But that wasn't the norm. It was a very rare occurrence.

Over the years, I've been researching these phenomena pretty extensively. Recently, I came across this article about Leonard Rowe. Leonard was from California. He had been catching hell promoting entertainment out there on the West Coast. I'd heard his name before and knew he wanted to do big-time promotions, but he faced the same roadblocks that I did in New York.

Leonard Rowe felt that racial discrimination against Black promoters in the entertainment industry was intolerable. So, he was instrumental in organizing a group of Black promoters to form the Black Promoters Association (BPA). The goal of the BPA was to secure equality and fairness for African American promoters in the concert promotion industry before we all became extinct.

He filed a lawsuit and had a strong case against the top two booking agencies (The William Morris Agency and Creative Artists Agency), all the booking agencies, and 26 White promoters in the concert business.

One of the things that struck me about Leonard's case, which was somewhat similar to mine, was that he was granted access to the plaintiffs' emails during the discovery phase of the case. He was asked to provide specific keywords to a data discovery company so that he could search through the emails belonging to the music agents. Specific keywords included racial slurs such as "nigger," "spook," and "Uncle Tom." Whenever those words were found, the emails containing the words would be revealed, and the data company would then be able to provide them with an accurate account of how many times each word was used and by whom.

Leonard was confident and did not doubt that the email search would uncover damaging and irrefutable evidence that racial animus and discrimination against Blacks existed at these White promotion companies.

A couple of weeks later, Leonard returned to New York for the email search results. Needless to say, the word "nigger" had been found *three hundred forty-nine* times in those emails. Hundreds of other racial slurs like "spook," "coon" and "monkey" were found as well.

Incredibly, these well-established White institutions were so racist. These agencies had offices all over the country. This was the same racist attitude that Black promoters were dealing with in New York. If you were a Black promoter, you were barred from promoting major acts at large venues. I realized early on what I was up against. Don't get me wrong, I loved the promotion business. I wanted to become a successful professional, but I wasn't going to allow the racist and ignorant-minded White establishment to put limits on my ability to promote entertainment.

Almost 40 years later, The Black Promoters Collective (BPC) was founded in 2020, during the pandemic, to address inequity in the live entertainment industry and promote independent Black promoters. I was happy to learn that the BPC is a 100% Black-owned company with six of the country's top independent concert promotion and event production companies. Although they didn't know it, this organization was so close to these old-school promotors that my heart and words couldn't describe it.

SportsTalk

1981 – *SportsTalk*: Art Rust Jr., a New York native born in Harlem, held numerous roles across many platforms in New York City. The one that stands out and inspired so many others was his gig as the host of a little radio show in the early 1980s called *SportsTalk*.

Art Rust had an encyclopedic knowledge of sports. He would talk in-depth about the Knicks, Nets, Rangers, Islanders, Jets, Giants, Mets, and Yankees.

I immediately liked Art Rust Jr. the first time I listened to him. He was my type of guy. I didn't even realize he was a Black Man at the time. For some reason, I figured he was White. Maybe it was how he sounded on the radio or the fact that Black news radio broadcasters weren't commonplace (at that time). Either way, I looked forward to his SportsTalk program every time it aired. It was great. Listening to his show made me feel like I was in the know about all things sports. For a sports fan, it was exciting to hear his broadcast every day.

I talked about sports every day on the train, commuting to and from work. And it didn't stop when I got to work. I was always talking with my coworkers about the latest episode of SportsTalk. Then, one day, my coworker Al told me that the show's host was Black. I couldn't believe it. It had *never* occurred to me that Art Rust Jr. was a Black Man before that moment. I saw him on a Yankees T.V. commercial with Billy Martin and George Steinbrenner sometime after that. I was *floored*!!! I was so proud of Art Rust Jr. that words couldn't express it. He was a brilliant sports mind and historian. As far as I was concerned, no one knew more about sports than Art. And he was a Black Man!

Journalist Stacy M. Brown once wrote about him, "Rust's "Sports Talk" was a game-changer, giving fans a platform to engage in conversation for three hours every night. Not to mention, guests would include legends like Muhammad Ali, Sonny Liston, and Joe DiMaggio.'

BRILLIANT MINDS, IGNORANT MINDS

The "Walking Encyclopedia of Sports" finally had his moment in the spotlight during the tumultuous 1981 player/owner strike in baseball. Rust was initially hired to host the Yankees pregame show. He was on air every night from 6 p.m. to 9 p.m. during the summer strike, which birthed an all-sports talk radio show that captivated disheartened baseball fans and laid the groundwork for the likes of WFAN, which emerged in 1988 with an All-White crew and not even a mention or an invitation to Rust.'

"Rust's impact remains undeniable. While Sirius XM's Chris Russo, who got his big break at WFAN alongside Mike Francesca and others, raked in millions, Rust set the stage for their success. Steve Somers, a host at WFAN, acknowledged Rust's role in shaping the station. "He certainly set the groundwork and the foundation for WFAN," Somers asserted."

Seven years later, an all-sports radio station, WFAN, launched. I can't tell you how angry I was that Art Rust Jr. was not on that station. It was inconceivable to me that he wasn't a part of an *all-sports station*. How could the most knowledgeable sports personality in New York City *not* be on the FAN? The brilliant minds decided to do an All Sports Radio format, a risky but brilliant idea. However, it was clear that the ignorant minds struck again, leaving one of the sports talk pioneers behind. I launched my own personal Art Rust Jr. campaign to no avail.

I and many other African American men (some women) are avid sports fans. Back then, we had little to no Black voices on the radio. We listened because eighty percent of the athletes discussed on the radio were Black. One morning, I listened to the premier New York City sports radio, and they hired this White guy. He was sort of a rock music radio icon and talk show DJ. In my opinion, the guy was an asshole who had *zero* knowledge about sports. But his ratings were so high in New York that the radio station owners marketed him as the marquee, the number one guy.

At the time, I was a commuter with an hour's drive to work every day, so I was pumped to listen to Sports Radio in the mornings. On my way to work one morning, I was listening to Sports Radio the way I always did, and this high-powered radio host decided to do a segment entitled "Ten Rap Records with the 'N' Word in the Lyrics." The next thing I heard was record after record after record being played with the 'N' word, all with bits of commentary between them berating and criticizing the music and the Black Community at large.

My first thought was, *what the hell does this have to do with sports?* My second thought was, what kind of message is this guy trying to send? To me, the message was as clear as day. That had nothing to do with sports. This radio host wanted to degrade Black people and then hide behind the record companies and Black rappers that authorized the release of these records. I was fuming as I listened to the broadcast, and all these White boys cackling and laughing behind the scenes as these songs played. I was angry, but I kept listening. And when they finally go to a commercial, I was like, *Wow!* These ignorant White minds. What were they thinking about allowing this type of music to be played on a sports radio station? To add insult to injury, when they came back from the commercial, they interviewed Art Rust Jr., and I was *appalled*. What was he doing there in the same room with these fools?

This Black Man, who had more sports knowledge on the tip of his finger than this radio host had in his whole body, wasn't fit to sit in the same room. It was a short interview. It lasted a few minutes, and I was sad for Art. Art Rust Jr. was on Sports Radio in New York before there was such a thing as Sports Radio. Here they had the Godfather of Sports Radio, and this major radio station relegated him to a five-minute interview with a jerk cracking jokes.

Twenty years later, that same White disc jockey made a racial insult about the Rutgers University women's basketball team, calling them "Nappy Headed Hoes." After he said it, his radio crew of sidekicks chimed in and said, "Yeah, they're like Spike Lee's jigaboos versus the wannabees in the 'Do the Right Thing' movie." (Kendi, 2019). I remember listening to these racist White boys and shaking my head. These idiots didn't even know the movie they were trying to reference was "School Daze." They knew nothing about the scene and what it represented in the Black community! They had no respect for Black people.

Gay Night at the Club

There was pushback from Black promoters nationwide for several years because we were shut out of all the major concert promotion events. Philly, Chicago, Atlanta, LA, Detroit, and New York. All over the country, Black promoters were locked out completely. We were looking to make up the difference for our bottom line.

John's mind is always thinking. One day, he came up with Plan B. "You know what? To hell with these bands. I've decided to promote 'Gay' Night.'

I stared at him for a minute, trying to see if he was serious. He was. "Really?"

"Yup, really! These gay promoters have been coming by the club for months now, telling me that they will pack the place if I give them a chance. Well, I'm going to give them a shot. Every Wednesday night, starting a week from this Wednesday, will be 'Gay Night."

I'll be honest: I was skeptical, but as they say, Beggars can't be choosers, and if those promoters said that they could pack the club, we'd be idiots not to try it. "Okay, let's go with it!

When the first "Gay Night" rolled around, John had us come to the club, set up, and talk about what we could expect…which nobody knew. I mean, we'd never done anything like this before. Still, the overall sentiment was, *well, let's see what happens.* About an hour later, people started rolling in. By eleven, over a hundred people were in the club. The line for admission extended around the corner. By midnight, the place was three-quarters of the way full and jumping. As a DJ, I was feeding off the crowd, and the crowd was pushing me to rock them, so that's what I did. It turned out to be the absolute hottest Wednesday night of my DJ career. That crowd was hyped, partying like Prince 1999. And the drinks were flowing. I don't think I've ever had so many people send drinks my way to the DJ booth.

That night, the party was jumping nonstop. Three in the morning, four in the morning, there was no sign of any letting up. And this was a *Wednesday night!* John had to pull the plug fifteen after four so we could get out before dawn.

It took a good thirty minutes to empty the club. Once everything was locked down, we sat around smoking, drinking, and counting money until six. That first night, there was no debate about it. That was the hottest crowd we've ever had. Hands down, we were onto something.

So that's how it went every week. Wednesdays were the hot night in town for us. By week four, John asked me to help the barmaid. I jumped right into it even though I never did it before then. My thought was that I could make some extra cash, and boy, did I! I was flipping the bottles behind my back like Tom Cruise in Cocktail and having a blast. And the crowd loved it. I had a lot of gay guys coming up to me and flirting with me, but hey, they were also tipping big. That was the first time I understood what the barmaids and waitresses already knew. Men who think you look good tip big.

Now, if you think this is some story about how I found my "true sexuality" or something like that, I'm sorry to disappoint you. Not a single man who ever hit on me did anything to change the fact that I'm heterosexual. As it turns out, that's not how that works at all. And if I'm being honest, I was flattered that those gay guys bought me drinks and tipped big. I was lining my pockets with their compliments.

I got teased by the waitresses and the barmaid, of course. But I wasn't mad about it.

"Wednesday Gay Night" was a huge success and a big money maker that the staff looked forward to every week. As a DJ, I loved the gay crowd. They came to party and dance, bringing out the best in me. And the best part? I even had a promoter hire me to do several outside gigs for them.

One night, one of my friends, a DJ, invited me out to his club for a party. I hooked up with my Godbrother, Ed, and we went to check out this party. The room was nice, and the crowd was beautiful. We were partying, having drinks, and generally having a great time when this sexy-looking White girl came up to me.

"Hello, D.J. Technician," she said with a smile. I smiled right back, and it occurred to me that she seemed to know me.

"Have we met somewhere before?" I asked her. She told me we met at the club where I DJ'd most nights, and she winked at me as she walked away. I stood there watching her walk away, trying to figure out how I missed somebody like her. She was *gorgeous*. Not the kind of woman that you could ever forget meeting. I walked over to Ed and asked him. "Hey, you see that woman?

Where do I know her from? Ed starts laughing. "Man, that ain't no woman. That's Marco. He's a female impersonator."

"Get the fuck out of here!" She had to be one of the hottest women in that place." My jaw hit the floor. "How can a man look better than eighty percent of the women in the room?"

"You should come to one of Marco's shows," Ed tells me. "He's terrific. One of the best in the show."

Later, we went to see Marco's show, which was one of the best times I had ever had. What you can discover is funny when you step out of your own world. You learn some new things, but many things are the same. Everybody wants to live, make money, party, and do their own thing. Once you start looking at it like that, you find out that people everywhere are just people, whether they're in a dress or pants.

Ripped off

A few months later, one of the major record companies started sponsoring a DJ mixing contest. They advertised it all over the radio stations and record pools so everybody in my world knew all about it. As soon as I heard about this contest, I knew right away I could win it! There was no doubt in my mind. I was putting mixes together in my mind as soon as I heard about the contest.

I had about three weeks to work on my DJ mix when I heard about it. I worked on it for several hours per day. I have always been a perfectionist when it comes to music and mixing. I had to get it just right. By the second week, it had gotten so bad that my girlfriend (who would eventually become my wife) started screaming at me, "Miles! Not again!!! Give it a rest, PLEASE!!!"

I turned down the volume and put on my headphones, but there was no way I could stop. It has to be perfect. Many nights, I stayed up working on it until early morning. I took a shower and went to work without sleep.

But it all paid off. Forty-eight hours before the deadline, I traveled to Manhattan and arrived at the record label headquarters to deliver my contest entry. I made sure the record company receptionist had all my contact information. I guaranteed her *this* was the winning entry, and I (certainly) expected to hear from her. Like I said. In my mind, I could not lose.

The deadline came and went. It seemed like I was listening to the radio twenty-four/seven, waiting for the contest results. Finally, about a week later, the announcement came! The winning mix will be played on the radio. I thought to myself, *Wait a minute. Nobody's called me yet.* I was confident that none of those other DJs could outmix me. I was wondering what happened to my phone call.

On the day of the big announcement, I waited with bated breath for the winning mix to be played. I sat there, glued to the radio, until they finally played the mix, and I almost passed out. It wasn't mine, but it sure sounded like my shit. *They stole my mixing ideas!* I couldn't believe it. I sat there with my mouth open, listening as all my creative mixing blended into a few different songs while the radio show host announced some other disc jockey as the winner. I was in a state of shock! I called the record company the next day about it, only to be told some bullshit story about my tape being submitted with all the others. All I could think was that these motherfuckers, stole my mixes and allowed one of their cronies to win the contest. That was the end of my days making tapes. If anyone wanted to hear a DJ Technician mix, they would have to listen to it live and in person. I worked too hard to build my brand and would never again put my best work on tape.

Maybe I overreacted a little bit. All DJs steal each other's mixes, but that contest incident drove me crazy. Whenever I heard a DJ make a nice mix, I might have copied it, but I made a point to perfect it and make it my own. I never straight-up ripped anybody off.

And it wasn't even the last time it ever happened. A short time after that, I decided to audition for a radio disc jockey job. I sent in my radio audition tape, but I found out later that the program director had stolen all my lines. I couldn't believe my ears. This guy who was supposed to vet me for a job was repeating all my slogans on "His" radio program. I couldn't seem to get a break!

The Death of Willie Turks

I dabbled in the promotion game for a few years. But, my heart was gravitating more towards being a DJ. A big heavyweight fight was scheduled in Vegas, so I decided to watch the fight at the Theatre at Madison Square Garden. The fight was between hometown boy Gerry Coney and the champion, Larry Holmes. But it was really the Black Guy versus The Great White Hope. The promotors really played up the racial overtones of this fight. The Champ called Cooney, The Great White Dope. What a night! Cooney hits Holmes below the belt during the fight, and the crowd goes wild. Holmes takes a few minutes to compose himself, he beats the shit out of Cooney, and the fight is stopped in round 13. After the fight, I head towards the LIRR Train station. As I approached the station right underneath the Garden, I noticed not many Black folks riding the train that night. All I see are drunk and pissed-off White boys shouting Nigger this and Nigger that.

I'm laughing my ass off because I'm drunk too, and in my mind, I'm preparing to knock one or two of these guys out before they jump me. As I boarded the train to Huntington, the entire train was packed. Gerry Cooney is from Huntington, too. He went to Walt Whitman High School, the rival cross-town school in Huntington. Lucky for me, none of these White guys messed with me—just a lot of shouting of racial epithets and cursing.

A week later, I heard about the murder of Willie Turks. He was a Black MTA train worker who was beaten to death by a White mob in Sheepshead Bay, Brooklyn. It was a story we often heard about a Black Man being in the wrong neighborhood at the right time. You see, they *hated* Black people in Sheepshead Bay. Remember when I mentioned the time I wanted tickets to the circus when I was a kid, and we couldn't go? Sheepshead Bay was the White racist neighborhood my cousin was referring to. This poor guy had just gotten off work from the MTA trainyard and was walking to his car with some coworkers. They stopped at the store, and when they came out, this group of twenty-something White boys beat the shit out of them for no reason. They beat him to death like a dog in the street. Damm! I was burning hot about it. I wanted revenge so bad I could taste it. I was still mad about being unable to go to that silly circus when I was a kid, and I was angry for Willie Turks. I remember being so mad that my parents had to calm me down.

It still pisses me off, even today. I don't have the patience to spend years fighting for what's right. That's an unfortunate character flaw I must unfortunately own up to. Racist and unjust policies would probably send me over the edge, like the Willie Turks incident.

Everything that happened up to this point boiled down to White people holding Black people down in any way they could. They beat us and kill us, and when that doesn't work, they hit us in our pocketbooks. White people financially benefited from Black people, which is the foundation on which the United States was built. There will always be unrest and violence in response to these problems, and no one seems interested in fixing them. Where are the brilliant White minds when we need them?

What I have realized is that so many industries in this country that still exist today have been built on the pain and suffering of Black and Brown people in this country, and we still have nothing to show for it. We have never gotten full reparations for the misdeeds done to Black people in this country. People think that reparations mean monetary gain, and they can, but it doesn't have to mean *just* that. Reparations are about *repairing* the damage done. Honestly, I feel our government should follow the example set in Germany in its measures to repair the damage done to the Jewish population during World War II. Germans put policies in place to educate the public and do away with racist policies that hurt their citizens, and today, they are stronger for it.

Where are our reparations? When will this country stop hurting its citizens and own up to the crimes that are still happening today?

Glory, Glory, Hallelujah

Looking back on my promotion career, I realize I was ahead of the curve. Since I was an established DJ, I knew all the major players. I'd paid my dues in the eighties. By the nineties, I was one of the more prominent players. It was still a segregated world. I hadn't broken through and was still promoting the smaller/less-known Black acts, but that was how it was.

I was able to promote a gospel show at the Westbury Music Fair. The White promoters didn't (seem to) care too much about gospel music, so it was reasonably straightforward. My partners and I did a bunch of events centered around the "Break Dancing" craze. It was great, but I needed more. I read an article once in some music publication about how Black promoters couldn't handle a large event at a stadium or major theatres. I couldn't believe what I was reading. There were ignorant White minds who did not know how brilliant Black minds could promote a stadium event.

I was pissed off and burning inside. I had a Rolodex full of professionals in the entertainment landscape—Black, White, Hispanic, Women, and members of the LGBTQ Community. Undoubtedly, I could have effectively and professionally produced a large-scale promotion. I had a Bachelor's degree in Business Administration, knew about contracts, understood entertainment law, and had several attorneys at my fingertips. I knew about the unions, I knew about building codes, I knew about the Fire Marshall, I knew *exactly* what the owners wanted. I even understood radio and advertising. Nobody could tell me that I didn't know what entertainers people wanted to see. And anything that I wasn't an expert on, I made damn sure one of my staff members knew about it. I wanted to tell the author of the article to remove the barriers and watch me work. From what I could see, those White boys who were promoting Black acts didn't even know what they were doing. Yeah, they had concessions and T-shirts and shit like that, but none of it catered to their fan bases, who were predominantly Black.

Promoters like me went to these large venues and put flyers on the cars of all the people in attendance. So let's say there was a hot band in town at the Coliseum like Earth, Wind & Fire, Cameo, Funkadelic, or Lakeside. (Or all of them. How's that for a rockin' 1980s show). The coliseum held sixteen thousand people, and the show sold out for weeks. My strategy was simple. I found a room in the vicinity that could hold four to six hundred people, and I rented the place out. Those big-time promoters didn't care about the scraps that fell off their table, so there was no problem renting a room to promote a smaller event. The trick was to get one of the bands to stop by the party, even if it was just for a minute or two. Sometimes, you get lucky, and a band member or two might pop into the party for a drink and a few photographs. That was gold for a promoter. It added to my reputation. The rumor of a celebrity stopping by one of my parties was enough to drum up business. That was the business of building relationships, and I not only loved it, I was damn good at it.

Mr. Livingston, It's Time for a Change

Somewhere in the middle of that, I had a lull in the promotion business. I found myself spinning my wheels in the music industry. I started thinking about becoming a healthcare professional. It was fun, but the older I got, the more I wanted a job with benefits, a 401(k) plan, life and health insurance, and maybe a credit union. You know, all the regular shit you don't get hustling around from gig to gig.

One day, I got a call from my cousin Tom Chase. He asked me about my career aspirations and job prospects, so I told him about my musical career as a DJ and promoter. Cousin Tommie counseled me about the importance of working for a company that provides benefits like health insurance, retirement, and a steady income to build a strong credit rating and stability.

It was the right conversation at the right time. I was becoming disillusioned with the music world and needed something more permanent. Tommie persuaded me to go and get "That good City of New York job," and I listened. On May 16, 1980, I was hired into a position as a "Hospital Care Investigator" (HCI) for the New York Hospitals Corporation.

Freedmont General Hospital. When I arrived at work on my first day, a Caucasian woman walked in and asked, "Well, who is Miles Livingston?"

I answered, "I'm Miles Livingston."

She looked at me, visibly crushed and horrified. "Oh, hi," she said in a sheepish tone. "I'm Irish, and when I saw the name Livingston, I thought a fellow Irishman had been hired."

I just smiled at her. "I am Irish!" I told her." I'm from the Black Hills of Ireland. It's so lovely to meet you."

She looked down at the ground and walked out. My supervisor, William, who happened to be in the office during this encounter, chuckled and said, "Hey Miles, that certainly went well. You're going to fit right in with us. I could tell she was so happy to meet you."

I laughed at this experience because it reminded me of when my Dad sat me and my brother down one day and told us about our Sir name. "The Livingston family," he told us, "Are from Montserrat West Indies. Your grandmother's last name is Livingston. She didn't have to change her last name when she got married to your grandfather. The important thing I want you boys to know is that Livingston is an Irish name. White people are going to see your name and think that you are White. It's happened to me all my life and will also happen to you." My Dad was so right. Sight unseen, this White woman thought I was White and almost passed out when she saw I was Black. I couldn't wait to tell my parents about my first day at this "Good New York City job."

As the weeks and months rolled by at my new job, I quickly realized that Black men hold very few management positions. There's a brother in Medical Records, another brother in the Admitting Department, and another brother in Linen/Laundry and Housekeeping. Four African American males in management at my job. Only four. I don't know what to make of it, but I do take note of it.

On the other hand, I worked under the umbrella of Hospital Finance. There were no Black men in management there. My cousin, who got me that job, eventually moved on to a Bronx Hospital while I stayed in Queens. Even though it's early in my career, I'm cognizant of my surroundings and work environment. I watch and see everything, and the wrongdoing towards Black men is glaringly obvious to me.

1983 – Trouble Brewing

As an upwardly mobile Black Man employed in the healthcare sector, I instinctively am looking for opportunities for advancement. Music was still my first love, but I was also ready to get serious about working as a healthcare professional. I've got a college degree, for Christ's sake. It was time I had a career. I'd been a temp for over two years, and it was time to take the civil service exam. New York City's civil service exam process was designed to ensure the hiring process was competitive and fair. It also meant better pay and opportunities. I studied hard for that exam. And when I took it, I felt confident that I was going to get a good score.

It took a little time, but eventually, I got my Notice of Result card from the DCAS (The Department of Citywide Admin Services). I scored a 98.1093%, which was…good. I looked at my scorecard and wondered *what kind of score is this*. Come to find out, over five thousand people took the exam… and my list number was forty-nine.

That doesn't sound great! Civil Service rules stated that people were hired based on the number. Well, number forty-nine at Freedmont Hospital was actually number one. Even so, I had to wait almost the entire year before they called me to attend the hiring pool interview.

Around this time, Michael Stewart was killed by police on September 15, 1983. He got arrested for spraying graffiti on the L train in Brooklyn. The police said Stewart resisted arrest, so they restrained him and tuned him up. Translation: the police beat the shit out of him while waiting for the police van. They took him to the hospital, but he was in a coma by the time they arrived. He lived for thirteen days and died before regaining consciousness. A minor petty offense and another Black Man gets killed by police. It was the first time I got involved in several events to protest Police brutality and support the Stewart family.

One day, I received a call while I was at the office. "This is Ms. Doledrum calling from the Dept of Personnel, Background Investigations unit."

"How can I help you?" What happened next was a barrage of questions about my resume. I answered her questions, and suddenly, she had an attitude.

"Mr. Livingston, it has come to my attention that you have misrepresented yourself on your resume. If you don't send me the necessary documentation, you will be terminated from your job."

I couldn't believe my ears. "Are you serious? Are you sure you're speaking to the right person?"

"Well," She responds, "Are you Miles Livingston?"

"Yes, I am."

"And do you reside at 436 East 16th Street?"

"Yes, I do."

"And you are employed at Freedmont Hospital Center?"

"I am."

"Alright then. I'm speaking with the right person. You have one week to comply with my request, or you'll be terminated."

A few days later, a certified letter from the Dept. of Personnel informed me that I had to comply or be terminated. Among the documents I needed to provide was proof of my last two places of employment. My previous two jobs were at the Dept of Labor and the Suffolk County Youth Development Agency. So, I called my old boss, Paul, who remembers me very well from those days.

"Hey, Miles," he said, "I've been expecting your call. Some hotheaded woman from the Dept. of Investigations called me and threatened to have you fired for falsifying your resume."

"What!!! I can't believe this! She called me with the same story."

"Don't worry, Miles. I wrote her a nice letter on my letterhead that should straighten everything out."

"Thank you, Paul. I appreciate it."

In addition to my boss's letter, I also answered my letter in a notarized document. As far as I was concerned, the matter was put to bed, but I couldn't help wondering why my integrity was being challenged. A few weeks later, a coworker approached me in the men's room. "Hey, Miles," he told me, "Watch your back. I don't know what you did to Jim, but he's out to get you." That's all he said to me before walking out…

The next nine months were hell for me at work. It started with my employment list number getting called. I was contacted to go down to the pool for a permanent position. I walked in for my appointment at the pool, suited up and ready to accept my job. I felt that even though I'd spent all that time as a "provisional" employee or Temp, now that I'd taken the civil service test, the rest should be simple. I belonged there. I thought I'd proven that.

I sat in a waiting room with about fifty other people before I heard my name called. I approached the front desk and was called into one of the offices.

"Hello," the woman who called me into the office said. She was a stern, older Black woman who didn't seem to have much patience or time for any bullshit. "You're Miles Livingston, right?"

"Yes, I am."

"Well, I have to tell you that you've been bumped."

I just stared at her. "Bumped? What's bumped?"

"It means that another employee has taken your spot. You work at Freedmont Hospital, right?" I told her yes, and she looked down at some paperwork in front of her.

"You have been bumped, and I can do nothing to help you."

I told her that HCI exam number forty-nine is number one at Freedmont Hospital. She told me it didn't matter because I had a "Bad" reputation. I couldn't believe my ears. Apparently, I garnered a reputation as someone who didn't complete their work. And, therefore, didn't deserve the position I'd been doing on a temp basis all this time.

I walked out of that building in Downtown Manhattan feeling like shit. Here I was, all pumped up when I went there because I'm the number one employee at Freedmont Hospital. I also tested higher than most people applying for the same position. And now, to be told that I have a bad reputation? What a terrible ending to a potentially great day.

What it worked out to be was that I was to be fired right before Christmas. A little while after that interview, I received an official termination letter by certified mail stating that December 23rd, 1983, was my last day of employment. It was unbelievable, but I didn't let it get to me, at least not while I was still working. I knew what kind of worker I was. I was prepared to fight for my rights.

The first thing I did was make an appointment to speak to the department director, who happened to be a middle-aged Black woman and a career city employee. She was as cold as ice toward me from the jump. But she told me there was nothing they could do for me.

I decided I would visit the Executive Director of Human Resources. My thinking was, how can they possibly fire me? This was wrongful termination, at the very least. How can they bump me out of my job without reason or evidence?

Anyway, the H.R. Director granted me a meeting. I arrived early, only to be kept waiting for nearly thirty minutes. The secretary ushered me into an opulent office – plush carpet and a fine mahogany desk. Degrees and certificates hung all over his walls in lacquered frames. Mrs. Gladstone sat behind a gigantic desk as I walked through the doors. She looked up and asked me to take a seat. I went through everything that happened so far, right from the beginning. I shared my high score on the civil service exam, the call from Mrs. Doledrum, the conversation about my "reputation" during the interview…all of it. I also brought a briefcase full of my credentials. I wanted to show her that I was a hard-working college graduate. Despite this unfounded claim that I didn't work, I had come to work every single day.

She listened, and when I was through, she carefully examined my paperwork. After several minutes, she looked at me and said, "I'm reinstating you, Mr. Livingston. Effective immediately." What stood out the most was the tip I got about my Patient Accounts Manager, "Jim," having it out for me. After she told me I was reinstated, she called her secretary and told her to get Jim on the phone. When her phone buzzed a few minutes later, she wasted no time.

"Hello, Jim, this is Samantha Gladstone. I'm here with your employee, Miles Livingston. I have just reinstated him to full duty, effective immediately. I'm sending him back to his workstation right now. You are not to harass him or intimidate him in any way. Do you understand me? I heard him say (something like), "I understand, but he got bumped, and his position is filled."

She responded sharply. "Well, I suggest you un-fill it because this employee has been reinstated. I expect his employment file to be on my desk in the morning. Are we clear, Jim?"

Wow!!! I finally found someone who was on my side, someone with power. It was an exhilarating, once-in-a-lifetime feeling. I walked back into my office with the swagger of a superstar. Deep down inside, I didn't think they could fire me on such bullshit, and I had the H.R. Executive Director behind me. It was a complete vindication for me. I never really had any more problems out of Jim Balvin after that. He left me alone, and I left him alone. And I continued to work in my full-time position as an HCI despite some efforts to get me removed.

1984 – Back to Basketball

It's '84. I met my wife about two years prior—the love of my life and the only woman for me. The moment I met her, I knew she was the one. During that time, life was good at home. She was my peace.

Outside of my home was a different matter. It was a crazy time in New York. Gangster John Gotti was running wild, and the media and press loved him. The news programs were inundated with coverage of Gotti. Then, in April, Marvin Gaye was shot to death by his father during a domestic dispute. The entire nation was in shock. They say that you always remember where you were during big events in the world. I was in my car when I heard about Marvin Gaye's demise. As soon as I got home, I immediately started pulling out all of my Marvin Gaye records and began working on a musical tribute mix in his honor.

I was an avid basketball player at the time, balling in the parks and various places throughout Long Island and Queens. The hospital happened to participate in the NY Hospitals Basketball League. I tried out for it when I learned that our hospital was assembling a team. After all, I was a beast on the court. They were going to need a guy like me on their team.

The hospital had this little dinky elementary school gym. Some of the other guys and I chuckled and joked about its size. It was what I'd call a "matchbox" gym, small and square with little room to move around in. It was all we had.

I try out, and, of course, I make the team. During one particular practice, this new guy showed up to play. He was about 6'5" and 270 lbs. A big bruiser type guy. Practice began, and he stepped out to guard me, but there was no way he could defend me. I was too nimble, and his size made him slower than me. I throw a "shak-n-bake" move at this big boy and blew right past him to score. He didn't appreciate that too much because he got me back towards the end of practice. I got the ball and drove to the hole to get another two points, but the big boy lumbered over to stop me at the last second. He grabbed me and slammed me down onto the court. I landed hard on my wrist. It hurt like a bitch, but I shook it off and finished the game. Afterward, the coach looked at my wrist to make sure I was okay. I told him I was fine and he took me at my word.

The coach (Also our new Human Resource director) gave us a nod and a "Good Practice, fellas" and told us that the season would start next week and we needed to be ready.

Around this same time, I enrolled in a computer programming class at the Albert Merrill Computer Programming School. I hustled out of practice, jumped on the train, and headed to class. As I rode the train to class, I slowly realized that I had a problem with my wrist as I reviewed my class notes. When I looked a little closer, I could see my wrist was starting to swell. By the time I got to class, I was in excruciating pain. It looked like class wasn't happening that day, so I excused myself and went to the nearest emergency room.

In the emergency room, they x-rayed my wrist and told me that it was fractured. The doctor shot me up with pain medication and wrapped my wrist in a Plaster of Paris cast. Then he wrote me a script and told me to come back in a month to have the cast removed. I rode the train home with my arm in a sling and a cast on my wrist.

When I showed up to work the next day with a cast on my wrist, My HR rep/coach said, "Hey, Miles. I'm not at all surprised. That was a tough shot you took last night. I'm going to put you out on workers' compensation until you heal. Don't worry about anything. I'll be your witness since I coach the team."

It sounded good to me. I returned to my department and went straight to my director's office. You know, my director Jim Balvin, who gave me so much trouble the year before? Yeah, that guy. So far, we haven't had any problems since then. I didn't think anything of telling him what happened and what the new HR rep had just told me.

I knocked on his door. "Hello, Mr. Balvin. May I speak with you for a minute?"

"Sure, come in. What happened to your arm?"

"I injured myself playing basketball for the Hospital Basketball Team."

He blinked at me like I'd started speaking another language. "I didn't know we had a basketball team."

"Yes, we do. I just stopped in to tell you that I'll be out on workmen's compensation for the next six weeks while I heal."

"The Hell you will," he scoffed. "Playing basketball isn't a work-related injury. I will certainly not approve a workmen's comp leave for you."

I could have argued or given him a hard time about it. But if I had learned anything by this point, I'd learned that having people on your side in high places spoke louder than anything else. I looked him straight in the eye, and with a smile, I said, "Thank you for your time, Mr. Balvin. The Director of Human Resources told me to tell you that he'll answer any questions you may have concerning my compensation claim." Then I turned around and walked out. My worker's comp was approved, and I was out for six weeks. I remember one of my coworkers (and very good friend), Al, seeing me as I walked out that day and asking what happened to my wrist. I told him the story, and he chuckled, shaking his head. "You really got over with that one. Take care of yourself, and we'll see you when you return to work."

I stayed home on paid leave until I got my cast removed six weeks later. It really is good to know the right people. It was seemingly a blessing in disguise because Jessie Jackson was running for President, and this time off gave me an opportunity to volunteer for the Jackson campaign.

1985/1986 – The More Things Change

By the end of 1984, I was engaged to my fiancée. We planned to get married in November that year, but it didn't work out because we still had some outstanding expenses. It's funny how money always seems to get in the way of love. We could have done a courthouse wedding, but this was our first marriage. We wanted it to be something special, shared with our friends and family, and that cost money.

My fiancée and I decided to pay off our wedding expenses (honeymoon and all) before we married. That way, we wouldn't have any bills or loans after the wedding ceremony. After pouring over our budgets, we concluded it would take about ninety days to pay off everything. We buckled down and started saving. It was hard, but we managed to get it done. We married on February 5, 1985, and had a wonderful honeymoon in the Bahamas. The best part was when we got home, we were debt-free from our wedding expenses.

On Oct 7, 1985, I went to see Minister Louis Farrakhan speak at Madison Square Garden. It was an enlightening and exhilarating experience for me to be inside a packed Madison Square Garden with over seventeen thousand Black people. Farrakhan passionately spoke on many valuable lessons for the Black community, energizing everyone in the building. His speech got national attention thanks to some controversial remarks he made about the Jewish community. Out of everything he said that night, the press corps chose to run with the negativity, and they painted him as being anti-Semitic.

The New York Times reported: "Louis Farrakhan, the Black Muslim minister, electrified an overflow crowd of 25,000 at Madison Square Garden last night with a message of economic and spiritual renewal coupled with a ringing denunciation of his critics."

Farrakhan was quoted as saying, "They call me racist, they call me bigoted, they call me anti-Semitic," Mr. Farrakhan said. "But I want you to listen very carefully tonight. If anything like that comes out of my mouth, I want you to raise your hand and stop me. That's what they say I am. Tonight, I want you to judge for yourself." (Roberts, 1985).

In January 1986, Martin Luther King Jr. Day was finally observed. The bill had been passed three years before. Still, it took a concentrated effort from politicians and celebrities (notably Stevie Wonder) to push it to be recognized nationwide. When it finally was, it was a great day.

By July, the one concert I regretted missing that year came through New York. Run-DMC rocked Madison Square Garden. At the time, they had a hit single, "My Adidas," that singlehandedly skyrocketed sales for the shoe company. I heard Russell Simmons invited the Adidas executives to the performance. Man, I wish I'd been there.

But by the end of '1986, things were back to business as usual. On December 20, A twenty-three-year-old Trinidadian immigrant named Michael Griffith was killed after being hit by a car as he was chased onto a highway by a mob of White youths who had beaten him and his friends. My brother and I attended a protest march with the Rev. Al Sharpton to support the family of Michael Griffith and protest racial violence against Blacks.

Griffith's death was the second of three infamous racially motivated killings of Black men by White mobs in New York City in the 1980s. There was Griffith, Willie Turks, who I already mentioned back in '1982, and Yusuf Hawkins in '1989. Seeing how much things were starting to change was funny, yet they stayed exactly the same.

Class Action

1984, the Acme DP Corporation sent me a $3,500 check to settle a class action discrimination case. You see, I applied for a job at Acme DP Corp back in 1981. It was the usual interview with the twenty-something White girl in Human Resources. The Newspaper advertisement was for a payroll analyst position with a "Bachelor's Degrees are preferred" tagline. So, I applied, got the interview, and never heard back. Two and a half years went by, and my phone rang. An attorney working on a class action discrimination suit called me to say that my resume became a focal point during an investigation of Acme DP, and he had some questions for me.

"Were you offered the position you applied for at Acme DP?"

I said no. The attorney replied, "Well, your resume was thoroughly examined, and you are qualified for the position you applied for. Mr. Livingston, may I ask your race?"

I answered, African American. The attorney asked if I had been called back for a second interview. I told him that I wasn't. At that point, the attorney told me about the class action discrimination suit that had been filed against the company, and I could be part of it because I met the criteria. I was one of many who qualified for the position but wasn't considered because I was an African American. Of course, I agreed to join the lawsuit. He thanked me and said he would send paperwork for me to sign off on and would be in touch.

A couple of weeks later, a thick package of non-disclosure agreements arrived for me to sign. I did not waste any time signing it and mailing it back. About ninety days later, a check for $3,500 arrived in the mail. That check was right on time since I was still out on workman's comp for my wrist.

And what do I do with the money? I head off to Atlantic City to do some gambling. My brother just bought a new Honda Civic and wanted to take it for a drive. What better way to test it out than a road trip? We hit the road, me, my brother, and my god-brother, Ed. As soon as we got on the New Jersey Turnpike, my brother hit the gas and started to air that Honda out.

"Let's see what this puppy can do," he said as he floored it. We were moving about a hundred and five miles per hour when I noticed we were coming up fast on a police car. My brother also saw them, too, just in time. We slowed down just as we got close to the cops, but it was too late. The second we passed them, the cops turned on their lights and followed us. My brother pulled off to the side of the road.

Both cops exited the police cruiser and approached the car. I'm like, *Oh Shit. We're in trouble now.* New Jersey Highway Patrol Cops were the worst.

"Stay calm, boys," said Ed. "Just get your documents ready."

The first cop walked up to the driver's side, and the second cop sidled up on my side. Here we were, three Black guys in a speeding car on the highway. It was a recipe for disaster. I can see the cop on my side has his hand on his sidearm from the driver's side mirror. My heart was racing. My brother rolled down his window and said, "Good evening, officer. How can I help you?"

"Did you realize you were speeding? I saw you in my rearview mirror approaching us so fast it was obvious you were speeding." He looks over at me and Ed. "Have you Boys been drinking tonight?"

"No, Sir," my brother said.

"License, registration, and insurance card, please." said the cop. As my brother went to get his papers, the cop glanced at the windshield. "I don't see your window sticker?"

"I just bought this car, and I wanted to take a drive to Atlantic City."

"Is that so?" The cop said. "Can you step out of the car for me, please?"

My brother complies. Once outside the car, the cop asked him to recite the alphabet. My brother was so surprised he replied, "What?"

"You heard me. Say your ABCs. *Now.*"

My brother gulped and started babbling like an idiot. *A bah, A bah, A bah, Bid ah, Bid ah, Zee…*

The cop leaned in and asked, "Try that again? Say your ABCs!"

Once again he starts stammering, *A bah, A bah, A bah, Bid ah, Bid ah, Zee.*

I couldn't hold it in any longer. "Billy, what the fuck is wrong with you???"

All of a sudden, Ed started laughing from the back seat, which made me laugh. And that made both cops start laughing. We're all laughing hysterically until we're practically crying. The cops finally composed themselves, and the first cop looked at my brother, wiping tears from his eyes. "All right, you sure you haven't been drinking tonight?"

My brother shook his head, no. The officer miraculously gave my brother his license and documents and said, "Slow down and have a good time in Atlantic City."

And it was over, just like that. The cops walked back to their patrol car and drove off. I swear I wanted to kick my brother's ass, but we were still laughing. "You know that no one will *ever* believe this story. What were you thinking? Why didn't you say your ABCs like the cop asked?

"I thought that if I said them super-fast, he would know that I wasn't drunk," my brother said.

I mimic him. "*A bah, A bah, A bah, Bid ah, Bid ah, Zee* is saying your ABCs super-fast??" And we all start laughing all over again.

Today, I shudder to think about how that situation could have escalated into something tragic because of nonsense and silliness. It's the luck of the draw when dealing with cops. Anything can happen.

Shortly after our trip to Atlantic City, news about the death of Len Bias spread like wildfire across the country. Len Bias was the Boston Celtic's number one draft pick, an All-American College basketball star, who died of a drug overdose. He was so happy the Celtics drafted him that he decided to celebrate with drugs and alcohol. Things got out of hand. The entire nation was shocked, especially basketball fans like myself.

The Mad Bomber

After a long day at work, I finished on time and caught my train home. That day, the train was full. It was rush hour, and I sat next to this middle-aged White man. Around twenty minutes into the commute home, I started to hear this guy whimpering and sobbing.

"Are you all right?" I asked him.

He turned to me and said in a thick Irish brogue, "You can't imagine the hell I've been through in my life. I was a soldier back in Ireland. A member of the IRA. I'm a bomb builder. I've killed many, many people." He broke down again, sobbing. "My brother is dead, my sister is dead, my parents are dead, I have no one, so I became a soldier and spent my life killing people."

I told him that you could start your life over again in America. I asked him, "How did you get out of the country?"

121

He told me about life in Belfast, Ireland, and how the Catholics and Protestants were at war with each other. He told me how he fought to end British rule in Northern Ireland. It's an incredible story. I sat and listened to him tell me his life story, hoping that might help him feel a little better.

He gave me a history lesson about the British rule in Northern Ireland and the dissident rebellion for Irish independence. He told me that he could relate to Black people's struggle in America. "I know about Martin Luther King and how you Black people have to fight for your equality. Discrimination is a terrible thing. I am a White Catholic, and the Protestants back home in Belfast hate me." He broke down once again.

I tried to console him by saying, "Look, you must begin a new life now in America. "What's done is done. You are a survivor. You made up your mind to make changes in your life, and you did that. Many people in this world don't have the discipline and determination to change their lives, and you did that. You've got to pull yourself together and be strong for your lost comrades and family members. It's time for a new beginning because the past will eat you alive and drive you crazy. Promise me you will let the past go and make a fresh start."

He listened to me, his tears hanging in his eyes. "Yes, I will. Thank you for that. I needed to hear it." The train pulled into my stop, and I turned to him and told him to take care of himself and that I would pray for him.

What an encounter. I never even learned his name. The mad bomber from Belfast who survived beat the odds and escaped to America.

BRILLIANT MINDS, IGNORANT MINDS

"Blacks Aren't Smart Enough to be Managers"

On a beautiful spring evening in April of '87, it was the fortieth anniversary of Jackie Robinson's integration into major league baseball. In 1987, several Black baseball players played professional baseball, but only one Black Manager (Frank Robinson) and one General Manager (Bill Lucas) existed. I was hanging out with my Dad that night watching Nightline when Ted Koppel asked Al Campanis why he thought there were no Black managers in baseball. He responded that Blacks didn't have the necessities or intellectual capacity to be Field Managers or General Managers.

Yeah! He said that in *1987*. My Dad and I looked at each other, like, *did you hear what that White man just said on national TV?* Then, to add insult to injury, a surprised Ted Koppel asks him again, "Do you really believe that?" And this White man, who was the President of the Los Angeles Dodgers baseball team, repeated it. "Blacks just don't have the intellectual capacity to be managers."

I mention this story to say that it's the same antiquated thinking that's still prevalent today at my organization and others. You have to understand. This statement wasn't made in 1935. This was in 1987—an age considered to be a modern one. The feeling is reinforced when you look at our leadership structure. It reflects the mentality caused by the lack of African American men in leadership positions. It's been my experience that Black men just aren't given a chance to lead. Diversity and Inclusion initiatives are fantastic, but I've found that they are used to promote women into management leadership roles while retarding the growth of Black men in the workplace.

123

In the world of sports, you always see that kind of thing. A year after Al Campanis stood ten toes down on his racism in front of God and everybody, one of my favorite football players, Doug Williams, became the first African American NFL Quarterback to win the Superbowl while playing for the Washington Redskins. I was so excited about it that I went right out and bought a Doug Williams Redskins hat. I wore that hat for the next five years until it practically fell off my head, and then I put it in the rear window of my car. That hat stayed with me for years. Doug Williams was my hero. Even though I couldn't play football in high school because of my hip injury, I understood the trials and tribulations of becoming a Black quarterback on an organized football team, even if it was on a smaller scale. Watching talented Black quarterbacks be turned into defensive backs while their teams languished in mediocrity because of racist decisions was the norm. Williams was one of the first Black quarterbacks to surpass that expectation. And while he wouldn't be the last. This situation was few and far between for several years. It was another way that White racists couldn't deal with Black men in leadership positions.

1988 - A Big Disease with a Little Name

My first cousin, Ronald (my dad's sister's son), was like my big brother. We were born three months apart, and while growing up, we were close. Our mothers would sometimes dress us like twins when we were little.

When I was at college, I really missed him. He worked as a personal shopper at Barney's Clothing Store back home in New York. And Ronald could dress. He was what we used to call a clothes horse. He had a style that was ahead of the game. Ronald's finger was on the pulse of New York City nightlife. He was always in the know about what was happening around town. Ronald knew all of the hot spots.

Ronald was also a gay man and a proud gay man at that. And me? I was your typical knuckleheaded, ignorant young man with no real-life experience yet. I didn't play about my cousin. I loved Ronald unconditionally. He was my brother in almost every way. We spent our whole lives together. Before college, he was a regular part of my life, and after college… Well, I wouldn't say we grew apart. It was just the way circumstances unfolded. I went to Missouri after high school; he stayed in New York.

But we always got together whenever I was home for semester breaks and holidays. I didn't care that he was gay. It was enough just to hang with him and enjoy life. Later, when I proposed to my wife, he helped plan my bachelor party and drove me around before, during, and after my wedding. Ronald made sure I was on time for every part of the wedding activities. He kept me out of trouble before I tied the knot. He was my true Road Dogg, D. O. double G!

One weekend, I went to get my Jheri Curl touched up. A coworker did my hair, so I usually went to her to give her some business. We started talking about family, and I told her about Ronald. At that point, he'd been sick with an ulcer for a year. I was talking about how we couldn't hang out and party anymore because he was sick, and I missed doing that with him.

"You know they can cure that with diet and medication," she'd said. "It's probably something more than an ulcer."

That got my attention. "What do you mean?"

"In this day and age, when people don't recover from minor ailments, it's a sign that something else is going on. You should tell your cousin to get an AIDS test." It was like she'd just called my cousin out of his name. I turned around and looked at her.

"What??? An AIDS test? Nah, my cousin isn't sick like that."

"I'm just saying, you never know. Better to be safe than sorry."

A few weeks later, my cousin called and asked me to come by. Of course, I was going. He lived in Uptown Manhattan, Washington Heights. That was an affluent neighborhood with a lot going on; it was a happening community. And since we hadn't been hanging out often, I was glad to see my cousin.

When I got there, he wasn't the same person I was used to. He looked sickly. A little too thin, his skin had taken on a dull color, like flat paint. He led me into the living room, stretched out on the couch, and got under a blanket. He told me that he just got home from the hospital.

"You all right, man?" I asked. "That ulcer still bothering you?"

He looked at me momentarily, like he was trying to decide how to tell me. Then, he blurted it out. "I got it, man. The doctors say I got AIDS."

I was sitting there in a weird space, trying to stay calm on the outside but going nuts on the inside. My mind was filled with questions. How did he get it? How long has he had it? How long does he have?

But this visit wasn't the time for all that. I couldn't wrap my mind around Ronald being sick. The first thing I said was, "You should get a second opinion. You know doctors get it wrong all the time."

He smiled and said, "I've suspected for a while. Getting sick like I have been… it's hard not to suspect that's what it is. I guess I avoided it until I had to deal with it…"

I couldn't believe what my cousin was saying and how calm he was. I wanted to flip out. I didn't get why he wasn't flipping out, too. I kept my cool. If he wasn't tripping, I didn't want to trip. "Does Auntie know?"

He nodded. "I told her this morning." He started coughing. The cough quickly devolved into a coughing fit, and I had to get him a glass of water to calm it down. Looking at him, I could see that he was sick.

I stayed with him for a while longer, and we talked. That year, he had been hoping that his ulcer would clear up. At first, it was just stomach pain here and there, but over time, it just kept getting worse and worse. It got so bad that he had to go to the hospital, and that's how he found out.

When I left, I felt like a part of my world was caving in. I didn't want to imagine a life without my cousin Ronald in it…but here I was, facing that reality.

The following month, at my daughter's baptism celebration, Ronald showed up looking well-dressed as usual but frail and weak. It broke my heart to see him like that. He moved slower and was less surefooted. He needed help standing up at times. It was like he was a shadow of his former self.

As time went on, Ronald had more and more hospital visits. Every visit turned into a longer and longer stay. One day after work, I went to see him. In the hospital, there was a special AIDS wing where all the patients went for care. It was a dreadful place. People from every race, creed, and gender, all wasting away, sores all over their bodies. Some were well enough to be awake, and others, I think you see the picture!

It was an awful thing to see. So many people died from this disease that was ravaging the community. It was hard for me not to be sad for Ron's sake.

When I saw my cousin, he told me about these special blood transfusions that he got every couple of weeks. Apparently, they made him feel better and gave him some energy. At that point, he lost so much weight. Ron went from six foot four and a hundred and ninety pounds to less than a hundred pounds. Now, he was bedridden and unable to walk.

That last time I saw him, he was discharged a little while after…and then he died later on Michael Jackson's birthday. He had asked me to do his eulogy and requested that we cremate him and sprinkle his ashes in the ocean of the West Indies.

Shortly after his funeral, my Mom sat me down for a talk. "Son," "I know you work hard and play your music on the weekends. Please be careful with the decisions you make. I would hate to lose you or your brother because you made a bad decision. You saw what happened to your cousin, Ronald. Your aunt is heartbroken."

Watching how my cousin died and seeing all the patients in the AIDS ward at the hospital…I can't imagine a more agonizing death. I never passed any judgment on my cousin or anyone else for having the disease, but I understood where my Mother was coming from. At the end of the day, it didn't matter how my cousin contracted AIDS. He was gone, and he suffered so much in the end. I could never put my Mother through that kind of agony.

I never really understood, until after his death, why Ronald and his Mother argued so much throughout the years. They bought a car together when he turned twenty-one. That was a disaster. My Aunt never wanted him to have the car in the first place. The only way she would agree was if they both owned it. Auntie would drive the car during the day, and my cousin would have the car at night. But that arrangement wasn't enough. They still argued constantly, and eventually, Ronald sold the car to my Mother.

When I think about that argument and all the others, I wonder if any of them were ever about the thing they were fighting about. My aunt was appalled that her son was gay. She couldn't handle it, and she never supported her son. At the time, I was oblivious to what was happening. Whenever we went out, my Aunt would start complaining about him using the car. My Aunt said things like; *I noticed a scratch on the car, don't get any parking tickets, please drive carefully.* And every time, I would tell her, "Auntie, don't worry. We'll be fine."

After the funeral, my Aunt asked me to come over to her place. She'd packed up and set aside everything of Ronald's that she still had. I'm talking about jewelry, clothing, and photographs. Every memory that she had of him was now set aside in cardboard boxes.

She asked me to take them. To take them away and out of her house. I was shocked…and a little hurt. You see, to my Aunt, Ronald passed away not because he'd gotten a terrible disease but because he'd "decided" to be gay, and that's what led to his illness. When I took his things, the tension was so thick in the air that you could have cut it with a knife.

Later, I talked to my Dad about it. Her grief had turned to anger and hate, and it made him worry about her well-being. I think it ate her up all along. Her son's death was just the catalyst that brought it out.

When I think of Ron, I know he wouldn't want us to be angry or sad about his passing. He lived his life to the fullest and wanted us all to do the same. One of the last things my cousin, Ron, ever said to me before his passing was, "Hey, Miles, thirty-four isn't a bad life."

For Ron, it wasn't about the quantity of his life but the quality.

4

The Nefarious Nineties

In the nineties, a ton of movies depicting African American life in the hood came out. One constant theme in almost every movie highlighted relationships between the Black Community and Asian businesses.

In the movie Menace II Society, two young African American men make a routine beer run to a convenience store owned by a Korean couple. An argument ensues after the store owner insults one of them, and the lead character, O-Dog (played by Lorenz Tate), murders the Korean couple. Spike Lee's Do the Right Thing covers the African American/Korean divide through the day-to-day interactions. There's one scene in particular where Radio Raheem (played by Bill Nunn) is trying to purchase batteries for his boom box and ends up in an argument because of the shared racist attitudes between them.

Those and many other scenes are reminiscent of an ongoing struggle between Blacks and Korean store owners in America. And they tell a story of racism that has carried over, even within the communities of the Global Majority.

In January 1990, The Red Apple boycott in Brooklyn started. It was a protest against a Korean grocer that allegedly assaulted a Haitian woman. David Dinkins, the mayor at the time (and the first African American to hold the office), crossed the picket line to prove he was non-biased. In his call for unity between Blacks and Koreans in the area, he called Brooklyn "A gorgeous mosaic." It was an unfortunate decision. And I loved Mayor Dinkins. I even volunteered to help his campaign. I understood what he was trying to do, but he totally missed the point. When he crossed that picket line, the Black community saw him as if he were picking a side and supporting the Koreans. It was a decision that cost him dearly. By the next election day, the turnout in the Brooklyn voting districts was almost non-existent. In the end, Mayor Dinkins lost his bid for re-election to Rudy Giuliani. I guess the road to Hell really is paved with good intentions.

Later, news media stories about the incident would characterize Dinkins as being slow to react, which is what ultimately cost him in the long run:

"The city's inability to end the Family Red Apple boycott has been politically embarrassing for Mayor David N. Dinkins, whose reputation as a consensus builder has been seen as one of his major assets. As that boycott has dragged on since January, critics of the Mayor have attacked what they say is his slow and overly cautious style." (Tyson, 2008).

The New York Times wrote:

"After eight months of procrastination, Mayor David Dinkins marched right into two boycotted Korean grocery stores yesterday, leaving no doubt that when he wants to be the healer and conciliator that so many New Yorkers had hoped for, he knows how to play that role."

Around the same time, I got into a back-and-forth with a Korean journalist who contributed to a New York Daily News column. I was trying to make the point that Koreans specifically came into African

American neighborhoods and opened up businesses. They didn't hire Blacks or anyone from the community, they contributed nothing financially to the Black community, and most importantly, they had no respect for Black people. It just incensed me.

I didn't understand why Koreans came specifically into our neighborhoods and sold us liquor, cigarettes, and drug paraphernalia. As I have said, I'm a Long Island kid. Whenever I was in a Jewish or Italian neighborhood, I never saw a Korean store. It felt like they were helping to destroy our communities for profit, and I just wasn't down with that.

The crazy thing was that it was happening all over the country. I remember being in my local record store one day after work, and the clerk clued me in on some new West Coast rap music. He put on Ice Cube, and after a few minutes, I realized that Ice Cube was rapping about Koreans. *Wait a Minute!!!* I walked over to the clerk and asked him to play that song again. Ice Cube was rapping about the same situation I was trying to explain to this Korean journalist. The song was called "Black Korea," and at that moment, I realized that the same level of disrespect towards Blacks in New York was happening in California and other major Black cities throughout the nation.

Huggy Bean and Mother Hale

My partner Harold, God rest his soul, was also a promoter. The day we met, we immediately gravitated toward each other. His goals and dreams aligned with mine, and it felt like the sky was the limit when we linked up. He had so many contacts that it made my head spin.

At the time, I was getting a little frustrated with the promotion business. I seem to be blocked at every turn. So, I decided to take another approach and teamed up with my partner Harold. Harold knew of a theater troupe that was developing a program for television around a character named "Huggy Bean." Around that same time, I was invited to the Hale House Christmas Party and introduced to Mother Hale.

Hale House was an organization built around helping disadvantaged children and babies with programs that provided child care and assistance to children addicted to drugs. In the 90s, there was an initiative to help children born with AIDS. It was a great organization, and Mother Hale was one of the kindest and most charitable people I have ever met. She truly was a blessing to the world.

After I met with the theater group, I realized exactly how I wanted to promote them. Meeting the theater troupe and Mother Hale around the same time wasn't a coincidence. I decided that their off-Broadway type of performances would lend themselves to the fundraising efforts for Hale House. I had to pat myself on the back for that idea. It was brilliant. It was just one way that fundraising enhanced my promotions. It's allowed me to see the bigger picture, and it's not always about the parties.

With the plan in motion, I wrote a grant proposal designed to promote multicultural theatre programs for children. The proposal outlined a plan to assist the Mother Hale House with their fundraising efforts for their initiatives towards helping babies and children born with HIV/AIDS. I was awarded a grant from NBC Television, which was the impetus for our promotion company to do fundraising for the Hale House Foundation. It was an extremely gratifying experience to have been able to raise funds for Mother Hale and contribute to her remarkable efforts to care for children with HIV and AIDS. Right around this same time, Magic Johnson announced that he was infected with the AIDS virus. WOW, I was shook. My Freedmont Hospital basketball teammates and the NBA basketball world were in a state of shock! I was scared to death for Magic, especially after experiencing my cousin's losing battle with HIV. As the rumors swirled around the cause of his diagnosis, I quietly prayed for Magic to weather the storm.

Hey Mr. DJ, the Remix

Shortly after the Mother Hale fundraising effort reached its peak, I settled back into my DJ gig. One night, out of nowhere, this promoter approached me. I took a short break and let my cousin Rob take over for me so I could talk to this guy at the bar. The first thing I notice is that he has a very distinct accent. Panamanian, I think. I had never heard it before. He hit me with compliments immediately, telling me that I was the absolute best out of all the DJs he heard play music. He was going on and on about how my mixes were so good and how I drove the crowd wild. In the back of my mind, I agreed with everything he was saying, but I was waiting for him to get to the point. He finally spits it out, saying, "I am the promoter of a brand new club opening next month. This club is going to be the hottest spot on Long Island, and I want you to be our house DJ."

He added, "Here is my card. I would like you to meet my partners and the club owner to discuss you joining our team."

It sounded intriguing, I have to admit. After hyping me up like that, I felt I had to check him out. So, I agreed to meet with him in the next couple of days.

I showed up at the address on his business card on a Wednesday evening after work. As soon as I walked into the club, it was clear the owners invested a tremendous amount of money to design and build the place.

There was one thing I noticed immediately: this nightclub had custom-built audio equipment that could play recorded music from several different sources simultaneously, so the DJ could mix the music to create seamless transitions between recordings and develop unique mixes of songs. This club had it all, and I had the knowledge and expertise to operate that kind of setup. I only mixed on my own high-quality Technics brand turntables, and the array of different club mixers you would find in a club of that magnitude was slim. Only the top two or three mixers could be used, and I was intimately acquainted with all of them.

I noticed that the mixing board, sampler, synthesizer, and equalizer were top-of-the-line quality, which is everything I had hoped to work with. I decided right there and then that this was going to be my new home.

The concept of this club included several unique design elements meant to distinguish it from any other club, even though it was not yet open to the public. The ambiance set the right mood for a fun party night—the strobe lights were in the right spots. Colored disco lights were all over the dance floor, all the proper lighting for a hype mood.

The DJ booth was encased in glass so everyone could see me above the dance floor. Also, interactive game-like lighting was built into the surface of the bar, in addition to the state-of-the-art lighting system. The place was *spectacular*.

The club owner walked over to me along with the promoter who invited me. He greeted me warmly as I introduced myself. To my surprise, he also had another accent I couldn't readily identify. His name was Logan, and he was from Australia. "Turn on the music and lights for Miles so he can experience the sound and ambiance of the room," he said to the staff after our introduction.

Club lighting is an essential ingredient in creating an atmosphere that can draw people in, and Logan understood that. Nightclub lighting is the first impression that a person gets when they walk into the club. It makes a statement and sets the mood for the rest of the night. The lighting guy turned on the club lasers, LED lights, par cans, and a ton of other special effects. There were fog machines, wall washers, black lights, and the club sound system. It was all just incredible! That was the type of club that would leave a lasting impression on the minds of its patrons, and with me supplying the soundtrack, that place was going to be the *shit*.

I think my favorite part of the light show was the club lasers. I was mesmerized by them. And so were the patrons. The party crowd loved lights, lasers especially. A good laser light show with a pumping sound system turns the dance floor from ordinary to extraordinary. Lasers can entertain your audience and keep them in the club for hours without them even realizing it. The fog machine was added to the mix, and suddenly, the laser effect was multiplied tenfold. Not only could I see the amazing and intricate designs on the floor, but the path the laser carved through the hazy room was now easily visible. Combine all this with an earthquake-like sound system, and suddenly, you have an electrifying and visually striking atmosphere.

Needless to say, it was a done deal. Of course, I agreed to become the House DJ for this new club. The owner hired an advertising agency that planned to shoot a T.V. commercial that would air during *Soul Train*, and they wanted "me" to be their house DJ in the commercial. All that with a substantial pay increase, I might add.

But leaving the club that gave me my shot in the first place to go to the one offering better money and (better) everything else wouldn't be easy. There's an old saying, "If you don't have a place to be bad, you'll never get good." The Native New Yorker was my training ground. It gave me the chance to really hone my skills. It will always have a sentimental place in my heart. As soon as I accepted the job, I immediately started thinking about how to tell John I was leaving to move on to a brand new opportunity. It was all good in the end. I mean, it's all part of the music business. Plus, at least two or three DJs were salivating at the opportunity to take my spot at John's Club. He wished me well and understood that, in the end, you gotta keep elevating. That's the way of the world.

New Decade, Same Old Racism

The year that jumped off the next decade was a full one. In June, I left work to go to Yankee Stadium to see Nelson Mandela. He was released from prison that February. By summer, he'd been on a world-speaking tour. Stadiums were packed all over the country to hear him speak. After all, he was a man who sacrificed twenty-seven years of his life to the apartheid regime in South Africa. There was no way I wasn't going to be there. It was history in the making.

By September, The Newsday newspaper published a weeklong scathing expose entitled "A World Apart- Segregation on Long Island." It covered school discrimination, housing discrimination, politics, All-White school boards, police harassment, and brutality. The article really showed how deeply embedded racism was in Long Island in the '90s. And really, it was a snapshot of the entire country. What's the saying? Things are tough all over, and they were for Black people in a lot of the same ways in different states.

I was riveted as I read story after story of overt racism. The article details various stories about real crimes and the struggles of racism in Long Island. I recall a story of one family's home that was vandalized and burned. Police harassed a prominent African American citizen because he decided to take a stroll down the street to his neighbor's house for a cookout. An African American woman was accused of shoplifting. Black students were placed into special education classes for their "attitudes." I read stories about redlining or affluent Blacks who were steered away from homes for sale in White communities and about a dozen other rampant acts of racism in my hometown. The worst part? These stories don't come as a surprise to us African Americans who live on Long Island. Or anywhere else in America. Racism is and always has been a way of life for us.

The Central Park Jogger case was front and center in New York City media coverage during this same period. Five innocent Black teenagers were wrongfully convicted of rape and assault of a White female jogger.

I marched and demonstrated against the conviction of these innocent Black boys. Deep down in my heart, I knew these boys were innocent. And so did the majority of the Black communities throughout New York. Those NYPD cops snatched up the first Black boys they could catch.

Interestingly enough, not one White teenage boy was arrested that night. Only Black males were arrested. Twelve years later, on December 19, 2002, the Central Park Five convictions were overturned. These young men were exonerated and released from prison. One of the Central Park Five, Yusef Salaam, actually ran for and won and is currently a member of New York City's 9th City Council District Seat.

A Celebration of Life

My son was born on December 13th. That day, I was sipping Cognac and smoking cigars with my big brother Bill. Not my little brother, Billy. I'm talking about Bill, my brother from another mother. I'd had a daughter about two years before my son was born. Now, I got the chance to be a father once more. I was even present at his birth. What a blessing to be a Dad two times over. It was one of the finest days of my life.

But two months later, as sometimes happens in the balance of life, my father-in-law passed away. My wife was beside herself with grief. Losing a parent has got to be the worst pain a person can experience. In spite of everything, she pulled herself together and coordinated his funeral. I did my best to support her by taking care of our children while she and her sister shouldered the task of making funeral arrangements.

As soon as we entered the church on the day of the funeral, our two-month-old son started to cry.

I took our son off her hands. She had enough to deal with that day. Luckily, my wife packed the baby bag with everything I could possibly need for him. This time, our little man was hungry. So I took him aside and gave him his bottle while my wife dealt with everything else.

There's a very special way an infant can affect a funeral. When the Reverend started the ceremony, Miles Jr. started fussing. He fusses and coos so much throughout the service that, finally, the Reverend acknowledged him as my father-in-law's grandson. I could almost feel the tension in the room dissipate. The levity and diversion of an innocent baby brought calm to the room. Maybe even a little relief.

Afterward, the funeral became more of a celebration of life than a funeral. While one life was lost, another life began. An entourage of people filed past us to console my wife and pay their respects to the family, but the focus for everyone was our infant son. Tears fell from my wife's face as she hugged our baby son tight. It's funny how someone at the beginning of their life can take away some of the pain of loss. It was a moment in time that will last in my mind forever.

1991 - Charity Starts at Home

The Rev. Jessie Lewis Jackson got involved in a hostage release situation when he made a trip to the Persian Gulf and asked Saddam Hussein to release several foreign nationals, including American and British citizens.

To a lot of laypeople, his presence seems like a strange one. Rev. Jackson was primarily seen as a civil rights leader. He was not someone you might expect to go overseas to negotiate with terrorist regimes. However, Rev. Jackson was not new to international hostage negotiations.

What the younger generation might not know is that Rev. Jackson was successful in the past in getting prisoners released in various situations. In the case of his presence in the Gulf, he didn't even have the blessing of the U.S. government. Rev. Jackson intervened on his own accord and was successful on the Global stage.

In following his example, sometimes you do something not for prestige or money or even for valor. You do it because it's the right thing to do. You stick your neck out because somebody has to. "Do The Right Thing" – Spike Lee.

1992 – The Right to Education

The New York Times published a story about my hometown. "Huntington, New York Schools accused of steering minority and foreign-born children into special education classes." Apparently, this was being done without proper screening or assessment to determine that the students were, in fact, disabled. It reminded me of how my school was set up twenty-five years before.

My school developed a tracking system when I was a kid. The educational tracks were labeled A–D. If you were in the Track A curriculum, you were considered "Smart." That is to say that those students were taught at a much higher level than the rest of the students.

Conversely, if you were in Track D, you were considered dumb or less intelligent. Those classes were little more than nonsense. It's like the kind of thing you'd find in a daycare. Needless to say, the majority of Track C and D students were Black. The school district had the audacity to mail letters to all the parents about this so-called tracking system.

When my Mom, along with other African American parents, got the letter that their child was being placed into a lower tracking system of education that segregated them from the White kids, they were *furious*. I remember my Mother taking me right into the guidance counselor's office and demanding that I be placed into regular classes with all of the other kids. She was determined that I would not be part of any tracking system. Not only would she not sign the tracking system document, but my Mom informed the school that she would not allow her son to return to school until this discriminatory tracking system was abolished.

Next, she went to my brother's school and demanded that he return to regular classes. My brother had recently been placed into the special education class with a bunch of other Black kids. Nope! Lucille wasn't gonna have it! "I will homeschool my boys until these racist policies are corrected," I remember her saying.

Needless to say, my Mom had us doing more reading and report writing at home than we did in school. The protest only lasted a few days, but the school board felt it. Most of the Black students stayed home during that time. They had no choice but to scrap the whole tracking system program.

Knowing that The New York Times wrote this article about my little ole' hometown school district was encouraging. The brilliant minds that ran the school district were ignorant about how to educate African Americans and other minorities. It was a truth that was finally brought to the light of day. It's like I always say, what does the remedy for this problem look like? How do you implement it? How would they punish an affluent White school district? What would be done for the students who were harmed by this discriminatory program? There were a lot of unanswered questions in my mind, and since I had a history with this school district, I was reticent about being optimistic when it came time to send my children to school.

Fifteen for a Seventeen-Year-old

I was watching the News one night, and anchorman Tom Brokaw went to a Virginia County jail to interview this seventeen-year-old high school athlete. I heard about this Black kid from Virginia who got arrested after a scrap at a bowling alley. I didn't realize, at the time, it was the eventual NBA superstar Allen Iverson. All I knew was that a 17-year-old high school athlete was sentenced to fifteen years in prison. He'd never been in trouble before. He just got caught up in a situation that turned into a brawl. Come on, had this kid been White, do you honestly think he would get a fifteen-year sentence? It was ridiculous.

The Tom Brokaw interview shed much-needed light on the injustice against this young Black teenager. After serving four months, Iverson was granted clemency and released. The charges against him were eventually dropped. Man, I was so glad they let this young man go. Thinking back on my childhood, White boys who got into trouble never seemed to get punished. It didn't matter what they did. They committed home burglaries, auto theft, drug arrests, rape, whatever. White boys never got into trouble. Their parents would hire a high-powered lawyer to make a deal for them and get them off every time. Have their records cleaned and sealed, a few months' probation, and they restart their lives again with a spotless record.

Meanwhile, if a Black boy steals a candy bar, it's off to reform school. If a seventeen-year-old Black boy gets into a brawl, he's charged as an adult and sent to prison. Amazing but true. Allen Iverson's case was a special one. So many of us never get to start over.

1993 – Ups and Downs in a Black World

By December, a crazed Black Man, Colin Ferguson, pulled out a nine-millimeter pistol and opened fire at other passengers on the Long Island Railroad. He killed six people and wounded 19 others before being stopped by other passengers. Ferguson's murder trial was crazy. He fired his defense attorney and demanded that he not only represent himself but question his victims on the stand.

For the next few months, riding the Long Island Rail Road every day to work was surreal. I almost always sat by myself. None of the White commuters would sit next to a Black Man. One day, I bumped into my friend Seymour. While we rode on the nearly empty train, I said," Well, at least it's nice to stretch out and relax every day on the train."

Meanwhile, back at work, I penned a complaint letter to the Freedmont Hospital Patient Accounts Director. My complaint was about the racial bias against Black men inside the department. No African American men were in management, so I decided to call them out on it. The director scheduled a meeting with me and assured me during that meeting that my allegations of racial discrimination were baseless and the department operated fairly and justly.

What a bunch of lip service! They can say that all they like, but there still weren't *any* Black men in management. I listened attentively to what he had to say, thinking the director was telling me what I wanted to hear. Six weeks later, a Haitian American brother gets hired into a management position. I'm happy for him. I'm also excited to know a Black Man is in a managerial position in our department, but I couldn't help but feel like the fix was in. They could have easily given me the position by promoting me. I was already working for the company. But that was never going to happen. I had become the troublemaker, the rabble-rouser, the malcontent. My hopes for a promotion went up in smoke the minute I filed that complaint.

1994 – *The White Bronco and O.J.'s Trial*

The day that it came out that O.J. Simpson allegedly murdered Nicole Brown Simpson and Ron Goldman happened to fall at the same time The New York Knicks reached the NBA Finals. That White Bronco slow-speed chase was all over every channel for hours. I was pissed that I couldn't watch the Knicks game. Cable television was coming into its heyday, but much of the platform operated like network television. Picture it. There were over one hundred channels to choose from, and The White Bronco Chase was on the other ninety-nine channels. Why can't I watch the Knicks Game? *WHY???* Listen, I know it's history now, but right then, I could give a rat's ass about it. All I knew was that my team was in the finals, and I was *missing it!*

Over the next few months, it becomes clear that this O.J. thing was a big deal. Everybody's calling it the trial of the century. And it was for the Black Community. It was the main talking point for a lot of us around the proverbial water cooler and a major point of division between Black and White people.

October 3, 1995, O.J. was exonerated in open court. I was watching the verdict at my aunt's house during my lunch break. When the verdict dropped, Black neighborhoods exploded—cheering, blowing their horns on the street, and celebrating all around. I was on my way back to work, blowing my horn like crazy. That's right, I was one of those hornblowers, and I was proud to blow my horn.

I know there's been a lot of discourse about the O.J. verdict over the years, but you have to understand something. For us, it was never about whether he did it or not. White people have the luxury of seeing a case where a millionaire is up for murder and focus on the justice or injustice of a verdict. They can look at it without choosing to focus on the person's race (or the opposite). That's not how it works in the Black Community. Race is always a factor for us. And when that millionaire is a Black Man, we already know that the odds are stacked against him regardless of how much money he has. The trial that we watched was about one of our own beating the system that routinely oppresses us day after day. He beat the system by using the same tools that White people have used to do it for centuries. Like it or not, that was cause for celebration, in my opinion.

The Boys in The Hood Are Always Hard

A few weeks later, in the wee hours of the morning, I was woken by the sound of gunfire. *Pop, Pop, Pop*! I jumped out of bed and ran upstairs. I looked out of the corner of the window to see a group of kids running away. One boy was down, and another boy was shaking him and pulling on him to get up. But I could see that the boy was dead. Shot down right in front of my home. I immediately called 911.

That killing was part of the infamous MS-13 gang activity that was on the rise in our town. Every day, it was getting worse. When I left for work about four hours later, the body was still lying in front of my house. The cops wanted to question me again as I was leaving, but I told them I had a train to catch. Nothing had changed since I called them earlier that morning, and I had nothing to add.

As the years rolled by, the FBI, ICE, ATF, and local law enforcement were rounding up MS-13 gang members. It was unbelievable that a rash of gangland murders started happening in Long Island. My neighborhood had never been a source of this kind of violence before.

At the time, The New York Times reported:

"Under Operation Matador, ICE has arrested 816 people suspected of gang affiliation. About 170 came to New York legally as unaccompanied minors, some of whom were also seeking asylum, and several dozen were still minors when they were detained. Roughly a dozen students from Huntington High were rounded up." (NY Times, 2019).

"In the last few years, Long Island's MS-13 members and victims have gotten younger. In 2016, MS-13 gang members murdered five Latino Brentwood High students with bats and machetes. In 2017, the gang killed three more local Latino students and left their macheted bodies in a park in Central Islip. Some two dozen young men from Brentwood and Central Islip were eventually charged with the murders. A few were as young as 16." This gang activity was allowed to fester and grow for over ten years in our community. It was a tough situation for law enforcement to deal with.

1995 – Little Boy Lost

A good friend of mine invited me to a special program for kids at her church. So, my brother and I rounded up our kids and headed out. We got there about ten minutes late, and it was packed. It was a large Church with more than fifteen hundred people in attendance. It turned out to be a wonderful service. At the conclusion, my son, who was four at the time, asked me to go to the bathroom. So I took him.

When we got to the bathroom, it was crowded. I guess everybody had to go. We found a stall, and I asked him if he needed help.

"I can do it myself, Daddy," he said. "I'm a big boy."

"Okay, call me when you're done. I'll be right by the entrance door. Remember to wash your hands."

"I know Daddy. I know."

I stood at the bathroom exit door, watching everybody that came out. Two minutes, four minutes, five minutes… I was standing there waiting, but I didn't see my son. Finally, I went in to get him. "Hey, Miles Jr., how are you doing in there?" No response.

I barged into the stall he was in, and he was gone. *Gone!* I started yelling for him. "Miles! Where are you?"

I looked all over that bathroom, in every stall, and under the sink. I was calling for my son, but he was not answering. Every second that passed, I was getting more and more panicky.

"Did anyone see a little boy by himself in here?" I asked the few guys who were in the restroom. Nobody had seen him. I rushed out of the men's room, looking and shouting for him. There were people milling around all over the place, and I asked whoever I ran into if they had seen him. Nobody had. It was like he'd vanished into thin air.

I made my way back to where we were sitting. My brother took one look at me and asked, "What's wrong?"

"Miles is missing. Did he come back to his seat? Did you see him?"

My brother shakes his head no. *Where is he???* I grabbed my daughter and my two nephews. "Listen, M.J. is lost. We have to find him. I want you guys to look around for him, bring him back to our seats, and wait for me. Do you understand?" They nodded, and off they went. "I'll look on the lower level," my brother said. "I saw some kids going down there." He ran off in the other direction. I immediately found the Reverend to tell him that my son was missing. He walked up to the pulpit and made an announcement that my son was missing. He gave out his name and a description of his clothes and his age. "Please bring him to the church office if you find him."

I thanked him and continued my search. The longer I looked, the more panic set in. I started to get frantic and think my son must have left the building entirely. I rushed onto the street and flagged down a police car. "Officer! Please help me! My son is missing!"

The cops questioned me briefly. Even though I would have to wait to file a missing person's report, they told me they would drive around the area and look for him just the same. My son had only been missing fifteen minutes. He couldn't have gotten far. I gave the cops his description, and they pulled off, leaving me to do my search on foot.

I must have run up and down a two-block radius of the church looking for him. I stopped strangers on the street, asking if they'd seen him. "He's a little boy about four years old, Black. Have you seen him?" Over and over again, I was told no. Nobody had seen him.

I rushed back to church, hoping my brother, daughter, or nephews had found him. I've never prayed so much in my life looking for my son.

When I finally found my daughter, she was playing tag and jumping rope with a bunch of other kids. Anger flashed inside me as I ran up to her. "Valinda!!! Where is your brother?" I shouted. "Did you see him?"

"No, Daddy," she answered, "I couldn't find him."

"So, you just stopped looking for him?"

She looked at me with big, worried eyes and shrugged. I had to take a breath. She was just a kid, after all. I told her to go back to playing with her friends.

I'm in an ice-cold sweat. What was I going to tell my son's mother, his grandmother, and the family if he was lost? What the hell was I going to do if something happened to him? I continued running around frantically, looking for some sign of Miles. My son had been missing for twenty minutes at that point. I found my brother downstairs. The second he saw me, he asked, "Did you see him?"

"No, not yet."

"All right, he can't be in the building anymore. Let's look for him outside."

Outside, we decided to split up. I told my brother I already circled the block looking for him. Now, I was going to look across the street. He walked off in the opposite direction on the next block over. The whole time, my heart was beating fiercely. My son was lost, maybe even kidnapped. What could I do? Where could I look? I was running around like crazy. Thirty minutes had passed by that point. Where was my son???

After circling the next block, I decided to head back to the Church and call the police. I felt like I was out of options. We've looked everywhere. I was out of breath and feeling defeated, but I didn't stop looking and running. I slowed down to look into parked cars and tried to take note of vehicles passing by, but there was still no sign of him.

As I approached the church, I saw my brother waving at me…and he wasn't alone. I sprinted up to him. Little Miles was standing by his side. I fell to my knees, hugging him, tears streaming down my face. "Miles, where did you go? Where did you go?"

"I was looking for you, Daddy."

I hug him and squeeze the breath out of him. "My son, my son, I thought I lost you."

I asked my brother where he found him. He pointed out a man standing nearby and said, "He brought him back to the church."

I walked up to him. "I've been looking for my son for damn near a half hour. Where did you find him?" The man told me that he found him walking down the street by himself. When he asked Miles where his parents were, he told him we were at the church, so he brought him back.

"Thank you. sir!" I shook his hand gratefully. "Thank you very much for bringing my son back to us."

When I questioned my son later about it, apparently, I'd missed him when he came out of the bathroom. He didn't see me, so he went looking for me. When he didn't find me in the church, he thought I'd left. My heart aches at the idea that something might've happened to my son. Thank God he was found by a kind stranger and brought back to me.

Walking back to the car, I felt exhausted from running around for the last half hour. But that was all right. As I squeeze my son's little hand, I'm looking down on the ground as I walk up on a little child's tie lying in the street next to a car. I stop and look closely at the tie, which is my son's. I hadn't noticed that he was missing his tie in all this commotion. We've walked about five blocks already towards where we parked the car. I'm shocked. I can't believe this; little Miles's tie is lying in the street. I sharply grab him and look him straight in the eye, "What is your tie doing here?"

"I was trying to find you, Daddy," he says as he begins to cry again,

"I thought you left without me, so I tried to get back to the car."

I look at him and reply, "Son, are you crazy? Did you think we would leave without you?"

"I would never leave you."

We both lost it, and we're crying and hugging each other once again.

I can't believe my little boy walked all this way by himself. It's unbelievable!!!

I remember thinking about how I was going to explain this little adventure to his mother and deciding that I would cross that bridge when I got to it. By then, I felt blessed to be heading home with my son. I remember looking back at him, his sister, and his cousins in the back seat and welling up with emotion. I had to turn back around to keep from crying again. I had my son back and everything was right with the world again. I was never going to let him out of my sight again.

To add insult to injury, I managed to get my hands on an NBA Playoff ticket a few weeks later between the Knicks and Pacers. Unfortunately, the Knicks lost the game. All I could remember was yelling at movie director Spike Lee, telling him to leave Reggie Miller (the Pacer's star player) alone. Spike was sitting courtside razzing and teasing Reggie Miller, and Reggie destroyed the Knicks that night and called us "Choke Artists." It was a humiliating night.

The Million Man March

October 16, 1995. My brother, a bunch of my homeboys, and I packed up and hit the road to Washington, DC, for the Million Man March. It was an event that brought Black men from all over the country together as a display of unity. It was an incredible weekend filled with memories that would last a lifetime.

The Million Man March weekend started when we jumped into our vehicles, prayed for traveling mercies, and hit the road. We were fueled by Minister Farrakhan's message for Black Men to come together for a day of atonement. As soon as we entered the Washington, DC, city limits, a warm sense of pride came over me. It was a beautiful site to see thousands and thousands of proud Black men loaded into cars and busses. We shouted out to each other, saying the names of our cities, dapping each other up, and saluting each other. We were all connected in a way I had never experienced before or since.

The Million Man March was a great experience for me. Being around a million Black men focused on self-improvement and positivity was inspiring. There was no strife or arguments. Everyone there was respectful and peaceful to one another. My only regret was that I didn't bring Miles Jr. with me. I didn't realize that so many fathers would bring their sons to the march. I imagine that was a core memory for a lot of children.

The atmosphere was like being at a giant family reunion of sorts. One that just so happened to be publicized all over the world. I remember walking through a sea of Black men a few hours into the march, and I happened to spot my Godbrother, Ed. "Ed, what's happening, bro?" We both dapped and hugged each other in jubilation. What a day. There was a line around the pay phones at one point. Men calling wives, kids, and parents...

"Turn on the television! Are you watching?"

"Look at all the Black Men! A million of us! We're here!"

Everyone back home is so proud of us. We were a part of history.

An all-star line-up of speakers were in attendance, Maya Angelou, Rev. Jessie Jackson, Rosa Parks, Rev. Al Sharpton, Benjamin Chavis, Dick Gregory, Martin Luther King III, and, of course, Minister Louis Farrakhan. The message was clear. It was time for Black Men to take responsibility for improving themselves and their communities. It was time for Black Men to stand up and become better fathers and husbands. Yes, and to stop killing each other. We had to fight racism and White supremacy and somehow overcome it. Minister Farrakhan made us all recite an oath to improve ourselves and our communities.

The thing about the Million Man March was that a million Black Men were all motivated to do the same positive action. When the time came, we dropped everything and rolled out. Black Men from all walks of life came together from all across the country. Gay or straight. Athletes and convicts. Pastors and Politicians. It didn't matter. People of all faiths and classes showed up to hear the message of unity and self-empowerment for all Black Men in America. We all gathered together to hear Farrakhan's message. It was a historic day.

Shortly after the march, racism still raged on. A rash of arson attacks against Black churches started to unfold. At the time, it seemed like every month, a Black church in the South was burned down, like Alabama, Mississippi, Georgia, Tennessee, etc. It made you wonder what was really going on. Do you remember "What's Going On" – By Marvin Gaye? Take a moment, look up that song, and listen closely to the lyrics. Then you will get my point! It got so bad that President Clinton had to pass the Church Arson Prevention Act. It made arsonists who burned houses of worship have to answer for it as a hate crime. It's unbelievable to think that a level of racial hatred still existed against Black people in this country. The New York Times reported Clinton making an announcement:

"These attacks against African American churches and other houses of worship are an affront to our most basic beliefs of religious liberty and racial tolerance,'' Mr. Clinton said in a ceremony in the White House Rose Garden."

"The announcement is the latest effort by the White House and other government institutions to show concern over the epidemic of fires and vandalism that has burned down or damaged 73 Black churches since the beginning of 1995. Congress will soon consider a $24 million appropriation over two years for the Bureau of Alcohol, Tobacco and Firearms to investigate church fires."

President Clinton took it further by establishing The National Church Arson Task Force to assist the FBI, ATF, and other law enforcement agencies in investigating these crimes.

I think about how we all came together. A million strong with the promise of being better men for our community and how, right after that, racism reared its ugly head on our community. I truly wonder even today what good it all did. In the moment, the world saw how organized we (Black Men) could all be when we set our minds to it. All of us in attendance were ready to step up to the challenge of being the bedrock for our families and communities. But just like a lot of things. It seemed like everybody forgot about the stand we made by the next month, and it was back to business as usual. When you hear about something like those church bombings and compare them to the level of racism that still happens to Black Men every day, it's not hard to make the comparison to the same kind of hatred that Blacks have to fight against inside the workplace. Ignorant racist minds were alive and well in the nineties, and they haven't gone anywhere.

1997 – Reading is Fundamental

My daughter dragged me to a huge Harry Potter and the Sorcerer's Stone Book event at the local Barnes & Noble bookstore. I bring Miles Jr along, thinking this would be a fun experience. When we got to the bookstore, there were several *hundred* people there. The line to get into Barnes & Noble wrapped around the block. We waited in line just like everybody else, and the whole time, I thought there must have been some celebrity or something inside for the crowd to be this big.

But what I really noticed was we were the only Black people in the crowd. I was shocked that we were the only Black faces in a crowd this size. I heard my mother's voice in my head, something she told me long ago. "You and your brother had better go to every activity and every event that this town or school has for kids. It's a big problem in our society that Black people don't participate in school events more." Mom was right. This bookstore event was important to my daughter, so I had to support her.

My daughter mingled right in with her classmates. I stood by and watched while these kids bubbled over with excitement. I thought, *"Who the hell is this Harry Potter guy?"* I admit, I didn't know Harry Potter from a hole in the wall. But what I did know was that everybody in that room was excited about him.

All the kids received their Harry Potter books and got in line to purchase them. Even Miles Jr. got one. Standing in line, I noticed these books were thirty dollars a pop. My son was a second grader. I thought there was no way he could read a three-hundred-page book, plus I wasn't expecting to lay out sixty dollars in a bookstore. When I reached the cash register, I told my son, "I'm only getting Valinda a book. Don't worry. When you're older, you can read her book."

"No, Daddy. I want my own book," he said.

"Miles, you can't read this book. It's over three hundred pages long."

"Yes, I can, Daddy. I promise I can read it."

It was a brand-new position I was being put in. There my son was, begging me for this Harry Potter book because he wanted to read it. And there I was, haggling over how much it was going to cost me. I had a moment of clarity right then and there. How can I possibly refuse to buy my young Black son this book that he wants so badly? This wasn't like some toy, video game, or something he might lose interest in as soon as he got home.

It was a book. How could I deny my son that for any price? "Okay, son. I'll buy you this book, but you better read it!"

VERNON M. O'GARRA

My son was over the moon. He was only seven years old, jumping up and down with this book that appeared bigger than he was, holding it in his arms. Shit, I had to cough up sixty-five bucks and some change. Sorry, kids, no ice cream today. They could have cared less. My daughter sat in her booster seat, reading the book to her brother, and Miles followed along. The picture of them both pouring over a book with so much interest is burned into my brain forever. The best sixty-five dollars I ever spent.

The moral of this story is that the following year, by the end of the third grade, my son gets off the school bus and bursts into the house. Daddy, Daddy, Daddy! What's wrong, Miles? He holds up the Harry Potter book. "I finished reading my book today." A gigantic smile comes over my face. I had forgotten all about that book. You know how your kid says they want something, and you get it for them, and then a week later, it's under their bed, out of sight, and forgotten about?

I ask, how did you do it? My teacher made us read our books each day for the reading lesson, and today, we finished the whole book. I am so proud of my son; I can't believe it. "You mean to tell me that you read all 300 pages Miles? Yes, I Did!!!! I told you, Daddy, I told you I would read it! WOW, he's happy, and I'm beside myself. I can't believe it. This 8-year-old kid, my son, actually read this book. Just then, my daughter comes into the room and says, oh, I read mine twice already. Dad, I'm reading the second one now, and she walks out. Show Off! What can I say? It's a win-win situation.

1999 – The Killing of Amadou Diallo

The Amadou Diallo police shooting happened, and it really shook up the community. Amadou Diallo was a Black Man standing on a street corner late one night after having dinner with some friends. Police saw him on the street and stopped him. When they told him to put his hands up, he ran for the entrance of the building he lived in. When he reached for his wallet, the police opened fire on him. When the smoke cleared, they shot forty-one rounds.

Journalist Bob Herbert wrote in an Op-Ed:

"The killing of Amadou Diallo was cold-blooded, but it probably wasn't murder. It appears that one or more of the officers genuinely believed Mr. Diallo had a gun and that all four officers, imagining danger when, in fact, there was none, panicked and began firing.

There is no doubt that the shooting was reckless and wrong. The 41 shots from the frightened cops turned a terrible mistake into a hideous one. But even a hideous mistake by police officers who think their lives are in danger falls short of the threshold for second-degree murder." (Herbert, 1999).

Those cops that shot him went on record as saying that he "fit the description" of a rape suspect they were looking for. Yeah, right. We knew that was bullshit because all young Black Men look alike to White cops. At that time, street cops were running wild under the rein of Mayor Giuliani.

I've seen these renegade Street Crime Units in action. Undercover cops running around African American and Latino neighborhoods harassing Black and Brown Men with impunity. It's all they did. I had never seen White men getting stopped and harassed that way. Never! Those Cops were out of control.

The death of Amadou Diallo was a sad situation. My brother and I took a trip to the Bronx to rally and protest his killing. The rally was organized by Rev. Al Sharpton, and several hundred people attended. Despite what was reported, it was a peaceful protest. That didn't stop the cops from arresting more than two hundred people.

The thing I kept thinking about was the fact that the cops who murdered Diallo shot him forty-one times. The poor guy was dead after the first or second shot, and these four White racist cops just kept shooting him. Diallo was an unarmed Black Man from Africa whose only crime was being in the wrong place at the wrong time. The cops lied and said he was reaching for a gun, but all he had was a wallet in his hand. He was attempting to produce his identification when they shot him down.

On the way home, we headed to my brother's house to have food and drinks and listen to music. We had been downloading music for the past few weeks, and I left some of my recording equipment at his house. After we finished eating, I told my brother that I was going to download some more songs that night and transfer the other songs onto my hard drive. To my surprise, my brother told me he erased all the music we had downloaded.

"Are you crazy? It took hours and hours to research and download all those songs! Why did you delete them?" That's when he told me about the Napster case verdict. Apparently, anyone caught downloading music was guilty of pirating.

I almost tipped over, laughing at him. "Are you serious? There are over twenty million people downloading music in America. What makes you think the music police will find you?" I was laughing, but I was very serious about music. Even though I was near the end of my music/DJ career, it still took me several hours to learn that whole new concept of music file sharing and downloading. Honestly, I was crushed that all our hard work was just gone.

The Williams sisters have taken the tennis world by storm. Venus and Serena won the 1999 U.S. Open women's doubles championship, and Serena won the singles championship. The following year, Venus won the Wimbledon singles championship and teamed up again with Serena to become the first sisters to capture the women's Wimbledon doubles championship. The sisters usually wear colorful beads and butterfly hair clips. Little Black girls all over the country are emulating them and playing tennis.

That was the nineties filled with highs and lows and everything in between. As it all came to a close, it was a decade of growth and discovery and a time when everything seemed like it was on the verge of change. It was hard to say if that was going to be for the good or not. For every good thing, an equally terrible thing happened. From the Yankees winning the World Series to Columbine. From Tiger Woods coming on the scene and smoking everybody to the death of Amadou Diallo. The Nefarious Nineties was quite a ride, and in the end, it left us wondering what was to come.

5

A Leap Of Faith

Ambition (noun) "a strong desire to do or to achieve something typically requiring determination and hard work."

– Oxford Dictionaries

The New York Yankees and New York Mets made it to the World Series in Baseball. It was a subway series, and the entire city was excited. The workplace where I was employed ran like nobody was in charge. The female management team did whatever they pleased, unchecked. The White male leadership team was cashing big ass checks, and rank-and-file union employees were out of control. It seemed like *nothing* could be done to curb the corruption around me. But then, in an environment like that, what could they expect from any of us? I was working without any discipline or motivation. I'd roll into work around eleven or twelve every day, but no one said anything to me about it.

I know some people might think that was a cool setup to have a job where they could just lay back and relax, but for me, it was a sign of something more profound. I had lost sight of my goals and aspirations for that job. Coming in whenever I wanted meant I didn't give a shit about showing up. Hell, they were lucky I even showed up.

But I knew I needed something more. Working like that made me feel like I was languishing instead of flourishing. I decided to enroll in grad school but soon stopped after a couple of classes. That's how profound my lack of motivation was. At that time, there were still only four African American men in management out of a thousand employees (give or take): The Admissions Manager, the Linen Supervisor, the Housekeeping Supervisor, and the Food Service Supervisor.

And somehow, I ended up being selected "Employee of The Month." I had forgotten about the interview I did a month before. Some H.R. person from the health network's Resource Newsletter interviewed me for the monthly employee spotlight editorial. It was a nice accolade to have, but I could hear my coworkers snickering behind my back. *How did he win? Why did they choose Miles?*

All the 'haters' came out of the woodwork. I loved it. There's nothing like pulling in every morning and parking my car in the Employee of the Month parking space right in front of the building.

As the months rolled by, the job I once loved became a hellhole. My coworkers didn't do a thing all day, every day. They came to work and sat down on their asses for years, waiting to retire on a nice City pension. The Health System was a bureaucracy that muddled along whether its' employees worked or didn't work. I felt like I was being held back. In the end, I couldn't take it any longer. It was time for a change.

VERNON M. O'GARRA

Eastern Mission Financial Services

I resigned from my job with Freedmont Hospital to pursue a career in sales. I accepted a position with Eastern Mission Financial Services. Making the move was met with some controversy in my family. My mother sat me down and asked me outright if I was "Out of my mind for quitting my good city job." I reassured her that everything was going to be all right, and I was confident in my decision. It's hard to explain to your mother that money doesn't mean anything if you've lost the motivation to earn it in the first place. I had to move on to something I felt I was going to thrive in. Little did I know that I would be in for a rude awakening entering the world of financial services and having to deal with racist White clients and Black clients who were suspicious of other Black people handling their money. I know how crazy that sounds, but internal prejudices within the community are sometimes just as bad as the racism outside the community.

I had to take a psychological exam and a sales assessment test before being hired for the position. Before taking the test, I decided to do extensive research about these exams, and I was pretty surprised by what I discovered. I uncovered many things these companies were looking for in their sales force. Many sales companies have developed testing methodologies that study a person's mental ability, personality values, vocational interests, and social adaptability, among other things. All prospective applicants must sit for a test designed to gauge varying levels of sales performance. Your scores are analyzed statistically to determine the psychological probability of success in the sales industry. You're not hired if you don't meet their minimum testing criteria.

I disagreed with some of the philosophies and points of view, but I embraced them anyway to get the job.

I figured the way to best get around it all was to parrot their philosophies back at them. It worked. At my interview with the agency's general agent, they told me I scored very well on my assessment exam and I was just the type of individual they were looking for.

As a professional financial advisor, I was licensed in several areas: Life Insurance, Mutual Funds, Variable Annuities, and Stocks & Bonds. Financial services sales was a very tough and challenging career. Even though it was a tough business, I was a pretty good agent. Twenty-three new agents were in my new hire group when. After six months, only ten of us remained.

The thing you have to realize is that, for people of color, there is always a racial aspect at play in everyday life—work, family, education, worship, athletics, *everything*. You try to escape it, and surprisingly, some people can, or they believe in their minds they can. But race is always there, whether lurking silently in the corner, screaming in your face, or waiting for you to drop your guard. It's just a matter of time before it's going to get you.

I was with this sales agency for six months, and we were off to Milwaukee for our company convention. It was a great experience. There were only two Blacks from my agency and a handful of brothers from across the country, but we were all together to learn. The Eastern Mission Financial Services Company was one of the largest employers in the state of Wisconsin, and, to my surprise, many African Americans worked there. There were way more Black EMF employees than agents.

They outnumbered the New York office by at least twenty to one, maybe more.

There was a wealth of learning available to us. Plus, I met many people, namely, the legendary Duke University Basketball coach, Mike Krzyzewski, and Mt. Everest survivor, Beck Weathers. They gave us impassioned keynote speeches and taught us lifelong lessons.

We all returned to New York, fired up, and hit the ground running. In spite of all the trials and tribulations a Black Man can have in a financial services firm, I forged ahead with renewed purpose. I kept a positive attitude and worked hard. Many White clients avoided me, and some Black clients reneged on me, but I kept going. These were just bumps in the road that came along with every endeavor.

I was also considering this Financial Advisor assistant position. Financial advisor assistants generally worked in an office environment during regular business hours. In some cases, the assistant's hours were timed to coincide with the stock market opening, which could result in early morning hours, depending on the time zone.

The qualifications required for this position vary by organization and openings. Some organizations require a two or four-year college degree in business or finance, while most at least prefer a degree. Experience in the financial service industry was highly desired, and marketing or public relations experience may also be helpful. A working knowledge of financial products is essential; securities and insurance licenses were highly desirable. If an opportunity presented itself, I would definitely consider it.

Sometimes, It's Your Own People

During that time, we were recovering from the effects of '9-11,' and the Black guys, such as myself, in the agency were catching hell. As I said, there were only two of us, and we were getting it from both sides of the aisle. You see, some Black people believe in the myth that if you do business with a Black person, you'll get ripped off, while a lot of White people don't have enough respect for a Black Man to trust him to handle their money and finances. It was a tough business, and with that dynamic, it was a lot tougher. Just the same, I was very good at what I did. Plus, I loved sales.

One day, a fellow sales professional, Josh, came into my office to shoot the breeze. He noticed some magazines on my desk and focused on one in particular. It was a Chase Bank brochure with a photo of my cousin Sharmelle and a bank executive on the cover. He asked me who the woman was and I told him it was my cousin.

"Oh, wow," he said. "Do you have any idea who that man is standing next to her?"

"No. I don't know him."

He smiled. "That's Saul Sapperstein. You know, he's one of Rob's clients."

I'm floored. I didn't know Saul Sapperstein, but suffice it to say, he was a big deal. "Get the fuck out of here," I said. I looked at the photo again. Rob was one of the top financial professionals in our agency. For Saul Sapperstein to be his client was a big deal. Wow. Josh nudged me and said, "Rob's in his office now. Let's go over there."

So, we walked down the hall to Rob's office. When we got there, he was on the phone. With the phone cradled on his shoulder, he saw us and waved us in while he finished his call. Josh showed him the magazine and asked Rob, "Hey, did you know this was Miles's cousin?"

Rob blinked, then smiled wide. "Holy Shit, she knows Saul? He's my best client." You can believe that. The man was a multi-millionaire. "Tell me about your cousin. How does she know Saul?"

I explained to him that she ran her own public relations and event marketing firm in the city, and Chase Bank was one of her clients. As soon as I said that, Rob's face lit up.

"Do you think you can get some referrals from her?" he asked me. "If she knows Saul, then she's got to know some bigwigs that we could work with. I'll work with you personally to develop and sell her referrals. Miles, this could be huge for you."

It sounded good to me. I told Rob I'd speak to my cousin and get back to him. I left the office with a spring in my step. Connections were everything in the business world.

But when I talked to my cousin a few days later, she was like, "Miles, there's no way I can give you any names."

I couldn't believe it. "Sharmelle," I added, "my associate Rob handles all of Saul's money and finances. I want you to meet him and talk with him to discuss your finances." She still said no. In fact, she was *adamant* about it. She told me there was no way, no how, she would meet with Rob or discuss her finances with me. And referrals? Out of the question. I could not believe my cousin was blocking me like that.

When I returned to the office and talked to Josh about it, he looked disappointed, but the next thing he said blew my mind. "The most important thing in this business, Miles, is that you have to establish integrity and credibility with your clients. If you don't have that, you have nothing. Do you have credibility with your cousin? Does she trust you?"

"Obviously not," I retorted,

"Then that's something you're going to have to work on."

That was a tough conversation to have. There I was, one of only two African American sales agents in our office, bearing my soul to the successful Jewish guy about credibility with a family member. I didn't like it at all, and it was a bitter pill to swallow. Well, it was just a matter of time before Rob stopped in for a visit. "Hey, Miles, how's it going? I had a chat with Saul the other day, and he spoke very highly of your cousin and her relationship with Chase Bank. Miles, I must tell you that the essence of our business here is referrals. Let me explain how it works..."

I sat and listened to Rob, but what did he think? I was brand new to all this. Of course, I knew how referrals worked.

"Miles," he said after explaining the concept that I was very familiar with, "You are one of the most knowledgeable incoming agents in the office. But if you don't get referrals, you can't be successful. Some of these guys are nowhere near as smart as you, but they get referrals. I suggest you go back to your cousin and set up a meeting with me. Saul will vouch for me, so there will be no problem there. Just set up the meeting, and I will do the rest."

I did try asking Sharmelle again, but it never happened. If I had to pinpoint a moment in time that marks the start of the end of my relationship with her, that would be it. It's a shame because you would think that she would give me the benefit of the doubt, being somebody who knew me well. The thing is, I don't feel that Sharmelle ever saw me outside of the childhood perception of who she thought I was.

Sharmelle was my cousin's wife; I met her when I was fourteen. For years, she only knew me as "Little Miles" from New York and not much else. Imagine only seeing somebody as the kid that you used to know, even when they're grown as hell. I was thirty-four at that time. I was twenty years from the kid that she knew. I mean, I had kids, was married, and was working in a financial firm. I wasn't that "go for coffee, go for donuts" kid anymore.

The straw that broke the camel's back in our relationship (although there were a few straws before this one) was when the Executive Director of Freedmont Hospital invited me to a Community Board Meeting. For the record, the Community Board served as a link between the hospital and the community, facilitating access to quality health care. How I got invited happened out of the blue. One day, the CEO asked me what I was doing after work. And when the CEO asks what your plans are, the only right answer is that you don't have any.

"I need some employees to attend our monthly Community Board Meeting to add support for the hospital."

"I'll be there," I said.

At the event, the CEO gave a masterful presentation to the board that elicited a standing ovation. I got the chance to meet one of the board members, Ms. Sylvia Watson. I introduced myself to her and told her I worked in the Finance Department, Patient Accounts, which she seemed very interested in. She was great. We chatted for a few minutes, and we were getting along great. She turned out to be a great connection to have.

Later that month, I was assisting my cousin Sharmelle during one of her events in New York. Now, my role at her event, or at least I thought my role, was to support her and possibly rub shoulders with some people I could use as referrals or make connections. It just so happened that Ms. Sylvia was also at the event working as one of the wait staff. When I saw her, we struck up a conversation. Everything was going well until my cousin walked up. Not wanting to be rude, I introduced them. Sylvia was very much still in work mode, so she asked Sharmelle what she needed. Sharmelle gave her a smile and replied, don't worry about it. I have Miles here. He can get me whatever I need."

Sylvia and I looked at each other with this expression that could only be described as *"Is she for real?"* Sylvia cleared her throat and responded with, "Actually, my job is to serve everybody. I'll be happy to get you something if you need it."

"I'm fine," said Sharmelle.

I was shocked but didn't want to make a scene, so I asked Sylvia to bring me a soda and a fruit cup. Before she left, Sharmelle asked her, "So, you know Miles?"

"Yes. From the hospital." Sylvia threw me a pleasant smile and a wink. "He's good people." She left to get my order, but I was fuming.

That's when I knew it. I would never be anything but "Little Miles" to my cousin. Sharmelle was never going to see me as an equal. At this point, I was almost *forty,* and she still treated me like a "gopher." I can't tell you how demeaning it was for her to treat me that way.

Over the next couple of years, we drifted farther and farther apart. That's how it is! Sometimes, you have to move on from people incapable of valuing the expertise you can bring to their table.

My cousin has a brilliant mind, but her mind is ignorant about my ability to bring value to her business endeavors and her personal finances. When you look at the big picture, she's falling into the same trap that a lot of Black people fall into. And it's all because of a stereotype that we never even invented, yet we perpetuate every day. My cousin sees me as just another Black person who doesn't add value to her life.

Trust

Around 2002, I was at the yearly Insurance Company Conference, where legendary college coach Mike Krzyzewski gave the keynote address. It was a great conference. I even got an autograph from Coach K. The event had various workshops that I decided to take in the interest of bettering myself for work. I took a course on how to be a productive "Insurance Agent Assistant." The whole thing was about how to help your sales manager double his or her income. Now, I hadn't planned on taking this workshop. I just so happened to be on my way to lunch when a couple of my associate agents saw me walking the exhibit hallway, and they convinced me to come with them. It turned out to be an interesting session. After all, we all had the mindset that we would need our own assistant at some point during our careers. Now, we'll know what skills and qualities to look for.

The justification for hiring an assistant in an insurance agency is that the assistant must increase your income by a thirty percent minimum jump for your boss to justify paying you for having the assistant. By the end of year three, your income should double. I listened intently, took notes, and purchased the assistant's manual.

At lunch, a few of us were discussing the seminar, and we all came to the realization that all six-figure earners in our agency have assistants. And most of those assistants make more money than we do without overhead. There I was, paying the monthly rent for my office, printing and copying fees, stationary, telephone bill, health insurance premiums, secretary costs (a secretary that I shared with two other agents), office supplies, gas for my car, licensing… the list goes on and on and *on*.

I was getting killed with fees and expenses. And after just barely surviving for twenty-four months as a full-time insurance agent, I was ready to make a change.

So, that conversation led me to a business relationship with a financial services expert…who also happened to be a personal friend of mine. I took a big leap and quit my agency to start something with him. The goal was to help him earn more income by closing business deals for him while he was out of state. Also, I was prospecting for new accounts by doing the leg work and outreach with Black Churches and businesses.

But he didn't make the job easy. For one thing, he had a commute that ate up much of his time and money. Four hundred miles every month from New York to Virginia and back again. Sometimes, it was more. I can't imagine how much he was spending on gas and car maintenance alone. It could cut back expenses significantly if I could convince him to generate new, more lucrative business ventures in New York. We'd had several meetings where I attempted to explain how to utilize my expertise to benefit himself, but he (clearly) kept missing it. When I think back on this relationship, it saddens me greatly that we could never make any real progress. I feel it's a classic case of two African American Men being held back because of the same stereotypical lack of trust and credibility. Then again, maybe I should say I was held back. He was doing fine financially speaking, but with my help, he could have been doing so much better.

My vision for that business relationship was to eventually build our own financial services agency. I mean, quite simply, that someone has to be the president, owner, senior partner, etc. And someone else has to fill that support role, such as an administrative assistant, second in command, etc. Now, I had no problem filling that role. I was qualified for that position, and I felt that it was the best possible way I could build up his business. But my associate had a Type A personality. Trying to tell someone with a Type A personality what's-what can be like talking to a wall sometimes.

The whole thing about my job as his assistant was if he was making more money, then so was I. If he made one hundred and fifty thousand dollars, and I made about seventy-five thousand, I'd be satisfied with that kind of cash coming in. But if I can help him make *more* money, I will make more money. It's a win-win all the way around. I was thinking big. Let's get to the one-million-dollar income mark and keep growing our agency. Why should we stay where we're at when we can keep shooting for the stars?

He never got what I was telling him. He didn't see that I was the catalyst for him to increase his income because I could see the big picture, but he couldn't.

After a few months of trying to convince my partner that I was not going to stab him in the back, it finally hit me that the whole problem was that he didn't trust me. You must trust when working with someone else in the financial services business. I couldn't be at a sales meeting trying to close a deal and worrying about my partner doing something unscrupulous that would undermine me. I have to have faith that he's got my back. Without trust, you have nothing, and he didn't trust me enough to close business deals for him when he was out of town. He didn't trust me enough to take my advice on his best options. The thing you have to understand about sales is that you have to build a strong foundation. There's plenty of food for everyone to eat. Just set up your business model correctly, and you will be fruitful. Sometimes, the ignorant mind gets stuck on stupid and can't see the forest for the trees. What can you do? It's the way life works sometimes.

Being stalled ended up working out for me. My backup plan to finish my master's degree was underway, and I decided to return to working in the healthcare sector.

The *"Wrong" Neighborhood*

While I was trying to process the ins and outs of my career, I started to come to the conclusion that these trials and tribulations would never end. I decided to go for a drive to clear my head, and I ended up going over to visit my brother and nephews. It was a great decision. My brother fired up his grill and threw some steaks on, and we had a barbecue going on. Perfect timing. We sat down and had some beers, and my brother told me about one of the PTA parents he met during the school year.

She was a White woman who was close in age to my brother; their kids were both around nine years old. As kids tended to do, they became the best of friends. One day, my nephew went to his friend's home for a sleepover, for which my brother gave him permission, not thinking anything of it. He'd met the other kid's parents a few times at PTA meetings, and she worked with him on a few school committees and class projects. Up until this point, she seemed all right.

"She drops Imen (his son) off," he said as we sat on his patio, talking while he entered the house. "I told her I'm glad the kids had a good time, and maybe we can switch up next time with Chad coming over here, alright?"

"Uh-huh. What did Chad's mother say?"

He shook his head. "This chick goes, 'Oh, no! That can never happen. My husband would never let our son (Chad) come over here.' You should have heard the way she said it like it was a joke or some shit. Hell, I thought it was for a second, so I laughed. And she's like, 'I'm not kidding. My husband wouldn't go for something like that.' So,

I'm like, 'Why not? They're best friends. Was there a problem or something when my son was over there?' And she's like, 'No, no. My husband's just not comfortable with this neighborhood. That's all.' What the fuck does she mean *this neighborhood*??"

My brother took a swig from his beer bottle, his face in a deep, bitter frown. "I told her that was fine and my son wouldn't be coming over to their home again. And I said make sure to let your husband know that."

"So, you know what's she saying?" I said. "There're too many niggers in this neighborhood for her? Is that it?"

He chuckled. "That's what I should have said. Just like that, too."

"Man, you know that's some bullshit. Imen can go over there, but it's too 'dangerous' for Chad to come here. You know what that was really about, right?"

He scoffed. "Hell yeah, I know. It's messed up."

It was. And when you think about it, this was a woman that Billy thought he knew pretty well that said that shit. The two of them worked side by side at the school and were a part of the same committees. And both of them were happy to encourage their kids to be friends. So, I thought, but now that's over. It's a shame. It could have been a treasure to have Chad and Imen become lifelong friends, but now both of them got cheated out of that friendship because of some ignorant-minded racists.

But the sick thing about it is that what happened to Billy and his son isn't an uncommon experience. I went through a similar situation with my son. I mentioned earlier that my Mother was big on us being a part of our kids' education. She was always preaching about Black Fathers and how they need to be more involved with their kid's school and activities. "You never see the Black dads at school events and activities. You boys better represent and show up for your kids!"

Those lessons about parental involvement resonated with us, and many times, my brother and I did turn out to be the only Black Men at PTA meetings, parent-teacher nights, and other events for our kids. When my son was about six or seven, he went on a class trip to the Bronx Zoo. The teacher asked if I would mind being a chaperone for the trip, and I agreed.

The trip there was on the train. I was surrounded by all these giddy second and third-graders, happy to be on a field trip to the Bronx. My son and I were the only African Americans attending, and I was a little surprised. I know there were Black kids in my son's class. *Where are all the other Black kids?*

I was one of six parents and the only male on this trip. Four of the other five moms had daughters, and guess who all their little White princesses wanted to play with? You guessed it. My Black son. Throughout the hour-plus train ride, it was "Miles, sit with me!" or "Miles, play with me!" All these White mothers were sheepishly looking at me, and I was cracking up. Those little White girls were crazy about my son, and I could see their mothers were appalled.

It's all fun and games until our Black sons get older. A few years later, when Miles Jr. was about eleven or twelve, he came home late from hanging out with a friend. I greeted him when he came into the house and asked, "What's up? Why are you late?"

"Dad, I had to walk home."

I looked at him, confused. "Did your friend's mother say something about driving you home?"

My son sighed and shook his head. "Megan's mom wasn't home. And when her dad came home, she flipped and told me she had to hide me."

"Hide you? What are you talking about?"

I sat my son down, and he told me the whole story.

"She told me if her dad found me there, he'd freak out. Bad. So, she told me to get in the closet, and I did. She piled a bunch of stuff on me and told me not to make a sound. I was there for a few minutes before she let me out and told me to go out the back."

I was shocked. My son was made to hide in a damn closet just because one of their parents came home? What kind of bullshit was that? And what kind of parents were they?

I told my son (Miles Jr.) he was forbidden to visit these so-called friends ever again. Those were the same classmates who played with him during that class trip to the zoo—all his so-called friends with the racist parents. I don't know what Megan's dad would have done to my son if he caught him there, but I didn't want to find out.

VERNON M. O'GARRA

Trials of a Single Dad

By this time, my wife and I separated. The thing about splitting up from the mother of your children is that those shared responsibilities get a dozen times harder to keep up with. Suddenly, I've got to have eyes in the back of my head (at all times) because it's now two households where there used to be only one.

One Friday night, when my son was a teenager, I got a call from him after ten at night. He told me he was walking home and needed me to pick him up. Let me preface this by saying that I've always told my kids they can call me for a ride, day or night if they're in trouble. His calling me like that had alarms going off in my head right off the bat.

I started thinking that if my son was *walking* home at ten o'clock at night, then something happened. Why aren't somebody's parents taking him home instead? When I asked him about it, he said his friend's parents couldn't drive him. Now, I'm extremely pissed off. Whenever their friends come over, I've always driven them back home. They can't extend the same courtesy to my son?

To make matters worse, he's walking in the Huntington Bay/Lloyd Harbor area, which is about as White as sour cream. There aren't *any* Black families out there. When I got in the car to get him, I was steaming. My Black son is walking through a White neighborhood at night, and not a single parent thought to offer him a ride for his own safety?

I know there are people out there who think that Black boys and men getting arrested, beaten, or killed just for walking down the street is some new thing. I'm here to tell you it's not. My son was in real danger that night from the Police (a private company that regularly patrolled that area) or any other racist person who thought that seeing a Black face at night was trouble. And it was his racist ass friend's parents who put him in that predicament.

It took me about forty-five minutes to get there and even longer to find him since he was walking. Every second I didn't see him was like a lifetime. A million different scenarios raced into my head, and none were good.

When I finally did find him, relief couldn't describe what I felt. I was still hot. I was ranting to him about these "friends" of his who didn't even bother to look out for his welfare. I'm telling you, I could have heated the car without a defroster that night.

On the flip side of that story is my daughter, who was fourteen and getting into a scene that was a little out of my purview as a music lover. She loved heavy metal and Gothic music and got deeper into it the more I saw her. Black clothes, spiked wristbands, heavy army boots. On her birthday, I bought her a pretty dress. Something I thought was the style for girls her age. She turned her nose up at it. I guess I should have got it in black.

She called me one day because her favorite band was in town. It was this all-girl, Canadian metal band named "Kittie." I looked them up, and none of the band members looked much older than my daughter—the bass player's even Black. Go figure.

The venue was a place I knew pretty well, located in the Village of New York City. I agreed to take her to the concert and my son came along.

Over a hundred people had to wait to get into this place when we arrived. And all of them were all flavors of rock fans. I saw spiked hair; some were every color of the rainbow. There were girls with ripped fishnet stockings and a ton of pancake makeup. People with face piercings and tattoos it was crazy. We got in line, and my kids were excited. I thought (maybe) I could use some of my DJ influence to move things along. I left my kids in line, went to the doorman, and flashed my "DJ Press" Credentials. He nodded and told me I could go right in. I told him to hold on a second and let me grab my kids because they were in the line. They were initially reluctant, worried they'd lose their place in line at a sold-out show. But once they realized I was getting them in VIP style, they came with a quickness.

We ended up getting third-row seats, and let me tell you, Kittie turned it out. They rocked the house, and everybody loved it, including my kids.

It's moments like those that live in my memory, and I carry them with me as the best times of my life. Through all the bullshit at work and the troubles with my ex-wife, even the near-constant racist shit that seems to wash up on my doorstep every day, I have moments like that with my kids. When I think back to that night, I was glad I could give them a piece of something that they would cherish forever. Everything I went through made it all worth it.

BRILLIANT MINDS, IGNORANT MINDS

I'm all wrapped up in this new series on HBO called "The Wire." It's a story about the drug-infested, crime-riddled city of Baltimore, Maryland. The characters in this show are incredible, and the series offers a compelling critique of systemic failure and the complexities of urban life in the hood. I would be locked into this program for the next five years.

6

Returning To A Career In Health Care

I firmly believe that everything you go through prepares you for something. You just don't know what that something is.

For me, that "something" turned out to be bringing a discrimination lawsuit against my employer and fighting against the marginalization and injustices against Black Men inside the workplace. I must tell you that I am the type of individual who documents *everything* that happens to me concerning my career while inside my workplace. I've been doing this since my days at Freedmont Hospital in the 1980s. I'm not sure why I do this other than to say it's something inside me that instinctively notices differences in the treatment of Black Men, and I want to document that.

My mind is brilliant when it comes to noticing the injustices against Black Men in corporate America and our battle to advance our careers inside a racist environment. But, my mind is also ignorant about the insidiousness that exists to keep me back and hold me down.

After a rocky road in the Financial Services field, I accepted a part-time position with Municipal Hospital and soon joined the 3609 MEIU Union Local. Healthcare was my backup plan just in case my career in financial services didn't pan out. I quickly learned about this female-dominated employment landscape and the pitfalls that lay ahead of me.

During a trip to New Jersey, I was using public transportation and was waiting at a rather large bus terminal. I think it must have been Newark, New Jersey. I had just exited the train and was waiting for the convention center bus. As I was waiting, it suddenly occurred to me, what's wrong with this picture? I was seeing African American women bus drivers. I didn't realize it until I subconsciously watched over a dozen women park these huge buses.

I certainly don't want this to sound the wrong way, but after I started to pay close attention, the majority of the bus drivers coming into the terminal were a majority of Black women. It struck me because I had never seen anything like this before. Sure, you see a woman bus driver every once in a while. But not fifteen out of every twenty buses. I was shocked. I wondered, don't Black men need these jobs? How many brothers are unemployed or laid off while all these women got these good city bus-driving jobs? I'm not hating on Black women. I'm merely pointing out a fact.

As a Black Man, you can't help but think, what are we doing wrong? We've got to compete with our own women for jobs. It's like I said before. Flawed legislation has allowed not just Black women but all women the opportunity to leap head and shoulders ahead of Black men. It's been a cumulative effect. Over the years, Black women becoming heads of households have become commonplace. By society legally discriminating against Black men, women have been more likely to have employment opportunities going towards them, more so than Black men. This phenomenon has created a major problem. "These differences in career entry alone help explain why Black men are slower to marry than White men. But a difficult transition to stable empowerment is an even greater barrier to marriage for Black men than it is for White men." (Raley, 2015).

Who wants to get married when you can barely support yourself? With all the headaches Black men have to deal with, the last thing you want is an unhappy wife who is supporting the household and nagging at you. It's a conundrum. I fully support Black women who climb the ladder of success. However, I am simply pointing out that the employment disparity between Black men and Black women is systematically unequal.

HBCU or Bust

Since I had attended an HBCU, it was also a dream of mine to have my daughter attend an HBCU. I decided to sign her up to take an HBCU college tour. These tours can provide African American students with an opportunity to visit several Black college campuses across the country. I was thinking that this would be a wonderful trip for my daughter to take. I saw it as a way for her to get the Black experience and quality education. Unfortunately, sometimes, when we make plans for our kids, things don't always go as planned.

I attended a few meetings with the organization that plans the tours, reserved a spot for my daughter with a down payment, and discussed it in detail with my daughter's Mother. To my surprise, she told me my daughter wasn't interested in going. I couldn't understand what the problem was. So I waited for my daughter to come home and explained the college tour details to her. She was totally against taking this trip. No matter how hard I tried to persuade her, she told me she wasn't going. It deeply saddened me. Just the same, I donated my trip deposit to another student. Even though my money was tight, I was happy to assist another student with the cost of covering a trip like this.

I concluded things with my daughter by telling her not to be sad or upset about it. After all, I should have discussed the whole thing with her sooner. As much as I believed she would benefit from the experience, it was on me to talk it over with her, and I didn't, and I apologized for that.

I'm like any parent. I only wanted what was best for her, and that's why I arranged everything the way I did. In the end, we hugged it out, and all was forgiven. I guess lesson learned. A few months later, she won her high school Veterinary Science Award. She placed # 1 out of 110 competitors. My daughter was also recognized as the Veterinary Assisting program's "Most Outstanding Student" of the year at graduation. Her mother and I were extremely proud as her teacher made glowing remarks about her excellence in class.

The Difference is Black and White

Around that time, I enrolled in grad school and started charting my course to success when Sean Bell was murdered by NYC undercover cops. I was especially concerned about this murder because the strip club where Mr. Bell was partying was directly across the street from the LIRR Train station. It just so happened that I frequently patronized the club whenever I was waiting for a train home or when I just missed a train home and maybe had an hour or so to kill before the next one. Needless to say, after the Sean Bell incident, I never set foot back inside of that club.

The Sean Bell incident was compared to Amadou Diallo's killing and was even a part of the campaign for Fernando Ferrer's run for mayor. But just like with Diallo, the cops that shot Bell went to trial and were declared not guilty. Bell was gunned down by five cops in a similar way; only he and his friends got more than fifty gunshots, and the cops got away with it. Only in America!

Shortly after that, the Duke University rape case was front and center in the media. Several members of the Duke University Lacrosse Team were accused of rape. The media portrayed the Duke athletes as privileged White boys who were good students. They just happened to plan a little party one weekend where they invited a Black female stripper. Something went awry at the party, and rape allegations were front-page news. The case was a media darling. It had a perfect race angle. An African American exotic dancer cries rape against an All-White college team of athletes. Plus, a crooked D.A. was later introduced into the case. The Black community throughout the country had an eye on the case, with everybody immediately believing that all the accused would be acquitted and fully exonerated. And the Black girl who brought the allegations would be embarrassed and humiliated.

Interestingly, this case took a twist when the District Attorney of North Carolina was found guilty of withholding DNA evidence. He ended up doing jail time, and eventually, he resigned. As for the case, it was dismissed, of course. The Duke athletes went free. It was the kind of thing you see so much of; you almost expect the same outcome. It was the same as with people like Brock Turner and Kyle Rittenhouse. A little bit of wealth and the right shade of White seems to change the minds of a jury faster than anything else. It was the same thing with the Duke case. The majority of African Americans felt the Duke players were guilty, but the D.A. withheld evidence. You absolutely cannot do that. What a case! It was definitely on my radar. I followed this case very carefully. Although the White athletes were declared not guilty, they had a wealth of legal resources behind them. That made all the difference in this case.

2008 – Barack Obama Makes History

I applied for a few more supervisory positions at work. However, I was primarily focused on school in 2008. I joined the effort to elect Barack Obama for president and became part of the Obama Volunteer Army. I had been an active member of my local democratic club and was a Committeeman in my community for several years. I was familiar with how to support and advocate for a political candidate, so it wasn't a stretch for me to volunteer for Barack.

I had become disillusioned with politics after volunteering for NYS Comptroller Carl McCall's campaign in 2002 to become Governor of New York. I believe Carl McCall, an African American, was the superior candidate in that race. He had single-handedly grown the NYC Pension system financials into the stratosphere. He was a brilliant money manager, NYS Senator, NYS Commissioner of Human Rights, and skilled politician. He would raise money and sponsor fundraising events and was really a man of the people, *All* the people! I was always shocked at the amount of Whites who supported Carl and attended his rallies. It seemed like he was the guy who could cross the color lines and get everybody's vote.

The only problem was, as soon as those White supporters stepped into the voting booth and closed that curtain, they all voted for the White guy and not Carl. Incredibly, Carl McCall lost the race by a landslide. I was so disgusted and disappointed with racist politics that I quit. I abandoned my committeeman position and disconnected from all political activities and groups. I was done!

Six years went by, and then Barack Obama came along. He was the only politician that could have drawn me back into volunteer service. I attended the Obama Academy and learned about social media campaigning and debating. We learned how to combat the John McCain point of view and cheerlead for Barack. It was an amazing experience. I wasn't into the social media thing too much, so this Obama Academy was a real eye-opener for me. Email, blogging, webinars, and text messaging were all so cutting-edge. I had just purchased a new smartphone and was only utilizing forty percent of what the phone could do. It was an enlightening three-day class. To my surprise, at the end of the academy, they requested that I go to Ohio. *Ohio????* The academy coordinator told me that Ohio was a "battleground" state. Barack had to win Ohio if he was going to be president. We were going to have to be trained to be boots-on-the-ground volunteers.

We had just finished this incredible training about how to increase voter turnout for the Barack Obama Campaign. The entire class was all revved up! We were ready to campaign and give it a hundred and ten percent effort. I thought they would turn me loose in my own community, but I later learned that New York was a Democratic State that already had Barack's support. He needed his volunteer army of people to be in battleground states nationwide. Ohio was in my geographic area, so that's where they sent me. The coordinator set up lodging and meals for us and told us that there would be a group of volunteers already there to help out, and some of them opened up their homes to us over the next week while we helped the campaign.

The next morning, I went to my local election office and picked up an absentee ballot since I would be in Ohio on election day. I requested a few days off work and called my contact person in Ohio.

When I got to Ohio, I was treated like a VIP. All of us out-of-state volunteers were treated well, and we received excellent accommodations and great hospitality.

My next four days of campaigning for Barack were exhilarating, and the Obama for President campaign headquarters in Cleveland ran exceptionally well. The individual who ran the headquarters was regimented and focused. He had very specific tasks for us to accomplish each day. Each day, he divided us into teams, and we were assigned to different voting districts and counties that needed the 'Obama presence.' We hustled all day, every day, right up until the election. It was a blast. The night of the election, all of us volunteers celebrated over our phones and social media as the votes started rolling in.

Barack Obama was elected the first Black president of the United States. It was probably one of the proudest moments of my life. I was glad to have been a part of the campaign and a part of history.

"Yes, We Can" – Barack Obama

Knocked Off Course

That same year, this White guy from Howard Beach, Queens, got convicted of assaulting three Black guys with a baseball bat. It was a hate crime conviction, and the guy ended up getting sentenced to fifteen years in prison. It was a high-profile, racially motivated crime, and many of us in the Black community had been following the case. The feeling among us was that it was about time a White man got convicted for assaulting a Black Man. This case is sensitive to the Black community because it happened before. Twenty years earlier, Michael Griffith was killed in the same town.

I had also become very comfortable in my position at work, so I applied for some supervisory positions to test the waters. I planned to enroll in grad school while I applied for managerial positions. The idea is that if I got both things moving, I'd have the academic credentials to back me up by the time I was in a higher position. I was lucky enough to be a member of a union that provided tuition reimbursement, so I was eager to begin classes. I decided to attend the University of Phoenix Online.

Needless to say, by the time I was back to focusing on school, it was more than half a decade later, and I had to start all over again from scratch. I didn't realize how rough and taxing the journey would be. I had sent them my transcript from six years ago, and they told me that too much time had passed and they couldn't accept any of my credits. So, I would have to retake those first bunch of courses.

Now, during that time, my diverticulitis condition was getting significantly worse. I experienced several hospitalizations over the past few years, and the doctors told me I needed surgery. If I prolonged the impending surgery any longer, there was a good chance my colon could burst, and I would require emergency surgery and a colostomy bag.

With all the stress at work and dealing with school, I was starting to get sicker and sicker. It became clear that I needed to have the surgery I should have had all those years ago. I scheduled the surgery, requested a leave of absence from school, and took a short-term disability sick leave from work.

The surgery turned out to be hell on earth. When I woke up in recovery, the surgeon came in to check on me and let me know that he had to remove almost ten feet of my colon because it was so severely damaged. I was in shock about that…but I was thankful I was going to be okay.

Eventually, they moved me out of recovery and into a room with another patient on a respirator. Let me tell you, if anybody thinks that a person can get some rest in the hospital, they are mistaken. Between the noises coming from the respirator keeping my roommate alive and the nurses coming in and out at all hours of the night, I think I was awake more than asleep.

I was moved to a private room before too long, which helped. The next morning, another doctor came to see me and explained the pain medication IV I was hooked up to. All I had to do was press a button to control my dose. I was so out of it that all I could do was listen and nod my head.

My entire abdominal area was wrapped, bandaged, and soaked with blood. The doctors didn't stitch me up after the surgery since it was an abdominal surgery. They had to use staples. I had about thirty-five stainless steel staples holding my abdominal area together, and I was in *excruciating* pain. The surgeon told me on several occasions that I would be hospitalized for only a few days, but the way I felt, I was very skeptical.

By day three, a rookie doctor came into my room and told me that my tests showed that I had internal bleeding and that a nasogastric tube needed to be inserted into my stomach to drain the blood. This doctor wasn't my regular surgeon, so I had a hard time processing why I would need something like that. I told him that he was making a mistake.

"No, Mr. Livingston," he said, "There's no mistake. You're bleeding internally and we have to remove the excess blood that's seeping into your stomach."

"Yeah, I'm gonna need my surgeon in here."

So, he went to get my surgeon. Forty-five minutes later, my surgeon came back and confirmed that I did need the tube. He also gave me a detailed explanation of what was going on. If I didn't get it done, I was going to bleed out and die. There was no other option. All right. I gotta get a tube up my nose.

So, the rookie doctor came back and tortured me. He sprayed a lidocaine anesthetic up my nose and down my throat, which by itself got me coughing. He waited until I was "numb," then pulled out a long plastic tube, squeezed some lubricant on the tip of the tube, and told me to lay back and relax. He inserted the tube into my nose. The tube was tough to get in because he started getting rough with it, and I was beginning to get uncomfortable. As he put more and more pressure on the tube, he was telling me to swallow. Keep swallowing, and the tube will go down. But every time I swallowed, he started ramming the tube harder and harder into my nose until it seemed to get stuck.

The whole thing went on for a minute or two until I finally told him I needed a minute to rest. "Do you know what you're doing?" That's when he admitted this was his first time doing it. I told him he probably needed to get some help because he was torturing me.

He called another doctor, who skillfully inserted the tube into my nose and down my throat. It was a terrible experience from the very beginning. Once it was in, I got to watch the blood getting sucked out of my stomach into a bag. It made me feel sicker than I was.

On day Four, the doctor removed my automatic pain injection device and told me that I would be given pain meds every four hours. The next day, I had a different nurse, and that went bad from the jump.

It got to be about time for my shot, so I rang the bell to call for a nurse to give me my pain shot. She came in and told me they would bring it. FIVE HOURS LATER, she finally comes back with the pain shot. By that point, my pain level was at a hundred!!! I absolutely lost it when she finally came into my room.

"Didn't you read my chart?" I screamed, "The doctor says I can get my meds every four hours! What's wrong with you? Can't you read?" There I was, a grown-ass man crying and yelling like a baby. That nurse needlessly allowed me to suffer, and I wasn't going to let her leave without giving her hell about it. I demanded to see my doctor after she administered the pain meds. It took me a good thirty minutes to get relaxed and finally fall off to sleep. I didn't want food. I didn't want T.V. I didn't want water. I just wanted to be left alone to sleep.

On Day Five, I woke up to the physical therapist wanting me up and walking. I tried, but I was so weak. I couldn't even walk to the end of the hallway. By the time I got out of bed and walked halfway down the hallway, I was exhausted and in pain. They took me for X-rays, and the doctor walked in when I got back to my room.

"Miles," he said sternly, "I see you've been pulling your gastro tube out."

"No, I haven't."

"Well, the x-rays show the tube is no longer in your stomach, and I taped the tube to your nose after I inserted it, so you must have moved it."

Damm, he busted me! Caught red-handed. Hey, I was tired of having that thing up my nose.

He helped me back into bed with my therapist and re-inserted about six inches of the tube back into my nose, then reordered more X-rays. "Ok, Miles," he said on his way out, "don't touch the tube. You still need it. I'm going to confirm the tube location with the X-rays before my next visit. Do you understand?"

"Yes, doctor. I understand."

On Day Six, I woke up with a sky-high fever and diarrhea. I'm also in excruciating pain. The nurse came in to take my temperature and blood. A couple of days had passed since I went off on her, and I was feeling bad about it, so I apologized. To my surprise, she admitted to misreading my chart and pain medication schedule and apologized.

About ninety minutes went by, and my surgeon came in. "I'm sorry to inform you that you have C. Diff."

"What is C. Diff?" I asked him.

Clostridioides difficile colitis, or C. diff, is a type of bacteria in my colon that happened to cause all my symptoms. "Your body has had so many antibiotic medications you were unable to fight off this type of infection. It also can have something to do with the cleanliness of the hospital, and individuals not washing their hands can spread this infection."

My surgeon told me that he was going to have to prescribe a special kind of high-powered antibiotic that should fight off the C. diff. I was moved into isolation, meaning I wasn't allowed visitors. I let my parents and other family members know the information, which was tough but necessary.

In the meantime, I was suffering. The pain medication was doing nothing for that type of pain. It seemed like I was spending hours on the toilet, not to mention the thirty-plus staples I still had holding my guts together. I was in constant pain and went without sleep for seventy-two hours. The infection started to subside, and finally, I tried to sleep. I was so weak I could barely make it to the bathroom and back. My surgeon told me to walk up and down the hallways to keep my body from atrophy, but I couldn't even do that. When my nurse took me for a short walk, it exhausted me.

The next time I went for an X-ray, I ended up cursing out the technician. I was so exhausted and in pain. I quickly realized that I was not myself. *Who have I become?* My surgeon came into my room after getting gowned up to protect himself.

"Miles, your labs and blood work are beginning to normalize. That's a good sign. You're still bleeding internally, so the gastric tube will need to stay in for a few more days. The x-ray looks good, so please don't touch your tube. Would you like something to eat?"

Eat. The last thing I want to do is eat! The doctor nodded, agreeing that he would let me rest. Before he left, I said, "You told me I'd be in the hospital for less than a week. I've been here over two weeks, and I feel terrible."

"Hang in there, Miles," he told me. "You'll be alright."

A few days later, the doctor finally took me out of isolation and allowed me to have visitors. My Mom, Dad, and Auntie came to visit me. I had been in the hospital for two weeks already, and we had a wonderful visit. I didn't allow them to touch me. However, they were senior citizens, and I just had this C. diff thing, so I dared not let them get too close to me.

Towards the end of our visit, my co-worker came in. Hello Miles, how are you?"

She came over to hug me. I stopped her and made a joke out of being contagious. She said, "Miles, I have something for you. We knew you were having surgery, so we took up a collection for you." She gave me an envelope stuffed with cash.

"Thank you so much, Michelle. I really appreciate this. Please meet my family." I introduced her. I gave my Mom the envelope after Michelle left, and she started to weep.

"Son, you are blessed," she said, "your co-workers must really love you. Look at this envelope and beautiful card. Get well and hurry home."

Recovery

It took me about four months to fully recover from my surgery. Once I recovered, I focused on completing my master's degree program, but unfortunately, I experienced another setback. My Mom, who was eighty-five years young at the time, was diagnosed with an artery blockage. The cardiologist recommended a cardiac catheterization procedure for Mom, and he explained that there were some risks to consider because of her age.

Needless to say, I was on edge the night before her procedure. I was still trying to keep going with my studies. Mom wouldn't want me to stop just because she was going to have surgery. Still, I stayed with her and helped out as often as I could. I was taking classes online, so I did a lot of my schoolwork while visiting her or helping her with her appointments. On the night before her surgery, I sat in her hospital room doing homework until I dozed off before submitting my assignment. I was totally exhausted. The nurse woke me up and told me to go home and get some sleep.

So, I called a cab and headed home. And early the next morning, I took the day off to see Mom before her surgery and be there when she got out. Thank the Lord, everything went well. Mom made it through the surgery with no issues. They expected a good outlook for her after recovery.

I felt so relieved. The weight of the world had been lifted off of my shoulders, and I could re-focus on school. I went to my Mom's room to wait for her to return from the recovery room. Since I'd brought my laptop, I decided to log into my online class. To my surprise, I had an email waiting from my instructor. It said, "Miles, I am waiting for your paper. What happened? You missed the deadline."

I'd been so preoccupied with my mom's health that I completely forgot to turn in my paper. I explained what happened to my professor, and she ended up giving me an incomplete for the class, even though I turned in the paper late. That immediately caused the university to place me on probation, leading to my suspension. You see, all the students had to sign a contract before starting classes, so we all know what criteria to follow. One of the things that could get you in trouble was getting an Incomplete in one of your classes.

I felt my situation was special with my Mom being in the hospital. So, I appealed the suspension and submitted my Mom's medical documentation. The dean upheld my appeal; however, I was still barred from classes for eight weeks.

I was extremely disappointed, but what could I do? Instead of lamenting about that outcome, I decided to immerse myself in work. I took some continuing education courses on emergency care protocols and admitting office procedures in addition to applying myself to everything in my normal workload. I wanted to become the absolute best Clerical Account Representative I could be. I also applied for the Municipal Hospital Administrative Internship Program, which was a fantastic program, but it only had six internships. Of the hundreds that applied, I sadly wasn't selected.

Eight weeks later, I was back in school. I finished my final five courses with straight A's and graduated in November 2009. I was an upwardly mobile Black Man employed in the healthcare sector, and I've gotten a master's degree in healthcare administration to advance my career. The way I saw it, my degrees had to set me apart from the crowd, or so I thought. Another happy moment was when my son, Miles Jr., became an NCAA Fencing Champion. Even though he was only a freshman at Penn State University, his teammates voted him onto the championship team because he won most of his fencing matches during the season. The entire family was very proud of him.

Advancement in the Workplace

Finally, I earned my Master's degree in Healthcare Administration. It was a labor of love, and now that I'd achieved that goal, I couldn't wait to restart my career. Deep down inside, I knew I had so much potential and so much to contribute to my organization. It was an incredible feeling.

One of the first things I noticed about the employment landscape is that many of my female colleagues (I'm not hating on them) had already entered the ranks of management. I should add that, of course, I noticed. I worked and went to school, so I saw these women moving ahead of me all the time. I applied for a few supervisory positions along the way, but nothing panned out for me, so my head stayed in the books. Many of my coworkers knew I was working towards getting a higher position, so they looked for management jobs for me. *Hey Miles, there's an opening here!* Or *Miles, they need a manager over* there. I inadvertently developed an insurance training grid for myself and the team in an emergency. I realized that I knew all of the health insurance codes.

Hey Miles, how is it that you know all of these codes? I dared not tell them the real deal. I was xeroxing every health insurance card that came into the E.R. so that I could study them. In those days, we were allowed to make copies of insurance cards. After about ninety days, I'd accumulated around forty cards in all. From there, I decided to memorize the codes and keep them in a grid inside a notebook in my locker. It was all fine and good until I got a call to leave work early for a family emergency, and I forgot my notebook.

When I arrived at work the next day, a Xerox copy of my grid was lying on the desk. I asked my co-worker about it.

"What is my grid doing here?"

My co-worker said, "The supervisor found it and asked me whose it was. I told them it was yours."

I was hot. I felt like my privacy had been directly violated. "This is private property," I told them. "How did they even get this? Did they go through my locker?"

Before he could answer me, I was called into the supervisor's office. He sat me down while holding another copy of my grid.

"You know," he said, "I understand this belongs to you."

I'm still steaming, but I know better than to go off on my boss, so I just nod. "Yeah, it's mine."

"I just want to let you know that this is a great idea. I love it."

Yeah, sure, I thought. *Your compliment and a subway token will get me a ride home on the train tonight.*

Nothing more came of that until about six months later, when all the new hires were given study guides with my grid included. Of course, it was all new and improved, but basically, it was my insurance grid. I do not doubt that somebody stole it and used it, claiming it as their own idea. I had bigger fish to fry. I let that one roll off my back and stayed focused on bigger and better things.

I quickly realized that a Black Man with a master's degree is basically the "kiss of death" in my field. The women hated me, White men despised me, the HR department didn't know what to do with me, and the hiring managers kept away from me like I had the plague. The contacts I used to work with were scared to death and intimidated by me. Here I was, running around like a chicken with its head cut off, and nobody would help me. Incompetent idiots got jobs left and right, but I was left on the line despite my qualifications. After a year of it, I diplomatically approached my leadership to ask them what the hell the deal was. I had been denied the last five supervisory positions I applied for. What did I need to do to get promoted at this institution?

Thanksgiving '09

For some strange reason, I decided to cook Thanksgiving dinner that year. My cousin Al usually hosted a traditional Thanksgiving Family Feast every year, but he lived in West Virginia. While we always had a good time at his house, I was tired of the yearly five-hour drive. On top of that, my parents and other elderly relatives were getting up in age, so I had to do all the driving. Usually, after dinner, when we were all relaxing and having drinks, inevitably, one of my family members was always ready to go home. Who wants to be on the road driving for five hours on Thanksgiving night? Certainly not me, but that had become my routine. As you can imagine, playing chauffeur to my family members had taken all the fun out of Thanksgiving for me. Getting up at the crack of dawn, driving around various boroughs to pick up relatives, and then driving from New York to West Virginia was a grind. I was done with that.

So, that year, I called my kids to tell them that I was going to stay home and cook Thanksgiving dinner. I let them know that it's not going to be an all-day thing, so if they wanted to, they could stop by for a plate and be on their way if they couldn't stay. At that point, I had about two weeks to prepare the dinner, so I was in no rush to get started. I called my dad, girlfriend, and a few other friends and began planning everything. I prided myself on cooking barbeque. I decided to fire up the grill for some chicken, ribs, and a turkey.

Thanksgiving Day arrived, and my kids stood me up. Hour after hour went by. I even called them up to ask when they were coming. All I got from them was a bullshit answer. Something about *maybe* stopping by and other similar excuses that did not sit well with me. After going back and forth with them, I finally told them to jump into an Uber or taxi at my expense and just come over and get some food because I had cooked so much. Even after I offered them a cab ride, they *still* didn't come. My dad and girlfriend were starving, so I invited them to go ahead and eat. It was the saddest Thanksgiving of my life. I was humiliated and embarrassed, but most of all, I was heartbroken that my own kids didn't want to spend the holiday with me. I could say that it was my ex-wife's fault and that she poisoned them against me, but if I'm honest, I don't know the real reason why they couldn't be bothered to spend Thanksgiving with their father. And in the end, the only thing that mattered was that they didn't come.

The holidays always feel like they're missing something without your kids around. Thanksgiving just exacerbates those emotions, and when my kids stood me up that one year, it devastated me. I felt like my kids didn't have enough respect for me to show up for Thanksgiving dinner or even call to say that they weren't coming.

Since that Thanksgiving, I've always chosen to work the Thanksgiving Holiday. That day is supposed to be about having those you love around you. Without my kids, it doesn't feel like it's worth the effort for me. Maybe that'll change in the future, but for the time being, I prefer not to put myself through it every year.

7

Black Lives Matter

"Anger is better. There's a sense of being in anger. A reality and presence. An awareness of worth. It is a lovely surging."

–Toni Morrison

I am so proud of these young up-and-coming African American leaders who established the Black Lives Matter movement. It's like someone was finally shouting what we've always known from the mountaintops. Finally, the world *has* to sit up and notice that there's a problem in this country.

We must never forget those who have died needlessly at the hands of bigoted and racist people, and we can *never* forget their names.

Sean Bell – On November 25, 2006, a shooting occurred in Queens, New York. Three males were shot when the New York City Police Department (NYPD) fired 50 shots in both plainclothes and undercover. Bell was slain the morning before his wedding, and two of his friends, Trent Benefield and Joseph Guzman, were seriously injured. The event provoked widespread criticism of the New York City Police Department, drawing parallels to the 1999 killing of Amadou Diallo. This police shooting touches me because I frequent the establishment where this killing took place.

Oscar Grant III – On January 1, 2009, a 22-year-old African American man was fatally shot by BART Police Officer Johannes Mehserle in Oakland, California. Following allegations of a fight on a crowded Bay Area Rapid Transit train returning from San Francisco, BART Police officers detained Grant and several other passengers on the platform at the Fruitvale BART Station. BART officer Anthony Pirone kneed Grant in the head and forced the unarmed man to lie face down on the platform. While Pirone held Grant in a prone position, Mehserle drew his pistol and shot him in the back.

Aiyana Mo'Nay Jones – On May 16, 2010, Officer Joseph Weekley shot and killed seven-year-old Aiyana Jones from Detroit's East Side during a raid carried out by the Detroit Police Department's Special Response Team. Her death attracted national media attention, prompting U.S. Representative John Conyers to request that U.S. Attorney General Eric Holder conduct a federal investigation.

Trayvon Martin – On the night of February 26, 2012, in Sanford, Florida, George Zimmerman shot and killed Trayvon Martin, a 17-year-old African American high school student. Zimmerman, a 28-year-old man, was the neighborhood watch supervisor for his gated community, where Martin was visiting family when he was shot. This murder and the subsequent trial shook the entire country. It was "Rodney King" and "O.J. Simpson" all over again.

Rekia Boyd – On March 21, 2012, Dante Servin, an off-duty Chicago police detective, shot and killed 22-year-old Rekia Boyd in Chicago, Illinois. According to authorities, Servin filed a noise complaint against Rekia and three of her friends as they gathered in Douglass Park, then drove out to where they were and confronted them. After exchanging words, Servin fired five shots from his car as Boyd and the others turned to leave. Boyd was struck in the head and killed.

Jonathan Ferrell – On September 14, 2013, police officer Randall "Wes" Kerrick shot and killed Ferrell, a 24-year-old former collegiate football player for the Florida A&M University Rattlers, in Charlotte, North Carolina. Kerrick had been charged with voluntary manslaughter. After being involved in a car accident, he went to the nearby home of Sarah McCartney, who called the police after claiming that Ferrell was trying to break in. When the police showed up, he reportedly ran towards them for help. Kerrick opened fire on him, shooting him twelve times.

Eric Garner – Eric Garner died on July 17, 2014, in the New York City borough of Staten Island after a New York City Police Department (NYPD) officer, Daniel Pantaleo, choked him while arresting him. Video footage of the incident drew broad national attention and highlighted concerns about law enforcement's appropriate use of force.

John Crawford III – On August 5th, 2014, Crawford, a 22-year-old African American male, was shot and killed by Beavercreek police officer Sean Williams in a Walmart store in

Beavercreek, Ohio, near Dayton. The officer claimed he was armed, but Crawford was only carrying a BB gun. A grand jury refused to indict the two officers on criminal charges.

Michael Brown – On August 9, 2014, Michael Brown Jr., an 18-year-old African American male, was fatally shot by Darren Wilson, a 28-year-old White Ferguson police officer, in Ferguson, Missouri, a suburb of Saint Louis. This killing would rekindle the Black Lives Matter movement in the United States.

Laquan McDonald – On October 20, 2014, Laquan McDonald, a 17-year-old African American, was killed by Chicago Police Officer Jason Van Dyke. The police had initially reported that McDonald was behaving *"abnormally"* while walking down the street and refused to put down a knife he was holding. Dashcam footage of the shooting shown thirteen months later, on November 24, 2015, revealed that McDonald was walking away from the police when he was shot sixteen times.

Akai Gurley – On November 20, 2014, a New York City Police Department officer shot and killed a 28-year-old man in Brooklyn, New York City, USA. Two police officers patrolling stairwells of the New York City Housing Authority (NYCHA)'s Louis H. Pink Houses in East New York, Brooklyn, entered a pitch-black stairwell, one of whom, Officer Peter Liang, 27, had his handgun drawn. Gurley and his girlfriend entered the stairway on the seventh floor, fourteen steps below them. The gunshot was ruled an unintentional discharge; the bullet ricocheted off the wall, killing Gurley once in the chest.

Tamir Rice – On November 22, 2014, Timothy Loehmann, a 26-year-old police officer, shot Tamir Rice, a 12-year-old African American, in Cleveland, Ohio. Rice was holding an imitation plastic Airsoft rifle when Loehmann arrived and shot him nearly instantly. Loehmann and 46-year-old Frank Garmback responded to a police dispatch call about a person with a pistol. A caller reported that a person was pointing "a pistol" at random people at the Cudell Recreation Center, a park run by Cleveland's Public Works Department. At the beginning and middle of the call, he states the pistol, "It's probably fake." The caller indicates near the end of the two-minute call that "He is probably a juvenile"; however, this information was not transmitted to officers Loehmann or Garmback during the first dispatch. The officers stated when they arrived, they both repeatedly demanded that Tamar Rice "Show me your hands" through the open patrol car window. When Tamar complied, the officer shot him twice in the chest.

Walter Scott – Walter Scott was shot on April 4, 2015, in North Charleston, South Carolina, after a daytime traffic check for a non-functioning brake light. Scott, an unarmed male, was fatally shot by North Charleston police officer Michael Slager. Slager was charged with murder after a video surfaced showing him shooting Scott from behind while he was fleeing, contradicting the police report.

Eric Courtney Harris – On April 2, 2015, 44-year-old Eric Harris was fatally shot during an undercover investigation in Tulsa, OK. Harris fled from authorities unarmed. While Harris was being subdued, Tulsa County Reserve Deputy Robert

Charles "Bob" Bates, 73, mistook his own firearm, a Smith & Wesson.357 revolver, for a Model X26 Taser. Bates shot Harris in the back while he was on the ground. According to the Tulsa County Sheriff's Office, he instantly stated, "Oh, I shot him! I am sorry." Bates was convicted of manslaughter and sentenced to four years in jail.

Freddie Gray – On April 12, 2015, the Baltimore Police Department detained Freddie Carlos Gray, Jr., a 25-year-old Black Man, and accused him of having a weapon. Gray went into a coma while being transferred in a police van and was sent to R Adams Cowley Shock Trauma Center. While police claimed no wrongdoing, the medical examiner's report listed Gray's death as a homicide. Criminal charges were filed, but thanks to mistrials and other legal misfires, none of the six officers involved were imprisoned. Gray died on April 19, 2015, from spinal cord damage.

Charleston Church Massacre – On June 17, 2015, a mass shooting occurred in Charleston, South Carolina, killing nine African Americans at a Bible study at the Emanuel African Methodist Episcopal Church. Clementa C. Pinckney, a state legislator and senior preacher, was among those killed; three victims survived. This church is one of the oldest Black churches in the United States and has long served as a focus for civil rights activism. After multiple people recognized Dylan Roof as the main suspect, he became the focus of a manhunt, which culminated the morning after the shooting with his arrest in Shelby, North Carolina. He admitted he carried out the shooting with the goal of inciting a racial war. To add insult to injury, the officers took him to Burger King when he was arrested.

Sandra Bland – On July 13, 2015, Sandra Bland, a 28-year-old African American woman, was discovered hanging in a jail cell in Waller County, Texas, three days after being arrested on a pretextual traffic stop. Though her family insisted she was a well-adjusted, happy person, her death was declared as suicide. The incident was followed by protests over her detention, a dispute over the cause of death, and allegations of racial violence.

Samuel DuBose – On July 19, 2015, Ray Tensing, a White University of Cincinnati police officer, shot and killed Samuel DuBose, an unarmed Black Man, during a traffic check for a missing front license plate and a suspended driver's license. Tensing fired his gun at DuBose after he started his car. Tensing reported that DuBose tried to drive away and was being dragged because his arm got stuck in the automobile. Prosecutors said that evidence from Tensing's bodycam indicated he was not dragged, and a grand jury indicted him for murder and voluntary manslaughter. He was later fired from the police agency but was released on bond before trial. A November 2016 trial ended in a mistrial after the jury was deadlocked.

Christian Taylor – On August 7, 2015, a 19-year-old college student was shot to death by Arlington, Texas, police officer Brad Miller at a car dealership in the city, adding to the ongoing debate fueled by Black Lives Matter and other social justice organizations about young African Americans dying at the hands of law enforcement.

Jamar Clark – On November 15, 2015, Minneapolis Police shot Jamar Clark, a 24-year-old African American from Minneapolis, Minnesota. The shooting included two police officers, Mark Ringgenberg and Dustin Schwarze, who were later placed on paid administrative leave. Clark died the night following the incident at Hennepin County Medical Center after being removed from life support. Black Lives Matter planned an 18-day protest outside the Fourth Precinct police station and other rallies and demonstrations throughout Minneapolis.

Alton Sterling – On July 5, 2016, two White Baton Rouge Police officers shot and killed Alton Sterling, a 37-year-old Black Man, at close range in Baton Rouge, Louisiana. The officers were attempting to hold Sterling's arms, and he was shot after allegedly grabbing for a loaded .38 caliber revolver in his pocket. The incident sparked protests in Baton Rouge and a request for a civil rights inquiry by the United States Department of Justice.

Philando Castile – On July 6, 2016, Philando Castile, a 32-year-old African American, was stopped while driving in Falcon Heights, Minnesota, and killed by Jeronimo Yanez, a St. Anthony, Minnesota police officer. Castile was driving a car at 9:00 p.m. with his girlfriend, Diamond Reynolds, and her four-year-old daughter. He was stopped by Yanez and another officer in a suburb of Saint Paul, Minnesota. The officer claimed he was in fear for his life and shot him in front of his little girl.

Paul O'Neal – On July 28, 2016, Paul O'Neal was shot in the back by Chicago Police Department officers after a grand theft auto chase. O'Neal, 18, drove a stolen Jaguar into two police cars, a parked automobile, and a police officer. Police claim O'Neal, who was unarmed, left the vehicle following the chase and refused to stop. The medical examiner classed the incident as a homicide. After a preliminary investigation, the three cops who discharged their firearms were relieved of duty. After an inquiry, no criminal charges were filed against the officers involved.

Terence Crutcher – Betty Jo Shelby, a police officer in Tulsa, Oklahoma, shot and killed Terence Crutcher, a 40-year-old motorist. When the encounter occurred, he was unarmed and standing near his vehicle in the middle of the street.

Keith Lamont Scott – Brentley Vinson, a municipal police officer, shot and killed a 43-year-old African American man on September 20, 2016, in Charlotte, North Carolina. Police arrived at Scott's apartment complex to look for an unrelated individual with an outstanding warrant. According to police, officers observed Scott exiting a vehicle in the parking lot while holding a weapon and refusing to comply with their directions. Scott's wife refuted the officer's account, stating he wasn't armed. Nonetheless, by November, the charges against Vinson were dropped.

Bettie Jones – On December 26, 2016, Chicago police officer Robert Rialmo killed an innocent bystander before also fatally shooting Quintonio LeGrier, age 19, in the 4700 block of West

Erie Street, where LeGrier was staying with his father. LeGrier's father called 911 from the city's West Side. According to initial accounts, Rialmo stated that LeGrier, who suffered from mental illness, was carrying a bat. When he arrived on the scene, he fatally shot Jones in the chest after she opened the apartment building door for Rialmo, who fired eight shots at LeGrier. Six shots hit LeGrier, killing him.

O'Shae Terry – On September 1, 2018, O'Shae Terry was shot and killed during a traffic stop in Arlington, Texas. Despite bodycam footage confirming the murder, Officer Bau Tran was sentenced to six years deferred adjudication and fined six hundred dollars. In other words, all he had to do was pay a fine. He didn't even serve a day in prison for murdering Terry.

Botham Jean – On September 6, 2018, off-duty Dallas Police Department patrol officer Amber Guyger entered Botham Jean's apartment and shot him fatally. Guyger claimed that she entered the flat thinking it was her own and shot Jean, assuming he was a burglar. Guyger was only charged with manslaughter, causing distrust in the process and indignation over the death of an unarmed Black man. This sparked demonstrations and charges of racial bigotry. Two months later, the charge was changed to murder.

Ronald Greene – On May 10, 2019, Ronald Greene, a 49-year-old Black Man, died after being apprehended by Louisiana State Police following a high-speed chase outside Monroe, Louisiana. During his arrest, he was egregiously assaulted. He was hit with a stun gun, punched, choked, and dragged along the ground while being handcuffed and shackled. At least six White troopers participated in the violent arrest. Instead of calling for medical assistance, the troopers left Greene unattended, face down, for more than nine minutes after the assault. When Greene's corpse was delivered to the hospital, police told doctors that his automobile had run into a tree. Medical examiners found this claim to be false. After an investigation, police adjusted their statement, saying that he died in the struggle during the arrest without acknowledging the officer's part in it.

Ahmaud Arbery – On Sunday, February 23, 2020, Ahmaud Arbery was shot and killed while jogging near his home on the outskirts of Brunswick, Ga. Three White men hunted him down in a pickup truck and shot him to death. The killers walked free for two and a half months before a video was released to the public on May 8, 2020, detailing Arbery's death. After that, it took seventy-six days before they were arrested.

Manuel Ellis – On March 3, 2020, police officers in Tacoma, Washington, killed a 33-year-old unarmed Black Man while attempting an arrest. The Pierce County Sheriff's Department initially claimed Ellis had attacked a police cruiser before attacking the deputies. Prosecutors cited civilian witnesses as indicating Ellis did not attack the police car or the officers and that the officers were the instigators of the violence towards Ellis. In addition, a video of the event backed up witness statements. Ellis, while pinned to the ground, cried out, "I can't breathe."

Daniel Prude – On March 23, 2020, Daniel Prude, an African American man, was killed after being forcibly restrained by Rochester, New York, police officers. Prude had a mental breakdown after swallowing PCP and was walking naked through the city streets. Police attacked him and held him face down on the pavement for two minutes and fifteen seconds before he stopped breathing. Prude underwent CPR on the scene before succumbing to suffocation complications after being removed from life support.

Breonna Taylor – On March 13, 2020, Taylor was fatally shot in her own home by police in Louisville, Kentucky. She was asleep when they burst through her door and invaded her home. She was only twenty-six years old and an EMT. This killing was the spark that rekindled Black Lives Matter protests around the country.

Rayshard Brooks – On the night of June 12, 2020, Atlanta Police Department (APD) officer Garrett Rolfe fatally shot Rayshard Brooks, a twenty-seven-year-old African American man. Devin Brosnan, an APD officer, was responding to a complaint that a man (Brooks) was sleeping in a car blocking a Wendy's drive-through lane. Brosnan radioed for help, and Rolfe arrived a few minutes later. Rolfe administered a breathalyzer test, which revealed that Brooks' blood-alcohol content was above the legal limit for driving. Rolfe and Brosnan began handcuffing Brooks, but Brooks seized Brosnan's taser and attempted to flee. Rolfe pursued Brooks on foot, and Brooks half-turned to discharge the taser at Rolfe's head. Rolfe then drew his gun and fired three shots at Brooks, hitting him twice in the back and killing him.

Jacob S. Blake – On August 23, 2020, police officer Rusten Sheskey shot and badly injured Jacob S. Blake, a twenty-nine-year-old African American man, in Kenosha, Wisconsin. Officer Sheskey shot Blake seven times in the back when he opened the driver's door of his SUV during a traffic stop. Three of Blake's sons were in the rear seat at the time.

Jonathan Price – On October 3, 2020, a White Texas cop killed Thirty-one-year-old Price after offering a handshake and asking whether the officer was "doing good." According to witnesses, Jonathan was behaving as a good Samaritan and attempting to halt a domestic attack inside the gas station's convenience store when the police arrived. Shortly after the handshake, Price was shot four times by Officer Shaun Lucas at a gas station in Wolfe City, Texas, according to bodycam footage.

Daunte Demetrius Wright – On April 11, 2021, police officer Kimberly Potter fatally shot Daunte Wright, a twenty-year-old African American man, during a traffic stop and attempted arrest for an outstanding warrant in Brooklyn Center, Minnesota. Wright was shot after a brief battle with officers. He drove away but smashed into another vehicle and collided with a concrete barrier. He was pronounced dead on the scene. The next day, authorities said Potter intended to use her Taser but accidentally grabbed her revolver, shooting Wright in the chest. Two days later, Potter and Brooklyn Center police chief Tim Gannon resigned, and Potter fled her house after her address was released on social media. Potter was eventually arrested and charged with second-degree manslaughter.

Andrew Brown Jr. – Andrew Brown Jr., a 42-year-old Black Man, was fatally shot in the head by a deputy sheriff on April 21, 2021, in Elizabeth City, North Carolina. Following the shooting, seven cops were placed on leave. Brown died one day after former Minneapolis police officer Derek Chauvin was convicted of George Floyd's murder and after the recent police shootings of Marvin Scott, Daunte Wright, Ma'Khia Bryant, and Adam Toledo. Brown was shot after his automobile "made contact" with law enforcement authorities who were serving a search and arrest warrant at his home, according to a prosecutor. A court has ordered that the body camera videos of the shooting not be made public.

Tyree Nichols – On January 7, 2023, at approximately 8:21 p.m. CDT, five Memphis Police Department (MPD) officers stopped Nichols at the Raines Road and Ross Road intersection on suspicion of reckless driving. Following the initial police physical assault, Nichols began sprinting from the vehicle, complaining of lack of breath. During the incident, Nichols managed to get away. When officers apprehended Nichols, they assaulted him for about three minutes, beating and kicking him in the head and hitting him on the back with a baton while they held him down. Three days later, Nichols died. After a few days of his passing, the officers involved were fired and charged with second-degree murder.

George Floyd – On May 25, 2020, Floyd died in Powderhorn, a neighborhood south of downtown Minneapolis, Minnesota.

Derek Chauvin, a White Minneapolis police officer, kept his knee on the right side of Floyd's neck for eight minutes and forty-six seconds during an arrest, including two minutes and fifty-three seconds after Floyd became unresponsive, according to the criminal complaint filed against Chauvin. Officers Tou Thao, J. Alexander Kueng, and Thomas K. Lane assisted in Floyd's arrest, with Kueng holding Floyd's back, Lane holding his legs, and Thao watching. The murder of George Floyd shocked the country. It shined a light on Police brutality against Black men. It was also the impetus behind efforts to heal racial discrimination in this country.

Financial Institutions, Retail, Tech, and other companies vowed to invest enormous sums of money into initiatives aimed at combating racial injustice. For many of these organizations, it was a nice sound byte for media and public relations purposes to pledge billions of dollars. These companies felt pressured to do something positive, so they jumped on the "George Floyd" Racial Equity bandwagon. The problem is they never really made a firm commitment and had no strategy or plan to give financial support.

"Many Black women found themselves on the "glass cliff" in 2020 when companies and public agencies scrambled to diversify their staffs and launch diversity and inclusion initiatives as the nation faced a reckoning on racism following George Floyd's death." (Ellis, 2022). The phenomenon coined by researchers as the "glass cliff " is essentially the opposite of the "glass ceiling"– the term that describes the barriers minorities face to advance in the workplace. Research shows that women and people of color are more likely to be appointed to poorly performing companies than White males. (Ellis, 2022).

"Now that we are a few years removed from the massive racial justice protests that gripped the United States, some corporations have backtracked on their antiracist commitments. Their financial pledges to antiracist causes have gone unfulfilled. Their promises to diversify their workforces have not been realized. Other corporate antiracist programs that were priorities in the aftermath of George Floyd's murder are no longer so." (Fletcher, 2024). Unfortunately, the attention and focus on race relations slowly faded away like a trend or the latest fad of the times.

And the list of African Americans killed by law enforcement goes on and on and on…

I'll end this chapter with my own dose of reality.

One night in 2010, my son called me. "Hey, Dad. The cops are pulling me over."

My heart dropped. "Put your phone on speaker and place it on the seat next to you in plain sight," I told him. Over the course of the next few minutes, I listened to my son ask permission to reach for his ID and insurance card. I listened to him address the cop with respectful terms like "Yes, sir" and "No, sir." I heard the cop ask my son if he had any weapons in the car and if he'd been drinking. If he had any illegal drugs. Every question my son answered calmly and respectfully…and it did nothing to help me stay calm. I listened in terror, praying that wasn't going to be the last time I ever heard my son's voice.

For Black parents, this is our reality. Anytime we get pulled over, it might be the last time we see our children again.

When the cops left to run his plates, I told him not to touch his phone. Keep talking to me on the speaker. I asked him if he was speeding, and he said he wasn't. He was just cruising along. I was starting to breathe hard, and my heart was about to jump out of my chest. As a Black Father, we all have that talk with our kids about the police— all of us. But when you're on the phone listening to a cop grill your son about what they think he might have in the car, all you can think about is what might go wrong.

So many Black men did everything right. Everything their fathers told them to do. So many of us complied with the police and were murdered, regardless! So many more are just walking, jogging, sleeping in our houses, eating, talking with friends, living our lives only to end up dead because some cop only sees a threat.

The cop returned to the car and told my son that he had a taillight out and to get it fixed. They let him go with a warning. Every day, I wonder if having me on speaker saved my son's life. Or if there was some other factor that saved him. I can't help but think about how my son could have ended up as one of the *hundreds of thousands* of names of Black men and women who have been killed by police.

It's a never-ending story of unarmed Black men being murdered by police officers in this country. It's woven into our daily lives. The advent of social media has allowed us to know about these unjust killings and violence perpetrated against Black men in this country, but the work is far from done. There is a problem in this country, and it needs to be solved. Let's not forget about the Black women who also were killed at the hands of law enforcement.

8

The Inmates Are Running The Asylum

"People do not choose rebellion; it is forced upon them. Revolution is always an act of self-defense."

–C. T. Vivian, Black Power and the American Myth (1970)

Looking back on my career, I would characterize myself as a late bloomer. I say that because now that I'm in my sixties, I have finally acquired the skill set I need to excel in hospital management. A skill set that, in my opinion, I should have mastered when I was thirty. I believe my delayed path is a direct result of having to fight through all the years I was looked over by my female and White male counterparts because of racial discrimination against Black men. It's a bitch to prove in a court of law. Some might say it's virtually impossible, but that's what we, as Black men, have to fight against. When I was around twenty-five to thirty years old, I should have entered into management. By thirty-five, I should have been the manager. By forty, I should have been running my own department. However, the lack of grooming and mentorship I was denied significantly affected my career growth.

"The lack of mentorship and guidance is not only a hindrance to individual growth but also to overall diversity and inclusion efforts within organizations. Without diverse perspectives and voices at the table, businesses miss out on the unique ideas and contributions that Blacks can bring to the table." (Solomon, 2023).

All throughout my career, I was looking for someone or some entity to rectify my situation. I discovered I was in a situation where the inmates were running the asylum. What I mean is that the ones running the show are the same ones keeping up the madness within any given system. When police officers break the law, other police officers cover it up. When racist Human Resource Departments hire only White males and women into management, the Company covers it up. When Major League Baseball players take steroids to get an advantage, MLB covers it up. NFL players with Chronic Traumatic Encephalopathy 'CTE' injuries and what the NFL knew and covered up. It's about corruption at the highest levels to keep corrupt systems going and going.

"Without third-party oversight and governance, powerful independent organizations will eventually self-destruct."

- Miles M. Livingston

Over time, many third-party entities had to be established to provide oversight to regulate these various organizations because they were incapable of governing themselves. They certainly couldn't police and discipline themselves. Without third-party oversight and governance, powerful, influential, independent organizations will eventually self-destruct. Well, it's the same principle inside Corporate America. Powerful White men, influential organizations governed by women, and powerful unions. All brilliant minds become ignorant when it comes to fairness for groups and individuals outside of their sphere of influence. Thank God for the Division of Human Rights organizations and EEOC.

Fight within the Workforce

I probably applied for over one hundred jobs in the four years leading up to my filing a discrimination lawsuit. I worked with several human resource Talent Acquisition Specialists who seemed to be intimidated by an upwardly mobile Black Man. They had no problem getting jobs for Black women and White males, but not somebody like me. And while it might sound like a problem that was unique to my situation, I know I'm not alone. The business of segregating Black men and women in the workplace and brewing dissent between us is an old tactic. It's a fight that's been raging on for at least twenty years. David J. Maume, a professor of sociology at the University of Cincinnati who specializes in gender inequalities in the workplace, said on the subject:

"White men resist attempts at gender integration in order to preserve their privileged positions within the firm. By segregating women into specific occupations with short job ladders, White men are free to compete among themselves for higher-paying jobs that offer better career opportunities. In this account, exclusionary dynamics extend beyond managers to blue-collar workers. This process is referred to as "social closure," in which employers discriminate in hiring and offering promotions, often at the urging of their (White) male employees." (Maume, 1999).

By 2009, President Obama signed the HITECH Act. My entire class was excited as our instructors explained the spirit and nuances of this Act. HITECH, or Health Information Technology for Economic and Clinical Health, basically stated that the entire healthcare sector would be mandated to adopt electronic health records (EHR). Healthcare entities such as hospitals, nursing homes, clinics, etc., would receive financial incentives for EHR adoption. Also, under the HITECH Act, all healthcare entities had to improve the security protection of healthcare data by following stringent guidelines detailed by the HIPAA Privacy and Security Act (which was initially enacted in 1996).

My graduate and workforce development classes were on the cutting edge of those learning and technological developments. We were under the impression that we would certainly be in high demand when we graduated. Or so you would think. I can't tell you how proud I was to put the letters MHA (Master of Healthcare Administration) or MS-HCA (Master of Science in Health Care Administration) after my name on my resume and email signature.

At that time, only two African American men were in the first cohort of the HITECH Workforce Development class at Columbia University in New York City. A few months after graduation, I reached out to my fellow African American classmate, and he (like me) was still in his same employment position. We both realized it would take some time to advance. We didn't know that we were both seen as Black men with too much knowledge. We were threats to the healthcare establishments that employed us.

I became so frustrated with the interview process I decided to give the White women interviewing me a taste of my reality. Probably ninety-five percent of the people who interviewed me were White women (Not quite sure why that was). And I was pretty sure that none of them ever had a Black male boss or supervisor. These were women who had never promoted or hired a Black male manager and probably never even had a Black male instructor in school. So, realistically, how much of a chance did I have to interview with them for a management-level position, and they would actually hire me?

It's a real problem! One that hasn't gone unnoticed even by researchers. An article in New York Newsday lays it all out:

"Exacerbating the lack of Black men in management positions and other factors,' experts say, 'are social perceptions of Black men that are often rooted in racial biases. Many potential employers would rather hire immigrants or women over Black men, who are viewed as 'not as compliant, more demanding, not reliable,' said Levitan, citing a large body of research."

"Black male job applicants, (particularly) if they are tall and muscular, need to be aware that many people immediately are intimidated by them,' said Chuck Hoffman, Director of Workforce Development Services at New York City College of Technology in Downtown Brooklyn. 'If they're going to an interview and it's a little White lady, I tell them, 'I would recommend you lower your voice and be aware,' Hoffman said. 'That's the reality." (Texeira, 2004).

"He who dares not offend, cannot be honest" –Thomas Paine

That being said, I went into my next interview, and I was waiting for that ten-million-dollar question. "Miles, your education is impeccable. You're intelligent, and you have a wealth of experience. So why have you remained in a clerical position and haven't entered the management ranks?"

"Well, that's a great question, and quite frankly, there are no Black male managers at my current job. I've applied for several managerial openings but have not been able to break through that glass ceiling. How many African American managers are employed here?"

And then that pregnant pause. I had usually researched the department, so I knew they had no Black managers. And for the hospitals that had Black women in management, I would change the question around and ask, "How many Black men do you have in management?"

And the thing is, I know that with them being White women, they already have an unconscious bias against me before I even open my mouth. And I know I'm not going to change their minds in the short span of a job interview, but I figure, why pretend? Let's just lay it all out and go from there. Maybe they won't hire me, but I gave them something to think about.

That's what Black men have to endure in these interviews. We're held back because of racism, and if we get the interview at all, we get asked the question, "Why have you stayed in a dead-end job for so long?" Like there's something wrong with us. Now, we have to defend ourselves and answer a bunch of questions that have nothing to do with our job qualifications.

One day after work, I went for a drive with a coworker. I told her about the issues I was having. Her response was to try to be 'nicer' when I go on these interviews. "Don't be so angry," she said. "Look at all the positive reasons why you stayed in the same job. A strong union, tuition reimbursement, excellent health insurance for your children." I took her advice into consideration, but I knew it didn't really matter. I could be nice or super nice. The way I saw it, if I showed up for an interview and the only Black Man I saw in the organization was the housekeeping guy, I already knew I wasn't getting the job. Around and around and around we go.

When I got home, I just wanted to relax. I turned on the television and saw a story about Henry Louis Gates Jr. getting arrested at his home. Gates is an author, college professor, filmmaker, and prominent in the Black community. The story had me wondering what in the world somebody like him could have been arrested for.

Come to find out that Dr. Gates had just returned home from a trip. When he tried to open the door, it was stuck. So, he had to break into his own home. One of his White neighbors called the police and told them they saw a Black Man breaking into a house. Need I say anything more? We all know how this story goes. The cops came, an argument ensued, and Gates was arrested. The police obviously didn't believe that this Black Man could own a nice house in this upscale Boston neighborhood, so they cuffed him and took him to jail. The charges were eventually dismissed, but had Gates been a White man, the cops would have verified who he was, which would have been the end of the situation.

It's always a double standard when you're Black. Dr. Gates was so well known that media outlets across the country were broadcasting the story. President Obama even weighed in, saying the Boston Police officers acted stupidly, and then he invited Dr. Gates and the arresting officer to the White House for a beer. I had mixed feelings about that. Law enforcement in this country was extremely biased when dealing with Black men in particular. From my point of view, it felt a little like the arresting officer was getting a reward for a wrongful arrest.

I was glad Dr. Gates wasn't shot or hurt by the police. After the dust settled, all the major news networks, FOX, MSNBC, and CNN, reported President Obama's popularity among Whites had dipped. Go figure, so much for a relaxing evening.

Dad Takes a Turn

My Father had always been an excellent driver with an impeccable driving record for my entire life. I don't remember a time when he even got a parking ticket. He's always been terrific on the road.

But time had a way of sneaking up on you. At this point, he was around eighty-nine years old and still driving. I don't think it ever occurred to us that Dad was beginning to slow down a bit. Sure, we all knew he was getting up there in age, but it's not something you think about until something happens.

Labor Day Weekend rolls around, and my brother convinces my Dad to drive him to Atlantic City (unbeknownst to me) to catch a plane. GPS was a thing by this point, but my Dad was set in his ways, so he didn't feel he needed it. He also didn't carry his cell phone with him.

My brother and I didn't have a great relationship at that time. We barely communicated on a good day. I had no idea of what was going on. I found out later that Dad drove him 150 miles to the A.C. airport and then drove back to New York by himself. I still don't know what my brother was thinking, letting our eighty-nine-year-old Father take the long drive alone. But then again, like I said, it's hard to see something like that until you actually see it.

BRILLIANT MINDS, IGNORANT MINDS

On Wednesday, September the First, my Dad left the Atlantic City Airport around two in the afternoon en route to his home in Greenlawn, NY (About 150 miles away). Dad should have arrived home between five and six in the afternoon but never did.

By Thursday, we were filing a missing person's report with the Suffolk County Police Dept. For two and a half days, we agonized and worried about him until we finally got a call from the Newburgh Police in upstate New York. They found my Dad walking alongside the highway. He was dehydrated, disoriented, and confused, but he seemed to be okay otherwise. When asked what happened, he couldn't explain anything or where he had been for those two days.

After speaking with the Newburgh Police precinct, I grabbed my daughter and godbrother, and we hit the road. When I finally got to the police station (About three hours away), my Dad told me that he thought he was down the street from his house and decided to walk home because the car would not start. He couldn't even remember where his car was.

I'm happy to say that this story has a happy ending. We drove back to Long Island, NY. I checked him into the hospital, where he ended up staying for three days. After getting his medications refilled and plenty of IV fluids, all the neurological tests and MRI brain scans returned normal. Dad was discharged home with a visiting nurse, and everything was going well. He still had some follow-up tests to complete with the neurologist. *Thank God* he was okay. His car was recovered a week after being discharged from the hospital. I had my nephew go pick it up and drive it back. Before I returned his car to my Dad, I had it checked out by a mechanic. As far as they could tell, the car was fine.

But what happened still had me unnerved, so I took him to a doctor myself in the hopes that he would check him out and agree that my father should not be driving. Surprisingly, the doctor told me that my ninety-year-old father was physically healthy. His eyesight and mental faculties seemed to be on track, so there was no basis for taking him out of the driver's seat. I couldn't believe it. After finding my Dad that way, I felt like I couldn't get anybody on my side.

So, as a last resort, I took my Dad on a driving test. And I have to tell you that it turned out to be the most fun I have had in years. He complained vehemently and kept reminding me that he was the one who taught me how to drive. It felt more like he was teaching me. My ninety-year-old father passed it with flying colors. Finally, my mind was at ease.

I think the stress of a six-hour drive, plus not taking his meds or eating and drinking, triggered something that caused him to become disoriented and confused. Thank the Lord he didn't get into an accident or pass out. The irony was that we found out later that Dad got stopped for running a stop sign at one point. The police officer said that he asked my Dad if he was feeling alright and asked him if he needed medical assistance. My Dad convinced him that he was fine, and the officer gave him a summons and sent him on his way. It was that summons that led us to him. It just so happened that a friend of mine, a police officer, saw my Dad's name in the system. It helped us track him down.

All I can say is that our collective Prayers were answered. We celebrated Dad's 90th birthday at the new Citifield baseball park to see the Mets play. We had a blast.

Back to the Asylum

Meanwhile, at work, the inmates were still running the asylum. The White women running the interviews were not looking to hire me. I knew it, and they knew it. What I also learned was that the entire process was bullshit. Hiring managers would rather hire an inferior, underqualified prospect than a qualified African American man. They want to put limits on the level of my participation in the organization because of the color of my skin and my gender. It was unconscious bias, plain and simple. I don't believe any of them knew they were being racist towards me. I think they were playing into a system that was already set up that way. They'd been conditioned to believe that a Black Man would be more trouble than it would be worth to hire me. It was ridiculous.

The American Sociological Review conducted a study about Race, Gender, and Workplace Power and discovered that "among White women, ascriptive similarity with superiors improves odds of attaining supervisory status with little work experience, but this benefit does not then open doors to managerial power, however, youth under White men does." (Elliott, 2004).

By the time I graduated, I was fifty-plus years old and had to compete with employees half my age. Healthcare is a sector where many people travel in similar circles, and I have been working at this network for eight years already. I probably knew a dozen women I'd personally worked with at that time, and every one of them had moved on to enter the management ranks. I also worked for NY Hospital Corp for twenty years. The White men and women who came up with me are now senior managers and directors making six-figure salaries. So when I say I know people, I really mean it. My LinkedIn contacts are full. People said they liked me. They said things like, I have a great personality. I'm smart, articulate, hard-working, honest, etc. But none of these people wanted to hire me for a management position.

At the time, I thought that, sometimes, a person could try too hard for something. I considered getting my project management certification (Project Management Professional). I was still a dues-paying union member in good standing, and they would cover my tuition, but I made up my mind that I wouldn't get my certification until I got hired into a project management position.

Don't get me wrong. Many of the women I encountered were very smart. However, that doesn't matter because we're all smart on this level. It's the opportunity that was needed, not smarts. They all were afforded the luxury of being allowed to grow into their positions. And the White men who came up with me back in the late eighties and nineties were all making six-figure salaries by that point. A major reason I went back to school for my master's degree was so I could compete with them. At the beginning of my journey, I had the mindset that I just had to work harder to get the same piece of the pie they were getting. Little did I know that the game was rigged against me all along.

Networking

I reached out to my director shortly after I graduated. She was a sixty-five-year-old White woman on the verge of retirement, set in her ways, conservative Republican; you know the type. I wrote her an e-mail that said, "Now that I have finally completed my master's degree program, I realize that over the past two years, I've been so focused on my studies that

I have taken little time out to meet the right people. I was hoping you could refer me to some influential individuals who could assist me with the arduous task of transitioning into management/administration within the Health System. I realize it will take more than academics for me to be successful. I need to meet and network with the right people in order to get my foot in the door of management/administration."

The definition of Networking is: "The action or process of interacting with others to exchange information and develop professional or social contacts." My thinking behind sending this e-mail was that people would refer names to me that I could (possibly) meet and network with. It was my sales background kicking in. I was prospecting for potential individuals who could help me during my job search. I sent out about twenty-five of these e-mails. A few were cordial and gave me friendly advice. Some referred me to others, and the rest didn't bother to answer me at all.

Of the ones that answered me was my director. "Miles, this isn't how things are done in this health system. You should go to the jobs website and apply for the jobs you are interested in. Once you apply, sell yourself during the interview."

I read her response, and my first thought was, *What kind of bullshit is this?* I know I would have been referred to several people if I had been one of her girls. I watched women and Caucasian men network and navigate their way around the health system all the time. They got promotion after promotion for themselves, which was all done by networking. She was saying (without saying) that networking wasn't the way it was done for African American men. It was a double standard for us.

The Panel Study of Income Dynamics (PSID) revealed that "Network assistance is increasingly effective among Black women, relative to White men, for moving into higher positions of power." (Elliott, 2004). This Networking concept also held true for White women as well. Trust me, as a Black Man, I knew the same set of rules didn't apply to me, but I had to play the game anyway and exhaust all avenues.

The person who initially hired me as a part-time employee when I first returned to healthcare was, at that point, a high-level healthcare manager within the Municipal Hospital System. And he was, no surprise, a White man. I reached out to him several times after earning my degree, and he never answered me back. He didn't even give me the courtesy of answering my emails. Unbelievable.

I couldn't help thinking, where are all the men? I was thinking that maybe if a man interviewed me, I would have a better chance at landing my dream job. I actually got interviewed by three men during my run of interviews at this organization. One, I believe, was a Filipino who was looking for a professional computer programmer for radiology department (which, to his credit, was clearly not me.)

The other two interviews were with a Latino gentleman I thought would hire me and a West Indian Black Man who I also thought would hire me. Neither person gave me an offer. I started wondering, "What's wrong with Me"?

That's the cancer that seeps into a Black Man's psyche. You prepare yourself for every pitfall and obstacle that may come your way at work or in society, but you still do not realize the success you expect. After being rejected and beaten down for so long, you start to wonder if the problem is you.

The reality is that we live in a racist society, and that's just the way it is. Racism translates into a system that pits us (Black Men) against one another. I'm sure the Black women hired into management wouldn't be there either if the racist Whites didn't feel like they had something to prove to the public. The bottom line is that hiring Black women looks better than hiring Black men. They're knocking out two marginalized parts of society with one stone, and when people figure out their game, they step back and say, "How can we be racist? Look at who's in management." It's nonsense. Scholar Pedro A. Noguera named the problem as early as '97:

"There is evidence in certain sectors that employers favor Black women over Black men as prospective employees." Healthcare happens to be one of those employment sectors. He went on to say, "White men do not fear Black women, but they do fear Black men and, hence, it is Black men who are the targets of 'severe physical and psychological enslavement and elimination." (Noguera, 1997).

We are up against a systemic racist mindset that's in power and will never change. We must, however, keep fighting.

The Workforce Development Program

In 2010, I attended a career fair at Columbia University shortly after graduation. I met Dr. Jillian Washington, who happened to be a White doctor. She introduced herself and explained to me that the Office of the National Coordinator for Health Information Technology (ONC) developed the Information Technology (IT) Professionals in Health Care Program (also referred to as the "Workforce Development Program").

The Workforce Development Program's primary goal was to train a new wave of health IT professionals ready to help providers implement and maintain electronic health records (EHRs) designed to improve healthcare quality, safety, and cost-efficiency. Despite my objections about returning to school, she convinced me to enroll in the program.

"Miles," she told me, "You're a recent grad student, you're employed at a hospital, and you are exactly the type of candidate we're looking for. It's 2010, and there are a lot of changes coming down the pipe in healthcare. We'll need qualified, educated, well-trained individuals to implement this program."

It was an excellent program and a great experience. It was too bad that the healthcare human resource machine was ignorant about this initiative. The brilliant minds behind it were ignorant about how to go about hiring this highly trained group of individuals into the workforce. It seemed like the healthcare hiring managers (throughout the country) were intimidated by us (Black men). They didn't know what we knew, they didn't understand the language we spoke, and they certainly weren't going to hire individuals who knew more than they knew. Needless to say, a Black Man like me talking about the interoperability of EHRs during a job interview was seen as a threat, and even though I was qualified for a myriad of positions, no one would hire me. My problem was trying too hard to qualify and represent myself to an employer that has no respect for African American men.

Mom Goes to a Nursing Home

It's amazing how life can totally interrupt your daily routine. My Mom's health had become a little more than we were equipped to handle, so it was time for her to go into a nursing home. I wrote a short message to my family on my social media account.

"Mom returned to the nursing home yesterday. It was a long and hard decision to make, but in the end, everything seemed to work out for the best. The cost involved in hiring a private nurse to care *for her was astronomical!!! Even though she has her own health insurance, plus Medicaid, they would only cover her for 12 hours of daily nursing care.*

Mom was diagnosed with Alzheimer's disease and requires 24-hour-a-day care. Since she was diagnosed in 2006, her disease has gotten progressively worse. The family has tried to help out as much as possible, but I was her primary care provider. So, after running around like a chicken with its head cut off, the stress and financial strain of caring for her ultimately caught up with me. I prayed about this situation long and hard for over six months, and this was a decision that I had to make.

The other side of the coin is that she is now a resident at one of the best nursing homes in New York State. The William O. Benenson Rehabilitation Pavillion. They allow their patients to have weekend, day, or hourly passes, which is great for taking her for dinner and family visits. The nursing staff and aides welcomed us with open arms the day we arrived. They all knew her because she had a short stay there about four months ago. She even got assigned to the same room and roommate she had back in March. She was smiling and in good spirits when I left her, and hopefully, she will make a smooth transition into nursing home life. It was a bitter/sweet day."

I gave Mom a few days to get settled, and then I took some time to spend a wonderful day with my Mom at the nursing home. We had lunch together. She wanted Chinese food, so I made a run to a nice restaurant for her. The nursing home was really nice. As the months and years passed, I realized how much of a blessing that decision was. Mom was being well cared for in a place where I could come and see her whenever I wanted. I was confident she would be better there than at home alone.

Tie a Knot and Hang on

A few days after I put my Mom into the nursing home, I got back to work. One of the management positions I applied for happened to be in the same department I worked in. I heard through the grapevine that instead of hiring me (or someone else qualified), they decided to hire somebody's relative, friend, or contact. She's a thirty-something White woman, who I heard had no experience in healthcare. Long story short, they wasted eight weeks training her for the position just for her to walk into work one day and tell the director that she was way over her head. She ended up resigning right on the spot after two months of training. How do you think I felt? I was burning up inside.

That's just one example of the nonsense that went on in the hiring department. Here I was, with a master's degree in Healthcare Administration, the same degree as my new director and CFO. I can't understand why my managers just kept passing me over. How can you go and hire someone clearly not qualified to manage the department when you have somebody *right in front of you* who could do that job? I even had one White woman tell me that I was the very first African American man she ever met with a master's degree. The interview had broken down. I guess she felt comfortable enough to tell me that. I remember thinking to myself, *does this woman live under a rock??* You work in a Human Resource capacity, and you've *never interviewed a Black Man with a Master's Degree?* It was unbelievable. How would I ever get a job within this institution? By that point, people were telling me I should quit and go to another organization altogether. They didn't realize it was a bigger problem than where I worked. Systemic racism is everywhere, and so long as it exists, marginalized individuals can't just go out and get another job, especially if you're a Black Man. The Bottom line was that there was no way I was quitting my job. I decided my only recourse was to fight these bastards from within.

It was a funky situation for me to be in. I busted my ass for three years to finally get my degree, went through a major surgery, my Mom's illness, being a single Dad, and paying child support (which meant I was broke all the time) in addition to being looked over for better positions that could change my situation. And all that wasn't even the half of it. It was a rough period of time in my life. The IRS had just seized all my income, and my landlord wanted to evict me… I was at the end of my rope but somehow managed to carry on.

In 2011, I applied for the Health System Administrative internship program. I was excited about the program. I applied for the program during my final year of grad school but wasn't accepted. I was hoping that the second time around would be the charm, but it was not!

As it turned out, I started a volunteer internship in the Health Information Management Dept. (Medical Records), which was an extremely rewarding experience. That staff embraced me, and I learned a lot of new things there. The director of my department gave me several challenging projects, and I embraced those assignments with a thirst for knowledge and understanding. I felt renewed in my mission to succeed and started interviewing for positions constantly.

By then, searching for management and administrative employment was a daily routine. It was approaching two years since my graduation, and I was beginning to feel a sense of urgency to land a job. July of 2011 marked the completion of the Columbia University Health Information Technology Certificate Program.

All in all, it was a great learning experience. I got to strengthen my concentration in project management and health information exchange and build my career toolbox. I'd been knocked down a lot, but after doing that internship, I felt there was still hope for me.

Mentorship

I've often said that mentorship has long been missing from the careers of many African American Men. We basically have to make it on our own and find our way in business and sometimes in life. I've always craved mentorship during my career. I've been lucky enough to have had a few. My cousin, Alford Ottley, for example. He was the most influential person in my life. Over the years, he taught me a ton of things. Had there been a person like him in my business life, I'm sure it would have made a difference in my career and the outlook I had on it.

Mentorship is something that I've always been jealous of with women in the workplace. My boss, at the time, a very successful and smart woman, would have lunch with the women in the office to uplift and teach them how to succeed in the workplace. I used to call them the "all-girls club". But the wisdom that she imparted to those women was invaluable to them. To this very day, all of those women who used to attend those meetings (many of them my peers and co-workers) are all employed in upper management as directors, VPs, project managers, etc., earning six-figure salaries.

Upwardly mobile Black men in corporate America are feared, so no one's giving us that kind of help. Had I been mentored while I was in my twenties and thirties, there was no doubt in my mind that I would have become a healthcare director, earning the big bucks.

Imagine two healthy babies born into this world. One baby receives love, nourishment, healthcare, and education. The other baby is neglected, malnourished, and left to his own devices. As the years roll by, the neglected baby is sick, hungry, and not thriving as he should. The other baby is strong, healthy, and happy. By the time these babies are ten years old, if the doctor who delivered them gave them both a physical examination, he would never believe they were the same children he delivered. One child would be the picture of health and have all the potential in the world to succeed. The other would be sickly, angry, and potentially uneducated. In ten more years, these children would become adults. Now, out in the world, only one would be ahead of the game and projected to succeed in life.

But, if someone intervenes with mentorship for the child without all the advantages, that can change the trajectory of his life. Suddenly, that child sees opportunities to improve and educate himself where he didn't before. All it took was someone to show him the door. So what happens if there's no one willing to do that?

This is my example of what racism can do to a person. This is my example of what a lack of mentorship can do. It can retard an individual's growth. That is the way I would describe my career in healthcare. I was treated like a neglected baby. One day, on the way home after work, I was riding the bus when four young White male students jumped on. They were excited about being chosen as interns to work in the Municipal Corporate Administration building. I immediately thought to myself, *where are the Black male interns?* There probably were none. Those young guys were being mentored by some of the best minds in the hospital network. Soon, they would all be earning six-figure salaries. And there I was, having already applied for two Municipal Internship opportunities over the years and hadn't been selected for anything. Seeing that small group of White guys validated exactly what I had been thinking when I applied for my internship. I don't fit the mold. I'm not what they're looking for.

The Price of Speaking Up

The Municipal Health System leadership team launched a new initiative called "LEADERSHIP Chat." It was designed for employees to be able to actually communicate with hospital leadership. I decided to take advantage of this new initiative, and I wrote them a letter in the hopes of voicing my concerns about racism within the organization:

November 14, 2011

Dear Hospital Leadership,

After noticing "LEADERSHIP Chat" on my screensaver over the past few weeks, I was compelled to learn more about it. When I listened to your message, I found it thought-provoking and innovative. I also realized that this approach was a very different way for leadership to communicate with their employees. Your willingness to reach out and connect with employees, to hear our thoughts and what we're thinking about, inspired me to heed your advice and respond to your request.

As I digested your message, it suddenly dawned on me that this was my opportunity to chat with the leadership team of this great health network. The message to allow our employees to be heard resonated with me.

My story is unique and probably unlike any you have heard before. As I reflect on my journey through the Municipal healthcare landscape, I find myself in a tremendous struggle to advance my career. I have a master's degree in Health Care Administration and a bachelor's degree in Business Administration. I graduated from Columbia University School of Biomedical Informatics with a Certificate in Health Information Technology. I have been focused on my studies over the past four years and have taken little time out to network and meet the right people who will give me a chance to prove myself as an administrator or project manager. It is clear that it will take more than academics for me to be successful.

I also volunteer/intern three days per week in the Municipal Hospital Health Information Management (HIM) Department. I am an extremely hard worker who has dedicated himself to a career in healthcare. I have been interviewing constantly for positions within the Municipal Health Network and have applied for countless others without much success. I've concluded that I need to find an open-minded individual who can judge me on my merits and give me a chance to join their administrative or project management team. I'm qualified, I'm a fast learner, smart, and I have a multi-talented skill set that will allow me to be successful. I can do the work. I'm not looking for a handout. I'm looking for an opportunity to prove myself.

Now that my academic foundation is strong, I am ready to advance to the next level in my career. Unfortunately, I have not been able to connect with the individuals that have interviewed me. In all fairness to them, I believe they have not been able to relate to a qualified minority male candidate like myself. I find myself searching for a unique individual who can think outside the box and who can relate to me as a qualified minority male candidate with great potential who wants to join an administrative or project management team.

There is no doubt in my mind that I can flourish as an administrator or project manager. I'm reaching out to you, in a professional way, in a sincere way, for a referral to someone in our vast network who can judge me based on my skills and abilities and provide me with an opportunity to advance my career. I believe that in a healthcare network that stretches from Staten Island to Stony Brook, there must be a place for a master's degree candidate who is well-versed in the areas of healthcare administration, information technology, finance, project management, health information management, and exchange.

More than anyone, I realize that this is quite a risky, unconventional, and somewhat unorthodox method of corresponding with a leadership team. But again, I was drawn to your "LEADERSHIP Chat" request for feedback and comments. I understand that our network is growing. I want to be a part of that growth as a representative of this great network and as an individual in my career. Unfortunately, dedication, persistence, hard work, and commitment have not yielded the career rewards I'm looking for. I need a little help to break through that glass ceiling. I hope you can shed some light on my dilemma and point me in the right direction. There is no doubt in my mind that I can prove myself once given the chance and opportunity. I know I can flourish in this healthcare field, which I love and have dedicated myself to. However, like everyone who has become successful, I will need some assistance and help.

In closing, let me say that I am happy to have been granted this opportunity to chat with you. Thank you so much for creating an official forum for employees to communicate their feedback, questions, comments, and concerns.

Sincerely,
Miles M. Livingston

About a week after sending that correspondence, I mysteriously received a call from H.R. Talent Acquisition Specialist Roxanne Moncrief. She let me know that she had been monitoring my submissions for Project Management jobs. My resume was suddenly not strong enough for a project management job. I responded, "That may be true, but I was ready for an entry-level position." Judging from the cast of characters I had seen on these project management teams, there was no doubt in my mind that I was qualified enough to be there. My coursework in project management alone put me head and shoulders above all the entry-level staff working at my Health System. And I would have no problem accepting an entry-level position at the measly clerical salary I was making. Ms. Moncrief responded by scheduling a meeting for us in the next few days.

But I finally realized what was going on here. My employer's attitude was, *let's get the Black woman to placate this disgruntled Black Man.* I was so angry and pissed off at the time that I didn't see it right away when she called me. The bullshit story she fed me was so convincing that I fell for it hook, line, and sinker. My subconscious mind wanted to believe she wanted to help me. After all, she was from H.R., where she was a Talent Acquisition Specialist, and they monitored all of the job application submissions. She convinced me that she wanted to work with me one-on-one after she met me and assisted me with my resume. That was the beginning of an extremely disappointing relationship.

A few days passed, and I arrived at her corporate office. It was the same scenario. There are no Black men in sight. It was a beautiful corporate suite of offices with a large pool of cubicles. There was a multicultural array of women, along with several White men. Ms. Moncrief had a very nice space with a secretary at her disposal.

Our meeting began with her review of my job applications; there were at least a dozen. After looking all of them over, she told me that I didn't have the skill set needed to be a project manager. Of course, I begged to differ. I explained my qualifications to her in detail. I included my course curriculum capstone project, which gave me more than enough project management experience to qualify for an "entry-level position." Even though my primary goal was to enter management, I was willing to accept a project management position.

I explain that during my time at Columbia University, our program offered four different areas of concentration. After the first week of study and research, I decided on project management. It was natural for me to organize and coordinate various projects. I was my workgroup's project manager, and I found it to be a perfect fit for me. More importantly, I fell in love with it. I also added information about my entertainment and music career, telling her I was a project manager during that time. Of course, that wasn't the official title; I was a promoter, but the difference was negligible.

Ms. Moncrief asked me for a list of contacts who had given me interviews. I gave her a list of ten names of prominent members of our health system, including a Vice President, Executive Director, Associate Director, Finance Director, Program Director, Lead Project Manager, and an Associate H.R. Director. I explained that as I reflected on my journey through the health system landscape, I struggled tremendously to advance my career. I had sacrificed so many hours to achieve academically; however, it was clear that it would take much more than academics to succeed. There was no doubt that I could flourish as a management team member, administrator, or project manager if given the opportunity.

When I made up my mind to get a Master's degree and seek out Management and Administrative opportunities, I knew as a Black Man that rejection would be an integral part of my job search experience. I have not let it deter me in the least. I expected it. I told her that I was planning my job search strategy for the upcoming year and would increase my activity and expand my contacts list.

I also told her that I had always maintained a positive mental attitude in spite of the pitfalls I had encountered. I said, "I know that racial discrimination is at play regarding my career path at this institution. With circumstances being what they are, I must say I am glad I met you. My colleagues and I have discussed seeking out Talent Acquisition Specialists on several occasions but never got around to doing it. Now that I have met you, I hope you can assist me in locating that open-minded individual who can judge me based on my abilities and allow me to join their management, administrative, or project management team."

The bottom line is that I believe the women who interviewed me have never had a Black Man as a boss or supervisor or had to deal with one in a leadership position. So which one of them is going to take a chance on me? To quote Texeira's article in Newsday:

"Black men represent a danger, a threat in a more immediate way. Employers don't even want to meet with them." (Texeira, 2004).

It reminds me of a friend, a brilliant African American man who was a high-level Corporate Executive Director for a major company. He was considering a transition to run a local Suffolk County Town Department. I remember this White woman who was a Town Supervisor at the time commenting that she would never support the decision to hire a Black Man to make that kind of salary. From my understanding, her comment was made in mixed company, and she couldn't care less about who heard it. She had the power, and she exercised that power. This is the kind of bullshit that Black men and women must endure inside the workplace: a Brilliant Black male mind and an Ignorant White female mind.

2012 – And the Beat Goes On

As the year began, I realized more and more that racial discrimination was at play in regard to advancing my career. As I went into interview after interview, the women who interviewed me could not relate to me. I noticed that in every hospital administrative suite or office I walked into, no African American men were in sight. The entire leadership team, including managers, supervisors, administrators, directors, and VPs, were all White men and women. The one common thread between myself and Municipal leadership was the Master's degree in Healthcare Administration. Most of them earn six-figure salaries. Why was I earning thirty-eight thousand a year as a clerk? I was dissatisfied with Ms. Moncrief, the talent acquisition specialist. She had done absolutely nothing for me.

I knew I was going to be in for a tough year all the way around. One night, I was watching CNN after work. I saw this White woman wagging her finger at President Barack Obama. Who does this White woman think she is? That was the President of The United States! You don't wag your finger at him! She turned out to be Arizona Governor Jan Brewer. Personally, I didn't give a fuck who she was. *Show a little respect.* I was really pissed off for myself *and* Barack.

About a month later, I was reading and hearing about this story about an unarmed Black teenager who got shot to death by some vigilante neighborhood watch commander. "Stand Your Ground," says Florida Law. I had never heard about this "stand your ground" law, but I immediately thought, *oh, it's another way for White people to shoot Blacks and get away with it.* That murder case was an American tragedy known as the Trayvon Martin murder.

Trayvon Martin was a teenager walking home from the store one afternoon. Reports say he was talking on the phone with his girlfriend when the neighborhood watchman, George Zimmerman, walked up to him and started harassing him. A fight broke out between them, and Zimmerman ended up shooting and killing Martin.

The Police in Sanford, Florida, where the incident occurred, didn't even arrest Zimmerman at first. They believed his bullshit story about a suspicious guy walking around the neighborhood that was up to no good. The cops allowed him to remain free for *six weeks* before public outcry forced them to arrest him.

It's unbelievable, especially when you have to work with a bunch of White people who didn't care at all about cases like this. As an African

American man, I try not to get too sensitive about these kinds of things, but after a while, it just becomes impossible. All of these racially motivated incidents affect you over time. I mean, these are my people. When I see Trayvon's parents, Sybrina Fulton and Tracy Martin, I see myself in them. I see my son in Trayvon. It was a situation that could have happened to any of us just because we're Black.

In typical fashion, the State of Florida found Zimmerman not guilty. The verdict ended up being the catalyst for the "Black Lives Matter" movement. The Miami Heat, Florida's NBA basketball team led by superstar LeBron James, all wore gray hoodies in support of Trayvon Martin and his family. It's a symbol of activism at its best and a call for social justice.

Published Op-Ed Article Writer

I had been occasionally in touch with my cousin Al during this time. He always seemed to be on the go, but that's how it is sometimes with successful people. He was all around the world and back. He came into town around Labor Day of that year and gave me a call. "Hey, Miles, I'm in New York. Let's meet for dinner."

I was good with that. After all, it had been a minute since I'd seen my cousin. We agreed to meet up at Applebees. I was pretty happy to see him. I always enjoyed my visits with my cousin. As my mentor and someone I admired, he was the one person I always felt was honest with me. Whether I wanted to hear it or not. He was the person in my life that told me like it was.

Over dinner, I explained that I had finally graduated from the University of Phoenix with my master's degree in healthcare and was having difficulty finding a management-level position. Al asked me what area of healthcare I was passionate about. I told him that after my involvement with Obama University, I was passionate about educating people about healthcare. I let him know that my employer was going to open a health exchange, and they just purchased an insurance company named Municipal SkyExchange. I told him that I was thinking about applying.

My cousin, Al, thought it was a good idea. "In fact," he told me, "I think you ought to write an article about this whole idea of the health exchanges. It's a brand-new initiative, and very few people understand it. If you can write and publish an article about the exchanges, you can position yourself as a health exchange expert. The lightbulb in my head lights up. That sounded like a fantastic idea.

My cousin Al always had a way of fueling me with enthusiasm and desire; he'd been doing it my whole life. I was so pumped up that I immediately started researching health exchanges and my employers' approach to how they plan on setting this whole thing up. I went to the NYS.gov website and found the Health Exchange workgroup recordings of their meetings. It was a great resource. Sitting in and watching them was an enlightening experience. A wealth of information was being shared right at my fingertips. In addition, the state experts had research papers and data about this new concept of health exchanges and how they were designed to work. It was a phenomenal concept. It makes me really appreciate President Obama's sheer genius and mental intellect in developing a healthcare system for the entire country.

It took me weeks to read and digest all the material about health exchanges, but as soon as I fully grasped the concept, it was time to write. My challenge was explaining the exchange in layman's terms and doing it within a six-hundred-and-fifty-word limit. However, I rose to the challenge and managed to get my op-ed article written.

I was super excited. After all, it had been twelve years since I published my first article. I created a mini press release package and sent out about ten email packages per day to various publications for about ten days straight. And then the waiting game began. Finally, after about three weeks, the phone rang. It was the editor for the Medical Business News. I was both shocked and happy to get her call. All in all, she seemed excited about the article.

"This is a great article, Mr. Livingston. Wonderfully written, brief, and to the point. It's exactly the type of piece we were looking for. We're going to go ahead and publish it in our November 9th, 2012, issue." I thank her profusely. Not too long after that, the Medical Business News published my op-ed article about Obamacare's SHOP Exchange.

Hurricane Sandy

I was over the moon about the article. I was brought back down to reality when Hurricane Sandy landed on the East Coast. If you've never lived through a natural disaster, I can tell you that it's what I imagine trying to survive an apocalypse has to be like. My employer arranged for a gas truck to come to the job because most gas stations were closed due to a massive power outage. It wasn't a bad idea, but the parking lot where the gas truck parked turned into a mob scene, with everybody panicking that they wouldn't be able to fill up their tanks before the truck ran out of gas. It got so bad that the truck driver panicked and drove off before anybody could get anything. There were swarms of vehicles surrounding this gas tanker. He didn't bother to try and wait for anybody to move out of the way. He pulled off, hitting a few cars on the way out of the parking lot. Luckily, I found a gas station on the way to work with gas cans for sale. I picked up three five-gallon gas cans for my daughter, Dad, and me. On my way home, I located another service station that had gas. I could tell they had gas by the line of fifty or so vehicles ahead of me.

It took me over three hours to get the gas. The lines at some stations were miles long, and that was if you could find an open gas station. I remember sitting in line, thinking, "I wonder if my Father and my daughter realize how much I love them to wait three hours to buy gas for them."

Since Hurricane Sandy was a category one storm, all the hospitals were on a Hospital Incident Command System (HICS) Level Three Emergency. HICS assists hospitals to improve their emergency management planning, response, and recovery capabilities for planned and unplanned events. All employees were required to work around the clock since the governor declared the Hurricane a state emergency.

Me and my coworkers had to sleep in the hospital until our relief showed up, which for me was about two days after I got there. I didn't find out how bad the damage was until I got home, crawled into bed, and turned on the news.

Over a *hundred* homes were burning up in the Breezy Point neighborhood of Queens—those poor people. Houses burned to the ground. They lost everything!

Kiss of Death

"Black people need to work twice as hard to compete in this country as white people" **–Tom Allison, Policy and Research Manager for Young Invincibles.**

Medical Business News
Health Care OP-ED Report

NOV. 9-15, 2012, I VOI. 100 I NO. 75 I $2.00 I MBN

FEATURED ARTICLE

Affordable Health Care

Miles Livingston

The Patient Protection and Affordable Care Act (PPACA or ACA), signed into law on March 23, 2010, mandates that states establish a Health Insurance Exchange. This new law allows states to create a virtual, hybrid marketplace for individuals, families, and small businesses to shop for health insurance. The goal of this initiative is to significantly reduce the cost of health coverage, provide individuals with a standard essential health benefits plan, and create a "one-stop-shop" marketplace for millions of uninsured consumers to obtain health coverage.

This health insurance exchange will be a predominantly web-based portal for health insurance quotes, coverage and billing options, premium tax credits, qualified health plans, links to brokers, and online and telephone call center customer service.

The exchange will actually encompass two health exchanges. 1) Individual Exchange, for individuals and families; 2) Small

Business Exchange, for small businesses. Individuals and families will be offered a variety of health plans from which to choose. The single mom applicant will be referred directly to the child health plus Medicaid option. Uninsured intact families and single entrepreneurs can shop competitive pricing among premier health insurance carriers. They may qualify for federal subsidies and tax credits designed to keep premiums affordable. Unemployed applicants will qualify for Medicaid health plan options.

Business owners will be referred to the - Small Business Health Options Program - or "SHOP" Exchange. This entity will allow small businesses to competitively shop health plan options in a competitive market environment. The SHOP exchange will consist of an online marketplace where companies can shop for cost-effective, qualified health plans (QHP) for their employees. Data will be securely exchanged electronically between businesses and the exchange to ease the burden of the application process. Customer service reps will be available to assist the small business owners. Tax incentives and cost-sharing subsidies are available for all businesses that qualify. Under this SHOP exchange model, businesses can make defined contributions, allowing employees the freedom to choose from an array of qualified health plans that have been benchmarked against the best, State health plans, Government health plans, and private health insurance HMO/PPO plans. The ACA also mandates that each QHP (and individual plan) must offer what is referred to as "Essential Health Benefits." This plan option must include ten essential benefits, such as in-patient hospitalization, emergency services, ambulatory services, maternity and newborn care, mental health and substance abuse services, preventative/wellness services, prescription drug plan, pediatric services (including vision and dental care), lab testing services, and chronic disease management.

The ACA is a very comprehensive and complicated law. There are several aspects to this Act; however, in my opinion, the small business community is a major driving force behind this health insurance exchange concept. The State exchange will market qualified health plans that will provide everyone with a standardized health insurance product that will include essential health benefits. This in itself is a monumental accomplishment.

Another caveat of the SHOP Exchange is that it provides health insurance brokers with the flexibility to transition into the SHOP program. Small business owners can maintain their relationships with brokers because the health exchange recognizes that these relationships are significant. This thing creates a win-win scenario. The brokers will market and promote the SHOP exchange, and small businesses can work directly with brokers who are familiar with the SHOP process.

The health insurance exchange is an innovative concept. The ACA has streamlined the health insurance process, but the debate against this legislation rages on. Major issues that come to the forefront include State-run exchanges versus federally run exchanges. What long-term effects will ACA have on Medicare, Medicaid, pay-for-performance, and fee-for-service?

Obamacare is certainly not the end-all, be-all solution. Still, with some tweaking and bi-partisan support, the ACA will transform healthcare delivery in these United States and become a leading model for healthcare delivery worldwide.

> **Livingston is a clerical account representative with Municipal Health**

****

November 4th finally rolled around, and I was on a mission to find the publication with my article. I went to a local newsstand next to my job and grabbed the December edition. I paged through the newspaper, and there it was. –by Miles M. Livingston.

Holy shit! I was so proud and happy I bought all twenty copies on the spot. I told the clerk I had an article published in the paper, showing it off to him with pride. He shook my hand and told me that he'd never met a real author before in his store. That was a great moment. I was a man on the rise.

I was ready to go and get my new job with my article in hand. I'm thinking, there's no way they can deny me now. Little did I know that a Black Man with a master's degree with the skills and knowledge to publish an article about this brand-new initiative was a very dangerous and intimidating individual.

You see, my thinking was, "Hey, my employer just purchased an insurance company for hundreds of millions of dollars, and they've got to staff it. This article is proof that I know my stuff. It's an easy in." Long story short, my employer hired over two hundred people to run the exchange. I applied for more than twenty different jobs, and still, nobody was looking to hire me. At one point, I walked into one of the senior manager's offices for an interview. He was a close associate of the G.A. at the insurance agency that I worked at a few years before, so I thought he had to know he had a winner. We talked for about thirty minutes, and he introduced me to one of his co-managers. I left their office thinking that I had the inside track.

My ignorant mind had me believing that I would be judged fairly and offered a position, and I couldn't have been further from the truth. Those high-level White men with their six-figure salaries avoided me like the plague. The only Black face I saw inside that office that day was the FedEx guy. It's funny. I knew more about health exchanges than probably their entire staff, but nobody would touch me with a ten-foot pole. I even reached out to the Executive Director of the health exchange prior to my interview and forwarded my article to him. His executive assistant received the article, so when I called, she knew exactly who I was. I also sent my article to the HR team in charge of hiring for the health exchange. But I soon learned I had done too much.

In hindsight, maybe I should have stayed in the shadows. I was a Black Man with knowledge and education, and that was too much for the hospital establishment to handle. I wanted a high-salaried management position just like the Caucasian men and multicultural array of women who went to school and worked with me. We had all worked hard to better ourselves and advance our careers, but I was left way behind them.

It was a sad commentary. To add salt to my wounds, my employer posted a screen saver on every desktop in the hospital saying, "We are happy to introduce our new Municipal SkyExchange staff." That's SkyExchange, which I'd applied to several times. To my surprise, it was a photo of nineteen women of different races and one White man. I was in a state of shock. Not one Black Man was on the team.

The writing was on the wall. I was working in a discriminatory work environment, and I have got to let my voice be heard. I start documenting every detail of my experience.

9

Formulation Of My Complaint

"I'm not 'gonna do anything other than what I think is worthy of being done."

–Harry Belafonte

Finally, after years of being passed over, discriminated against, and feeling hopeless, I couldn't take anymore. Lesser qualified individuals had gotten jobs ahead of me. I watched the friends and family of my bosses jump ahead of me. Mediocre White men and women who were less educated or less experienced than I was had taken the fast track to management positions. At the same time, I stayed languishing in a lowly clerical position. Enough was enough. By that point, I had been employed at Municipal Hospital for twelve years. The time to call out the bullshit was long overdue.

To my surprise, my employer hired an African American man into one of the supervisory positions I had applied for. That blindsided me because all of my superiors knew my credentials. They knew I was ambitious and had an upwardly mobile point of view, and, most importantly, I was seeking advancement into management. They didn't even consider me for the position. Instead, they hired some random Black guy out of the blue who had no hospital experience. Now, I could see this was personal. My employer was targeting me as someone they wouldn't promote, no matter what.

The first thing I did was write my complaint and march into the NYS Division of Human Rights Office on April 8, 2013. I'm not going to lie; I was nervous about taking this route. I was trembling like a leaf every step of the way. I had to do it! Somebody had to say something.

The Complaint

I walked into the Division of Human Rights building with shaky hands. All I could think about was after I filed this complaint, everything was going to change. When you stand up to a system bigger than yourself and speak truth to power, you run the risk of putting yourself in deeper trouble. I knew I could lose my job, reputation, and everything else just for doing this. Walking into that building wasn't about filing a complaint; it was about slaying a dragon.

But the alternative was to continue to sit back and let them keep their feet on my neck. When I thought about how hard I worked and how far I had come in my education over the last twelve years just to be held back for something I couldn't change or control, I had to do something. I couldn't spend another minute stuck at the bottom of the heap when I had all the tools to dig myself out.

I walked into that office, signed in at the security desk, and went to the third floor.

I attached a narrative to my complaint document, and it reads as follows:

I am an African American male with an undergraduate degree in Business Administration, a master's degree in health care administration, and a Certificate in Health Information Technology

267

from Columbia University (CU). While attending CU, I did extensive studies in Health Information Technology, Health Information Exchange, and Health IT Project Management. I was also an Administrative Intern in the Health Information Management (HIM) department for 14 months. I consider myself a well-rounded healthcare professional who is an effective communicator, team builder, and problem solver. I am experienced in revenue cycle management, patient accounting, health insurance, staff supervision, medical billing, and patient customer service.

In an effort to "self-promote" and market my career, I was successful in getting a healthcare article (I wrote) published in the *Medical Business News.* In spite of my successes, none of my hard work has paid off, and I have remained in a low-paying clerical position for the past (12) twelve years. In my opinion, mine is a clear case of race discrimination where an African American male with a master's degree in health care administration can't get a promotion and advance himself. The following is a history of the myriad of positions I have applied for. On or about the indicated dates are descriptions of my job applications.

I chronicled the history of my job applications and kept a journal of all the jobs I applied for. The human resource system my employer uses produces a record of each position an applicant applies for with the click of a mouse. So, I keep a diary of every job I have applied for.

Beginning in May 2006 - prior to enrolling in grad school, I chronicle every job that I apply for. I feel confident in my knowledge of the job and certainly can supervise my peers. I'm considered somewhat of a leader among my co-workers, who routinely seek out my opinions and advice concerning work-related matters. I applied for several

Supervisor positions in the Admitting office and the Emergency Dept., but one of my female co-workers got the job every time.

The clerk inside the Division of Human Rights office officially time-stamped my complaint and gave me a packet of information to fill out. I completed the packet of information and signed all of the necessary documents.

The following is my original discrimination complaint.

ORIGINAL COMPLAINT SUBMITTED:

DESCRIPTION OF DISCRIMINATION – for all complaints (*Public Accommodation, Employment, Education, Housing, and all other regulated areas listed on Page 3*).

Please tell us more about each act of discrimination that you experienced. Please include dates, names of people involved, and explain why you think it was discriminatory.

PLEASE TYPE OR PRINT CLEARLY.

The reason for filing this complaint is based on what I believe to be both gender and racial bias in the hiring and promotion process at my employer, Municipal Hospital System (MHS). I would estimate that over the past (8) eight years, all of the supervisory positions I applied for within my immediate department (Admitting) have been filled by female candidates with less qualifications than me. I have also applied for several administrative and management positions and have not been hired.

I am an African American male who recently graduated from the Columbia University School of Biomedical Informatics with a Certificate in Health Information Technology. My undergraduate degree is in Business, and I have a master's degree in Health Care Administration. I was also an Administrative Intern in the Health Information Management department for 15 months. While at Columbia University (June 2011), I did extensive study in health information technology, health information exchange, and health IT Project management. I am an effective communicator, team builder, and problem solver, and I am experienced in patient accounting, financial analysis, staff supervision, medical billing, and health insurance reimbursement.

In an effort to "self-promote" and market my career, I was successful in getting a healthcare article I wrote published in the *Medical Business News.* However, to date, none of my hard work has paid off, and I have remained in a clerical position for the past (10) ten years at my present employer. The following is a history of the myriad of positions I have applied for. On or about the dates indicated are descriptions of my job applications.

If you need more space to write, please continue writing on a separate sheet of paper and attach it to the complaint form.

PLEASE DO NOT WRITE ON THE BACK OF THIS FORM.

MAY 2006: Applied for Supvr position Admitting office: Janie Doe - **Hired**

SEPT 2006: Applied for Supvr position Admitting office: Jane Doe - **Hired**

JAN 2007: Applied for Supvr position Admitting office: Mary Jackson - **Hired**

NOV 2007: Applied for Supvr position Admitting office: Janetta Doe - **Hired**

FEB 2008: Applied for Supvr position Admitting office: Joyce West - **Hired**

JUN 2008: Applied for Supvr position Admitting office: Chandra Doe - **Hired**

FEB 2009: Applied for Supvr position Admitting office: Mindy Doe - **Hired**

DEC 2009: Applied for Supvr position Admitting office: Karen Smith - **Hired**

JAN 2010: Applied for Supvr position Admitting office: Wendy Jones - **Hired**

(At the start of the interview, my director says to me, "Miles, I'm not going to hire you for this position! It's nights and weekends; it's not for you." I respond to her by saying, "This supervisor position is a

*step up for me, and I am confident that I am qualified for this job; that's why I applied.) – **Result: Not Hired**.*

MAR 2010: Applied for Supvr position Admitting office: Juanita Rodriguez - **Hired**

MAY 2011: Applied for Supvr position Admitting office: Dorinder Doe - **Hired**

JUNE 2011: Applied for Supvr position Admitting office: Cynthia Jones - **Hired**

MAR 2012: Applied for Supvr position Admitting office: Natalia Doe - Hired

MAR 2013: Applied for Supvr position Admitting office: Thelma Wilson - **Hired**

MAR 2013: Applied for Supvr position Admitting office: Maria Doe - **Hired**

I also applied for various other jobs via the Municipal Hospital Careers' website and directly with HR reps, hiring managers, and administrators.

MAY 2010 – Applied for Municipal Hospital (paid) Administrative Internship Program.

Marjorie McDougal, Admin Mgr. Not Accepted into the program.

MAY 2011 – Applied for Municipal Hospital (paid) Administrative Internship Program.

Marjorie McDougal, Admin Mgr. Not Accepted into the program.

JUL 2010 – Interviewed with Mary Cross, Assoc. HR Director and was referred to Michael Shauvell, Exec. Dir. Municipal Hospital, Great interview. Not Hired. Re-called for a follow-up interview on 12/16/11 with Mr. Shauvell, still not offered a position.

JAN 2011 – Began a (volunteer) administrative internship with the Health Information Management (HIM) Dept, which lasted until April 2012. Excellent experience.

APR 2011 – Referred to Rosa Lander, Exec. VP PAANS/MUNICIPAL: This lady was a cohort of one of my instructors at Columbia University. Great interview, Not Hired.

MAY 2011 – Referred to Allscripts/MUNICIPAL (Electronic Health Record EHR Company)
Interviewed by P. Jannings and J. Barney (via telephone). Not offered position.

JUL 2011 – Referred to Debra Morgan, Program Director Allscripts/MUNICIPAL: Applied for an EHR implementation position, I was never contacted or interviewed.

JUL 2011 – Spoke directly with Admitting Director, Cynthia Euestheim (7/28/11) and expressed my concerns about not being hired. She referred me to Ann Johnson, Siemens Municipal

Health-e project director. Eventually, I interviewed with her on (8/16/11) for a project manager position. Great interview. Not Hired. Also, I should mention that a few female employees who worked with me in admitting went on to obtain management positions with this Health-e initiative. Cynthia Jones and Doreen McDonald).

SEP 2011 – Referred by Ann Johnson to Steve Roenia, Dir Clinical Practice, Siemens Municipal. Applied for applications analyst position. Great interview. Not Hired.

SEP 2011 – The Exec. Director of Finance Harris Goldberg forwards my resume to Karen Henriss, I.S. Project Controller. She e-mailed me to say she received my resume and would give it to her boss. She will contact me when suitable positions are available. I never heard from these individuals again.

NOV 2011 – The Municipal Hospital network CEO introduces a new way to communicate with employees called "LEADERSHIP Chat." I submitted a very diplomatically and politically correct letter to him describing my situation.

NOV 2011 – I finally met a Municipal Hospital HR Talent Acquisition Specialist, Roxanne Moncrief, on (11/28/13). I explained my situation to her, saying I felt I'd been passed over for various positions. I need an HR professional like her to help me navigate through the Municipal Hospital System employment landscape.

DEC 2011 – The Talent Acquisition Specialist arranges an interview with Stella Grenfeld, Director of Municipal PAANS (Physician and Ambulatory Network Services). Great interview. Not Hired. I applied for a position and submitted my resume to Ms. Grenfeld's office in May 2010. Received a call from her HR person named Phillip Wagner. However, I was never interviewed in 2010 and was told that my resume would remain on file until a suitable position became available.

MAR 2012 – I attend the Columbia University career fair (3/21/12) and meet Cree Hoffman, Municipal Hospital /Allscripts HR rep. She encourages me to apply for several available positions at Municipal, which I do. A year goes by, and I apply for several positions via the Municipal Hospital System Careers website and never get hired.

AUG 2012 – I am totally dissatisfied with the assistance Ms. Moncrief has provided for me. After eight months, she only arranged one interview for me. I'm wondering what the problem is. I've got a master's in healthcare administration and a certificate in health information technology from Columbia. I have over 15 years of experience in the healthcare industry and am employed at a hospital. I expressed my discontent with her performance, and she sent me to a totally inappropriate interview in the radiology department. They're looking for a computer tech that can debug all the radiology software in their department and troubleshoot computer hardware issues. This job is definitely not for me, and I chatted cordially during this interview, which lasted about five minutes.

NOV 2012 – In an effort to promote myself and my career, I published a healthcare article in the "Medical Business News." While researching the article, I discovered that my employer partnered with United Health to market a new health insurance product. The Municipal Hospital System Sr. VP, Mr. Henry Goldman, is in charge of this initiative, so I immediately contacted his office. I'm referred to the Admin Assistant, Tom Sussman. We chat two or three times over the next two weeks. I e-mailed my article and resume to him, and he e-mailed me the municipal health insurance exchange information packet. Tom says he forwarded my resume to Mr. Goldman.

JAN 2013 – I send an e-mail to the director of Municipal Hospital System Talent Acquisition, Pamela Bronson, explaining my frustration with talent acquisition. Within two hours of sending this e-mail, I received a call from Roxanne Moncrief on my cell phone. (The talent acquisition person that I'm unsatisfied with. She has stopped taking my calls and answering my e-mails. I have not heard from her in six months). She complimented me on my article, which I sent her three and a half months ago. Then, surprisingly, she referred me to Carmen Dunson, the HR person in charge of the managed care department, which SVP Henry Goldman runs.

JAN 2013 – I e-mailed my resume to Ms. Dunson. On (1/24/13), I spoke directly with Ms. Dunson, who seemed impressed with my credentials and article. She told me that Mr. Tom Sussman was now in charge of staffing the new Municipal Health Insurance Exchange initiative and that she would forward my resume to him. I told her that I spoke with Tom in November.

She advises me to follow up with him. I called Tom but couldn't reach him. I sent a follow-up e-mail to Tom stating I spoke with Carmen Dunson.

FEB 2013 – I cannot contact Tom Sussman for some unknown reason. I've called him three or four times already. I also left a couple of messages with his secretary. Three weeks go by and he has not even answered my e-mails. I contacted the HR person (Ms. Dunson), who said she thinks Tom is considering me for one of several positions and that I should call him directly. I called him immediately and left him another voicemail message, but Tom never called me back. I officially applied for the Managed Care Executive Assistant position via the Municipal Hospital System careers website on (2/1/13).

MAR 2013 – I decide to visit the managed care office in person and introduce myself to Tom Sussman. To my surprise, he's out of the office that day. The receptionist is very friendly and says she will let Tom know I came to see him. I sent Tom another e-mail when I reached my office, but he never replied.

MAR 2013 – Three brand new female Admitting Supervisors are hired and introduced to the staff on or about (3/21/13). Knowing that I have applied for all three of these supervisory positions, it becomes crystal clear that management is blatantly discriminating against me. I notice these (3) ladies are all 20-something. I finally made up my mind to file this discrimination complaint.

APR 2013 – As the new Municipal Hospital System (MHS) Children's Hospital prepares for its grand opening, numerous positions have been posted on the Municipal Hospital Careers website.

There is not a day that goes by when my phone doesn't ring or a co-worker doesn't stop by to inform me about an available management or supervisory position. The entire department knows about my situation. I have applied for so many positions over the years. I have lost count! It has taken me a few days to prepare this complaint document, and I have not applied for any positions this week. That certainly does not mean I don't intend to keep job hunting. As soon as I submit this complaint, in spite of everything that will happen to me going forward, I will still keep searching for that elusive management/administrative position in health care.

If you need more space to write, please continue writing on a separate sheet of paper and attach it to the complaint form.

PLEASE DO NOT WRITE ON THE BACK OF THIS FORM.

To the best of my ability, I have chronicled my journey for career advancement over the past seven years at the Municipal Hospital System (MHS). I am sure there are other employment discrimination incidents during my tenure, but they are far too numerous to remember. I have dedicated myself to a career in healthcare.

I've always been a hard worker and a fast learner. I enjoy helping people and always give my best effort in the workplace. Unfortunately, hard work and dedication have not yielded the successes I felt I earned. Over the years, many of my colleagues have gone on to positions and promotions that have enhanced their career development at Municipal Hospital System. Over my many years of employment, this has not been the case for me.

As a minority male candidate seeking an administrative or management position, it's been a rough road.

In my letter to the municipal CEO, I explained that many of the individuals who interviewed me had problems relating to me because very few African American male candidates have my credentials. The majority of minority males employed in the Municipal Hospital Health System work as Housekeepers, Maintenance staff, Food Service, Patient Care Associates, Mail Room clerks, Shipping & Receiving, and Transport workers. All admirable positions were held by upstanding men earning hourly wages.

Conversely, high salaried Administrators and Directors are primarily females who do not view minority males as equals. Thus, this is the reason for the dilemma I find myself confronted with. There is no doubt in my mind that I can be a productive member of an administrative team, project management team, or management team. I have the intelligence, the skill, and ability to do so. All I need is the chance to prove myself, and I have been searching for the individual who would give me that chance to make my case by my work ethic.

Submitting this complaint is one of the hardest decisions I have made in my life. I honestly believe that I have been discriminated against because of my gender, race, and age. I was so happy and proud when the Municipal Hospital System (MHS) hired me. I have always given my best effort to represent my employer professionally.

I've dedicated myself to a career in healthcare and will continue to work hard in my search for career advancement. However, I believe this situation needs to be examined by a third party with an impartial point of view.

Respectfully submitted,
Miles M. Livingston

ADDITIONAL INFORMATION

*The next three pages are for the Division's records and **will not be sent out** with the rest of your complaint.*

Contact Information

My Primary Number: (631) 999 9999 (Cellphone)

My Secondary Telephone: (718) 555 5555 (Work phone)

My Email Address: mlivingston@anywhere.com

Last Four Digits of My Social Security Number: XXXX

Contact Person (someone who does not live with you but will know how to contact you if the Division cannot reach you):

Name: My Daughter

Telephone number:

Relationship with me: Daughter

Special Needs – N/A

Settlement/ Conciliation:

To settle this complaint, I would accept:
(Please explain what you want to happen as a result of this complaint. Do you want a letter of apology, your job back, lost wages, an end to the harassment, etc.?)

I would accept an estimated amount of wages lost (with interest and inflation adjustment) at a management/administrative salary for eight years. Also, I would want an administrative, management, or health IT project manager position.

Additional Details:

Did you report or complain about the discrimination to someone else?

(If you told someone, filed a report, or sent a letter about the discrimination, please indicate whether you went to a supervisor, a manager, the owner of the company, your human resources office, your union, your housing provider, the police, etc.).

YES! By the time I enrolled in grad school in 2006, I began to voice my concerns about not getting promoted. I complained about my feelings of being discriminated against to my supervisor, my manager, my director, and my union representative. I had been employed for over (3) three years and noticed that a few of my female co-workers had gotten promotions to supervisor positions.

Date you reported or complained about discrimination:
May 12, 2007.

How exactly did you complain about the discrimination?

(Who did you talk to about it? Who did you file a report or make a formal written complaint or union grievance with? What did you say?)

There were several incidents of complaints that occurred. To the best of my recollection, I first complained to my union reps. Oryan Johnson and Alston Cummings. During this period of time I was reluctant to officially put anything in writing. I told them my female co-workers were being selected over me even though I had more qualifications for a supervisory position than they did. My director, Cynthia Euestheim, has always maintained an "open-door-policy" and I would occasionally chat with her about departmental hiring practices and whether or not I should apply for inter-departmental positions. She always encouraged me to apply but never ever hired me. As the years rolled by (2007-2010), I earned my master's degree, and I expressed to her in writing that I am still very interested in being promoted to management. The tone of my correspondence is not really a complaint more of a request for help. She agrees to help me but does nothing. A few conciliatory interviews are arranged but nothing ever develops. (Needless to say, during this period of time, at least (10) female individuals are promoted into management positions).

What happened after you complained?

(Was your complaint investigated? Was any action taken in response to your complaint? Did the discrimination stop? Did you experience retaliation for complaining?)

Nothing happened!!! Business as usual. In hindsight, I wonder if my director did retaliate against me. Only (14) days ago, 03/21/13: Three (3) brand new female supervisors were hired in my immediate department. All supervisory positions that I applied for.

If you did not report the discrimination, please explain why:

I was always taught that hard work and perseverance are the way to success. I always felt I could outwork my competitors and prove my self-worth. I honestly believe that because I was a minority male in a female-controlled environment, my academic accomplishments and networking contacts were not yielding the results I was expecting.

By this point (2011), it wasn't about applying for a job anymore. I had worked hard to build a solid academic foundation, and I also networked even harder to compile a cadre of contacts that included SVPs, VPs, Sr. Managers, Exec. Directors and Administrators. These types of individuals don't usually do interviews! They agreed to meet with me only because of the relationships I had built and the qualifications I had acquired. I was confident that one of them would hire me. I was not willing to file a discrimination complaint and forfeit all my hard work by being "black-listed." I was confident in my skill set and ability to perform various administrative and management functions. I was now searching for an individual that could "think-outside-the-box" and hire a qualified African American male. Unfortunately, I have not yet met that individual.

That's the reason why I didn't file a complaint. I can get my (proverbial) foot in the door but never get offered the position. So now it is my time to "officially" complain in the biggest way I can!!! I'm not getting any younger.

I can't help thinking, "When are people going to put this racial prejudice and skin color issue aside?" If I was *not* a minority male or a woman, there is no doubt in my mind that I would have been a member of Hospital management or administration years ago. It is my hope that this complaint will become an eye-opener so my employer can look closely at my situation.

Did the person you are complaining against touch you, hurt you, or physically harm you?

No (N/A)

If yes, please explain:

_____

_____

Examples of other people who were discriminated against in the same way as you were:

(For example, people who were harassed by the same manager, disciplined or terminated for the same reasons, did not receive an accommodation for the same reasons, etc.).

If you are complaining about discrimination relating to race, national origin, age, religion, etc., please describe their races, national origins, ages, religions, etc.

All I can attest to is how my employer has treated me. If there are other incidents of discrimination at my employer, they have not been brought to my attention.

Examples of other people who were treated better than you were:

(For example, people who were not fired for doing the same thing you were fired for, people who were doing the same job but making more money, people who were allowed to stay in the store while you were told to leave, etc.)

If you are complaining about discrimination relating to race, national origin, age, religion, etc., please describe their races, national origins, ages, religions, etc.

Many of the women mentioned on page 9 - of this complaint were and still are my colleagues. They have all been treated very well, in my opinion. They have grown in their careers; some are managers or supervisors, and some have gone on to work as project managers. All of them are paid more than I am. I would describe them as a multi-cultural array of WOMEN. Some are smart, some not so smart. Some have degrees, and some do not have degrees. The common thread among them is that they are all female.

The clerk made copies of all the documents in my complaint and sealed them inside a manila envelope. She handed it to me and told me I would receive a certified copy by mail in a few weeks.

I walked out of there, a nervous wreck. My head was spinning, and my palms were sweating. A big part of my brain was screaming *what have you done??* My heart was racing with panic.

I took a seat at a bus stop to calm myself down. I closed my eyes and took some deep breaths, settling into the fact of what I'd just started. I did what I had to do. I did what I believed was the right thing. I'm fighting the good fight. That's all there was to it.

I didn't know what work would be like in the coming days, but I knew I would have to get ready for the backlash. The battle had begun, and I'd just fired the first shot.

"The most important thing is you must put everyone on notice that you're here and you are for real."

–Kobe Bryant

The Upward Climb Begins

It was business as usual at work over the next few weeks and months. Management had nothing to say to me, and I had already done my talking. Three weeks later, I received the following correspondence from the Division of Human Rights. I also received correspondence from the Equal Employment Opportunity Commission (EEOC):

EEOC – New York Division

New York District Office

Miles M. Livingston

Anytown Ave.

Anywhere, USA

EEOC Charge Number: 987XYZ654ABC

NYSDHR Case Number: 999900XB

NOTICE

This office has been informed that you filed a complaint of employment discrimination with the New York State Division of Human Rights (NYSDHR).

The purpose of this letter is to inform you of your federal rights pursuant to one or more of the statutes under which you may have filed. Please be advised that your complaint will be investigated by the New York State Division of Human Rights, not the Federal

Equal Employment Opportunity Commission (EEOC). All questions, correspondence, and status reports with regard to your case must be directed to the NYSDHR Office where your complaint was filed.

Your Federal Rights (if you filed under):

Title VII – of the Civil Rights Act of 1964, as amended: If I want to file a private lawsuit in federal district court with my ***own private attorney*** because I do not want the New York State Division of Human Rights to conduct an investigation, I may request from EEOC a ***Notice of Right to sue, 180 days after you have filed your complaint.*** Once the EEOC grants your request, it is only valid for ninety (90) days from the date the Notice was issued, after which your time to sue expires. If you want the (NYSDHR) to conduct an investigation, you do not need to make this request or to contact or write either agency. The NYSDHR will contact you and/or advise you in the near future of their investigation and determination of findings.

The Americans with Disabilities Act of 1990 (ADA) is the same as Title VII above.

The Age Discrimination in Employment Act of 1967 as amended (ADEA) - If you want to file a private lawsuit with your own private attorney, you could do so any time after 60 days from the date you filed your complaint with the New York State Division of Human Rights. This is only if you do not want the New York State Division of Human Rights to conduct an investigation; otherwise, you do not need to do anything at this time; the New York State Division of Human Rights will contact you or advise you in the near future of their investigation and determination of findings.

EEOC REVIEW PROCEDURE

If you want the EEOC to review the New York State Division of Human Rights final determination because you are not satisfied with their final findings, you may request that the EEOC conduct a substantial weight review. This request must be made in writing to the EEOC within fifteen (15) days from the date you received the New York State Division of Human Rights final determination. Otherwise, we will adopt the state findings.

Your review requests must specify the reason(s) why you do not agree with the New York State Division of Human Rights final determination.

Mail your request for substantial weight review to:

Equal Employment Opportunity Commission

Attn: State and Local Unit

Anywhere Street, 3rd Floor

Anytown, New York 01234

This address is for review purposes only. Remember, if you have questions concerning the status of your case, you must contact the New York State Division of Human Rights.

Date: April 14, 2013

Their letter basically says that the EEOC office had been notified that I filed an employment discrimination complaint with the New York

State Division of Human Rights (NYSDHR). They also want to inform me of my federal rights and that I have the option to file a private lawsuit in federal court with my own attorney if I do not want the NYSDHR to conduct an investigation. If I decide to sue my employer privately, I must request a Notice of Right to sue from EEOC (180) days after I file my complaint. Once the EEOC grants the request, it is only valid for ninety (90) days from the date the notice was issued, after which the time to sue expires.

I was very encouraged by the notice because I knew for sure my employer was aware that what they were doing was a federal crime. I definitely got their attention, and now they would have to answer for their actions. I called my buddy to give him an update, and he gave me some crucial insights into what was coming.

"Just remember, Miles, you're not hiring Johnny Cochran or Perry Mason. Division of Human Rights Attorneys are overworked and underpaid. They've only got a handful of litigators, and they hand off most of their cases to their underlying newbie attorneys. I'm telling you this so you can be prepared. You may have to hire your own private attorney."

That's a tough pill to swallow…but I needed to hear it. He let me know that I'm in for a fight. I thanked him for the information and wondered what was in store for me next.

A few days later, I got a call from an NYSDHR investigator named Ms. King. The phone call was about an hour of questions and conversation that went into detail about my complaint. It was a wonderful and stimulating conversation that left me feeling validated.

After all, I had an encyclopedic knowledge of every detail of my complaint, and I was overjoyed to have the chance to tell everything to someone willing to listen. Ms. King absorbed everything I had to say, and when it was all said and done, she reassured me that an investigation would take place. She did, however, ask for my patience. It was going to take several weeks before I heard anything.

I was good with that. Knowing the wheels of justice were turning was enough for me then. The ball was finally rolling.

A few weeks passed, and the new Municipal Women's Hospital Grand Opening Event was scheduled right down the hallway from my office at the hospital's main entrance. One of the largest Wall Street Banks had financed this new hospital, and they spared no expense. The event was a big, fancy, catered affair with all the heads of the hospital in attendance and press coverage as well. If somebody had told me there was a red carpet out front with celebrities coming in, I'd have believed them.

Our CEO introduced the keynote speaker for the event, Dr. Josephine Mottley, as Chief Diversity & Inclusion Officer. To my surprise, she was an African American woman. She gave a powerful speech that day that resonated with everyone in the crowd. I was eager to meet her, and so was everyone else. After her speech, there was a line of people looking to shake her hand, and I was no different. I got in line and introduced myself, being sure to thank her for such an inspirational speech. I also asked to connect with her to talk about the Diversity and Inclusion programs and initiatives that she was getting behind.

I thought this woman was too busy to be a Chief Diversity & Inclusion Officer at the time. After all, Dr. Mottley was the Medical Director of Cardiology for a dozen hospitals. She taught at the School of Medicine. She also sat on the development task force for healthcare literacy for the community, *and* she was an active volunteer with several agencies. Plus, she wrote a book about Black and Latina Women's Heart Health that she just so happened to be promoting.

Dr. Mottley was obviously a brilliant and gifted individual, but she was also just a token Black Chief Diversity & Inclusion Officer. I'm not trying to take away from her accomplishments in saying that. I thought then and believe now that Dr. Mottley is a great woman with the best intentions in mind. But when a Municipal Hospital Network is run by multimillionaires who all fit a single demographic – rich, White, and male – eventually, someone is going to point out the racism in their employee lineup, and they know it.

So, what do they do? They find a Diversity Officer that no one will question them about. Somebody accomplished and, more importantly, fits the description to quiet their detractors. Dr. Mottley fit that description, and then some, being both Black and a woman.

Studies have found "that even a single female token in organizational leadership will positively impact effective organizational change and address tokenism—and that a single high-status-female in corporate leadership is enough to bridge the gap between qualified female professionals being promoted to senior-level managerial positions—even in male-dominated industries. The implication for practice with Black females is that White men may be most willing to help sponsor and mentor them in White-male dominated environments for career advancement, and not other Black females. As such, Black female professionals may bode well relative to professional development and career advancement through mentorship when mentored by senior White male executives. The implication for business and the organization at large is that it should engage, incentivize, and recognize diverse mentors, namely White male senior executives, when they participate in mentorship programming to improve their (White male) vested interest." (McIntyre, 2022).

Anyway, with all that was going on, I penned the following e-mail to Dr. Mottley:

Ms. Josephine Mottley, MD
Chief Diversity & Inclusion Officer

Dear Dr. Mottley,

I was surprised and intrigued by the 2013 Diversity Report that was posted on the MHS Website. It was interesting to learn that the Municipal Hospital System (MHS) was voted number nine on the Diversity Inc.—top 10 Hospital Systems list. I was shocked when I learned that the rankings were based on four key areas of diversity management, notably "Human Capital," which is five levels of management and promotions in and into management. Transitioning into management or administration has been a primary goal of mine for the past eight years. After reading the Diversity article, I'm convinced that this is a program I need to get involved with. Up until this point, I only had a cursory understanding of workforce diversity. I respectfully request the opportunity to briefly chat with you about this initiative so I can determine how diversity can help me advance my career here at Municipal Hospital Systems.

As an African American male, I believe I have worked very hard and taken several steps to overcome the barriers I have been faced with. Unfortunately, I have not gained the success I've been looking for. My search for a management position has been unsuccessful, and I have remained in a clerical role throughout my tenure at Municipal Hospital. My hope is that this Diversity program can assist me in my quest to transition into a Management or Administrative position here at Municipal Hospital System (MHS). I am not looking for a handout. I am qualified to make the next step in my career. According to diversity leaders, "formal mentoring with a cross-cultural component is the most effective method to improve the pipeline of talent to management, especially senior management." I was encouraged when I read this, and I would certainly be interested in a program that could help me get on track to a management position. I'm reaching out to you because I'm curious to know how (an individual with my ethnic background and academic accomplishments) can begin the process of reaping the benefits of workforce diversity. I also read that Municipal Hospital has two resource groups. My understanding is that these groups are designed as resources for identifying and developing diverse talent. As a minority candidate, I would definitely consider myself to be a talented individual who meets the diversity criteria. I certainly could benefit from the mentoring, talent development, and recruitment a diversity resource group could provide.

I came to Municipal Hospital in 2003 with a bachelor's degree in Business Administration and a background in hospital finance. After two years of part-time employment, I began applying for supervisory and management positions. I entered graduate school in 2006 and earned a master's degree in Health Care Administration. Even with a master's degree, I was denied promotion after promotion. In 2008 and 2009, I applied for the

Municipal Administrative Internship. Both times, I was not accepted. In 2010, I was recruited into the Columbia University (Health Information Technology) HIT Certificate Program, which was sponsored by the HITECH – ONC Workforce Development initiative. When I completed the program at Columbia, I decided to do some volunteer work.

I was working a 3 to 11 PM shift, so my mornings were free to job search and interview. I contacted several departments, and finally, the director of Health Information Management was gracious enough to offer me the opportunity to volunteer as an Administrative Intern. I worked three days per week from 10 to 2 PM for fourteen months, and it turned out to be one of the most gratifying experiences of my career.

As the years rolled by, I continuously applied for management, supervisory, and administrative positions without any success. I had begun to notice that individuals inside the Admissions Department, with fewer qualifications than me, were being promoted into management and supervisory positions.

In an effort to jump-start my career, I began to write. I wrote an article about a healthcare topic that was published in the "*Medical Business News*." My thinking was that writing an article would help my credibility and make me more marketable. This was *not* the case at all. People seemed to be impressed with my credentials but not impressed enough to promote me or hire me.

To date, I am still employed in a clerical role. There is no question in my mind that I need your help, and based on what I read about Municipal Hospital and diversity, I'm confident that this is the right place for me to continue my journey toward career advancement.

I thank you in advance for your time and consideration. My tenure at Municipal Hospital has been agonizing and very difficult. I hope the tone of my correspondence has not offended you, but it's a frustrating time for me. I would sincerely appreciate the opportunity to meet with you to thoroughly understand how workforce diversity can improve my job experience here at Municipal Hospital.

Thank you,

Miles M. Livingston

****

To her credit, Dr. Mottley followed up with me promptly and referred me to her VP of Diversity, Caroline Minter. I sent Ms. Minter an email and a follow-up with a second email a week later. She responded and scheduled a meeting with me. Ms. Minter basically spent the meeting blowing her own horn about how successful she had become. She went on and on about when she started out at Municipal, and her White male superiors courted her for an administrative position because she was so diverse and smart. I sat there listening to her bullshit, hoping she'd get around to the point of why we were meeting in the first place. How it all ended was with her telling me about her H.R. contacts and how she was going to assign one of them to work personally with me. She also told me that she was going to review my resume and map out a job-search strategy for me to follow. Before I left her office, she convinced me to join the BERG group. (Business Employee Resource Group).

I had heard all the talk about diversity, and I had educated myself on Title VII case law, but none of it spoke to equality for African American men. As an African American man employed at a rather large Health System, I had several questions about diversity that I hoped to get answers to. I made some observations over the years about the staffing at my place of employment that seemed unsettling to me. From what I could tell, African American men were generally channeled and clustered into labor force sectors that paid the least.

The majority of Black men at my employer worked as Housekeepers, Maintenance staff, Food Service workers, Patient Care Associates, Mail Room clerks, Shipping & Receiving, and Transport workers. Now, all these positions are admirable and held by upstanding men. But for that to be the case, and there still being no Black Men in upper management was suspect to me. Conversely, high-salaried V.P.'s Directors and Managers are mostly White men or Multi-ethnic women, and from what I could tell, none of them saw Black men as equals.

The fundamental problem is that the language of diversity speaks to individuals who fall into what is known as "protected-class" status, which, legally speaking, excludes Black men. Diversity programs are supposed to be more focused on the inclusion of underrepresented individuals. However, diversity held a smaller scope of interest at my company. My observations revealed that true diversity doesn't exist at the management levels of many organizations. The only diversity that is recognized is a multicultural array of brilliant, influential, and successful women who have all achieved management and leadership positions within their respective companies.

Corporate America isn't really interested in true diversity. They make sure that they hire some Black woman as the Chief Diversity Officer, and then check off the compliance diversity box, and it's back to business as usual.

Two months went by, and I hadn't heard a thing. I went to work daily, and management was cordial and friendly towards me as if nothing happened. However, I knew they all had to know about the complaint against them. I was sure that they couldn't say anything to me, and I certainly wasn't about to say anything to them.

Finally, on or around June 15, 2013, I received a letter from the Municipal Hospital Office of Legal Affairs. I had been eagerly anticipating that correspondence. It came by certified mail with a disclaimer that I had a two-week time period to respond:

VERNON M. O'GARRA

Office of Legal Affairs

Gladstone Mitchell, Esq,

Municipal Hospital System

June 14, 2013

New York State Division

Of Human Rights

Mr. Regional Director

Re: Miles Livingston v. Municipal Hospital System

Case No. 9999000XB

Dear Mr. Director:

This letter responds to the allegations made by Miles Livingston – Clerical Account Representative at Municipal Hospital, that he was subjected to discriminatory treatment – namely, denied promotions to positions – because of his race, age, and sex.

As set forth below, Mr. Livingston's allegations that he was subjected to discriminatory treatment are completely without merit. Indeed, rather than point to any evidence of discrimination, Mr. Livingston (i) lists a number of positions for which he allegedly applied, (ii) identifies the employee who he believes received the position for which he applied, and (iii) in a wholly conclusory manner, draws the impermissible inference that he must have been denied the positions because of his age, race, and sex. It is well-settled, however, that in the absence of evidence of discrimination, an employee cannot meet his burden of establishing a discrimination claim under these circumstances. Quite simply, Mr. Livingston does not offer one shred of evidence that he was subjected to discriminatory treatment because of any protected characteristic.

In addition, as set forth below, Mr. Livingston cannot maintain a discrimination claim before the (SDHR) State Division Of Human Rights with respect to the vast majority of the positions he cites in his Complaint. Consistent with the applicable requirements of the Executive Law, and as set forth below, those claims concerning positions for which Mr. Livingston allegedly applied more than one (1) year before he filed his Complaint are untimely and, therefore, must be dismissed as a matter of law.

Background

Mr. Livingston was first hired by Municipal Hospital – his employer – in May 2003 as a Clerical Account Representative.

Notably, the individual Mr. Livingston claims discriminated against him – Ms. Euestheim – was responsible for hiring him.

As a Clerical Account Representative, Mr. Livingston was responsible for, among other things, interviewing patients (or their designees) when they came to the Hospital seeking care to obtain appropriate demographic, employment, and financial sponsorship data (concerning, for example, insurance coverage); providing the patient with information that the patient is required to receive pursuant to Hospital policy; verify financial/insurance information; collecting point of service payments from patients; and providing financial counseling, as necessary.

Discussion

Distilled to its essence, Mr. Livingston's claim in this matter is that beginning in May 2006, other employees were promoted to supervisory positions in the Admitting Office that he claims he should have received. He also complains that despite his efforts to seek "promotions" to other positions in the Municipal Hospital System, he was not promoted. According to Mr. Livingston, the failures to promote him are attributable to discriminatory animus against him because of his (i) race, (ii) age, and (iii) sex.

a) Mr. Livingston's race discrimination claim is demonstrably false.

Even a cursory review of the facts in this case established that Mr. Livingston cannot meet his burden of establishing that he was subjected to discriminatory treatment. First, he has not offered any evidence which even remotely suggests that anyone took any adverse employment actions against him – such as denying him a promotion for which he applied – because of his race. Rather, Mr. Livingston simply appears to offer only faulty reasoning in support of his discrimination claim. As set forth below, however, it is well settled that such reasoning is insufficient – as a matter of well-settled law – to support a discrimination claim.

Second, and in any event, the relevant facts establish that there cannot be any basis for Mr. Livingston's race discrimination claim. For example, although Mr. Livingston cites race as a factor in a number of decisions to promote other employees to positions that he believes he should have received, the irrefutable facts establish that a significant number of the employees whom Mr. Livingston claims were promoted into positions that he believed he should have received are – like Mr. Livingston – African American. For example, each of the following employees (all of whom are specifically identified in Mr. Livingston's Complaint as having received a promotion that he believed he should have received) are Black:

i.   Jane Doe

ii.   Chandra Doe

iii.   Mary Jackson

iv.   Cynthia Jones

v.   Juanita Rodriguez

vi.   Thelma Wilson

Thus, of the fourteen individuals named by Mr. Livingston in this Complaint who received positions that he believes he should have received, the race of a majority of those individuals is the same as Mr. Livingston himself. Of the remaining employees, five are White (the second largest group by race), two are Asian, and one is Hispanic. 1

These facts – which are taken as they are alleged in the Complaint – demonstrate beyond any doubt that Mr. Livingston cannot establish the existence of any circumstances that give rise to any inference of race discrimination. 2

    a. *Mr. Livingston cannot establish any circumstances,*
       Which gives rise to an inference of age discrimination.

Similarly, any notion that Mr. Livingston was subjected to discrimination because of his age is belied by the fact that the individual whom Mr. Livingston claims was responsible for the discrimination against him – Cynthia Euestheim, the Director of Access Services – is herself <u>older</u> than Mr. Livingston. Indeed, Ms. Euestheim is 64 years of age and, further, has recently retired from her position with the Hospital.

---

1. The Hospital has responded to the allegations as set forth in Mr. Livingston's Complaint and reserves the right to submit additional information regarding any of the alleged promotions should it be necessary. With respect to the position referenced in Mr. Livingston's complaint concerning a promotion that occurred in March 2013 where the recipient of the promotion is

not identified, this may refer to, based upon information and belief, Jon Lee, who is Asian.

2. It is well-settled that in order for a complainant to maintain a claim in a promotion case, he must establish that he applied for the position at issue. See Howe v. City of New York, 2010 WL 3825730, *7 (S.D.N.Y., Sept. 29, 2010) (to establish a prima facie case in a failure to promote case, the plaintiff must establish that (1) he is a member of a protected class; (2) he applied for and was qualified for the job; (3) he was rejected for the position; and (4) the rejection occurred under circumstances giving rise to an inference of discrimination). Notwithstanding this requirement – and without prejudice thereto – Municipal Hospital has assumed, for the sake of this submission only, that Mr. Livingston did, in fact, apply for each of the positions referenced in his Complaint but reserves the right to submit additional information concerning Mr. Livingston's applications (or the absence thereof) for each of the positions at issue. The critical issue, as set forth herein, is that Mr. Livingston cannot establish the existence of circumstances that give rise to an inference of discrimination.

In addition, any possible inference of age discrimination is further refuted by the fact that Mr. Livingston is hardly the oldest employee in the Clerical Accounts Department. Indeed, there are a number of employees in the Department who are older than Mr. Livingston. In particular, there are 11 employees who are as old or even older than Mr. Livingston, the oldest among them being a 78-year-old Clerical Account Representative. Similarly, in addition to Ms. Euestheim, the Department employed other supervisory employees who were either older than Mr. Livingston or who were his contemporaries. For example, one Supervisor, Deena Miller, is

66yrs old; Lynnis Bailey, a Black female who is a Manager in Clerical Accounts, is 57 years old (and currently Mr. Livingston's immediate supervisor); and Pat Bragbile, a White female, is 58 years old. These facts establish that Mr. Livingston's suppositions regarding alleged discrimination because of his age are completely without merit.

> b. There is no basis for Mr. Livingston's claim that he was subjected to discriminatory treatment because of his sex.

With respect to Mr. Livingston's claim that he was subjected to discriminatory treatment because of his sex, there is no evidence that any of the decisions about which he complains were attributable to sex discrimination. Indeed, while one would believe from Mr. Livingston's complaint that the Hospital has no interest in hiring males as supervisors in the Clerical Accounts Department, the facts establish that this allegation is false. For example, the Clerical Accounts Department's Administrative Director, Emanuel Gornstein – who was promoted to Ms. Euestheim's position when she retired – is male. In addition, Stefanos Maaravi, one of the Clerical Account Supervisors, is also male. Similarly, Leroy Simpson was also hired as a Clerical Account Supervisor and is – like Mr. Livingston – a man.

In addition, it should also be noted that Mr. Simpson was hired into his role in April 2013, **during the same period of time** that Mr. Livingston alleges that he was not being hired **because of his sex**. Mr. Simpson's hiring establishes beyond any doubt that Mr. Livingston cannot establish the existence of any sex-based discriminatory animus.

    c. Mr. Livingston's claims concerning positions outside the Clerical Accounts Department should also be dismissed.

The same grounds outlined above for rejecting Mr. Livingston's race, age and sex discrimination claims concerning the Clerical Accounts Department also apply to positions in which Mr. Livingston complains concerning positions in the Hospital System. For example, although Mr. Livingston assigns discriminatory motives to his frustration about finding a promotional opportunity at Municipal Hospital System, the fact is that he cannot establish that any of those decisions were attributable to invidious discriminatory reasons.

For example, although he claims that he was subjected to racial discrimination, he notes that he had interviews with, among others, Mary Cross. Ms. Cross – like Mr. Livingston – happens to be African-American and, as indicated in Mr. Livingston's Complaint, in a senior position at Municipal Hillside Hospital. 3 Nor can Mr. Livingston claim that there was a female cabal aligned against him because – even in his version of events – a number of the individuals with whom he met were themselves male. 4

It should also be noted that although Mr. Livingston met with some of the individuals mentioned in his Complaint, he did not meet with others, and they would not have had any idea, for example, how old he was or, for that matter what race he was, based on telephone conversations that they had with him. For instance, although Mr. Livingston recounts discussions he had with Carmen Dunson, all of those discussions were over the phone. Surely, Mr. Livingston is not claiming in this case that Ms. Dunson somehow guessed at Mr. Livingston's age (or his race) and made the decision that he would not be considered because of any of these factors. Even repeating the basic premise of Mr. Livingston's case reveals its absurdity. 5

Finally, Mr. Livingston simply has not met his burden of coming forward with any information which even remotely suggests that his age was a factor in any decision that may have been made concerning Mr. Livingston in his search for a promotional opportunity.

---

1. Ms. Cross was, in fact, the Associate Executive Director for Human Resources at Municipal Hillside Hospital and has since been promoted to a new position as the Associate Executive Director for Human Resources at Municipal Dennox Hills Hospital. Similarly, Mr. Livingston concedes that he spoke with and met with other African Americans in the course of his efforts to find a job. For example, Roxanne Moncrief, Senior Talent Acquisition Specialist, is African-American as is Pamela Bronson, Director in the Talent Acquisition Department.

2. In particular, Mr. Livingston notes that he met with Steve Roenia, Harris Goldberg, Michael Shauvell, and Tom Sussman, among others.

3. Similarly, it should be noted that while Mr. Livingston expressed general interest in being hired by the Municipal

Hospital System's Insurance Company, scores of other individuals – many of whom had insurance company experience – expressed general and specific interest in working for the insurance company and were not interviewed or hired. Quite simply, for Mr. Livingston to claim that he was somehow subjected to discriminatory treatment under these circumstances is simply absurd. In any event, Mr. Livingston was eventually interviewed by representatives responsible for the new Insurance Company (not Ms. Dunson) in April 2013, a step which many applicants fail to reach, and Mr. Livingston was specifically informed that the Insurance Company was still developing its staffing plans. Thus, Mr. Livingston's sense of umbrage (what he describes as "frustration") is misplaced because, as he was informed, the Municipal Hospital is still actively looking at candidates as it continues to hire for the Insurance Company. In this regard, the early hiring decisions have been focused on individuals with extensive insurance industry experience, which Mr. Livingston does not possess.

As set forth above, the faulty logic upon which Mr. Livingston relies to support his discrimination claim – that discrimination <u>must have been</u> the reason for him not being promoted – is not sufficient, as a matter of well-settled law, to meet his burden in a discrimination case. *See, e.g., Peter v. Mount Sinai Hospital,* 2010 WL 1372686

(S.D.N.Y.) (rejecting "the familiar plaint of, "I am a member of a protected class; something bad happened to me at work; it must have happened because I am a member of that protected class" and holding that "[t]his sort of *post hoc, ergo propter hoc* reasoning has been rejected as insufficient again and again in employment discrimination cases....") (citations omitted).

d. The vast majority of Mr. Livingston's promotion claims are untimely.

It appears from Mr. Livingston's Complaint that he claims that he applied for positions in the Clerical Accounts Department beginning in May 2006. The irrefutable facts establish, however, that Mr. Livingston

did not file his Complaint in this matter until April 8, 2013. Thus, consistent with Executive Law, any claims relating to alleged promotions that Mr. Livingston did not receive occurring before April 8, 2012, are untimely and must be dismissed. *See* Executive Law, 297(5) 6.

Conclusion

There is no basis whatsoever for Mr. Livingston's claim that he was subjected to discriminatory animus because of his race, age, or sex. The irrefutable facts establish that while Mr. Livingston may have applied for various positions during his tenure with the Hospital, the positions that he believed he should have received were most often given to employees who were of the same race as Mr. Livingston. In addition, the relevant facts establish that Mr. Livingston's claim that he was subjected to age discrimination and sex discrimination are also completely without merit because, for example, even while he claimed that he was not being given a position because of his sex, the Hospital hired two male employees into supervisory positions and, further, continues to employ individuals in the Department who are either contemporaries of, or older than, Mr. Livingston. Similarly, while Mr. Livingston assigns a nefarious discriminatory motive to his frustrations about finding a promotional opportunity, he did not – in some cases – even meet with the individuals so that they could have any idea regarding his age or his race. For all these reasons, therefore, Mr. Livingston's claims in this matter should be immediately dismissed.

---

1. Again, as set forth above, Mr. Livingston cannot establish – with respect to any claim within the limitations period – that he was subjected to discriminatory treatment because of his race, age, or sex. Indeed, as set forth above, with respect to the positions in Clerical Accounts referenced in Mr. Livingston's

complaint for which he applied after April 2012, one of those positions was granted to an employee who was the same race as Mr. Livingston.

The Hospital reserves the right to submit additional information to supplement this submission.

Sincerely,

Office of Legal Affairs

Office of Legal Affairs

****

Section 5 of Executive Law states:

"Any complaint filed pursuant to this section must be so filed within **_one year_** after the alleged unlawful discriminatory practice."

Well, Well, Well. Who the "fuck" knew that?! I certainly didn't know that I had to file this complaint within a one-year time period. Shit. I realized my employer had been jerking my chain around for years, and I knew something was WRONG! That's what I knew! And no one told me anything along the way. My union rep never told me, and my friends and colleagues never told me. *No one* informed me that I only had a year from the date of the discrimination to file.

The worst thing is that I believed my employer would finally realize that I was wronged and would finally try to correct the error of their ways by giving me a shot at management. So, I kept waiting year after year, giving them the benefit of the doubt. Come to find out that my employer didn't give a fuck about me.

"Wait" has almost always meant "Never." We must come to see that, "Justice too long delayed is justice denied." –Martin Luther King

It was a hard and bitter lesson to learn about the bigger picture of racism in the workplace. I could use that moment as the beginning of my real education in what they defined as "Human Rights." It most certainly wasn't the same thing as what the rest of us thought. Either way, I was opened up to a whole different ballgame.

I submitted my rebuttal to the Human Rights Director as follows:

VERNON M. O'GARRA

July 9, 2013
Mr. Miles M. Livingston, MHA,
123 Anywhere Drive,
Anytown, New York.

New York State Division
of Human Rights,

Mr. Regional Director
Re: Miles M. Livingston v. Municipal Hospital System
Case No. 9999000XB

Dear Mr. Director:

As per the instructions from your office, I am submitting my rebuttal regarding the discrimination complaint filed against Municipal Hospital System. Let me begin by thanking the Legal Affairs Office for their response to my complaint. I have been anticipating a response for several weeks. I am not an attorney, and the legal jargon written into the document was quite a mouthful for a layperson to swallow. I am not familiar with the "applicable requirements of Executive Law." However, after reading and digesting the essence of the response, I believe that my employer has misunderstood the basic premise of my complaint. I am completing the Human Rights complaint form as it relates to my tenure over the past (6) six years at my employer, not one year. My complaint establishes a pattern of behavior towards me. My thinking was that maybe an employer can have a bad year or make some improper decisions over a period of time with regard to hiring and promotions. But a period of time that spans over (6) six years clearly demonstrates discrimination against me! Please let me clarify…

Point One - Gender

The point I'm trying to make with regard to gender is that throughout my tenure at the Municipal Hospital – Clerical Accounts Department, all of the promotions awarded have been to women. I might also add that these women are made up of a multicultural array of backgrounds. Of course, African-American women are among them, but that's not the point here. My point is that many of these women did not have the same qualifications I had. So, although I was qualified for the supervisory and management positions I applied for, I was not selected because I was a male. More importantly, I'm talking about an approximately six-year period.

In summary, the majority of positions that I applied for were filled by women. That has been my experience during my tenure at Municipal Hospital. Legal Affairs says that I offer faulty reasoning to support my claim. I don't know how they can say that. These are the facts.

Point Two - Age

The age criteria I spoke about pertained to the last group of supervisors hired over the past three years. I would guess that the last six or seven supervisors that were hired were all twenty or thirty-something-year-old women with less qualifications and experience than me. I will add that the women mentioned in the response document, whose names and ages were indicated, were unprofessional and unnecessary. Why reveal personal information about women employed before my arrival at Municipal Hospital? These ladies are in no way relevant to this complaint. My complaint only speaks to individuals "promoted" into supervisory and management positions during my tenure there. Again, the age of the department director and associate senior managers who have been employed prior to my hiring have absolutely no relevance to this complaint.

Point Three - Race

The racial aspect of this complaint is simply this: African-American men are grossly under-represented in supervisory, management, and administrative positions at this job. Why is this? Maybe racial discrimination, perhaps not, I don't know. I'll leave it to my employer and the Human Rights representative to come up with an answer.

Legal Affairs makes mention of (14) African-American women in the response document. They have totally missed the racial point here. Women of all ethnic backgrounds have achieved career success at Municipal Hospital. Again, the issue is that there are no African-American men in supervisory or management positions in the Clerical Accounts department. The response document also mentions the two gentlemen that were hired after I submitted this complaint. I am not privy to who is hired or when they are hired. I had no control over that. I am happy for these gentlemen. If this complaint has led to the hiring of an African-American male supervisor, I think that's wonderful. If I have created an atmosphere of apprehension and subjected myself to retaliatory measures by filing this complaint, that will be my cross to bear. I want to make a point that a third party needs to look at this situation and make a ruling. Whether or not the ruling is in my favor or not, I believe some changes need to be made.

Summary

I remind the Municipal Hospital Legal Affairs office that the NYS Human Rights Division is a mechanism designed to help employees who feel that they have been discriminated against. This process is not personal. I harbor no malice, ill feelings, or animosity towards anyone. I am simply following the guidelines that are in place.

My goal in filing this complaint is to have an impartial set of eyes from the Human Rights office take a look at my situation, evaluate it, and advise me about how I need to proceed with this matter. I have talked to a myriad of people at Municipal Hospital in regards to furthering my career. It's not like I woke up one morning and decided to file a complaint. I've been employed for TEN years!!! All my experiences throughout the years are germane to this complaint. This complaint is based on all my experiences and observations at Municipal Hospital and what has happened regarding promotions in my department. The prevailing message throughout my career has always been to work hard, go the extra mile, provide good customer service, and professionally represent my employer.

Following these basic principles are the keys to success. I believe that I have always done this. But it's hard to dedicate yourself to your career, work extremely hard, return to school, earn a master's degree, and not be able to reap the benefits of all your hard work and sacrifice.

It's frustrating and very disappointing. I need to understand why I find myself in this dilemma.

When one reads through the Human Rights Complaint Form as I did, I answered the questions as honestly and forthcoming as possible, based on *"my experiences, observations and treatment I received"* at my employer.

An example of some questions read;

I believe I was discriminated against because of my Age, Race/Ethnicity, and Sex (I honestly feel that I fall into all three categories). What did the person/company you are complaining against do? Please check all that apply. (I selected "Denied me a promotion or pay raise").

I would ask my employer what I am supposed to think. I'm an intelligent guy. I've studied health care in great detail. Healthcare is my career love and passion. I've probably applied for 50 positions over the years at Municipal Hospital, but I've certainly lost count. You're telling me I'm not qualified for any of these jobs? I don't accept that logic! I believe I am qualified.

My experience at Municipal Hospital has shown that most women get these jobs. I believe I have been discriminated against. African-American men are under-represented in supervisory, management, and administrative roles at Municipal Hospital. I don't know why that is. Hopefully, filing this complaint will reveal the answers.

Wow, it's 2013! I am very surprised that I actually filed this complaint. It's amazing that this type of stuff still happens. I sincerely hope Municipal Hospital and the Human Rights representative can sort this out. I, as an African-American male, have experienced some serious problems at this job where career advancement is concerned. This is a fact. I very much want to continue working at Municipal Hospital, and I want to have a rewarding career, just as members of Legal Affairs and others have had. I will continue to work towards achieving the goal of obtaining a challenging and rewarding career in health care at Municipal Hospital. Legal Affairs suggests that my complaint "Should be immediately dismissed."

I totally disagree. All aspects of this complaint have merit. Why not allow my experiences at Municipal Hospital to be used as a teaching moment to explore why African-American men are underrepresented in management, supervisory, and administrative positions.

In closing, I appreciate the Legal Affairs response and the opportunity to have this dialogue. Dismissing this complaint would only turn a blind eye to a situation that needs to be addressed and rectified. There are very intelligent individuals employed at Municipal Hospital. HR professionals, Diversity professionals, Legal professionals, and others. Why not get several opinions along with the Human Rights representative and collectively find a solution to my problem?

Thank you,

Miles M. Livingston

Miles M. Livingston.

VERNON M. O'GARRA

The Long Road to Validation

Shortly after I submitted my rebuttal, I received a call from Ms. Roberta Samuels, Senior Attorney for the NYSDHR. I made an appointment with her over the phone, but we chatted briefly about my case. After our chat, I follow up with an email:

On Jul 9, 2013, at 03:45 PM, "Livingston, Miles" enterprise vault archive < Mlivingston@MuniHosp.orj > wrote:

From Livingston, Miles
To Samuels, Roberta
Subject Re: Rebuttal to Municipal

Ms. Roberta Samuels, Esq.
New York State Division of Human Rights

Hello Ms. Samuels,

Thank you for reaching out to me. I have submitted the rebuttal to my employer's response to my filing a discrimination complaint against Municipal Hospital (see attached).

I was offended by my employer's response. I felt that the tone of the remarks in the document was insulting and condescending. This is the type of language and attitude that is representative of the very treatment I am subjected to at my place of business. In my opinion, this is the kind of rhetoric that exhibits the entrenched racial bias that exists against African American males at my employer. The culture that exists at Municipal Hospital fosters an atmosphere of workplace segregation that keeps African American men in low-paying jobs and women and Caucasian men in high-salaried jobs.

322

I look forward to our consultation meeting.

Sincerely,
Miles M. Livingston
Miles M. Livingston, MHA
Admitting/Emergency/Ambulatory Surgery
Municipal Hospital Systems
Anywhere, New York
(519) 888-9999 – w
mlivingston@munihosp.orj

■■

During the attorney meeting at the Division of Human Rights Office, Ms. Samuels acknowledged the level of detail I put into my complaint, saying that she'd never seen that degree of meticulousness since she started working for the NYSDHR. I'm flattered, but I only wanted to know if anything could be done for me. She told me. "Your case will definitely go to a hearing. My guess is that they will want to settle with you as soon as possible, but let's wait and see what happens."

And so, my faith was restored. I knew if I could get a fair and open-minded judge who would listen to my side of the story, I would be confident that I would prevail.

I returned to work the next day, and all was a status quo. In my job, I usually ran the entire office, however unofficially. At that time, I was training a new employee two or three times a week.

I routinely went to other department areas (like Cardiology, Pre-Surgical Testing, and such) to pick up overtime. I was a well-rounded employee who could be deployed to any department to provide support. The fact is that I loved my job in the healthcare/hospital industry.

Three weeks later, another certified letter arrived from the NYSDHR. I immediately ripped open the envelope:

FINAL INVESTIGATION REPORT AND BASIS FOR DETERMINATION.

NEW YORK STATE
DIVISION OF HUMAN RIGHTS

To: Miles M. Livingston   Region: New York

From: Regional Director   Date: August 2, 2013

SDHR Case No: 9999000XB -13 EXO8

Subject: Miles M. Livingston v. Municipal Hospital System

**FINAL INVESTIGATION REPORT AND BASIS FOR
DETERMINATION**

I.   Case Summary

This is a verified complaint, filed by Complainant Miles M. Livingston, on Fri 4/8/2013. The Complainant is an African American male. DOB is XX/29/1955, charges the Respondent with unlawful discriminatory practices in relation to employment because of age, race/color, and sex.

II.   Summary of Investigation

Complainant's Position

The complainant alleges that for the past few years, he has attempted to obtain a supervisory position with Respondent without success. Further, Complainant claims that he has applied for several supervisory positions that he was qualified for, however, all of the positions he applied for within his assigned department (Admitting Office) were filled by younger Black females with fewer qualifications. Complainant also asserts that he has not been promoted to supervisor because most of the high-salaried directors and administrators are females who do not see Black Males like Complainant as professional equals.

Complainant states that he took many steps to promote himself before many administrators and managers; he let them all know that he was interested in career advancement. Specifically, Complainant states that after one of many communications with senior managers, he was referred to HR Representative Roxanne Moncrief, who referred him for one

325

interview in over a year. and after Complainant expressed his frustration in an email during August 2012, she then referred him to an inappropriate position in the radiology department that required a skill set that Complainant lacks.

During January 2013, and receiving an additional area of responsibility (ambulatory surgery), the Complainant reached out to the Director of Talent Acquisition and again expressed his frustration with the department and dissatisfaction with Ms. Moncrief. Soon after, he received a call from Ms. Moncrief, who referred him to the Municipal Hospital Insurance Company.

The same HR Representative that was impressed with Mr. Livingston's credentials and stated that she would forward the Complainant's resume and recently published health-care-related article to Mr. Tom Sussman, who was then in charge of Respondent's new Health Insurance Exchange Initiative. Also, during this period of time, the Complainant applied for the Managed Care Executive Assistant position via the Respondent's careers website.

During March 2013, Complainant made several unsuccessful attempts to contact Mr. Sussman via emails and voicemail messages. During this same time period, Complainant states Respondent hired (3) three new Admitting Supervisors, all females in their twenties. Since management was aware of his long-held interest in a supervisory position, the recent hires clearly demonstrate clear discrimination against him.

Complainant states that between June 2012 and March 2013, he applied to four (4) supervisory positions, the most recent during March

2013, all were vacancies within his department, and all were granted to females.

Respondent's Position:

Complainant was first hired by Respondent in May 2002 as a Clerical Accounts Representative. Notably, the individual whom Complainant claims discriminated against him, Ms. Euestheim, was responsible for hiring him and is herself older than Complainant at 64 years of age. Ms. Euestheim recently retired from her position.

As a Clerical Accounts Representative, the Complainant was responsible for, among other things, interviewing patients (or their designees) when they came to the hospital seeking care to obtain appropriate demographic, employment, and financial sponsorship data (concerning, for example, insurance coverage); providing the patient with information that the patient is required to receive pursuant to Hospital policy; verify financial and insurance information; collecting point of service payments from patients; and providing financial counseling as necessary.

Firstly, the Complainant presented only statements for which he relies on to make the instant claims of employment discrimination by Respondent. Secondly, the relevant and irrefutable facts establish that a significant number of employees, such as the Complainant claims, were promoted into positions he believed he should have received.

For example, the following employees have all been identified by the Complainant as having received a promotion that he believed he should have received: **Jane Doe, Juanita Rodriguez, Mary Jackson, Thelma Wilson, Hope Williams, and Cynthia Jones.**

Thus, of the fourteen individuals named by the Complainant in the instant complaint who received positions, five are Caucasian, the second largest group by race, two are Asian, and one is Hispanic. Regarding the position that the Complainant sites, he applied for during March 2013.

In addition, any possible reference to age discrimination is further refuted by the fact that the Complainant is hardly the oldest employee in the access services department. Indeed, there are a number of employees in the department who are older than the Complainant. In particular, there are 11 employees who are as old or even older than the Complainant, but among them is a 78-year-old access service representative; similarly, in addition to Ms. Euestheim, the department employed other supervisory employees who were either older than the Complainant or who his contemporaries.

For example, one supervisor, Deena Miller, is 66 years old. Lynnis Bailey, a Black female manager in Clerical Accounts, is 57 years old (and currently the Complainant's immediate supervisor), and Patricia Abernathy, a Caucasian female, is 58 years old.

Investigator's Observations:

While the Complainant alleges herein that he applied for numerous supervisory positions with respondent beginning in May 2006 through May 2011, and all were filled by females. The instant investigation focuses on the applications by applicants that fall within the period of March 8, 2012, through March 8, 2013, only.

Comparative Data

Respondent provides that of the fourteen (14) employees that Complainant identifies in the instant complaint as having received promotions that he should have received, six (6) are African American/Black like the Complainant (Jackson, Wilson, Doe, Jones, Rodriguez, and Small); five (5) are Caucasian; two (2) are Asian; and one (1) Hispanic.

The person that the Complainant claims discriminated against him, Cynthia Euestheim, the director of the Clerical Accounts Department, is herself older than the Complainant at 64 years of age. In fact, the Complainant is far from the oldest employee within his department; currently, there are eleven (11) employees who are as old or even older than the Complainant.

Respondent provides that the access service department maintains male supervisors. As an example, the Clerical Accounts Department's Administrative Director, Emanuel Gornstein, who was promoted to Ms. Euestheim's position when she retired, is male. In addition, Stefanos Maaravi and Leroy Simpson, both male, are department supervisors. Similarly, Mr. Simpson was hired into his role in April 2013, during the same period of time that the Complainant alleges that he was not being promoted because of sex.

In conference, the Complainant confirmed Respondent's assertions that Ms. Euestheim, who served as his director during his entire employment until she retired, also participated in hiring him for the Clerical Accounts Representative position. Further, the Complainant confirmed that at some point during the spring of 2013, the Respondent, in fact, promoted and hired three males to the department as director and supervisors, respectively; these men are White, Asian, and Black.

The Complainant provides that he was repeatedly encouraged by Black female administrators, including former director Euestheim, to seek supervisory positions at work. Clearly, the respondent's record supports the Complainant's allegations that the Respondent failed to promote him to a supervisor position because of his race and sex. Respondent's records show that Respondent promoted only Black females (not Black males).

Respondent admitted that when the Complainant raised the issue of not being promoted to a Supervisor's position because of his sex and race, a Black male was hired from the outside to the position of supervisor. However, the Complainant was not offered the opportunity to interview for that same position.

Serena Chappel
Submitted by:
Serena Chappel
Human Rights Specialist I

I. **Basis for Determination**

The investigation failed to support the Complainant's allegation of age discrimination.

Nevertheless, the investigation and Respondent's records support the Complainant's allegation of race/color and sex discrimination. The Complainant is an African American/Black male and has been employed by Respondent as a Clerical Accounts Representative since the year 2002; during his employment, the claimant has been a satisfactory employee and furthered his education by obtaining a master's degree.

While Respondent argues that a Black male was hired as a supervisor during the same time period as the Complainant alleges he was denied a promotion due to his race/color and sex, this male was a new hire and not promoted, which is what the Complainant alleges he has been denied.

It is reasonable to believe that the hiring of a Black male in a supervisory position was a ***smoke screen designed to mask a discriminatory act.***

The Complainant alleges that he has been repeatedly denied a supervisory position with Respondent despite numerous networking efforts/applications and that he has been denied promotional opportunities because he is an African American/ Black male.

Respondent denies the instant allegations and provides information that shows the Complainant was initially hired by an African American/Black female. The Complainant states that his long-term director and many of his networking efforts were with African American/Black females.

Further, Respondent provided, and the Complainant does not dispute, that Respondent's Clerical Accounts Department is overwhelmingly racially/ethnically diverse, including African American/Black females.

Moreover, the department has never promoted an African American male to supervisor.

A review of the record reveals that there are material issues of fact involved, which are best resolved at a public hearing before an administrative law judge, where testimony is taken under oath, witnesses are subject to cross-examination, and a full record is made.

Based upon the above information, the investigation supports the complainant's claims of unlawful and discriminatory practices in relation to employment on the basis of his sex, race/ color.

Reviewed & Approved: *Margaret Smith-Jones*

Margaret Smith-Jones
Human Rights Specialist II

I.   **Determination**

Based on the foregoing, I find **PROBABLE CAUSE** to support the allegations of the complaint.

HDavid
_____

Harrison David
Regional Director

STATE OF NEW YORK

DIVISION OF HUMAN RIGHTS

ANYWHERE, NEW YORK 16666

September 12, 2013

Re: Miles M. Livingston v. Municipal Hospital Health Systems

Case No. 9999000XB

To The Parties Listed Below:

Please be advised that the respondents application dated October 24, 2013, in which reopening of the above-referenced proceeding was sought pursuant to Rule 20(b) of the Rules of Practice of the Division of Human Rights (9 N.Y.C.R.R. § 765.30(b)) in order to vacate a probable cause determination issued by the Division August 26, 2013, is hereby denied and that, therefore, the matter should proceed to public hearing.

Probable cause to believe that unlawful discrimination occurred exists when, after giving credence to the Complainant's version of the facts, some evidence of discrimination exists. *Robertson v. State of New York*, 240 A.D.2d 504 (2d Dept. 1997). A complaint may not be dismissed for lack of probable cause unless the facts revealed generate conviction in a persuade of Fair and detach factfinder that there is no substance to the complaint. *State Division of Human Rights (Thompson v. Hatch Association Consultants, Inc.,* 110 A.D.2d 1049, 488 N.Y.S.2d 907 (4th Dept. 1985). A determination of probable cause is not a final adjudication but merely a determination that there should be a formal hearing on the matter. *Board of Education v. State Division of Human Rights,* 68 Misc.2d 1035, 330 N.Y.S.2d 274 (Sup.Ct. West. Co. 1972).

A review of the record reveals that there are material issues of fact involved, which are best resolved at a public hearing before an administrative law judge, where testimony is taken under oath, witnesses are subject to cross-examination, and a full record is made.

These issues include but are not limited to, whether the Respondent discriminated against the Complainant due to race/ color and sex. In any event, the Respondent will have a full and fair opportunity to present witnesses and any other evidence deemed relevant to the presiding administrative law judge at the hearing.

Very truly yours,

General Counsel

General Counsel

VERNON M. O'GARRA

I read the determination from the Division of Human Rights and the follow-up letter, and I was jumping for joy inside like a little kid. I knew these motherfuckers were guilty. I knew it! I was so glad the Division of Human Rights was able to look at my case objectively and not be dissuaded by high-powered attorneys who spoke proficient legalese. It was truly validating for me.

I wondered what my director was thinking. I wondered what my managers and immediate supervisor thought. Most importantly, I started wondering what the Municipal Hospital System's attorney was thinking. I imagined that he was thinking that some disgruntled employee just kicked his ass and shot holes all through his legal argument against said employee. I was certain everybody on that side of the office knew they were all about to be investigated, and they were sweating about it.

Even though nobody could talk to me directly, I knew I was the subject of many closed-door conversations. Eventually, I'd find out exactly what they thought of me, but I'm getting ahead of the story.

There was still so much for me to learn and discover about human rights law. I lived a short distance from a law school, and the security guard knew me from the many nights I studied there when I was in graduate school. The law school library was open until a quarter to twelve every night and contained a wealth of knowledge. With the help of the librarian and even a few attorney friends, they pointed me in the right direction, which would end up providing me with nuggets of information about human rights law. Who Knew? The attorneys knew, but I was clueless about the law. I was fascinated as I researched the treatment of Black men in the Corporate American workplace.

After some research, I wrote another detailed letter to the Regional Director of the New York State Division of Human Rights. I wanted him to understand exactly who I was and let him know that this was not some "willy-nilly" complaint submitted against an employer by a disgruntled employee looking for money. My argument was serious! My employer was guilty of racial and gender discrimination, and I wanted to bring this egregious wrongdoing to light.

VERNON M. O'GARRA

September 28, 2013
Mr. Miles M. Livingston, MHA
123 Anywhere Drive
Anytown, New York

Mr. Harrison David, Regional Director
New York State Division of Human Rights
Re: Miles Livingston v. Municipal Hospital System (MHS)
Case No. 9999000XB

Dear Mr. David:

Since the submission of my complaint against the Municipal Hospital System, I decided to do some additional research regarding racial discrimination and the treatment of African-American men in the workplace. The data that I uncovered was very troubling and disconcerting. There are a plethora of studies that have been conducted that support my personal experiences of racism.

However, a major problem is that the "LAW" doesn't always recognize the injustices that are perpetrated against Black men in the workplace or in society.

After examining some of the Title VII case law, it was clear to see that some decisions adopt the theory of *"Colorblindness," and* some look at discrimination from a *"Protected-Class"* view. In contrast, others derive their decisions from the *"Reverse-discrimination* or *"Anti-discrimination"* case law. It's all very convoluted to a layperson like myself.

338

"Title VII prohibits a covered employer from considering race when making an employment decision, whether the race be Black or White." (Schwartz).

However, under the colorblind premise, "A law designed to benefit a traditionally disadvantaged racial minority would be seen as unfair special interest legislation. The colorblind vision holds that discrimination against minorities and women is no worse than discrimination against White males; affirmative action in any form is prohibited; and reverse discrimination claims are fully embraced. It is the colorblind theory, however, that has dominated Supreme Court doctrine in affirmative action cases." (Schwartz).

I quickly realized that these laws were designed by the dominant culture, with loopholes, for employers to hide behind and escape racial discrimination complaints in the eyes of the law. This colorblindness "Theory is a very effective strategy for preventing the truly harmful sort of discrimination, the oppression of one race by another." (Schwartz).

Reading this information was a bitter pill to swallow, but this is the reality that we all must live with.

"Racial/ethnic minorities in the United States face high levels of segregation in their employment opportunities, and in some cases such segregation implies an exclusion from better jobs, thus reducing their labor market opportunities." (Gradin, 2012).

Based on the number of times I was denied promotions over the years and the lack of African American men in supervisory, management, and administrative positions at my employer, I felt there was another agenda in play, even more insidious than racial discrimination.

It is my contention that the Municipal Hospital Systems Human Resource Department and several departmental hiring managers also acted in collusion against me. To quote the definition of the law, "Collusion occurs when two persons or representatives of an entity or organization make an agreement to deceive or mislead another. Such agreements are usually secretive and involve fraud or gaining an unfair advantage over a third party." (USLegal). This is exactly what happened to me. HR and management representatives within the Municipal Hospital System entity deceived and misled me. Furthermore, research has shown that "Black males with relatively high educational attainment are disproportionately distributed into lower-paying managerial and professional occupations" within their occupational sector. (Austin, 2011).

It is my belief Municipal Hospital System is guilty of "occupational sorting," which is the practice of steering Black men into lower-paying jobs, which, in effect, is a form of wage fixing. Labor market collusion is an anti-trust law infraction which is illegal. When H.R. representatives collude with hiring managers to occupationally segregate Black men into low-paying positions and also deny them promotional opportunities, they break the law.

"Minorities employed in the health care sector work in lower-skilled health care occupations such as nursing assistant and home health care aid." (Gabard, 2007). This finding is consistent with previous research by (Queneau 2006), "That minorities are over-represented in the lowest compensating health care occupations."

340

Employment and salary data will support the fact that (with the exception of doctors) there are no African-American men earning six-figure salaries at Municipal Hospital System. The next salary tier of $80K to $99K still will not produce one African-American male. This is because we have been barred from entering senior management and administration. This form of labor market collusion in wage/salary setting is unlawful. It has resulted in African-American males suffering reduced compensation because of racial discrimination and collusive employment practices.

I have always received encouragement from my employer. My superiors, hiring managers, and HR representatives have all encouraged and supported me during my struggle to obtain a master's degree. They made me believe that a master's degree was the key to my career advancement.

But all along, they knew they would never promote me. They deceived and misled me, which caused me to suffer severe wage suppression. They secretly agreed never to promote a Black male into a management position at Municipal Hospital System because they acted in collusion. "These actions are usually surreptitious, either because they are illegal under anti-trust laws or because they are intended to be kept secret from the victims." (Carter, 1978).

The law further states that parties in collusion against a third party have agreed to limit open competition by deceiving, misleading, or defrauding others of their legal rights. This part of the law also applies to me since my employer misled me into believing I was openly competing for the many positions I applied for. My employer blatantly defrauded me of my legal right to equally compete for a promotion by colluding and discriminating against me.

All of the female and White male employees with a master's degree in Health Care Administration are (all) high-salaried employees in senior management and Administration. "Across occupational sectors, regardless of degree requirements, Black males are underrepresented in high-wage occupations." (Austin, 2011).

My feeling is that if Black men are looked upon as the "affected group" of employees that the Municipal Hospital System has conspired against to fix wages and segregate into low-paying occupations, then they are guilty of labor market discrimination.

"Labor market discrimination is the key explanation for a racially segregated labor market that systematically crowds Black men into low-paying, less desirable jobs and out of high-paying, more desirable jobs." (Austin, 2011).

Over the past (10) years, I have spoken to various individuals throughout the Municipal Hospital System. Some female co-workers promoted into management told me they started out as clerks and worked their way up through the ranks. I've also talked with some of my White male counterparts who have progressed up through the ranks into administration. Some had advanced degrees, and some did not. The common thread among them was that early on in their careers, one of their superiors gave them an opportunity to advance. None of them stayed in a non-management position for eight years, as I have. They were allowed to develop, learn, and grow in various positions and then expelled.

BRILLIANT MINDS, IGNORANT MINDS

At my director's retirement party, they teased her about only having a high school diploma. Everyone laughed. But the point of the story was that she made the most of the "chances" she was given. African-American men never get those chances!!! The message was clear: hard work, dedication, an advanced degree, and perseverance are the keys to career advancement. I made up my mind I would follow the same model and plot my course for career success. It took plenty of hard work and dedication, enrolling in graduate school, supporting my co-workers, learning all aspects of my job, volunteer service, writing a healthcare article for a major publication, enrolling in the Obama "workforce development program, and persevering. After completing this, I continued to apply for all suitable promotional positions. I knew I was an African-American male, so I had to outwork my competition. But no matter how hard I worked, none of the Municipal Hospital System hiring managers would hire me.

In my opinion, what is happening to me is obviously a case of "collusive employment practice." An unspoken and secretive tacit agreement exists between the HR department and the various hiring managers within the hospital. This agreement is designed to collude against and racially discriminate against Black men who are seeking promotional opportunities in management and administrative positions. I believe that this tacit agreement has purposely barred me from promotions over the past eight years, in spite of the fact that I possess a bachelor's in Business administration and a master's in Healthcare administration. Individuals with my same credentials or less are employed in management and/or administration, earning at least twice my salary and more. This is a clear violation of the law because the goal of this secretive agreement was to collude and bar Black men from entering into management positions. I am of the opinion that my employer is guilty of collusive employment practices.

As far as gender is concerned, I have a healthy respect for women. I personally harbor no malice or ill-will towards women. I have a wife, mother, daughter, aunts and a host of multi-cultural women I work with on a daily basis. Municipal Hospital System leadership has done a masterful job in integrating successful and intelligent women into their workforce over the years. I applaud their efforts. A finding from a study by "Huffman, Cohen, and Pearlman (2010) shows that the greater the share of female managers, the greater the gender integration of non-managerial workers overtime." (Skaggs, 2012).

"The presence of women in high-level positions not only creates opportunities for similar others at lower levels through hiring, recruitment, and promotions but also has the effect of reducing discriminatory practices that keep women out of management." (Skaggs, 2012).

This female-friendly environment has created an atmosphere that encourages female hiring managers and human resource professionals to hire "similar other" female candidates.

Unfortunately, this evolution of female diversity is oftentimes bias towards Black men. In my opinion, female hiring managers require additional diversity training to realize there are qualified African-American male candidates within the pool of applicants.

More importantly, a cursory interview will not be enough. For God's Sake, It's 2013. It's time to actually "HIRE" and promote qualified Black men into management and administrative positions so that we can also be integrated into the Municipal Hospital System culture on levels equal to White men, just as women have. A reality in our society and workplace is that "Black males live in a sexist society, and a sexist culture, that doesn't allow Black males to express themselves," (Feagin, 1998). This culture causes a lot of problems for Black men, including oppression and racism, but even more importantly, being denied career development and advancement. It's what I would characterize as reverse gender bias against Black men.

According to a study conducted by Tulane University sociologist Dr. James Elliot and City University of New York professor Dr. Ryan A. Smith, "Racial and gender inequality are alive and well in U.S. workplaces. Black men with the same skills as White men are only half as likely to rise from supervisor to manager," provided the Black men even get to a supervisory level occupation. (Cox, 2004). Their findings also "Suggest that race and gender are not separate sources of discrimination but compound each other in limiting access to power and promotion. Elliot and Smith found that superiors are much more likely to fill positions of power with subordinates of the same race and sex as themselves. This tendency toward in-group favoritism is stronger in filling higher-level managerial positions than in filling lower-level supervisory positions." (Cox, 2004). This practice supports the theory that superiors often participate in "collusive employment practices" against qualified African-American male candidates who are also striving to advance their careers.

Hiring practices that treat all employees equally (especially African-American men) will make our institutions more diverse and stronger. This is a good thing, but unfortunately, even today, in the year 2013, "White

Americans continue to express support for negative stereotypes of minority groups in surprisingly large numbers, even though few of these individuals would identify themselves as bigoted or racist." (Smedley, 2003).

In 2004, a labor market study examined the effect of "Black-sounding" names (like Jamal Jones or Lakisha Washington) on receiving a positive response from employers. "Researchers sent out similar resumes with "Black-sounding" and "White-sounding" names to employers in Chicago and Boston. Resumes with "White-sounding" names received 50 percent more callbacks for interviews.

Similar studies using actual working individuals as a sample have returned similar results. In Milwaukee, Black and White males applied for jobs and presented similar qualifications in comparable ways. The White males received a higher rate of callbacks. In this study, half of the time, the males indicated they had a criminal record. The results showed that although ex-offenders received a lower rate of callbacks, White ex-offenders had a callback rate equal to Blacks without a criminal record. The study was replicated in New York City and returned the same results." (Bertrand, 2004). It was very troubling to learn that 'Whites' resistance to racial change reflects their perception that Blacks pose real and tangible threats to their personal lives, to their neighborhoods, their jobs, their children's education, and their safety." (Kinder, 2010)

Unfortunately, the results of these findings are still prevalent today. After reading these studies, I remembered a few years ago when Municipal Hospital System sent secret shoppers to evaluate patient care and customer service. I wonder what would have been revealed about our own culture had the secret shoppers been deployed to the Human Resources department like in the Milwaukee experiment.

SUMMARY

Racial discrimination has been thrust into the mainstream with President Obama's comments about the Zimmerman verdict, the U.S. Attorney General's comments about the Justice system, a Cheerios T.V. commercial, a U.S. Federal Judge's ruling that repealed the "Stop-and-Frisk" policies in New York City, and most recently the 50th Anniversary of Dr. King's March on Washington. Racial issues are alive and well in our everyday society.

Three presidents effectively reflected years of turmoil in the civil rights movement in a ceremony for the 50th anniversary of the March on Washington, where Dr. Martin Luther King gave his historic "I Have a Dream" speech. President Obama urged everyone in the crowd to become a modern-day marcher for racial harmony and economic justice. President Carter, the White Southerner who appointed more African-Americans to high-ranking positions than any of his predecessors, said, "In truth, Dr. King helped to free all people." "This march, and that speech, changed America," President Clinton declared, remembering the impact on the world and himself as a young man.

In the wake of the Zimmerman verdict and the Trayvon Martin killing, President Obama talked about being racially profiled and being followed when shopping in a department store. "He expressed his concerns about the welfare of African-American boys and wondered if business leaders, local politicians, clergy, celebrities, and athletes could collectively figure out how we could do a better job helping African-American men feel that they're a full part of this society and that there are pathways and avenues for them to succeed." He also expressed apprehension about convening a conversation about race. He feels that it may not be particularly productive since these kinds of conversations end up being stilted and politicized because folks are locked into positions they already have.

The United States Attorney General Eric Holder addressed the American Bar Association. The essence of his message was that the American Legal system, as it currently stands, "Our system is in too many respects, is broken." He implored the legal community to "Identify those areas we can improve in order to better advance the cause of justice for all Americans." I would certainly characterize Human Rights as a part of the legal justice system, and I believe that Mr. Holder's comments are also germane to my complaint and overall point of view.

Just look at the controversy surrounding the recently aired Cheerios commercial that featured a bi-racial family with an African-American dad, a Caucasian mom, and a bi-racial child. This ad led to a barrage of racist and offensive remarks on social media. It's unfortunate and very troubling, but many White Americans were very uncomfortable with this commercial and the revelation that the father of the little girl was a Black Man. The VP of marketing for General Mills, Camille Gibson, said, "We were trying to portray an American family, and there are lots of multicultural families in America today."

Time magazine columnist Eric Liu stated, "Our inherited and often unspoken notions about the U.S.'s fundamental Whiteness, about the alienness of brown and yellow skin, about the indelible stigma of Blackness, all are falling away, their adherents dying off. To be sure, we are not beyond race in the U.S. A glance at how power flows in any institution still reminds us that race matters, and darkness disadvantages." (Liu, 2013). I must say that I'm not sure I share Mr. Liu's optimism that the indelible stigma of Blackness is falling away. It's 2013, with the election of a bi-racial president, we're supposed to be living in a post-racial society. That being said, in my opinion, we still have a long way to go to achieve racial equality in our workplaces and in our nation as a whole.

U.S. District Court Judge Shira Scheindlin ruled that the New York City Police Department's stop-and-frisk tactic was unconstitutional. Police officers would decide who is suspicious based on race. Approximately 90 percent of the individuals stopped and frisked were Black and Hispanic men. This practice is a direct violation of the Fourth and Fourteenth Amendments. Judge Scheinlin said, "The stop-and-frisk tactic was indirect racial profiling."

These are not my words. These occurrences are well-documented facts. Unfortunately, racial discrimination has permeated our entire society. It is painfully obvious to me that our system of hiring and promoting minorities is also broken. There are many highly educated and talented African-American men, myself especially, that remain under-employed because of the color of our skin. This is fundamentally wrong on all levels. "Despite the decline of overt racism, systemic racial bias remains a subtle yet stubborn problem in American Society." (Levinson, 2012). "Nearly 90 percent of U.S. occupations can be categorized as racially segregated." (Austin, 2011).

I am not an individual that will allow this situation to stand!!! I'm going to fight against what I fundamentally believe is an injustice perpetrated against me because of my race and sex.

As I write these words, I can't help but imagine myself working on some hospital policy document or project management report for a colleague or administrator. Researching a discrimination complaint was the farthest thing from my mind. Up until a few months ago, I could never have imagined it. I was rocked to my core as I read through document after document of discrimination studies and analysis. It was unbelievable!!! I guess to say I was naïve about racial discrimination in the workplace would be an understatement. Racial discrimination couldn't be happening to me??? I was in complete denial. I've worked hard and studied hard. I couldn't believe that in the year 2013, I was being denied promotion after promotion because I am a Black Man. The empirical data presented here is absolute proof that I am a victim of workforce discrimination and collusive employment practices. The law states that because there are successful African-American "WOMEN" employed in administrative and managerial positions throughout the Municipal Hospital System, it is not a racist or discriminatory environment. The law does not recognize discrimination against African-American "MEN."

To this law, I would tell all Black men to "Stand Your Ground" and continue to fight against the discriminatory practices against us. "The economic marginalization of African American men has been studied in a variety of contexts, from joblessness to disparate wages and mobility. The prevalence of discriminatory firing, with ongoing racial harassment and discriminatory promotional and hiring practices, are quite evident in the workplaces in this country." (Mong, 2010).

I don't know what the future holds for me. I imagine at some point; I will be forced out of this job because I have the same career aspirations as the many women and White men that I work with. Only time will tell. I do know that having battled racism throughout my healthcare career,

I have to wonder, as I watch events unfold, how this wonderful nation can overcome its obsession with skin color. This bias against African-American men must stop. We need to learn to work together. If we are to survive, we will have to figure out how to get it right. Difficult discussions on these issues are necessary to effectively deal with the racism that exists within and among us. The fight is more challenging now with 24-hour television news coverage and radio talk shows that often seem designed to promote division and hate. When the public debate is poisoned by polarizing and hurtful speech and behavior, the work is more complex but just as necessary.

Finally, the overall goal of this document is to bring to light the egregious practice of labor market collusion, which I am a victim of, in addition to racial discrimination. My employer, Municipal Hospital System, has adopted these illegal practices and victimized African-American men for years. I respectfully request assistance from the Division of Human Rights to prove these allegations.

Thank you,

Miles M. Livingston

Miles M. Livingston

I ended the letter with a reference page so he knew I wasn't playing around.

I felt as though I had to take a deep dive into this protected class law and educate myself about this whole discrimination arena I had entered. I was pumped. I wanted the NYSDHR Director to understand my point of view concerning this matter. I was compelled to write a follow-up letter to him.

The NYS Division of Human Rights ended up agreeing with me. They found "Probable Cause," which led them to decide not to dismiss my case. This was all the fuel I needed to fight this battle. I had a legal entity on my side. For the first time, I'd been validated.

I finished the year 2013 by applying for more positions.

The Essence of Discrimination

As I was writing my rebuttal letters and living through that entire experience, I couldn't help but think about the movie *Philadelphia* and the scene where Tom Hanks and Denzel Washington were sitting in the Law Library reading from a law book.

"The essence of discrimination is formulating opinions about others not based on the individual merits, but rather on their membership in a group with assumed characteristics." –The Rehabilitation Act of 1973

That statement described my case to a tee. My employer formulated an opinion about me that was *not* based on my merits, graduate degree, or intelligence. They did not consider the fact that I was a published author or any other accomplishment I achieved while in their employ. The decision on whether or not I was qualified or not to advance was based on my membership in a group. I am an African American man, and members of my group are not allowed into management. At the time of my discrimination suit, there were no African American men as managers or Administrators, so Municipal Hospital felt that they had to continue the status quo and keep Black men out of high-salaried management positions.

It was a sad but true realization that my employer sanctioned this type of behavior, and I was the employee who had to bear the brunt of their racial discrimination. As I mentioned before, I struggled with the fact that so many African-American women were on the opposite side of this equation. I was just one lonely Black Man standing up to the establishment. I was a nobody to them. I understood they were all very successful Black women with career aspirations and families to support. It was just disappointing for me that they were unable to see the big picture of racism against Black men.

I've read somewhere that African American women have multiple identities. The Black woman is a mother, a wife, a sister, a daughter, as well as being a boss at work. She's an administrator, a manager, a Vice President, a Senator, a Legislator, a Congresswoman, a School Board President or member, a PTA member, a Doctor, a Lawyer, etc., etc., etc. She can wear all of these hats, but being Black happens to be one of the identities that she has, and it's an identity that is not very high on her priority list. Don't get me wrong. They are strong and proud to be Black, but inside Corporate America, when she has to deal with Black Men, her Blackness is suddenly not much of a priority. I understand that she's got to do what she's got to do. Support her family, get that next promotion at work, increase her income, and lead her multi-cultural and multi-racial teams at work. The Black woman is an expert in the execution of her duties. She knows how to move in boardrooms led and run by White men.

Black men don't have the chance to get that far. However, where Black women are being praised, Black men are being blocked by a corporate world that is dead set against them. We are underpaid and overworked. Our ambitions are blocked at every turn. And with all that working against us, you would think that Black women would be looking to help elevate us as a sign of unity. In my experience, nothing could be further from the truth. As a Black Man, you're on an island all by yourself.

It's a Catch-22 situation. I realize Black women have to protect their paychecks. But all Black men are asking for is to acknowledge our struggle. We're running the same race. I don't understand why Black women can't do more to give us a leg up. The powerful Black women that I have encountered in the workplace have all turned their backs on me.

Don't get me wrong. I never asked for a handout, and I'm not asking for one now. It's just that I've seen how other races work to help each other out while we remain divided. In my observations, I feel like I'm their enemy when I should be an ally. We should all be working together.

Instead, I'm perceived as a threat. By both Black women and White men, and that perception has kept me from advancing. I expected it from the White folks. Never from my own. Never from the women that we're supposed to love and protect.

It's hard out here for African American men, and all I'm saying is that we would appreciate some workplace support, especially when we are qualified to handle the job!

The Question of Racial and Gender Discrimination

My employer's attorney, Gladstone Mitchell, made a salient and reoccurring comment in his depositions and rebuttals against me. "The Law, when distilled to its essence," does not recognize Black Men specifically. It speaks to the African American race of people." He went on to mention fifteen to twenty women with their names and ages in his rebuttal to make his point that my employer does not discriminate as if to say, "There's no discrimination here. Look at all these Black women who have flourished in their roles."

I responded by pointing out that therein lies my point. In Gladstone Mitchell's listing of successful African Americans within the company, there were no men of African descent. Not a single one had "flourished" at this job. The sad part for me is that the attorney who was defending my employer was Black. I know that the rule of law has no color, but does this Black Attorney honestly believe that men like Martin Luther King or Frederick Douglas or any of the countless Black men through history who fought and (some) died to combat racism in this country didn't fight for all of us? Black men and women? Give me a break! They would all be turning over in their graves to see how Black men have been marginalized and held back in today's society. The ignorance of that law is clear in that it excluded African American men from protection. Once again, the brilliant legal minds crafted the law to identify all women as minorities. In that way, they can use African American women to meet both the racial and gender criteria for discriminatory purposes. To add insult to injury, the attorney knew that he could prove his case because the Black women hired by the hospital had flourished, and since everyone was focused on just the racial aspect, he could argue that discrimination was not an issue. The ignorant minds do not care about Black men and the discrimination laws. They have failed to see the ramifications of ignoring us. These legal minds are brilliant and ignorant, and we can see the impact of their decisions on our society today.

Why would legislators pass a law that benefits women and is biased toward Black men? Only brilliant/ignorant minds could answer why they would construct a law that benefits other people of the global majority over Black men. It obviously demonstrates the hatred and animus against Black men because we are not treated equally.

Long story short, when I, as a Black Man, claimed discrimination against my employer, I was quickly told that African American Men were *not* a protected class and that there were several African Americans in management positions at my job. I didn't understand what they were trying to say. After all, I was an African American man, and I was being discriminated against for that.

The attorney for my employer stated that several African American women have been promoted into management and have done very well for themselves and, therefore, they were not discriminating against Blacks. While reading the rebuttal to my discrimination complaint, I couldn't understand why the defense council kept harping on women. In particular, Black women. Did he not understand my grievance that no Black men were part of management? Did he even read my complaint? I had to educate myself to understand this law about protected class.

It was a real eye-opener. I quickly understood why discrimination cases like mine are almost impossible to win. The laws favor women. That's how they were written. As a Black Man, there are no protections that exist for us. The attorney knows he doesn't even have to address my concern of being a Black Man who has been wronged. He only has to prove that Blacks were hired into management. That's the law.

With that kind of faulty logic and legal precedence, they were able to win their case. The message was clear: as an employer (in corporate America), they don't have to treat Black Men fairly. They only have to treat women fairly and "Fuck You" Black men, and there's nothing you can do about it. It's the law. Again, the brilliant legal minds that legislated this law were ignorant about the effects this law would have on African American men. Or were they?

I received the "Final Investigation Report and Basis of Determination" four months later. It was a seven-page document:

NEW YORK STATE
DIVISION OF HUMAN RIGHTS

MILES M. LIVINGSTON   -   Complainant

-vs.-

MUNICIPAL HOSPITAL   -   Respondent

DETERMINATION AFTER
INVESTIGATION

Case No. 123XXX456
Federal Charge No. 987XYZ654ABC

On 04/08/2013, Miles M. Livingston filed a verified complaint with the New York State Division of Human Rights ("Division"), charging the above-named Respondent with an unlawful discriminatory practice relating to employment because of age, race/color, sex in violation of N.Y. Exec. Law, art. 15 ("Human Rights Law").

After investigation, the Division has determined that it has jurisdiction in this matter and that **PROBABLE CAUSE** exists to believe that the Respondent has engaged in or is engaging in the unlawful discriminatory practice complained of.

Pursuant to the Human Rights Law, this matter is recommended for public hearing. The parties will be advised of further proceedings.

VERNON M. O'GARRA

Dated: *August 26, 2013,*

New York

To reiterate, the Determination, signed by the Regional Director of the New York State Division of Human Rights, stated that there was **<u>PROBABLE CAUSE</u>** to support the allegations of the complaint. Those big, bold letters were never so beautiful. It was a huge step for me, and I was ecstatic. The idea of sticking it to my employer had my adrenaline pumping.

10

Flawed Legislation

"Our struggle is not the struggle of a day, a week, a month, or a year, it is the struggle of a lifetime."

–John Lewis

The entire year passed before I finally got a court date. I had been working every day wearing a proverbial "Mask" to keep up appearances and stay out of trouble. I was still consistently interviewing for positions as well. I joined a professional healthcare organization. I attended conferences, volunteered my services and expertise, and read and studied several healthcare journals. While keeping up the façade that everything was business as usual, I chose to make myself a better healthcare professional. For me, this wasn't just a job. This was my career. I also enjoyed traveling and attending conferences. It was refreshing to meet other healthcare professionals from other states. There were only a few African American men, but we are a very strong select few with similar journeys. We were hard workers dedicated to our respective companies. And we worked just as hard or harder than anyone else. We loved our careers.

NEW YORK STATE
DIVISION OF HUMAN RIGHTS

NEW YORK STATE DIVISION OF
HUMAN RIGHTS on the Complaint
of

MILES M. LIVINGSTON,

Complainant,

vs.

NOTICE OF HEARING
Case No. 9999000XB

NOTICE OF HEARING
Case No. 9999000XB

PLEASE TAKE NOTICE that, pursuant to Section 297 of the New York State Human Rights

Law (N.Y. Executive Law, Article 15), the above-referenced matter has been officially scheduled for a public hearing before **Magistrate Judge**, an Administrative Law Judge of

New York State Division of Human Rights to determine the charges of unlawful discriminatory practices alleged in the verified complaint filed in this case.

The public hearing has been scheduled as follows:

Date(s): Mon 5/23/2014 – Tue 5/24/2014
Time: 9:00 AM – 5:00 PM
Place: NYS Division of Human Rights

The first hour of the first hearing day may be considered a preliminary conference, at which the parties should be prepared to discuss the legal and factual issues in the case, should present all documentary evidence in their control which is to be offered in evidence, and should provide a list of proposed witnesses, with explanation of their identity and the scope of their knowledge of the facts of the case. 9 N.Y.C.R.R. § 465.12(h). Please note that documents should not be submitted to the administrative law judge prior to the hearing.

At least two (2) business days prior to the hearing, Respondent shall, and any necessary party may, file a written answer to the complaint, sworn to and subject to the penalties of perjury, with the Administrative Law Judge and shall serve a copy upon each of the other parties to the proceeding. The answer shall contain all affirmative defenses.

Mail to the Administrative Law Judge should be addressed as follows:

Magistrate Judge, Administrative Law Judge
NYS Division of Human Rights
Anytown, New York

A failure to answer the complaint shall be deemed an admission to the allegations of the complaint; the Administrative Law Judge shall note the default and the hearing shall proceed on the evidence in support of the complaint.

All parties appearing at the public hearing shall be allowed to present evidence in accordance with the Rules of Practice of the Division (9 N.Y.C.R.R. § 465).

If upon all the evidence at the hearing, the Commissioner finds that respondent has engaged in an unlawful discriminatory practice as defined in the New York State Human Rights Law (N.Y. Executive Law, Article 15), the Commissioner will issue an order against Respondent, as **provided** for by Section 297 of the New York State Human Rights Law, requiring such Respondent to cease and desist from such unlawful discriminatory practice and to take such actions as in the judgment of the Commissioner will effectuate the purposes of the law. This may include the payment of monetary damages and/or civil fines and penalties.

Requests for adjournments must be in writing to the Administrative Law Judge assigned to the case, <u>with a copy to all parties.</u>

No adjournment of the public hearing shall be granted except for actual engagement before a higher tribunal or for other good cause shown. <u>Please be advised that settlement discussions do not constitute good cause.</u>

Dated: April 3, 2014

Anytown, New York

Yours truly,
Chief Calendar Clerk

Flawed Legislation. It reflects the flaws in the Constitution, Declaration of Independence, and Bill of Rights, all written by the slave-owning forefathers of the United States. The laws in this country were designed to uphold White dominance and Black subjugation. This is the essence of Critical Race Theory. For those unfamiliar with it, Critical Race Theory (CRT) is an academic field of study at the college level, designed to teach students the full scope of our American history rather than the whitewashed version many of us learned. In my view, the contribution of CRT lies in highlighting that the founding fathers of the United States supported slavery, and the laws they crafted were intended to maintain political, economic, and social dominance over Black slaves. That's it in a nutshell. It's not rocket science.

"This normalization of expected, race-based practices in employment, housing, and education makes the racism that fuels it look ordinary and natural, to such a degree that oppression no longer seems like oppression to the perpetrators." (Taylor, 1998).

What is Critical Race Theory, and where did it come from? A group of esteemed scholars comprised of law professors and students from Harvard School of Law also discovered that: "Flawed legislation" existed within the laws that governed our society. They uncovered that "Racism in the law" was the governing factor written into a myriad of legislation that was passed in the United States. CRT's mission is to recognize and bring to light that there are racial disparities written into law, and they want to create a framework to rectify this problem. CRT scholars sought "To understand how a regime of White supremacy and its subordination of people of color have been created and maintained in America." (Parker, 2003).

"Critical Race Theory, as a critique of racism in the law and society, emerged as an outgrowth of the critical legal studies movement that took place at Harvard Law School in the early 80s. The law professors and students in this group began to question the objective rationalist nature of the law and the process of adjudication in the U.S. legal system. They criticized the way in which the real effects of the law served to privilege the wealthy and powerful (Whites) in U.S. society while having a deleterious impact on the rights of the poor " especially African Americans.

This working group of legal scholars argued that "The law, particularly civil rights law of the 1960s, was targeted to combat classical racism, the type of racism characterized by overt acts, such as grossly offensive behavior toward others, legal segregation, and discrimination or acts of racial violence," like lynchings, beatings and rapes of Black people. (Parker, 2003). Civil Rights Law was important, but it didn't address the subtle actions associated with everyday racism. "Like nonverbal exchanges and societal practices that maintain racism firmly in place. Furthermore, everyday racism is incessant and communicative and is seen in everyday actions by individuals and groups as well as institutional policies and administrative practices." (Parker, 2003). Racism remains alive and well in America "Not because of some philosophical contradiction between equality and justice but simply because the larger social order was willing to tolerate and accept racial inequality and inequity." (Parker, 2003).

One example of racial disparities written into law is the National Interstate and Defense Highways Act of 1956, signed by President Eisenhower. The federal government subsidized the construction of the interstate highway system, and these highways were frequently built through Black neighborhoods, many of which were physically destroyed in the process. Some local officials deliberately used highways to separate Black and White neighborhoods, reinforcing residential segregation (Ware, 2021). This is a clear example of how racially motivated laws were used not only to discriminate against Black people but also to economically harm them. Under Eisenhower, these practices were sanctioned and subsidized by the federal government.

The Supreme Court Plessy v. Ferguson decision "provided the foundation for a system of segregation and exclusion that adversely affected African Americans throughout the twentieth century." The ruling itself established the doctrine of "Separate but equal," meaning that racial segregation was legally permissible as long as the separate facilities for Black and White people were supposedly equal in quality. In reality, this often led to Black Americans being provided with inferior services, facilities, and opportunities in nearly every aspect of life, from education and transportation to housing and employment. This decision entrenched racial discrimination and inequality, shaping the social and economic landscape of the United States for decades.

During the 1940s and 1950s, the federal government facilitated the construction of suburban communities with the Veterans Administration and Federal Housing Authority-insured mortgages. These agencies invented redlining and required lending institutions to insert racially restrictive covenants in deeds for properties they insured." (Ware, 2021). Plessy did not directly cause residential segregation, but it did legitimize the laws, customs, and practices that established the Jim Crow regime." (Ware, 2021). These so-called laws, customs, and practices lead to present-day redlining, mortgage predatory lending, unfair home appraisals, schools, and a host of other racially motivated laws and infractions against

Black people. This climate of racial injustice was perpetuated by a system of White privilege that failed to correct this unjust legislation.

"For more than half of the twentieth century, policymakers at the federal, state, and local levels pursued development strategies that had a devastating effect on African American families. These policies included redlining, restrictive covenants, the interstate highway system, urban renewal, and exclusionary zoning. Federal housing policies barred Black families from the largest wealth-producing program in the nation's history—single-family homes in suburban communities. In 2016, the median Black family wealth was $13,460, less than 10 percent of their counterpart's $142,180 White family wealth. Slightly more than 25 percent of Blacks had no or negative wealth, relative to only a little more than 10 percent of Whites." (Ware, 2021).

"Segregation is a tool used to promote and preserve White supremacy. Racial separation makes it easier to isolate, surveil, and police Black people concentrated in inner-city communities. Plessy v. Ferguson provided the legal foundation for a discriminatory structure that continues to burden the lived experiences of African Americans to this very day." (Ware, 2021).

There are other examples of race-based law-making in the United States that warrant review. Historically Black Colleges and Universities are consistently underfunded throughout the United States. "The Supreme Court's decision in Brown v. Board of Education outlawing segregation in public schools has had a negligible impact on longstanding practices of unequal funding of publicly operated state universities. Today, by any measure, Black colleges and universities in many states continue to receive significantly less funding than their predominantly White sister institutions." (Sav, 1997).

"A federal lawsuit alleges that the state of Georgia, along with other states, has failed to fund its three public historically Black colleges and universities at the same levels of other institutions in the state's University System." "The suit came after federal officials told Georgia and 15 other states in '2023 that they had underfunded their land-grant HBCUs by more than $12 billion in recent decades in comparison with their non-HBCU land-grant peers." (The Atlanta Journal, 2023).

"Sundown towns" were not uncommon across the Midwest. In some cases, signs were posted at city limits warning African Americans that they were not welcome at night (Loewen 2006). In other towns, it was simply understood that Blacks were not welcome after sundown." "Interestingly, Asians and Hispanics may be accepted in towns that remained sundown toward Blacks. Also, as a side note, Highland Park, Texas, former home to President George W. Bush and Vice President Dick Cheney, was a sundown town until 2003." (Loewen 2006). It's unbelievable that this law remained on the books in Texas until 2003, and both former President Bush and Vice President Dick Cheney were unaware and did nothing to eradicate such a vicious and racially motivated law.

My point here is not to give a Black history lesson. My point is to highlight the rationale behind Critical Race Theory. This is the world we live in. This is our combined history, White and Black. As a Black Man, I find myself fighting racial discrimination as I coexist with my Caucasian brothers and sisters who enjoy their White privilege. America is a country that has "in effect, two criminal justice systems: one for

Whites and another for Blacks."(Ware, 2021). There is certainly enough proof in our history to validate that there are racial disparities written into law. Banning books about African American history and removing dialogue about race inside the classroom will do nothing but inflame the situation, making racial tensions worse. We should not underestimate the intelligence of our young, multicultural array of future leaders. For example, consider the number of White citizens, both young and old, who joined the George Floyd protests. I witnessed several protests where White participants outnumbered Black participants, which was remarkable. This showed me that many White people not only understand the realities of racism but are also willing to stand in solidarity with marginalized communities. They are open to engaging in meaningful conversations about race relations in America and are committed to working towards a more inclusive and equitable society. This willingness to learn and advocate for change is a promising sign for the future of race relations in our country.

Now that 'Critical Race Theory' has entered mainstream conversation, the dominant power brokers throughout the country are attempting to shut it down. In my opinion, the critics of CRT, led by Florida Governor Ron DeSantis, have overreacted. DeSantis wants to prohibit colleges and universities in his state from having programs on diversity, equity and inclusion, and critical race theory. "Several Republican lawmakers have proposed new bills regulating the discussion of race in the classroom. Twenty-six states have either proposed legislation, taken other measures to restrict the teaching of CRT or placed restrictions on how instructors can address racism and sexism in the classroom (Parker, 2003).

"The attack on CRT is evidence of the ways the system of White privilege attempts to silence those who experience racism and to attribute innocence to those who are active or complicit participants." (Parker, 2003). Critical Race Theory is nothing more than truth-telling. Racism and Bigotry is woven into the fabric of American history, so obviously, this phenomenon affects our laws. Why not explore, fix, and improve these legislative problems?

As American citizens, we must face facts objectively, as "The law serves to rationalize the wealthy and powerful in U.S. society." That's just how it is. Many of the Founding Fathers of America were slave owners, and the laws in this country were initially written to protect the rights of White male landowners, not enslaved people or other marginalized groups.

An important aspect of Critical Race Theory is the understanding that in America, "The sociological myth of racial categories is a powerful primary socialization tool that has a tremendous impact on social perceptions, social status, and social identity of all societal members. Racial categorization is a part of our cognitive psychological thinking." (Parker, 2003).

This is a very powerful theory. The bottom line is that we as a society must learn from our past and stop perpetuating the sins of our forefathers. CRT strives to bring to light and correct the injustices of racial discrimination, which will undoubtedly make us a stronger and more inclusive society.

The primary issue with CRT is not whether it exists or not. It's quite evident that it exists. The problem is how we add it to the dialogue of

American Society. Don't we want our children to learn the truth about American history?

That's the Ten Million Dollar Question.

I recently watched an interview with billionaire Elon Musk. He was asked about his comments about the Duke University Medical School's D.E.I. program. The Duke University Chronicle newspaper reported that derogatory D.E.I. "Allegations were recently repeated by billionaire Elon Musk, who replied to Ben Shapiro's thread that "People will die because of this," referring to the alleged new standards. In a recent interview with former CNN host Don Lemon, the Tesla and SpaceX CEO said that "they have literally lowered the standards at Duke University" in an exchange on whether DEI policies in medicine harm patients. (Lu, 2024).

"The Duke University Chronicle newspaper reported that "Duke University's School of Medicine has not lowered its standards for medical school admission or graduation, and continues to rely on GPA and MCAT scores, among other criteria," the Duke Health statement read.

This story captured my interest for two reasons. First, I could have been a DEI student or hire. Second, these two influential White men feel so negatively about DEI. As a Black male minority, I became a healthcare professional, but I could have also pursued a career in law or medicine.

What these influential White men fail to realize is that most minority candidates, myself included, have already gone through and passed the most rigorous and challenging academic criteria just to get our proverbial foot in the door. Duke would be fortunate to admit a potential African American male med-student. Because of the racial discrimination we endure, he was likely at the top of all his classes just to earn a seat next to the mediocre legacy of White men and White women in the class.

There is no good reason to attack DEI programs. A properly run DEI program does not lower standards. It delivers the best of the best African American students and/or job candidates. We enter our roles at various universities and Corporate American companies with superior expertise. We bring not only diversity but excellence to our chosen fields. We are not "Token Hires." We are extremely qualified men and women from diverse backgrounds with impeccable credentials. We bring value to our respective organizations and make them better. It's deplorable that a Billionaire business leader like Elon Musk, who employs thousands of people, totally missed the concept of diversity, equity, and inclusion. His mind is brilliant about building businesses, but his mind is ignorant about the power and credibility diversity can bring to his businesses.

What D.E.I. detractors and White male industry leaders don't understand or realize is that the initial spirit of Affirmative Action, Diversity, and Diversity Equity and Inclusion (D.E.I.) programs was to integrate the Lilly White sectors of Corporate America that run the country. African Americans, especially Black men, have been segregated out of administrative and leadership employment opportunities within these sectors. In America, discriminatory practices were uncovered nationwide, and subsequently, affirmative action was written into law.

Properly administered D.E.I. programs allow corporations to recruit and hire the next Michael Jordan of technology, the next Bernard Shaw of journalism, the next Ben Carson of medicine, the next Susan M. Collins of economics, the next August Wilson of Stage and Theatre, the next Thurgood Marshall of Jurisprudence, the next Robert Smith of business, the next Barack Obama of Politics, the next Langston Hughes of Literature, or the next Jacob Lawrence of Art. But if Corporate America is allowed to continue the lock-out of excellence from Black people and other minorities, the entire country will feel the effect. D.E.I. is a good thing if run properly. It's not a mechanism for token or quota hires. It's not an initiative to hire only women. These D.E.I. abuses have fueled anti-D.E.I. actions from both politicians and industry leaders.

A correctly implemented D.E.I. program examines industry leadership through a racial equity lens. The era of all-White CEOs, board members, management teams, and administrative teams is over. These positions of corporate leadership must be integrated with qualified African American men and others because diversity fosters innovation, improves decision-making, and reflects the diverse customer base and workforce of America, ultimately strengthening American industry.

During the 50s and 60s, the women's movement took hold, and the civil rights movement was in full force. However, it's important to remember that figures like Frederick Douglass, Martin Luther King Jr., Malcolm X, Marcus Garvey, Stokely Carmichael, H. Rap Brown, Bobby Seale, Thurgood Marshall, Medgar Evers, Muhammad Ali, and many other influential African American men weren't just advocating for women.

They were primarily fighting for the rights of all African Americans. While they sought equality for all Black people, including women, much of their focus was on the rights and equality of Black men, reflecting the broader social dynamics and priorities of their time.

While it is true that women in our society continue to struggle for inclusion, the Civil Rights Act of 1964 supports this struggle by protecting the rights of all enumerated protected categories: race, color, religion, sex, and national origin. Corporate America must understand that the Act mandates diversity and inclusion for all these groups.

I understand that women who have battled sexism, oppression, and unequal pay may primarily see diversity efforts as beneficial to themselves. However, corporate leadership must recognize that diversity must also include other underrepresented individuals, not just women, especially in management and leadership positions. Diversity initiatives should encompass all protected categories to (truly) reflect the spirit and intent of the Civil Rights Act of 1964.

The brilliant legislative minds of the times recognized that the Civil Rights Movement was progressing alongside the Women's Rights Movement. Courts conflated the protected categories in a way that allowed companies to meet Title VII requirements by hiring Black women while excluding Black men. This approach effectively overlooked Black men as a distinct group within the protected category of race. The Civil Rights Act of 1964 was enacted to address discrimination, but in practice, it enabled companies to diversify the workforce without truly addressing the exclusion of Black men. Consequently, companies could comply with the law by hiring Black women, thus appearing to meet diversity requirements while still sidelining Black men and not recognizing them as part of the protected category in hiring decisions.

While disparate impact analysis can be used to litigate this issue by showing that seemingly neutral employment practices disproportionately exclude Black men, it has its drawbacks. Neutral policies and employment practices, such as standardized tests, specific educational requirements, or particular hiring procedures, may appear unbiased on the surface. However, these practices can have a discriminatory effect if they disproportionately exclude certain groups, such as Black men, even without intentional bias.

To prove disparate impact, comprehensive statistical data and sophisticated analysis are required, which can be complex, time-consuming, and costly. One common method is the "Four-fifths rule," which states that a selection rate for any race, sex, or ethnic group that is less than 80% of the rate for the group with the highest rate will generally be regarded as evidence of adverse impact. For example, if 50% of White applicants are hired, but only 30% of Black applicants are hired, this would be less than 80% of the White applicant rate, indicating a potential disparate impact.

Employers can sometimes manipulate data to circumvent Title VII requirements. They might adjust hiring practices or selection criteria to ensure that they meet the minimum threshold of the four-fifths rule without genuinely addressing underlying biases. For example, they could hire a small number of Black men to create an appearance of compliance while maintaining overall practices that still favor other groups disproportionately.

In contrast, disparate treatment analysis focuses on intentional discrimination and often relies on circumstantial evidence. This can make it easier to litigate in cases where direct evidence is not available. Demonstrating disparate treatment involves using circumstantial evidence to show intentional discrimination against Black men compared to Black women, which can be more effective when explicit discriminatory actions or statements are absent.

Thus, while disparate impact analysis is valuable for uncovering systemic discrimination through neutral policies, it is less effective in achieving positive outcomes compared to disparate treatment analysis, especially in situations where clear evidence of intentional bias is lacking. This highlights the need for more inclusive and equitable hiring practices that truly reflect the intent of anti-discrimination legislation and ensure that Black men are recognized and protected as a distinct group within the protected category of race.

"Protected class" is a legal term related to anti-discrimination laws and policies. It means that employers, supervisors, and other figures are prohibited from discriminating against individuals based on their membership in specific groups. These protections extend beyond employment to areas like housing and government benefits.

Protected classes include race, national origin, color, religion, sex, age, and disability. States also have their own protected class laws, which can be more inclusive than federal statutes. For example, some state laws protect ancestry, sexual orientation, marital status, and arrest/court criminal records.

Long story short, when I, as a Black Man, claimed discrimination against my employer, I was quickly told that African American men are not a protected class and that there were several African American women in management positions at my job. At the time, I was unaware of the specifics of anti-discrimination laws, and I responded, "The point I am making is that only women and Caucasian males are part of the management team. I, as an African American man, am being discriminated against."

The legal proceedings associated with my case against the Municipal Hospital System were eye-opening, revealing how courts analyze facts and apply civil rights laws. After educating myself about the concept of protected classes and understanding how courts assess facts within anti-discrimination laws, I learned why the attorney for my employer emphasized that several African American women had been promoted into management and had done well for themselves. They argued that this demonstrated they were not discriminating against Blacks.

At the time, while reading the rebuttal to my discrimination complaint, I couldn't understand why the defense counsel kept focusing on women, particularly Black women. It became clear why discrimination cases like mine are almost impossible to win. It is not that Title VII of the Civil Rights Act favors women and provides no protections for Black men; instead, it is the interpretation of the laws by conservative judges that makes it almost impossible to prove discrimination. Defense attorneys know they don't even have to address the specific concern of a Black Man being wronged in the workplace. They only have to show that Blacks, in general, were hired into management, and the only method to counter this is through disparate impact evidence, which is difficult to uncover.

With such legal engineering by the courts creating adverse precedents, defendants like the Municipal Hospital System can win cases by settling them at a steep discount. The message was clear: as an employer, we don't have to treat Black men fairly. We only have to treat women fairly, and there's nothing Black men can do about it. It's the law. The brilliant legal minds that legislated these laws either were ignorant of the effects on African American men or perhaps were fully aware of the consequences.

Furthermore, historical context shows that governmental actions have long supported racially motivated policies and laws. This issue reflects the flawed legislation and critical race theory principles combined. According to the Economic Policy Institute, President "Woodrow Wilson not only took steps to segregate the federal civil service but set a tone that encouraged anti-Black activities across the country." (Rothstein, 2015). Since Wilson left office in 1921, the country has done very little to change the racist policies instituted during his administration.

Real estate companies across the country were particularly biased against Blacks and wielded significant power. They began re-zoning cities along racial lines, subjecting African American neighborhoods to new ordinance-designated zones earmarked for future industrial development. "Not only were these neighborhoods zoned to permit industry, even polluting industry, but taverns, liquor stores, nightclubs, and houses of prostitution were permitted to locate in African American neighborhoods but prohibited as violations of the zoning ordinance in White residential districts." (Rothstein, 2015).

As I read through this research, I said to myself, wait a minute, wasn't prostitution illegal in the 1920's? It is clear to see that governmental and state legislation was purposeful in their racially motivated approach to destroy African American communities all across the country.

Although there were a few court case victories that overturned some racially motivated efforts to maintain segregation, many cities, "Mostly in the south, ignored the court's ruling and continued to enforce racial zoning ordinances." (Rothstein, 2015). These zoning decisions significantly contributed to degrading African American neighborhoods. As the decades rolled by, many African American communities were declared "Slums" under racially targeted urban zoning maps and earmarked for demolition under the guise of urban renewal and slum clearance projects.

"Deeming Race irrelevant in law, does not make it so in life."
–Justice Ketanji Brown-Jackson

Another example of "Flawed Legislation" was the Supreme Court decision that struck down affirmative action with regard to college admissions. In the words of Justice Ketanji Brown-Jackson's dissent, "No one benefits from ignorance. Although formal race-linked legal barriers are gone, race still matters to the lived experiences of all Americans in innumerable ways, and today's ruling makes things worse, not better."

As you can imagine, I was in lock-step agreement with Supreme Court Justice Brown-Jackson's opinion. It was refreshing for me to know that someone with her encyclopedic knowledge and understanding of the law could recognize the damage this verdict could do to African Americans who wanted not only racial justice but also to attend elite universities throughout the country.

On June 29, 2023 – "The Supreme Court held that admissions programs at Harvard and the University of North Carolina that relied in part on racial considerations violate the Constitution's guarantee of equal protection, a historic ruling that will force a dramatic change in how the nation's private and public universities select their students."

"The student must be treated based on his or her experiences as an individual - not on the basis of race," Justice Roberts wrote, joined by Justices Clarence Thomas, Samuel A. Alito Jr., Neil M. Gorsuch, Brett M. Kavanaugh, and Amy Coney Barrett. "Many universities have done just the opposite for too long. In doing so, they have concluded, wrongly, that the touchstone of an individual's identity is not challenges bested, skills built, or lessons learned but the color of their skin. Our constitutional history does not tolerate that choice."

I totally disagree with the Supreme Court decision. My opinion about this ruling is these Republican, conservative right-wing Justices want to go under the assumption of what is known as a "Color-blind" theory or "Color-blind" racial ideology. This color-blind premise is derived from the "Critical perspective of color-blind theory, and color-blind racial ideology is based on the assertion that race no longer "Matters" as an obstacle to social and economic success in the United States, that substantial racial barriers no longer exist to keep historically oppressed groups from realizing the "American dream." Color-blindness provides White Americans with an ideological tool kit (cognitive frameworks, discursive devices) that can be used to defend White supremacy and advantages by denying the existence of racism and presenting "nonracist" counterarguments to policy proposals and other claims to redress racial inequalities and promote racial justice." "Two commonly held ideologies have contributed to the backlash against civil rights litigation, the myths of meritocracy and color blindness. By relying on merit criteria or standards, the dominant group can justify its exclusion of Blacks to positions of power, believing in its own neutrality." (Tayor, 1998).

Renowned Pulitzer Prize-winning author and civil rights journalist Nikole Hannah-Jones stated, "Today we have a society where constitutional colorblindness dictates that school segregation is unconstitutional, yet most Black students have never attended a majority-white school or had access to the same educational resources as White children. A society with a law prohibiting discrimination in housing and lending, and yet descendants of slavery remain the most residentially, educationally, and economically segregated people in the country. A society where employment discrimination is illegal, and yet Black Americans are twice as likely to be unemployed as White Americans, even when they hold college degrees." (Hannah-Jones, 2024).

So now that we have established a foundation for color-blind racial ideology, I can explain my point of view, which is that this color-blind theory does not work for African Americans, especially Black Men. Let me tell you why. Black people have been racially discriminated against for over 200 years. Racism is born into the DNA of America. My great-grandfather couldn't get into medical school to become a doctor. He couldn't get into law school and study law, he couldn't purchase a home, he couldn't purchase land, he couldn't even learn to read, all because of racial discrimination. All Black people could do in his day was provide slave labor and learn what they could under the radar.

Fast forward to the present day, and we're expected to embrace a so-called color-blind approach that ignores the 200-year history of racism and the harm it inflicted on Black people. This perspective pits Black students against Caucasian, Asian, or Jewish students, arguing that a Black student took their spot at prestigious institutions like Harvard. This reasoning is arbitrary and capricious. It overlooks the fact that, for 200 years, Black people were not only barred from entering prestigious colleges but were also held back by institutional racism. Meanwhile, many White individuals acquired wealth by profiting off slave labor. This flawed way of thinking fails to address the historical injustices that continue to impact educational opportunities today.

To adopt a theory of color-blind racial ideology, we would need to live in a race-neutral, non-discriminatory society. If Harvard, Yale, and Princeton were truly diverse, with equal representation of White, Black, Asian, Jewish, Indian, and female students, then color-blind admission criteria could be viable because racism would not exist. Under such circumstances, a color-blind approach might work. However, racism is still prevalent today. This is why "Affirmative Action" was enacted in the first place: to address the racist practices that prevented African Americans from entering predominantly White institutions (PWIs). For example, The "Flexner Report" was a landmark document of its time and was responsible for the closure of several Black Medical Schools throughout the country. "In 1905, seven Black medical schools led by

Howard University College of Medicine in Washington, DC, and Meharry Medical College, established in Nashville, Tennessee, were in existence. These Black medical schools enabled Black students to have access to medical training in greater numbers. By 1910, those Black medical schools had trained 1,465 doctors, and then, that promising legacy was abruptly extinguished." "Abraham Flexner, employed by the Carnegie Foundation and the American Medical Association, harbored strongly racist opinions on the role of Black people in medicine. He wrote that Black students should be trained in "hygiene rather than surgery" and were best employed as "sanitarians" who could help protect White people from common diseases such as tuberculosis." (Washingtonpost.com, 2024).

The long-term effects of this Flexner report were not only the closure of five African American Medical schools but a cumulative reduction of thousands of Black physicians practicing medicine over the years. Had this egregious racist offense been averted, health disparities in African American communities would look increasingly better than it does. During the time Flexner published his report, the only option African American medical students had was to attend Black colleges. The White medical schools didn't allow Blacks admission to their schools because of racial segregation. His recommendation to close five of the seven Black medical schools meant that thousands of Black medical students were forbidden from fulfilling their goals of becoming doctors.

That's why, in '2008, the "American Medical Association (AMA) realized that the Flexner Report was responsible for more than a century of racial inequity and bias. They finally understood the ramifications of the report and tendered an apology to African American physicians."

385

(Schneider, 2008). They also instituted measures to ameliorate (reform) discrimination in medical school admissions. This apology was issued to Black doctors, not White doctors, or Asian doctors, or Jewish doctors, or Indian doctors. The Black doctors were irreparably harmed, and this is exactly why Affirmative Action admissions for Black medical school students were initiated. You can't just start color-blind or non-racial decision-making for school admissions in the middle of the stream. Black students have been discriminated against in this country for over a century. That being said, as hard as it is for Whites, Asians, and others to realize, African American students deserve preferential treatment as far as admissions are concerned.

The Citigroup Global Perspectives & Solutions (GPS) report from 2020, titled *Closing the Racial Inequality Gaps*, indicated that improving access to higher education—across colleges, graduate schools, and vocational institutions—for Black students could potentially increase their lifetime earnings by an aggregate of $90 to $113 billion (Contify Banking News, 2020). This study, conducted by a team of distinguished economists and banking experts, focuses explicitly on Black students. It highlights that the significant economic benefits of enhanced educational access are not similarly quantified for other racial or ethnic groups. This underscores the argument for considering preferential treatment for African American students in admissions processes.

The American Nurses Association (ANA) has issued an apology to Black nurses and nurses of color for the racism they have faced, both historically and currently. As the country's largest and most prestigious nursing organization, this apology marks a significant step toward addressing these issues.

Similarly, major banks such as Wells Fargo and Bank of America have been implicated in predatory lending practices, subprime mortgages, and discriminatory redlining that disproportionately affected Black individuals. These institutions have been required to pay millions in damages to those impacted.

The remedies implemented were aimed at addressing injustices faced by African Americans and can be seen as forms of Affirmative Action. These measures were intended to counteract racism and support Black individuals. Affirmative Action, rather than being harmful, was beneficial. It served as a corrective tool to address the damage caused by decades of racial discrimination. The law was designed to help Black people advance in society and bridge the wealth gap. The dominant society in America introduced it to level the playing field and address inequalities. Removing Affirmative Action could lead to further discrimination and undermine the progress African Americans have achieved. According to renowned sociologist James R. Kluegel, Black men experience lower income returns in positions of authority compared to their White counterparts, with the income disparity growing at higher authority levels. Kluegel estimated that excluding Black men from leadership roles accounts for about one-third of the total income gap between Black and White individuals (Smith, 2002).

Race-conscious admissions at prestigious universities will increase diversity and integrate student bodies. The influx of Black and brown students will make our universities more well-rounded and stronger.

Basically, Whites will support initiatives that support White society. The problem that Whites fail to realize is that many of their so-called White initiatives and antiquated laws must be rewritten and modernized.

Because they don't understand this, racist Jim Crow laws are still on the books. For example, the ability to enforce voter suppression and gerrymandering makes it all right in their minds because these laws were never repealed and rewritten.

When we view the landscape of these United States, research supports the fact that White male dominance is in control of all American economic, political, educational, corporate, and media institutions.

"Currently, White men make up more than 80% of Congress, 78% of State political executives, 75% of state legislators, 84% of mayors of the top 100 cities, 85% of corporate executive officers, 100% of CEOs of Wall Street firms, 95% of Fortune 500 CEOs, 73% of tenured professors, 64% of newsroom staffers, 97% of heads of venture capital firms, 90% of tech jobs in Silicon Valley, 97% of owners of television and radio licenses, 87% of police departments and 68% of U.S. Circuit Court Judges." (Feagin & Ducey, 2017)

White leadership will never be able to right the wrongs of the White male elite group.

The renowned U.S. sociologist Joe Feagin, who also happens to be White, theorizes that "The central problem of the 21st century is elite White men. They long ago created what we term the elite-White-male dominance system, a complex and oppressive system central to most Western societies that now affects much of the planet. This small group of elite White men rule actively, undemocratically, and globally, yet remains largely invisible to the billions of people they routinely dominate." (Feagin & Ducey, 2017).

This White oligarchy has influenced the legal, political, and employment landscape since the inception of our democracy. This is the reason why systemic racism is so deeply entrenched in the everyday lives of African Americans. When you hear me using the term "Inmates running the asylum," what I mean is that the powerful White men who run the Corporate American industry cannot police themselves. When Blacks or Indigenous people complain about discrimination, the power structure we complain against can't relate to our concerns. They can't see it, and they can't understand it. They've made significant progress with women's diversity, so they don't even see the injustices that are perpetrated against Black and other minority men. (Feagin & Ducey, 2017).

I don't want to belabor (argue) this issue, but this is the very essence of critical race theory. An American President who supports segregation and signs legislation and policies into law that foster racism. The point I need to make here is that these laws and policies are flawed and have made their way into the workplace. Corporate America follows the lead of the U.S. Government, so how do you think African Americans are treated in the workplace? They're treated the same way society treats us.

As an underemployed Black Man, I'm complaining to my Union leadership, Human Resource Department, and Senior Management, but I can't get any justice. Systemic racism is deeply entrenched in our society. "The Inmates are running the Asylum." This is a bureaucracy that certainly cannot govern itself. I'm fighting an insurmountable battle.

"Institutionalized racism refers to differential access to the goods, services, and opportunities of society by race and is often normalized and legalized."

–Camara Phyllis Jones

Rocky Landscape

Upon completion of my NYSDHR rebuttal document, it became clear to me that the landscape in the corporate American workplace was stacked against us. By us, I mean Black Men. We have been placed into a pick 'n choose category. At best, all we could hope for from most companies is to be selected as their one token Black Man for a mid-level management job, and that's it. If you're an upwardly mobile Black Man like myself, you won't have a snowball's chance in hell as being that token Black management hire. Why? Because a man like that is considered a troublemaker. Black men who are successful business owners in the community can hold their heads high and be a badass without having to answer to anyone. The question is, how many Black men fit into these categories? Unfortunately, only a select few of us.

In an article written by Ellen Boneparth on the subject back in 1960, she wrote: "As members of the Black middle class, Black businessmen have the potential to play leadership roles within the Black community. They have the resources (time, money, education, contacts, and organizational skills) to affect social and political organizations at all levels of Black life." (Boneparth, 1960).

The Constitution and Bill of Rights are flawed and steeped in racism. The problem in our country is that the current White establishment realizes that many laws are unjust and racist, but they stand idly by and do nothing to rectify the problem.

Laws that target African Americans strip away our rights. Laws that are written so that perpetrators can hide behind are unjust. Unlike other career avenues, discrimination in the business and corporate world is covert and hidden extremely well. These days, racial discrimination in careers like law enforcement is heavily documented through body cams, social media, and a variety of modern technology that helps to maintain checks and balances. Sure, they can be disputed, and often are, but to the public, discrimination is as clear as day. In agriculture, when you see these poor Black farmers who have to fight for the same subsidies that the White farmers get, the way that their loan applications are denied, again, the discrimination is blatantly obvious. With voter suppression, when you look at the gerrymandering that occurs in Black districts and the petty laws that are passed to suppress the Black vote, it's blatantly obvious that discrimination has occurred. When you look at the education system in this country, you see the school-to-prison pipeline in which racist policies are aimed at young Black men and designed to send millions of young Black boys to prison. Again, it's blatantly obvious and in your face.

However, in the business world, there are so many curtains an unscrupulous employer can hide behind that makes it easy to get away with discriminating against Black men. By using Diversity and Protected Class laws to justify their racist agenda, they end up creating a maze of smoke and mirrors that specifically target Black men.

These policies are infused with discrimination and bias towards Black men. Efforts to correct them are nowhere to be found. In addition to formulating my rebuttal document, I took a serious look at this new buzzword concept, "Diversity."

I wrote the following article and sent it out to dozens of publications:

One Man's View of Diversity

The term Diversity has a very broad meaning. It seems like every organization attaches their own definition to this term. Diversity can encompass awarding a contract to a minority firm. It can include an initiative to hire and train U.S. Veterans or individuals with disabilities. It can mean providing seminars that train the workforce on how to treat people from various cultures.

Some diversity programs teach employees from different ethnic backgrounds how to respect each other and work together more efficiently. Is diversity meant to incorporate management, or is it just for rank-and-file employees? Diversity is a mixed bag of things. However, the foundation of diversity initiatives has been driven by women's rights and equality for women inside the workplace.

I am an African American man with a Bachelor's degree and a Master's degree. Needless to say, I am qualified for various management-level and administrative positions within my company. In spite of my qualifications and experience, I continually experience challenges with advancing my career. My employer promotes diversity in newsletters and social media, but it's an outdated view of diversity. By today's definition, diversity programs are supposed to be more focused on the inclusion of underrepresented individuals. However, at my company, diversity is still all about women. I say that because my observations reveal that true diversity doesn't exist at the management levels of many organizations, "The 'C' Suites." The only recognized diversity is a multicultural array of brilliant, influential, and successful women who have all achieved management and leadership positions within their respective companies.

Women have been empowered to become the primary practitioners and recipients of diversity initiatives throughout corporate America. It is obvious that women have received preferential diversity treatment with regard to career advancement when compared to minority males. The evolution of women's diversity oftentimes creates a female-friendly environment that is bias towards African Americans and other minority men who have been consistently marginalized and denied opportunities to advance their careers and earn higher salaries.

Understanding these dynamics, it's clear to see that women who have had to battle sexism, oppression, and unequal pay only see diversity for themselves. Corporate leadership has lost sight of the fact that diversity must also include underrepresented individuals who are not females, especially in management and leadership positions. Management teams comprised of all women and Caucasian men is really not diversity. On paper, it is, but in reality, it's not. What about adding Veteran males, African American males, Disabled males, Hispanic males, and Native American males to the team? What's both surprising and troubling is corporate leadership won't recognize that there are well-educated and qualified minority males within their organizations who are willing to contribute their expertise to the management ranks, but they are denied the opportunity.

A notable concern with diversity programs is their regulation under Title VII of the Federal Civil Rights Act, which I believe has limitations. Title VII's employment discrimination laws, along with affirmative action and diversity initiatives, classify women as a "protected class." This designation can facilitate quicker entry into the workforce and more rapid advancement into management roles for women. Consequently, women, including those from diverse backgrounds, may experience accelerated career progression and increased representation in management positions compared to minority men.

Under Title VII of the Federal Civil Rights Act, which protects individuals from discrimination based on race and sex, both African American women and men are covered under these provisions. However, the application of Title VII and related diversity programs often places significant emphasis on addressing barriers faced by women, including African American women, who have historically been excluded from many professional opportunities. This focus can inadvertently create challenges for African American men, who may also face both racial and gender discrimination.

Although Title VII protects both men and women, the specific design and implementation of diversity programs often prioritize the experiences of women, potentially overshadowing the unique challenges faced by African American men. As a result, African American men may encounter difficulties accessing career advancement opportunities, particularly in management and leadership roles. Studies suggest that hiring and promotion practices can be influenced by unconscious biases, leading to a preference for candidates who share similar race and gender characteristics with those making the decisions. This tendency for in-group favoritism can further limit opportunities for qualified minority men, making it harder for them to secure positions of power and influence compared to their peers.

The brilliant minds that run Corporate America have turned a blind eye and a deaf ear towards the racial injustices that qualified and highly skilled minority males suffer inside the workplace. When corporate leadership sits idly by and maintains a status-quo attitude, they are complicit in the discriminatory treatment that African American and other minority men must endure every day.

It is an affront (Insult) to the very idea of diversity when certain members of the workforce don't have access to the same opportunities as everyone else. Managing diversity is more than simply promoting women. Diversity involves recognizing the value that qualified minority men can bring to the table.

There is a troubling racial climate that is prevalent in our society and inside Corporate America. Diversity programs must do more to combat discrimination and promote inclusiveness. It's almost 2016. How long can we continue to bury our heads in the sand about the treatment of minority men? Title VII legislation and Diversity took a stand to rectify the mal-treatment of women inside the workplace. Now, it's time to address the unfair treatment perpetrated against qualified minority males with aspirations of career advancement.

Miles M. Livingston

I submitted this article to various diversity publications throughout the country but never got one response. I wasn't the least bit surprised. I was the angry Black Man, and the tone of my article was angry and borderline chauvinistic. But it was real, it was authentic, and it was how I felt as a Black Man in America who has to battle day in and day out for respect and equality.

"Your actions speak so loudly, I can't hear what you are saying."
— Ralph Waldo Emerson

Zero Sum Game

I was going to interview after interview to no avail. I walked around the vast hospital campus and visited the administrative corporate office areas, but I still didn't see any African American men. I perused the Municipal Corporate Directory that they posted on the Municipal website and employee portal only to find no Black men on the corporate team. I realize my employer hated me, at least enough not to promote me, but it's like I've always said, I wasn't the only Black Man out here.

My employer's actions spoke much louder than their "Diversity" and "Inclusion" words. They didn't value Black men or the potential we have to better our organizations. I couldn't hear their words because they didn't speak to me. I, on the other hand, would speak to them. My court date finally came around a whole year after that first hearing. It was scheduled for May 23, 2014.

True to form, my employer hired a high-powered employment law firm, Jessing Shabinov, to defend against little old me. I used the Division of Human Rights attorney, who did her best to represent me. Personally, I decided to do a little research about the "Jessing Shabinov" LLP law firm. They weren't a small-time firm at all. These were lawyers on the American Lawyer's Who's Who List and among the top labor relations and employment litigators in the country. They had generated over five hundred million in gross revenue and had unlimited money and resources. Several Fortune 500 companies were on their client list, and the accolades continue to go on and on.

I'm not going to lie. I was shaken. *This is what I'm up against??*

The hearing started with the judge identifying everyone and swearing me in. Then, to my surprise, the Judge asked me to step out of the proceedings. The bailiff escorted me to a lounge waiting area and told me to feel free to have some refreshments and relax.

I took a seat and remembered reading on the appearance document that my hearing was scheduled for two days. All day. From nine to five. I wasn't too rattled by that. I was prepared to miss a couple of days of work to get this settled.

I sat there in that lounge area rehearsing my discrimination speech over and over. I believed in my mind that, at some point, the Judge would put me on the stand to tell my side of this story. In addition to my speech, I was planning on telling the judge that I believed I was also a victim of reduced compensation and wage suppression. My plan was to request a financial settlement award that had to be structured very specifically. Some kind of deferred compensation or defined benefit plan that would reduce my taxable income. I expected punitive damages and back pay that would be invested into a tax-deferred retirement investment program. I also wanted to meet with a financial advisor to discuss and review the various payout options available to me. Finally, I was going to ask for a promotion into management with a substantial increase in salary, benefits, 401k plan, and a line of credit to purchase a new vehicle.

I know now that I was dreaming. As ready as I was to speak up for myself, I didn't even consider the possibility that I would never have the chance. As I had previously learned, these types of cases only consider a 12-month period of time, and so do any monetary calculations for settlements. I also learned that the courts cannot compel an employer to offer any employment opportunities or promotions to a complainant.

Long story short, my employer, through my DHR attorney (Roberta Samuels), offers me a measly seventy five hundred dollars to settle the case. I basically told them to go fuck themselves. I wasn't looking to be paid off. I wanted to work for my money. I wanted the promotion into management that I deserved. They told me that if I didn't settle, they would tie up this case in court for years. Obviously, my employer decided ahead of time that they would settle the case. They had completely prepared this "Stipulation of Settlement" document. I take about 30 minutes to digest the agreement. What it boiled down to was that my employer must agree to adhere to Human Rights Law. They *do not* have to admit to any violations of the law, which they clearly violated, or else I never would have sued them in the first place.

NEW YORK STATE
DIVISION OF HUMAN RIGHTS

NEW YORK STATE DIVISION OF
HUMAN RIGHTS on the Complaint of

MILES M. LIVINGSTON   -   Complainant
-v-
MUNICIPAL HOSPITAL   -   Respondent

STIPULATION OF SETTLEMENT
Case No. 9999000XB

On 04/16/2013, complainant Miles M. Livingston ("Complainant") filed
a verified complaint with the New York State Division of Human Rights

VERNON M. O'GARRA

("Division"), charging Respondent, Municipal Hospital System with unlawful discriminatory practice relating to employment in violation of N.Y. Exec. Law, art. 15 ("Human Rights Law").

After investigation, the Division found that it had jurisdiction over the complaint and that probable cause existed to believe that Respondent had engaged in unlawful discrimination. Thereafter, the division referred the parties for a public hearing.

Before the commencement of the hearings, the parties reached a Stipulation of Settlement. The terms of said Settlement agreed upon by the parties are as follows:

1. The Respondent agrees to continue to adhere to the Human Rights Law. By entering into this Stipulation, the Respondent does not admit to any violation of the law, including, but not limited to, the Human Rights Law, or to any liability for the charges of the complaint.

2. The Respondent agrees to pay, and the Complainant agrees to accept a total amount of $7,500.00, less payroll taxes, withholdings, and other deductions as required by law, made payable to "Miles M. Livingston." Respondent will issue, or cause to be issued, an Internal Revenue Service form W-2 for this sum and payment. This amount is accepted in complete satisfaction of this complaint.

3. In addition to the terms outlined in this Stipulation, the parties are also executing a Private and Confidential Settlement Agreement, attached hereto as a Rider (the "Rider"), the terms of which are incorporated hereto and which shall be binding upon the parties.

4. Both parties agree that payment of the aforementioned sum will be made by Respondent within 30 days after Respondent's execution of this Stipulation, provided that Complainant does not exercise his revocation rights in the (7) days following the execution of this Stipulation, as outlined in the terms of the Rider. Said payment will be made by bank or payroll check payable to Complainant and delivered to the Roberta Samuels, Senior Attorney – NYSDHR, to be held until the issuance of an Order After Stipulation by the Commissioner of the Division, and to be provided to the Complainant thereafter.

5. Both parties agree that they are entering into this stipulation willingly, without any coercion or duress, that this stipulation and the Rider attached hereto contain all of the agreed upon terms and no other promises have been made outside of this stipulation, and that this stipulation, upon approval by the Commissioner, completely resolves and terminates the complaint pending before the Division.

6. (a) In exchange for and consideration of the terms and benefits outlined in this Stipulation, the Complainant hereby withdraws the complaint before the Division, and before the United States Equal Employment Opportunity Commission, EEOC case number 987XYZ654ABC, with prejudice, and releases and discharges the Respondent, and Respondent's affiliated companies, subsidiaries, parent companies, and directors, shareholders, officers, employees, attorneys, agents, representatives, predecessors and successors and assigns, and all persons acting with or on behalf of them, from all charges, complaints, claims, liabilities, obligations, promises, agreements, actions, or causes of action, debts, attorney fees or other costs or expenses, of any nature whatsoever, including but not limited to employment discrimination claims arising under local, state or federal statute, regulation, or ordinance relating to employment discrimination claims or other employment conditions, or prohibiting termination or retaliation for reporting

a violation of the law, or any other claim related to or arising out of the Complainant's employment by the Respondent, known or unknown, which the Complainant may ever before have had or claim to have had, from the beginning of the world through the date of this agreement.

(b) In further consideration of the terms and benefits outlined in this Stipulation, the Complainant further agrees to execute and be bound by the terms outlined and included in the Rider, attached hereto and incorporated by reference.

7. The Complainant and Respondent agree not to disclose any information relating to the contents of the Stipulation other than disclosure required by law or disclosure to a party's immediate family, accountant, attorney, or medical or counseling professional. It is understood by the Complainant and Respondent that the Commissioner of the Division of Human Rights is not, and by law cannot be, bound by the confidentiality provisions of this stipulation.

8. A facsimile copy of this agreement will have the same force and effect as the original.
9. The parties understand this stipulation of settlement is subject to the approval of the Commissioner of the Division of Human Rights. The Respondent and Complainant consent to the entry of an order of the Commissioner of the State Division of Human Rights in accordance with the terms set forth in this Stipulation.

10. Respondent agrees to cooperate with the Division of Human Rights in any compliance review.

11. By signing below, the signatory for Respondent, Municipal Hospital System, warrants and represents that he or she has the authority to sign on behalf of and to bind Respondent, Municipal Hospital System, to the terms and conditions of this agreement,

to agree to all of the terms and conditions of this settlement agreement on behalf of Respondent, Municipal Hospital System and to ensure that Respondent, Municipal Hospital System, fulfills all of the terms and conditions set forth herein.

The subscribing parties hereby agree to the above terms.

6/10/2014   *Miles M. Livingston*

Date   Miles M. Livingston

6/10/2014   *Gladstone Mitchell*

Date   Municipal Hospital System
                                   By: Gladstone Mitchell, Esq.
                                   Legal Dept. MHS

VERNON M. O'GARRA

This is Private and Confidential Settlement Agreement (the "Agreement") is made and entered into this 10th day of June 2014 by and between complaint, Miles M. Livingston ("Complainant"), and Municipal Hospital System. ("Respondent").

WHEREAS, Complainant commenced in action by filing a Complaint with the New York State Division of Human Rights (Case No. 9999000XB) on or about April 8th, 2013, and with the United States Equal Employment Opportunity Commission (EEOC case number 987XYZ654ABC) against Respondent; and

WHEREAS, Complainant and Respondent desire to fully resolve the claims between them and any and all other disputes in connection with the above-referenced matters.

NOW, THEREFORE, in consideration of the mutual promises, covenants, representations, and other considerations contained in the New York State Division of Human Rights Stipulation of Settlement, dated June 10, 2014 (the "Stipulation") Complainant and Respondent agree as follows:

1. In exchange for and in consideration of the terms and benefits outlined in the Stipulation, Complainant irrevocably and unconditionally releases and discharges Municipal Health System, its subsidiaries, divisions, parents and member companies, institutions, affiliates or related business entities and any and all of their past and present administrators, officers, trustees, directors, agents, representatives, employees, board members, successors and assigns, jointly and individually, from any and all actions, causes of action, grievances, obligations, liabilities, judgments, suits, debts, attorneys' fees, costs, sums of money, wages, bonuses, benefits of any type, accounts,

reckonings, bonds, bills, specialties, covenants, contracts, controversies, agreements, promises, variances, trespasses, damages, extents, executions, claims and demands relating to any claims of discrimination on the basis of age (including, without limitation, any rights or claims under the Age Discrimination in Employment Act), which Complainant, his heirs, executors, administrators, successors and assigns, ever had, now have or hereafter can, shall or may have for, from the beginning of time to the date of this Agreement.

2. By signing this Agreement, Complainant acknowledges and agrees that:

(a) He has been afforded a reasonable and sufficient period of time for review, for deliberation thereon, and for negotiation of the terms thereof, and he has been specifically urged by Respondent to consult with legal counsel or representative of his choice before signing it;

(b) He has carefully read and understands the terms of this Agreement, all of which has been fully explained to him;

(c) He has signed both the Stipulation in this Agreement freely and voluntarily and without duress or coercion and with full knowledge of its significance and consequences and of the rights relinquished, surrendered, released, and discharged hereunder;

(d) The only consideration for signing this Agreement, all the terms and benefits set forth in the Stipulation, and no other promise, agreement, or representation of any kind has been made to him by any person or entity whatsoever to cause him to sign this Agreement; and

(e) He was offered a minimum period of twenty-one (21) days after his receipt of this Agreement to review it, but he has chosen to waive such minimum period because he did not wish to wait the full twenty-one (21) days and that such waiver was initiated solely by him, was voluntary on his part and was made without any duress or coercion of any kind.

3. Complainant acknowledges and understands that this Agreement may be revoked by him in writing at any time during the period of seven (7) calendar days following the date of his execution of the Agreement by delivering such written revocation to Jessing Shabinov LLP. If such seven (7) day revocation period expires without Complainant exercising his revocation rights, the obligations of this Agreement and the Stipulation will then become fully effective.

4. Complainant understands and acknowledges that the Confidentiality requirements set forth in Paragraph 7 of the Stipulation shall equally apply to the terms of this Agreement.

The subscribing parties hereby agree to the above terms;

6/10/2014 _____   *Miles M. Livingston*
Date   Miles M. Livingston

6/10/2014 _____   *Gladstone Mitchell*
Date   Municipal Hospital System
                                   By: Gladstone Mitchell, Esq.
                                   Legal Dept. MHS

I took umbrage (offense) with this "Stipulation of Settlement" document. I essentially have to agree to a slew of legal restrictions just to receive a sum of money that I didn't even want. So there it is—my complaint is basically swept under the rug for a modest payout. What really bothers me is that Black men are uniquely burdened by situations like this. Caucasian men run the workplace, women are now fully accepted, and immigrants have been elevated within the workplace, often surpassing Black men. LGBTQ employees have also made tremendous strides over the years. It's a rough situation in corporate America for Black men.

The Jessing Shabinov attorneys, on behalf of Municipal Hospital, pressured me to sign—or instead, strongly encouraged me to sign—this Stipulation of Settlement agreement right then and there on the spot. Municipal Hospital must pay me $7500 within 30 days, and I must withdraw my complaint and willingly, without any coercion or duress, sign a "Gag Order" stating that I cannot disclose any information relating to the contents of the stipulation agreement or any details of the case.

"This is a victory, Miles. You won!"

"Yeah? And what did I win?"

"They didn't admit any guilt."

"They didn't confess to any wrongdoing."

"What exactly did I win?"

It gets better. She also mentioned that the Jessing Shabinov attorneys pointed out that I hadn't filed a grievance with my union. They tried to use this as leverage to reduce my settlement amount, arguing that I hadn't exhausted all available options before filing my complaint. That's not entirely untrue. Although I spoke to my union reps, it never occurred to me to file a formal grievance. Our conversation ended with her telling me, "Look, Miles, if your employer continues this type of discrimination against you, just sue them again next year."

I researched and read through my employer's Policy and Procedure manual when I returned to work. The "Compliance & Grievance Procedure" section stated, "It is the health system's policy to foster sound employee relations by encouraging open communication and reconciliation of work-related problems or concerns. The purpose of this policy is to provide a process where employees and employers can address workplace disputes. If an employee feels that they have been treated unfairly or differently, they may file a grievance." The more I read, the more I realized that the Municipal attorney was right. I should have filed a grievance.

I wasn't deterred; as far as I could tell, my employer got away scot-free. What's seventy-five hundred dollars compared to the millions they were making? They tossed a pittance at me and expected me to be satisfied. It was an insult. It's more than an insult! In many ways, it was worse than losing because they didn't have to admit any guilt for what they were doing. It was wrong. And I wasn't about to let them sweep this and me under the rug. It was time for another battle.

My Brother's Keeper

President Obama's "My Brother's Keeper" was a fantastic program. Launched in 2014, President Obama's visionary program focused on young Black boys who were vulnerable and at risk. Most African American men in the country could see that our boys needed help. As adults, Black men were often at the bottom of the barrel when it came to opportunities, education, employment, healthcare, finances, and just about everything else. Growing up in a racist society is no joke. To compound that, Title VII of the Civil Rights Act, while intended to protect all marginalized groups, sometimes fails to address the specific challenges faced by Black men. These boys are in for a rough life, and President Obama could see it. The President coordinated the "My Brother's Keeper" initiative, which was designed to help young men of color by mentoring and educating them.

The initiative was designed to include corporations and business leaders in various communities throughout the country that would mentor and educate young men of color. The focus on young boys included how to avoid trouble and stay out of the criminal justice system, in addition to being prepared for and engaged in school.

"More than 1,000 women of color have signed a letter calling for gender equality in President Obama's "My Brother's Keeper" program, putting the White House on the defensive about its initiative aimed at improving the lives of at-risk boys and young men." (Henderson, 2014). Those naysayers couldn't wait to come out of the woodwork against this program. Some said the "My Brother's Keeper" program to help young Black men unfairly excluded Black girls who experienced the same issues. Which, in my opinion, couldn't be further from the truth. There were programs for Black women and girls all over the place. For example, the American Association of University Women (AAUW) sponsored several programs for women nationwide. The National Association of Colored Women's Club, The Essence Magazine Organization, The National Coalition of 100 Black Women (NCBW), Black Girls Rock, The National Black Women's Justice Institute, the list goes on and on and on. All these programs for Black women, and the second one comes out for Black boys and men; people lose their minds. It didn't make sense.

I was surprised and disappointed that some African American women did not fully support the President's initiative. While African American women have achieved significant success in the workplace, education, media, and business, surpassing Black men in some areas, it's important to understand the broader context of their position on this issue. Some African American women felt that "My Brother's Keeper" did not adequately address the needs of Black girls, who also face significant challenges. They were concerned that focusing solely on boys might overlook the systemic issues affecting both genders.

While President Obama recognized the importance of getting young men of color on the right track, some women believed that both boys and girls needed support and resources to thrive. Many African American women have worked hard to overcome obstacles and may have felt that more comprehensive initiatives were needed to uplift the entire community.

The concern that Black girls might be left out of similar opportunities is valid, given the struggles they face. However, the President's initiative aimed to address the specific challenges young Black boys encounter, recognizing that these issues could ultimately impact the pool of eligible men for successful Black women. While some women may have felt their concerns were not addressed, others understood the long-term benefits of supporting young Black boys.

Supporting young Black boys is essential and does not diminish the importance of addressing the needs of Black girls. Both efforts are crucial for the community's future. By fostering understanding and acknowledging these dynamics, we can build solidarity and cooperation between Black men and women, ensuring that all members of the community can thrive and succeed together. It's important for all of us to seize opportunities to uplift young Black boys, recognizing that their success benefits the entire community and helps address the concerns about being "equally yoked" in relationships.

11

The Essence Of Law

"Condemnation without investigation is the highest form of ignorance."
— Albert Einstein

I was listening to an interview on the radio one morning, and this guy, a prominent African American businessman and media owner, was being questioned about racism in the media and television industry. He was explaining that when Black men take a stand against racist and discriminatory treatment, the establishment would come after them with the four Ds: Dismiss, Discredit, Demonize, and Destroy.

DISMISS: to decide that somebody or something is not important and not worth thinking or talking about.

DISCREDIT: to make people stop respecting somebody or something.

DEMONIZE: to describe somebody or something in a way that is intended to make other people think of them or it as evil or dangerous.

DESTROY: to damage something so badly that it no longer exists, works, etc.

It was like a lightbulb went off in my head. When I filed my complaint against Municipal, their legal team asked for a dismissal.

Then, they tried to discredit me by saying that I failed to follow the proper channels prior to filing my complaint, that I ignored union protocols and filed a baseless complaint.

Then, as my complaint began to get some legs, they tried to demonize me by implying that I was an angry Black Man who tried to intimidate and coerce people. They characterized me as a malcontent employee in an effort to destroy my credibility.

All of a sudden, I was being micromanaged to death. Things like how often I was late for work or how many errors I did or did not make were under close scrutiny. I was even written up for wearing headphones at my desk while I worked. The funny thing about that is that the supervisor who questioned me caught me with the headphones as I was coming into work. I wasn't even signed in yet. Still, she wrote me up anyway.

Things like that were retaliation, plain and simple. I had a target on my back all because I had the nerve to call out the discrimination against me. This is the kind of thing that only marginalized communities can relate to. You're expected to keep your head down and keep quiet even when they're stepping on your neck. The minute you cry foul, that's when they start picking at you. Every little thing you do is a blemish against you and becomes documented on your record. By characterizing me as a malcontent, they attempted to knock me back down or put me back in my place. They were still hiring lesser qualified employees over me and passing over me for promotions. It became clear that the end goal was to make things so inhospitable for me that I would either shut my mouth or quit altogether. It was a nice try, but I wouldn't be easily defeated.

VERNON M. O'GARRA

"Be true to what you said on paper."

–Martin Luther King

The Handbook

I researched a copy of my union's collective bargaining agreement and my employer's Human Resource policy and procedure manual, and I read them thoroughly. I was determined to write a grievance that would make my employer's head spin. Imagine those lawyers telling me I failed to file a grievance. They probably weren't expecting me to follow up on that.

The Union's Collective Bargaining Agreement and Municipal's Human Resource Policy and Procedure Manual made for some very interesting reading:

COLLECTIVE BARGAINING

Agreement

between

League of Municipal Hospitals and Nursing Homes

and

3609 MEIU Municipal Employees International Workers Union

March 1, 2008, through October 31, 2015

COLLECTIVE BARGAINING AGREEMENT

<u>Article IV</u>

No Discrimination

1. Neither the Employer nor the Union shall discriminate against or in favor of any Employee on account of race, color, creed, national origin, political belief, sex, sexual orientation, citizenship status, marital status, disability or age.

I skimmed through the document and focused on article four and the section entitled, "No Discrimination." As you can see, it was clear what constituted discrimination. I was confident that the statement supported my grievance and decided to cite it in my grievance document.

I began reading the Municipal Human Resource Policy and Procedure Manual. I focused on four policies that were relevant to my grievance.

1. Complaint and Grievance Procedure
2. Equal Employment Opportunity / Affirmative Action
3. Non-Discrimination and Non-Harassment
4. Recruitment and Hiring

Again, I was confident that these four policies supported my grievance, and I decided to cite these policies in my grievance document.

Municipal Hospital Health System
Human Resources Policy and Procedure Manual

Policy Title:	Part:	V	Revised/ Reviewed:*
Complaint and Grievance Procedure	Section:	1	03/15/05 08/01/06 11/05/07 04/05/09 09/15/11 12/24/13
Category:	Effective Date:	1999	
Discipline and Standards of Conduct	Page:	1 of 2	

Policy

The health system's policy is to foster sound employee relations by encouraging open communication and reconciliation of work-related problems or concerns. Misunderstandings or conflicts can arise in any organization. *It is the health system's belief that most complaints about working conditions, supervision, co-workers, or other work-related problems can best be handled through informal and private discussions between the employee and his or her supervisor or department head.*

Purpose

The purpose of this policy is to provide a process where employees and employers can address workplace disputes.

Scope

This policy applies to all the health systems' benefit-eligible, nonmanagerial employees who have completed an assessment.

Procedures

Step 1: An employee should first discuss any complaint with his or her immediate supervisor in person or communicate it in writing. This must be done within 10 working days of the occurrence. Issues can best be resolved at this stage, and every effort should be made to bring about a resolution.

The supervisor must give his or her verbal or written decision within 10 working days of receiving the complaint. If the complaint is not resolved to the mutual satisfaction of the employee and the supervisor, the employee may then present the complaint to his or her department head.

If an employee reasonably believes that discussing his or her complaint with his or her immediate supervisor would be futile, the employee may move to the next step in the grievance process. The employee must ask for a Step 2 Grievant within five working days of the supervisors response to the initial complaint.

Step 2: *Grievant must put request in writing and be advised that hearing will be limited to issues stated therein, including remedies sought.*

The department head will discuss the complaint with the employee and obtain pertinent information regarding the complaint. Within five working days after the discussion with the employee, the department head will give his or her decision to the employee. If the employee is still not satisfied, he or she may proceed to the Step 3 grievance within ten work days of the department head's decision.

Step 3: The department head will submit a written request for the employee to meet with Site Human Resources (HR) designee.

The employee may ask a co-worker to attend the meeting. After the grievance has been heard, the employee will receive a written decision within 15 workdays.

If the problem has not been resolved to the employee's satisfaction, he or she may take the grievance to Step 4 within five working days of receiving the Step 3 determination.

Step 4: The site HR designee will schedule an appointment with the Vice President, Human Resources designee, and the Executive Director designee.

The employee may ask a coworker to attend the meeting and must be available to testify. After the grievance has been heard, the employee will receive a decision within 15 workdays after the meeting.

Employees must exercise good faith in processing complaints and cooperate in any investigation. *The employee submitting the complaint will be encouraged to provide relevant information, including documents, names of witnesses, etc.* An employee does not have the right to have an attorney or other outside individual (non-employee) present during the internal investigation or during a grievance meeting.

The health system will not tolerate any form of coercion or retaliation against an employee who processes a complaint under this policy or who cooperates with an investigation. This policy and its procedures should not, however, be construed as preventing, limiting, or delaying the health system from taking disciplinary action against any individual in circumstances where such action is deemed appropriate.

Municipal Hospital Health System

Human Resources Policy and Procedure Manual

Policy Title:	Part:	III	Revised/ Reviewed:*
Non-Discrimination and Non-Harassment	Section:	3	11/01/05 08/01/07 11/05/08 04/05/09 10/13/11
Category: **Legal/ Regulations**	Effective Date:	1998	
	Page:	1 of 3	

Policy

The health system is committed to maintaining a work environment that is free from unlawful discrimination and harassment. In keeping with this commitment, *the health system will not tolerate unlawful discrimination or harassment against its employees by anyone, including any supervisor, co-worker, patient, or vendor where such discrimination or harassment is based on employee's age, race, creed/religion, color*, national origin, alienage or citizenship status, sexual orientation, military or veteran status, sex/gender, gender identity, disability, genetic predisposition or carrier status, marital status, partnership status, and victim of domestic violence, or any other protected status.

Additionally, *the health system does not tolerate retaliation against any employee* for making a complaint about or opposing discrimination or harassment or for cooperating, assisting, or participating in an investigation of a discrimination.

Purpose

The purpose of this policy is to ensure that individuals covered by this policy are provided with equal employment opportunities and a workplace that is free from all forms of prohibited discrimination and harassment in compliance with the applicable laws and regulations regarding non-discrimination and non-harassment.

Scope

This policy applies to all health system employees, job applicants, vendors, agency staff, volunteers, and outside contractors.

Definitions

The term "discrimination" as used in this policy refers to the <u>*different treatment*</u> *of an employee, in any respect of employment, because of the employee's age, race,* creed/religion, color, national origin, alienage or citizenship status, sexual orientation, military or veteran status, sex/gender, gender identity, disability, genetic predisposition or carrier status, marital status, partnership status, and victim of domestic violence, or any other protected status. *The range of employment practices where discrimination is prohibited includes but is not limited to:* (i) hiring and firing; (ii) compensation, assignment, or classification of employees; (iii*) transfer, and promotion, layoff, or recall;* (iv) job advertisements; (v) recruitment; (vi) testing; (vii) use of health system facilities; (viii) training and apprenticeship programs; (ix) fringe benefits; (x) pay, retirement plans and disability leave; and (xi) any other terms and condition of employment.

Municipal Hospital Health System

Human Resources Policy and Procedure Manual

Policy Title:	Part:	IV	Revised/ Reviewed:*
Equal Employment Opportunity/ Affirmative Action	Section:	12	03/15/05 08/01/06 11/05/07 04/05/09
Category: **Legal/ Regulations**	Effective Date:	2001	07/18/11 12/24/13
	Page:	1 of 2	

Policy

It is the policy of the health system to provide equal employment opportunity and treat all employees equally regardless of age, race, creed/religion, color, national origin, alienage or citizenship status, sexual orientation, military or veteran status, sex, gender, gender identity, disability, genetic information or genetic predisposition or carrier status, marital status, partnership status, victim of domestic violence, or other characteristics protected by applicable law.

Personnel policies and employment practices including, but not limited to, those relating to: (i) hiring and firing; (ii) compensation, assignment, or classification of employees; (iii) transfer, and promotion, layoff, or recall; (iv) job advertisements; (v) recruitment; (vi) testing; (vii) use of health system facilities; (viii) training and apprenticeship programs; (ix) fringe benefits; (x) pay, retirement plans and disability leave; and (xi) any other terms and condition of employment, will be administered consistent with equal employment principles and applicable affirmative action requirements.

Purpose

The purpose of this policy is to describe the health system's commitment to comply with federal, state, and local laws and regulations governing equal employment opportunity and affirmative action requirements.

Scope

This policy applies to all health system applicants, employees, volunteers, students, and medical staff.

Procedures

1. All managers, supervisors, and employees are required to apply this policy in their day-to-day programs and employment decisions.

2. Corporate Human Resources, Site Human Resources, and Administration will ensure adherence through the health system's mission and responsibilities.

Municipal Hospital Health System

Human Resources Policy and Procedure Manual

Policy Title:	Part:	VIII	Revised/ Reviewed:*
Recruitment and Hiring	Section:	1	03/15/05 08/01/06 04/05/09
Category:	Effective Date:	1999	09/15/11 12/24/13
Recruitment and Hiring	Page:	1 of 2	

Policy

It is the policy of the health system to give equal consideration to all applicants for employment. Employees will be selected on the basis of qualifications that meet the specifications and essential job responsibilities of the position for which they are being considered.

The health system will recruit, employ, evaluate, compensate, transfer, promote, and educate personnel without regard to race, sex, religion, creed, color, gender, gender identity, national origin, marital status, age, sexual orientation, alien or citizenship status, disability or Vietnam-era veteran's status, and treat all employees equitably. State labor laws must be adhered to in relation to the employment of minors who must obtain working permits prior to employment. The health system's minimum hiring age is 16.

Purpose

The purpose of this policy is to provide guidelines for selecting, recruiting, promoting, and employing best-qualified candidates for available positions at the health system facilities.

Scope

This policy applies to Talent Acquisition staff and/or hiring department heads and designees.

Procedures

A. General Procedures

1. *The health system makes every effort to select the most qualified individual for every job opening.*

My summary assessment of the Municipal Human Resources Policy and Procedure Manual was nothing to write home about. These policies did not support the rights of African American men.

426

The Complaint and Grievance Policy states that the purpose of the policy is to provide a process where employees and employers can address workplace disputes. I could appreciate the spirit of this policy; however, I had already established a relationship with my leadership team and communicated with them. They all knew I was qualified and was actively seeking a management position. I guess I needed to file a grievance to let them officially let them know how I felt.

The Equal Employment Opportunity Affirmative Action policy states that the health system will provide equal employment opportunities and treat all employees equally regardless of age, race, creed/religion, color, etc. I certainly felt like I could definitely file a grievance based on Municipals noncompliance with this policy and my ignorance about protected class law. After reading this section, I felt EEOC was on my side when they ruled against Municipal when I filed my discrimination complaint.

Under the Non-Discrimination and Non-Harassment Policy, the health system is committed to maintaining a work environment free from unlawful discrimination and harassment. In keeping with this commitment, the health system will not tolerate unlawful discrimination or harassment against its employees by anyone, including any supervisor, co-worker, patient, or vendor, where such discrimination or harassment is based on the employee's age, race, creed/religion, or color. My employer was definitely in violation of this policy. It was a no-brainer.

Finally, the Recruitment and Hiring Policy was a joke to me—just meaningless words on paper. The policy stated, "It is the policy of the health system to give equal consideration to all applicants for employment. Employees will be selected on the basis of qualifications that meet the specifications and essential job responsibilities of the position for which they are being considered." In practice, however, the policy was ignored when it came to African American men. Women hired and promoted other women, and Caucasian men hired and promoted other Caucasian men. They exploited the ambiguity in the implementation of "protected categories," focusing on gender and race in ways that sidelined Black men. Legally, there was nothing a Black Man could do but file a complaint.

Clearly, I wasn't being treated equally in the eyes of these policies!

One of the things that really annoys me in the workplace is the fact that when I complain about the lack of Black men in management, I always get bullshit answers to my questions. I realize that my employer dislikes me, possibly for several reasons. I'm upwardly mobile, I have a Master's degree, I'm intelligent, I intimidate people (so they say), I don't take shit from people. That being said, I'm not the only Black Man employed at this institution. You mean to tell me that no African American man has ever been promoted within the history of this department since the hospital's inception. That's crazy to me. At the time I filed my discrimination case, only White men and females earned six-figure salaries (in non-clinical jobs) at this institution. That's a sad commentary.

The lack of respect for Black men in the workplace fosters an attitude of resentment toward us. Our educational accomplishments are marginalized, while those of others are embraced. We are not recruited or promoted. When this type of bias is condoned and not addressed, organizations miss out on the valuable contributions we (Black Men) have to offer.

After reviewing all the union agreements and policy procedures, I drafted my grievance document and submitted it to my union leadership representative and my immediate management team.

"Corporate leaders may find implementing antiracist policies to be challenging or even inconvenient. But if corporate leaders find it difficult to transform their corporate practices now, imagine how difficult it was during the civil rights movement. If these leaders find it uncomfortable to shift their corporate climates, imagine the racial discomfort stakeholders of color have endured for many years. True corporate leadership requires positive and decisive action now. As Dr. King proclaimed, "The time is always right to do right." (Fletcher, 2024).

Date: July 14, 2014

GRIEVANT:

Name	Miles M. Livingston
Job Title:	Clerical Acct. Rep
Wage Rate:	$20.25 hourly
Work Phone:	(718) 999- 9999
Shift:	8AM – 4PM
Department:	Admitting
Location:	Admission Office
Seniority Date:	March 6, 2003
Admitting Deptt.:	Emanuel Gornstein
Job Title.:	Dept. Director
Hrs. of Duty.:	9AM -5PM
Work Phone:	(718) 999- 9999

****

Statement of Grievance:

<u>Denied Promotion Because of My Race & Gender</u>

WHEN did the problem (s) occur? (Most recent) May 2014

WHERE did the problem(s) occur? Admitting Department

WHY is this grievance? Violation of HR Policies and Procedures

HOW to remedy? Requesting promotion into management

BRILLIANT MINDS, IGNORANT MINDS

I filed this grievance against my Employer on **July 14, 2014:**

Upon reading the Hospital Union Collective Bargaining Agreement, Article IV, "No Discrimination" section states: *"Neither the Employer nor the Union shall discriminate against or in favor of any Employee on account of race, color, creed, national origin, political belief, sex, sexual orientation, citizenship status, marital status, disability or age."*

In addition to the Union CBA document, the language in the Municipal Human Resources Policy and Procedure Manual, sections concerning EEO/Affirmative Action and the Non-Discrimination and Non-Harassment Policies state: *"It is the policy of the health system to provide equal employment opportunity and treat all employees equally regardless of age, race, and sex/gender, in regards to personnel policies and employment practices including, but not limited to, those relating to (iii) transfer and promotion."*

After reading these documents, it is my contention that the Municipal Hospital Admitting Office is in violation of these policies, and I exercise my right to file a *Grievance* on the grounds that I was; **"DENIED PROMOTION BECAUSE OF MY RACE & GENDER."**

This grievance is being filed against (Municipal Hospital Admissions Department), my department Director, associate director, managers, and supervisors for singling me out and discriminating against me. And also, for failure to promote me into a supervisory or management position. I have applied for several supervisory and managerial positions within this department and have been denied promotion because I am an African American male.

431

When I researched the promotional history of this admitting department, I discovered that no African American male has ever received a promotion in this department! I personally find this practice to be racially discriminatory because I have been singled out and denied career advancement simply because of my race and gender. I do understand that African American men are not part of the "protected class" status. However, I do belong to an "affected group" of employees that have been barred from promotion into management within this department.

Even though I am not part of a protected class, it is against Municipal policy to single out any particular group of employees and discriminate against them. The policy states:

The health system will not tolerate unlawful discrimination or harassment against its employees by anyone, including any supervisor, co-worker, patient, or vendor, where such discrimination or harassment is based on employees' age, race, sex, or gender. All managers, supervisors, and employees are required to apply this policy in day-to-day programs and employment decisions. The term "discrimination," as used in this policy, refers to the different treatment of an employee in any aspect of employment.

In spite of giving my best effort and working extremely hard for this department, I have received "different treatment" because only African American men are barred from promotion. I have learned the job duties of 'Clerical Account Representative' very well. I have been asked several times to assist in training new hires and cover various work areas throughout the department. (ex. ER, pre-surgical testing: surgical admitting, front desk admitting, cardiology, etc.) I have always happily fulfilled any request from management and have established a great working relationship with management and my fellow employees. I consider myself a versatile team player who is knowledgeable, dependable, and highly qualified for promotion.

During my initial interview, when Municipal first hired me, I asked if there were opportunities for advancement and career growth. I was told, "Absolutely, yes, there is opportunity to grow and flourish at this institution." My question is, when will I get the opportunity to begin my career growth at Municipal? I have an undergraduate degree in Business Administration, a master's in health care administration, and a certificate in Health Information Technology from Columbia University.

I've published a healthcare article in the Medical Business News. I have a background in revenue management and finance. I attend healthcare conferences annually. I did a volunteer internship for 14 months in the Medical Records Dept. and also volunteered for the "Get Covered New York" initiative.

All of my work performance evaluations throughout my tenure here have been satisfactory. I am a hard-working and dedicated employee.

I state these accomplishments about myself, not in a braggadocious manner. But to highlight the fact that leadership in this department harbors an extremely low opinion and disrespect for me because I am an African American man seeking career advancement. I have been stuck in a low-wage, clerical role in this department for years while my female and White male colleagues have matriculated into higher-salaried management-level positions. I feel I have a wealth of experience and would greatly contribute to our institution as a manager or administrator if given the opportunity to gain the necessary experience.

But, I have been barred from getting promoted or getting hired into a management or supervisory position only because of the color of my skin and gender. The problem in this department is my superiors do not view African American men as equals. They cannot fairly and objectively evaluate the skills and abilities of African American men and, subsequently, are incapable of exercising fairness and making race-neutral decisions as far as promotions are concerned. I can't imagine why there haven't been any African American men ever promoted within this department.

What other conclusion can I draw? Lesser qualified female candidates have been promoted ahead of me, and I don't understand why. Everyone deserves an opportunity to learn and grow to enhance their career. It's 2014. Isn't it time for race to be a non-factor so African American men can be fairly judged by our ability and intelligence?

Quite frankly, I don't know what else I can do to prove my self-worth to this organization. If it's not racial discrimination, then please tell me what the problem is. I have followed the same "work ethic" model as my female and White male cohorts, and still, I was left behind. This type of behavior is certainly not in line with Municipal policy.

Miles M. Livingston

12

National Action Network Legal Night

"Adversity does not build character; it reveals it."

–James Lane Allen

I was super pissed off at this point in my career and with good reason. I decided to speak with Reverend Al Sharpton at the National Action Network. I told him my story, and he referred me to NAN attorney Michael Hardy, who invited me to Legal Night. I attended the legal night event, and it was an incredible experience. I listened to a half dozen attorneys who gave excellent presentations in their respective areas of expertise. There, I ultimately met the attorneys that would represent me, Ellis & Mavericks LLP.

It's around 2016, and police brutality and murders of unarmed Black men seemed like they were rampant throughout the nation. High-profile shootings of Alton Sterling and Philando Castile sparked nationwide protests across the country, especially in Louisiana and Minnesota. There was even violence against the police as five cops were gunned down in Texas, and a week later, three more cops were killed in Baton Rouge, Louisiana. The country was in turmoil.

Colin Kaepernick was taking a knee during the National Anthem, Trump was running his mouth talking shit while campaigning for president, and I was still sitting at work with a Master's degree talking

435

to my female counterparts with High School diplomas that make double my salary.

I was completely done. Year after year was rolling by and I couldn't even pay my bills. At my attorney consultation meeting, I stressed the point about how broke I was. I asked them to work out some sort of contingency payment plan since I had just come out of bankruptcy. My son was in college, and I lived in a shared space. I was in bad shape. I had no car or credit cards, and my bank account was habitually overdrawn. I was struggling for real.

Round Two

The attorneys at Ellis & Mavericks LLP were so impressed with my legal binder of information that they decided to take my case. The way I saw it, I had exercised my *Right To Sue* with the EEOC, and my attitude was that I had nothing left to lose. The worst they could do was fire me; they weren't about to do that because it would be a wrongful termination. So what the fuck? Let's go for it.

This time around, it was like a courtroom drama that you would see on television, only without a jury. I sat in a gigantic courtroom with an opulent law library and a ton of conference rooms, and I got grilled for eight hours a day for the next two days. And that's not an exaggeration. They questioned me for a full seven hours for two days, minus a lunch hour. It was grueling.

Then, over the next ten days, a litany of witnesses and testimony was heard, and the case was eventually settled.

The Smoking Gun/e-mails

This is the start of my second lawsuit against my employer. All the necessary paperwork was filed by my attorneys this time. The one thing that annoyed me was that the NYSDHR had hired an interim commissioner who dismissed my second case. The Municipal attorney basically submitted the same document as before, requesting a dismissal, and this time it was granted. I immediately exercised my right to sue option, and away we went. The following are notes and files from that case.

01/09/14 – EEOC Case dismissal and Notice of Rights. (Reason) The EEOC has adopted the findings of the state or local fair employment practices agency that investigated this charge.

(The fix was in. They rubber-stamped my employer's objection).

04/03/14 – NYS Division of Human Rights public hearing: Livingston -v- Municipal Health System. You must appear on Wednesday 06/18/14 and Thursday. 06/19/14 from 9 AM – 5 PM: New York Regional Office.

06/18/14 – "Judge, can I ask a question?" I stood up in court and spoke out of turn. I couldn't take listening to the Executive Director of Human Resource's bold-faced lie on the stand like that. My attorney is asking her about emails from my employer, and she keeps saying she doesn't recall them. It's bullshit.

"Please sit down, Mr. Livingston," the judge admonishes. "You will not be asking any questions during these proceedings. Do you understand?"

I told her I understood, and I sat down, but, man, I was hot. My attorney had just subpoenaed several emails from my employer, but to our surprise, many had been redacted. I read over a dozen emails, and the only readable thing on any of them was my name, the person's name who sent the email, and the individuals who received the email.

About ten days before, my attorney sent me a copy of those emails to review. I remember going through them and wondering *what they were saying about me.* It was clearly a big topic that warranted discussion. Every week, they had a meeting or Zoom, and the topic of each correspondence was "Miles Livingston."

Still, what I did read was a cold splash of reality for me:

On Dec 24, 2014, at 12:45 PM, "Harris, Mabel" enterprise vault archive <MHarris@MuniHosp.orj > wrote:

From: Harris, Mabel
To: Amstel, Nigel Talent Acquisition
Subject: Re: don't we need to talk about Miles tomorrow? I will call u.

Nigel, do you want to talk now as in today, or can we talk on Friday? If you want to talk today, please call me on my work cell, 599-114-4399. I am not recommending Miles Livingston for the position.

sent from my iPhone On December 23rd, 2014, at 8:07 PM Nigel Amstel <NAmstel@MuniHosp.orj > wrote:

REDACTED

BRILLIANT MINDS, IGNORANT MINDS

On Nov 12, 2014, at 11:17 AM, "Cohen, Maureen" enterprise vault archive <MCohen3@MuniHosp.orj> wrote:

From: Cohen, Maureen
To: Weiss, Martin, Executive Recruiter
Subject: Re: Miles Livingston

Hi Martin,

We're going to pass on Miles Livingston. His credentials are impressive, but the hiring manager feels that he is not a good fit for their department. We are keeping Janet Josepp, Thomas Pempert, and Stewart Leggit on our shortlist, but we want to see more candidates. I had asked Nigel to schedule Karen Johnson to interview with Chris Bacon and me, who was referred by Chris Pataleo. Are there any other resumes we can see?

Thanks,
Maureen Cohen
Director, IS PMO

Note: By the time my case went to trial, my attorney told me that the individual selected by talent acquisition, Karen Johnson, was no longer with Municipal. The plan was to subpoena her and question her about her credentials and job experience, but she was no longer employed. I began wondering what kind of individual gets a primo project management position with one of the top companies in the state, only to end up gone in six months. Of course, there could have been a myriad of reasons. Still, she was not the only candidate chosen over me who was no longer employed or otherwise unavailable for subpoena when my trial date rolled around.

In my opinion, this was also a smoking gun. These individuals were hired into these positions but couldn't do the job. This was all proof that my employer was retaliating against me. I prayed that my attorney could see through this maze of bullshit. It was blatantly obvious to me.

Note: This email was from a hiring manager who was sent my resume by Talent Acquisition Specialist Roxanne Moncrief, who also referred me to a job opening in his department.

BRILLIANT MINDS, IGNORANT MINDS

On September 19, 2014, at 09:06 AM, "Codrington, Henry" enterprise vault archive webmail/

    <HCodrington@MuniHosp.orj > wrote:

From: Codrington, Henry
Sent: Friday, September 19, 2014, 09:06 AM
To: Moncrief, Roxanne
Subject: RE: Miles Livingston

Hello, Ms. Moncrief,

This candidate applied for one of our positions. Although his resume meets our criteria, I was advised to steer clear of Miles Livingston, and we will pass on this candidate.

Henry Codrington | Director, Revenue Cycle
Municipal Hospital Health System
Tel: (888) 099-9911
Email: hcodrington@munihosp.orj
www.munihospcareers.com

Note: During my quest to enter management, I conduct a search of the Municipal Hospital Revenue Cycle / Finance Department leadership hierarchy. I came across Vice President William Stenson. I write him a letter and enclose my resume. He responds to me:

441

VERNON M. O'GARRA

On Mar 3, 2015, at 09:28 AM, "Stenson, William" enterprise vault archive
<WStenson@MuniHosp.orj > wrote:

From: Stenson, William
Sent: Tuesday, March 3, 2015, 09:28 AM
To: Livingston, Miles
Subject: Revenue Management Opportunities

Thank you, Miles,

Your background is very impressive, and I will share it with our leadership and
patient accounts and keep you in mind when we have something that may fit. I also
will share your status with Sara Liu, V.P., in RIT area, for I think she may be helpful
in regard to finding work in the project management team.

Good luck,

William Stenson

William Stenson, Vice President
Revenue Cycle Management

BRILLIANT MINDS, IGNORANT MINDS

On Mar 3, 2015, at 10:43 AM, "Stenson, William" enterprise vault archive <WStenson@MuniHosp.orj > wrote:

From: Stenson, William
Sent: Tuesday, March 3, 2015, 10:43 AM
To: Livingston, Miles
Subject: Revenue Management Opportunities

Hello Miles,

The only management position I have (presently) in our department is a full-time position in our pre-registration insurance verification unit, the CBO. The position is full-time, though it covers weekends and holidays. If you are interested in it, please reach out to me.

Thanks,
William Stenson, Vice President
Revenue Cycle Management

VERNON M. O'GARRA

On Mar 3, 2015, at 11:08 AM, "Livingston, Miles" enterprise vault archive <Mlivingston@MuniHosp.orj > wrote:

(My response email)

Hello Mr. Stenson,

I would definitely be interested in this position. Feel free to forward my resume to the hiring manager. I would be happy to come in for an interview at your convenience.

Thank you,

Miles M. Livingston

Miles M. Livingston, MHA
Admitting/Emergency/Ambulatory Surgery
Municipal Hospital Systems
Anywhere, New York
(519) 888-9999 – w
mlivingston@munihosp.orj

Note: The point I need to make here is who gets recommended for a job by the V.P. of Revenue Management, and that individual does not get the job? Has that ever happened before? Do you mean to tell me that this Vice President allows his staffers to ultimately make the decision not to hire the person he recommends for the position? Smells fishy to me. Only a Black Man would experience this type of disrespect.

BRILLIANT MINDS, IGNORANT MINDS

On May 25, 2015, at 09:05 AM, "Sara Liu" enterprise vault archive <SLiu3@MuniHosp.orj > wrote:

From: Liu, Sara
Sent: Monday, May 25, 2015, 10:38 AM
To: Stenson, William
Subject: Project Management Opportunities

Hello William,

Thank you for recommending Miles Livingston. Although his credentials are impressive, I don't feel he would be a good fit for our team.

Sincerely,

Sara Liu

Sara Liu, Vice President
Revenue Cycle Management

Note: If I hear or read that I am not "a good fit" one more time, I'm going to pull out what little hair I have left on my head! This is such bullshit. I interviewed with this woman who had an all-female project management team, and these women were getting paid. I knew Ms. Liu was not going to hire me, but I went on the interview and answered all of her questions. And, YES, I was happy, friendly and courteous.

More REDACTED e-mails. . .

On Dec 17, 2014, at 03:08 PM, "Grayson, Robert" enterprise vault archive <Rgrayson@MuniHosp.orj > wrote:

From: Grayson, Robert
To: S███████████████████████████
Subject: Miles Livingston's email

Ms. Roberta Samuels, Esq.
New York State Division of Human Rights

███████████████████████████████

██

Sincerely,

██████████████████

BRILLIANT MINDS, IGNORANT MINDS

On Jan 28, 2015, at 09:45 AM, "Opilsner, Dontay" enterprise vault archive <Dopilsner@MuniHosp.orj > wrote:

From: D.O.

Subject: Re: Miles Livingston

Ms. Roberta Samuels, Esq.

Note: These emails were redacted and presented as evidence. I couldn't imagine why the Judge allowed my employer to get away with withholding evidence.

In my opinion, these emails could prove my allegations of collusion and retaliation. What were they saying about me that the attorneys didn't want to reveal?

Note: This email was from a recruiter who contacted me shortly after I applied for a Project Management position.

BRILLIANT MINDS, IGNORANT MINDS

On Nov 11, 2014, at 11:16 AM, "Messenger, Martin" enterprise vault archive webmail/

    <MMessenger@MuniHosp.orj > wrote:

From: Messenger, Martin
Sent: Tuesday, November 11, 2014, 11:16 AM
To: Livingston, Miles
Subject: Introduction

Miles,

I have been assigned to work on the role IT Project Admin, which I understand you have interviewed for. Please get in touch with me when you are able to discuss the next steps.

Martin Messenger | Executive Recruiter / IT
Municipal Hospital Health System
Tel: (897) 099-9911
Email: mmessenger@munihosp.orj
www.munihospcareers.com

VERNON M. O'GARRA

On Nov 12, 2014, at 02:47 PM, "Livingston, Miles" enterprise vault archive webmail/ < MLivingston@MuniHosp.orj > wrote:

From: Livingston, Miles
Sent: Wednesday, November 12, 2014, 02:47 PM
To: Messenger, Martin
Subject: Interview

Martin,

I have *not* been interviewed for the IT Project Admin position. Hopefully, you will be able to arrange an interview for me.

Thanks,

Miles Livingston, MS – HCA
Admitting/Emergency/Ambulatory Surgery
Municipal Hospital Health System
Tel: (897) 099-9988 - w
Email: mlivingston@munihosp.orj

BRILLIANT MINDS, IGNORANT MINDS

On Nov 12, 2014, at 05:26 PM, "Messenger, Martin" enterprise vault archive webmail/ < Messenger@MuniHosp.orj > wrote:

From: Messenger, Martin
Sent: Wednesday, November 12, 2014, 05:26 PM
To: Livingston, Miles
Subject: RE: Interview?

Miles,

It is an auto-generated email; please answer the questions in the email.

I know you have not been interviewed.

Martin Messenger | Executive Recruiter / IT
Municipal Hospital Health System
Tel: (897) 099-9911
Email: mmessenger@munihosp.orj
www.munihospcareers.com

Note: This recruiter claimed he sent me an auto-generated email, but the second email didn't have any questions attached. It had me wondering what was going on with this guy, and before I could respond, he sent me another email that stated the following:

451

VERNON M. O'GARRA

On Nov 13, 2014, at 03:06 PM, "Messenger, Martin" enterprise vault archive webmail/ <Messenger@MuniHosp.orj > wrote:

From: Messenger, Martin
Sent: Thursday, November 13, 2014, 03:06 PM
To: Livingston, Miles
Subject: RE: Interview?

Miles,

There is no further interest in your resume at this time. Thank you for your interest.

Martin Messenger | Executive Recruiter / IT
Municipal Hospital Health System
Tel: (897) 099-9911
Email: mmessenger@munihosp.orj
www.munihospcareers.com

Note: This was the type of crap I had to deal with on top of everything else in my life. I sent out a complaint email to my union representatives, Mary Kenia and Rakmann Khan.

BRILLIANT MINDS, IGNORANT MINDS

On Nov 19, 2014, at 09:08 AM, "Livingston, Miles" enterprise vault archive <MLivingston@MuniHosp.orj > wrote:

From: Livingston, Miles
Sent: Wednesday, November 19, 2014, 09:08 AM
To: Khan, Rakmann; Kenia, Mary
Subject: Re: Meeting Request

Dear Mary and Rakmann,

This is typically what happens to me periodically during my job search at Municipal Hospital. I receive a call or email from an HR representative or hiring manager telling me they have received my resume and want to interview me for a prospective position. Then, a day or two goes by, and suddenly, they're no longer interested in seeing me. The attached emails represent perfect examples of my experiences at this institution. As you know, I constantly network and make contacts with people by making calls and sending emails, all designed to advance my career.

I can honestly state that my opinion about this situation is a little biased for obvious reasons. This is the type of treatment I have experienced in the past, and it seems to be happening again. It smells a little fishy to me, but I will reserve my true feelings until I've had the chance to discuss this with you. As I have stated, this is the norm for me. I can't help but wonder what's going on regarding my situation at this hospital.

My first impulse was to vehemently correspond directly with this HR representative, but I had second thoughts because I was not in the best of moods. I know I have a history here, and there seems to be nothing I can do about that. In spite of my best efforts, I'm heading down that same road I just traveled.

I know that my experiences at this institution have not been positive. In my opinion, the circumstances surrounding my career advancement have been discriminatory. I would understand if you decide to distance yourself from me. I know I'm in a precarious situation. That being said, I respectfully request the opportunity to meet with you once again, and hopefully, you can give me your points of view concerning my future here.

I have attached the emails in question for you to review. They seem unusual to me, but I would like your opinion.

Thanks,

Miles M. Livingston

Miles M. Livingston, MHA
Admitting/Emergency/Ambulatory Surgery
Municipal Hospital Systems
Anywhere, New York
mlivingston@munihosp.orj

Note: It was obvious that as soon as the recruiter figured out who I was, or maybe one of his colleagues told him who I was, there was no further interest in me. This was clear and obvious retaliation. Another smoking gun example that I vehemently complained to my attorney about. My union representatives sides with Municipal Talent Acquisition and told me it was just a mistake, a computer glitch. I wasn't not buying it.

BRILLIANT MINDS, IGNORANT MINDS

Here are the emails:

On Feb 25, 2015, at 02:45 PM, "Livingston, Miles" enterprise vault archive < MLivingston@MuniHosp.org > **wrote:**

From: Livingston, Miles
To: Weiss, Martin
Subject: **Re**: Follow-up

Mr. Martin Weiss, Executive Recruiter / I.T.
Municipal Hospital – Talent Acquisition

Dear Mr. Weiss,

My name is Miles Livingston. We briefly corresponded in November concerning the Assoc Project Manager and Admin I.T. Project positions. I recently met with Ms. Marilyn Friedman, Director of I.T. services, who suggested I contact you.

I am still very interested in transitioning into the role of Project Manager, and I am eager to gain an opportunity to do so. I have tweaked my resume to make my skill set a little more marketable for a career change into project management.

I have an open mind in terms of obtaining a suitable position. I am not above an entry-level or assistant project management opportunity.

Please feel free to contact me at your earliest convenience.

Regards,

Miles M. Livingston

VERNON M. O'GARRA

Miles M. Livingston, MHA
Admitting/Emergency/Ambulatory Surgery
Municipal Hospital Systems
(519) 888-9999 – w
mlivingston@munihosp.orj

On Feb 25, 2015, at 02:55 PM, "Weiss, Martin" enterprise vault archive <**Mweiss2@MuniHosp.orj**> **wrote:**

From: Weiss, Martin
To: Amstel, Nigel
Subject: ACP --- Follow-up re: Miles
Attachments: MLIVINGSTON_Resume.docx

How do I respond?

Martin Weiss | Executive Recruiter IT
Municipal Hospital Systems
Anywhere, New York
(519) 888-9999 – w
mweiss2@munihosp.orj

Note: That was their actual response. I was like, "What kind of question is this? You respond by finding me a job. You're a trained HR Professional, do your fucking job!" I had already spoke with him four months earlier, so we weren't strangers. However, now that I was on

Municipal's radar, it seemed like Human Resources refused to work with me. That's clear retaliation! When Martin consulted with his leadership, and they made the decision not to do their jobs and help me, they committed "collusion" against me. I cried like a baby to my attorney, he was sick of my constant bitching and complaining, but this was another smoking gun. I wanted him to hammer my employer at every turn since now we had the ammunition. A blind man could see how guilty they were, and I only hoped the judge could.

I reached out to one of my previous supervisors, another Black woman who was climbing the ladder to career success. She had just gotten a promotion and transitioned into the Municipal Hospital behavioral health division, and she now ran her own department. Naturally, I sent her my resume so she could inquire about any available positions. She never answered me, so I left it alone. I could see the writing on the wall. I had been relegated to the role of "troublemaker," "rabble-rouser," and "malcontent" in the eyes of Municipal leadership.

VERNON M. O'GARRA

On Apr 27, 2015, at 10:38 AM, "Bailey, Lynnis" enterprise vault archive webmail/
<Lbailey@MuniHosp.orj > **wrote:**

From: Bailey, Lynnis
Sent: Monday, April 27, 2015, 10:38 AM
To: Khan, Rakmann
Cc: Swazee, Jane
Subject: Good Morning
Attachments: MLIVINGSTON_Resume

Good Morning Rakmann,

I hope all is well with you.

I would like to bring this to HR's attention regarding Miles. He sent me a similar email on the 14th. I was very busy and did not respond. Here is another email that was sent this morning. I am reticent with Miles sending me these emails because he has already brought a case against the Management team when I just left Municipal.

Although I was already here at Municipal Hillside, I had to give statements regarding why he was never considered for a Management position while I was there. I am going to respond that there are no positions here at Hillside at this time. I just wanted to bring it to someone's attention.

Have a good day
Thank You,
Lynnis

Lynnis Bailey | Manager
Municipal Hillside Hospital

458

BRILLIANT MINDS, IGNORANT MINDS

Tel: (897) 099-9911

Email: Lbailey@munihosp.orj

Note: This woman was my immediate supervisor for the past five years. She knew me, my work ethic, my personality, my skillsets. She had written two excellent referral letters for me over the years. So, of course, I thought she would be in my corner. Big Mistake. Did she think I would no longer work hard because I filed a complaint? Who knows what she or anyone else in management thought? I was a pariah among them, and the stain of my complaint would follow me for the remainder of my career.

Note: When my attorney successfully subpoenaed all of these emails, I penned the following letter to him after reading them.

Jeffrey,

I wrote these words five years ago in a letter to the Regional Director of the New York State Division of Human Rights. I could very well have written this yesterday. These e-mails prove beyond a shadow of a doubt that my employer colluded and retaliated against me.

"It is my contention that the Municipal Human Resource Department and several departmental hiring managers also acted in collusion against me. To quote the definition of the law: "Collusion occurs when two persons or representatives of an entity or organization make an agreement to deceive or mislead another. Such agreements are usually secretive and involve fraud or gaining an unfair advantage over a third party." (USLegal). This is exactly what happened to me. HR and management representatives within the Municipal Health System entity deceived and misled me. Furthermore, research has shown that " Black males with relatively high educational attainment are disproportionately distributed into lower-paying managerial and professional occupations" within their occupational sector. (Austin, 2011).

Labor market collusion is an illegal anti-trust law infraction. When H.R. representatives collude with hiring managers to occupationally segregate Black men into low-paying positions and also deny them promotional opportunities, they broke the law. "Minorities employed in the health care sector work in lower-skilled health care occupations such as nursing assistant and home health care aid." (Gabard, 2007). This finding is consistent with previous research by (Queneau 2006), "That minorities are over represented in the lowest compensating health care occupations."

We must prove to the Judge that Municipal Hospital is guilty of Retaliation and Collusion against me. I have sorted through the e-mails, and I was able to select the most incriminating ones. I look forward to discussing this with you.

Thanks,

Miles

****

As I look back on this letter I wrote, it strikes me how disheartening this situation had become for me. Deep down in my soul, I knew I would win my case. The issue for me was that there were so many African American women involved in the discrimination against me. The Executive Director of Human Resources was a Black woman.

The Executive Director of Diversity and Inclusion was a Black woman, the talent acquisition specialist assigned to me was a Black woman, one of the union officials I had to deal with was a Black woman, and one of my department managers was a Black woman. They were all brilliant women with brilliant minds, yet, like their White male

461

counterparts, they were ignorant about the workplace challenges faced by Black men.

The Municipal attorney who prosecuted the case against me was a Black Man. All of these Blacks were against me, not one ally in the bunch. I was a pariah inside my own company. Couldn't they see that there was a lack of Black men in management? Were they blind? I could understand the attitude of White men, that was easy, but this attitude of entitlement from Black women just rubbed me the wrong way. Brilliant, but ignorant minds.

If I could have only seen other Black men in management at Municipal, I would have been satisfied to know that my complaints had been heard and proven wrong. But there were no Black men in management for me to see.

A Bend in the Road

My experience was bittersweet. I had just gotten my settlement from the first case against Municipal. Now was round two. The interesting thing about this case was that I was qualified for jobs that would have only paid me maybe four or five thousand more than I was currently making. I would have been happy to take those jobs. The cost of giving me a management position would have been substantially less than the two settlements and legal fees that my employer had to pay. It's amazing to me that they decided to fight me to the end instead of doing the right thing!

I was really focused on this whole idea of collusion. It was very clear to me; however, I later learned that proving collusion in a court of law was a totally different story. From what I could see, we had the smoking gun emails, we had the Human Resource Director perjuring herself, and still, it wasn't enough. It was time to settle the case. We completed the depositions for that day, and the judge called me and my attorney into chambers for a conference. "Mr. Livingston, your employer wants to settle this matter. I'm going to set a date on my calendar for a settlement conference, and I will notify you by mail, Thank you."

I was still angry; I wanted my attorney to pounce on those lying bastards. How could the judge allow redacted emails into evidence? Those email correspondences were the evidence to prove my collusion and discrimination case. They proved that my employer was meeting secretly about me, to discuss how they would impede my growth into management. I felt that the judge was not only wrong but ignorant. She should have compelled my employer to submit unredacted emails and come clean about what they were discussing. Instead, every time my attorney brought up the subject of emails during the deposition, my employer was always allowed to skirt through the issue with bullshit responses, lies, and untruths, and the judge allowed it to happen. It made me sick.

One of these "Law Review" publications weighed in on the judge's decision concerning discovery rules and what information to allow and disallow in my case. They referred to our request for documentation from my employer as a *"fishing expedition,"* which I totally disagreed with. I was not fishing; I knew exactly what I wanted. However, the judge, in my case, allowed my employer to withhold evidence and redact critical data in the form of emails, which reduced the amount of damages I would have received when my case was settled. That's what happens to Black Men in my situation. I believe the term that was used was

"Gamesmanship." All I know is that my employer was allowed to get away with it. It was a brilliant strategy.

This is the brief that my attorney prepared for the court:

UNITED STATES DISTRICT COURT
EASTERN DISTRICT OF NEW YORK

MILES M. LIVINGSTON,	)	
Plaintiff	)	Index No.: 465 Civ 37499
	)	(HGBF69)
MUNICIPAL HOSPITAL (MUNICIPAL	)	
HEALTH SYSTEM, INC.)	)	
Defendant.	)	
	)	
_____	)	
	)	

**PLAINTIFF'S RESPONSE TO DEFENDANT'S MEMORANDUM OF
LAW REGARDING DISCOVERY DEFICIENCIES**

VERNON M. O'GARRA

TABLE OF CONTENTS

POINT I

DEFENDANT'S REQUESTS FOR PLAINTIFF'S PERSONAL FILES OF HIS CURRENT EMPLOYER IS AT ODDS WITH THE DISCOVERY LIMITS OF RULE 26, WHICH DEMANDS RELEVANCE AND PROPORTIONALITY 470

POINT II

IN RESPONSE TO POINT II, TO THE EXTENT THAT PLAINTIFF CAN
FIND COMPLETE DOCUMENTS; THEY WILL PRODUCE THEM 476

CONCLUSION 477

TABLE OF AUTHORITIES

Cases

Federal Rules

VERNON M. O'GARRA

PRELIMINARY STATEMENT

Plaintiff Miles M. Livingston ("Plaintiff") by his attorneys Jeffrey Elden Associates, pursuant to the Court's Oct 4, 2017 Order, submits this response to the defendant's memorandum of law regarding discovery deficiencies and in response to the defendant's motion to compel plaintiff to execute and authorization for the release of his personnel records from Revenue Management Group, his current employer.

It appears that there may be some "gamesmanship" at play concerning the defendant's requests for authorization to receive the plaintiff's personnel file. The plaintiff has offered to personally provide the relevant documents from the file, which makes the authorization unnecessary. The plaintiff wonders whether the doubling down of this request through seeking records and resume interview notes that are not proportional and arguably entirely irrelevant is simply a ploy to play on the plaintiff's concerns that his employer will retaliate against him because he filed a discrimination claim against Municipal Hospital, which is Revenue Management Group's contractor for services.

SUMMARY OF RELEVANT FACTS AND PROCEDURAL HISTORY

To avoid redundancy, the plaintiff respectfully incorporates their declaration as a recitation of the statement of facts and procedural history. Other facts relevant to this motion are incorporated in the body of this memorandum.

ARGUMENT
POINT I

THE REQUESTS BY THE DEFENDANT FOR THE PLAINTIFF'S PERSONNEL FILES OF HIS CURRENT EMPLOYER IS AT ODDS WITH THE DISCOVERY LIMITS OF RULE 26, WHICH DEMANDS RELEVANCE AND PROPORTIONALITY

Defendant's insistence upon Plaintiff's signing and authorization releasing his personnel file from his current employer is unnecessary and arguably retaliatory. As stated in the party's joint letter, the defendant proposed the following language for revised authorization for the Plaintiff's personnel records from Revenue Management Group.

Any and all documents relating to [Miles Livingston's] salary, compensation end, or benefits associated with his employment with Revenue Management Group and any and all documents related to [Miles Livingston's] application for employment and hiring by Revenue Management Group, including but not limited to his resume application interview notes any references or recommendations submitted on [his] behalf in [his] offer letter for the time period 2016 to present.

[Elden Dec. 14]

The defendant argues that the files are relevant to the mitigation of damages. The Plaintiff agrees to the relevance of these files, which is why the Plaintiff will provide these mitigation documents to the defendants, *albeit* from his own possession. [Elden Dec. 25].

The Plaintiff argues that the production request is over burdensome because the information can be provided directly by the Plaintiff. The Plaintiff warned the defendant during their meet and conference that Plaintiff fears retaliation from his new employer. [Elden Dec. 21].

The plaintiff is concerned that if Revenue Management Group learns he is complaining of discrimination from his prior employer, it may adversely affect his employment relationship. [Id.]

Accordingly, in response to the defendant's mitigation of damages justification for his authorization, the Plaintiff will produce his Revenue Management Group W-2s and his offer letter to the defendant for the calculation of damages. [Elden Dec. 25].

The Plaintiff will also provide the defendant his Revenue Management Group offer that's relative to his entitled benefits. [Id.] Consequently, there is no further information to produce regarding mitigating damages. Admittingly, the Plaintiff's new job pays more in all respects to his previous employment with the defendant.

To bolster their need for this authorization, the defendant now claims they want to fish through the plaintiff's personnel file to identify whether any Municipal Hospital employees supported the Plaintiff's application for employment with Revenue Management Group. The defendant wants to discover if any Municipal Hospital employees previously accused by the Plaintiff of discrimination wrote a reference letter supportive of the Plaintiff. The defendant is clearly on a fishing expedition and at great prejudice to the Plaintiff's current employment opportunities at Revenue Management Group. There is less burdensome information there, and there is a less burdensome way to discover this information short of sending his new employer and authorization for the Plaintiff's personnel file. The Plaintiff will commit to providing all references provided by Municipal Hospital employees. [Elden Dec. 26]. The Plaintiff will provide this information even though Municipal Hospital has this information in its possession and control since Municipal Hospital could simply ask each of the relevant hiring managers and talent acquisition specialists whether they provided the Plaintiff with a recommendation.

The Plaintiff's willingness to cooperate with the production of documents eliminates the need to allow the defendant to fish through the entire personnel records of the Plaintiff's new employer.

Certainly, if the Plaintiff provides these documents, there is no prejudice to the defendants. Therefore, a mass production of this authorization is not needed.

Nevertheless, the Plaintiff's resume, application, and interview notes have little, if any, probative value to their defenses. The Plaintiff should not be prejudiced by Municipal Hospital's fishing expedition. The defendant has not provided a single justification for this data.

As pursuant to rule 26(b)(1), the defendant has the burden to "illustrate exactly why and how the personnel files sought a relevant, material, and proportional to their claims." See *Williams v. Fire Sprinkler Associates, Inc.*, CV 15-3119 at (ADS) May 27th, 2016). The defendant's request for his employment application resume and interview notes from his current employer does not support their defense. It cuts against their defense because Revenue Management Group hired the Plaintiff. The Plaintiff's case follows in most respects *Bernie v. Town of Cromwell Board of Education*, 243 F.3d 93, 103 (2d Cir. 2001), where this Court stated that a fact issue regarding the plaintiff's job qualifications could be found. "[if] the Plaintiff's credentials would have to be so superior to the credentials of the person selected for the job that no reasonable person, in the exercise of impartial judgment, could have chosen the candidate selected over the plaintiff for the job in question." The discovery of a reference letter from Municipal Hospital clearly supports Plaintiff's argument that he has superior credentials. Therefore, the letter is relevant to the Plaintiff's claims but lacks relevance. More importantly, it is proportionately respective to the defendant's defense. The Plaintiff's resume did not change from the many times he provided this resume to the defendant during his application process at Municipal Hospital.

---

1. The current version of Rule 26 defines permissible discovery to consist of information that is, in addition to being relevant "to any party's claim or defense," also "proportional to the needs of the case." Fed. R. Civ. P. 26(b)(1), See also *Id.* Advisory Comm. Notes (2015) (noting that amendment "restores the proportionality factors to their original place in defining the scope of discovery" and "reinforces the rule 26 (g) obligation of the parties to consider these factors in making discovery requests, responses, or objections"). The specific proportionality factors to be assessed when considering the scope of discovery are:

- The importance of the issues at stake in litigation
- The amount in controversy
- The parties' relevant access to relevant information
- The parties' resources
- The importance of discovery in resolving issues. And,
- Whether the burden or expense of the discovery is outweighed by the benefit

Fed. R. Civ. P. 26(b)

Relative to relevance and proportionality, and similar to the reference letter, the Plaintiff's resume helps the Plaintiff's burden, not the defendant's.

The application, interview notes, and resume sought by the defendants are simply irrelevant to their defenses or fail to proportionately test. The material issue of the case is whether the Plaintiff's paper qualifications stack up against the applicants selected for the job.

The problem with the paper qualifications and interview notes sought from the Plaintiff's new employer is that they bear no probative weight to the case issues at bar. The Plaintiff applied and was denied by the defendant, not Revenue Management Group.

Why the defendant is seeking these documents is a mystery because they never gave an explanation in the first place, and if they did, it should not be one this court should find legitimate.

As the Plaintiff's response suggests, the facts and circumstances of this case are easily distinguishable from the cases presented by the defendant. The Plaintiff will provide the mitigation data concerning his damages from his employer because it is directly relevant to the damages calculation. However, the Plaintiff's resume, interview notes, and employment application are not proportional; it has little or no probative value to the defendant's defenses since it's an apple-to-orange comparison on the issue of paper qualifications concerning similarly stipulated applications in a failure to promote case, thereby there is no benefit to its discovery. Nevertheless, as a less burdensome alternative, he will produce the resume. [Elden Dec. 16].

Relative to the mitigation data (salary, compensation and/or benefits associated with [his] employment with Revenue Management Group), the Plaintiff's less burdensome alternative to this discovery request should be accepted by Municipal Hospital. The documents sought can be provided directly from the Plaintiff. Further, the Plaintiff will provide the reference letters and the resume provided to Revenue Management Group directly. [Elden Dec. 26]. However, the defendant's request for the personnel file documents concerning his employment application, resume, and interview notes from the Plaintiff's new employer is at "odds with the discovery limits of Rule 26, which proscribes relevance and proportionality in civil cases." *Quoting Williams,* CV 15-3147 at 7. The Defendant provides no justification for the relevance of the interview documents. Therefore, the Court should reject the defendant's request to compel the Plaintiff to sign an authorization for these documents and accept the alternatives suggested.

POINT II

TO THE EXTENT THAT PLAINTIFF CAN RESPONSE FIND COMPLETE DOCUMENTS THEY WILL BE PRODUCE THEM

During prior meet and confers and during the conference call which preceded this Order, the Plaintiff stated that he would review his files and correct any deficiencies relative to missing documents. [Elden Dec. 27]. Therefore, as stated in the defendant's case examples (Def. Brief, p.9), and as stated by the Plaintiff's counsel, to the extent that the Plaintiff can find complete documents, he will produce them. Otherwise, as stated to the defendant in prior meet and confers

[Elden Dec. 9]. Most of these documents appear to be emails from the defendant's system. Thereby, these documents are already in the defendant's custody and control.

<u>CONCLUSION</u>

For all the foregoing reasons, the defendant should be denied the production of the Plaintiff's personnel file by way of authorization, and a less burdensome method should be adopted as stated by the Plaintiff. However, the application, interview notes, and other items loosely referenced as part of the application are irrelevant or proportional to the defendant's defenses and should not be compelled.

Dated: June 14, 2017, New York, NY.

Respectfully submitted,

Plaintiff Attorney

Jeffrey Elden, Esq.

Of course, I may be a little biased, but I felt that my attorney described this situation pretty well. My employer wanted me to authorize them to fish through my records to gather dirt against me. The thing is, I didn't have any dirt for them to dig up. I was one of the good guys, an honest, hard-working, and responsible employee.

It was like one of these police brutality murder cases where the Police wanted to blame the victim for his own death—assassinating the character of the victim, which, of course, has nothing to do with the victim being murdered by the police.

So, here's the thing that happens in these types of discrimination cases. The employer adopts the point of view that this Black Man can't possibly have the resources to fight us, so let's bury his attorney in paperwork. So that's exactly what they did.

My employer's attorney requested that one hundred and twenty-four records be released to Jessing Shabinov, Municipal Hospital's attorney. Those records were to include all my medical records (including any psychiatric or psychological) as well as any social media of mine. Basically, they wanted to find out any information relating to my physical or mental state starting from 2014.

First of all, as I was told by my attorney, I would never post anything work-related on social media. Secondly, I was sure their attorneys already scoured through the internet looking for my social media pages anyway, so I didn't understand why they made a written request for it in the first place. Sure, I imagine it was for the sake of privacy law, but they didn't find anything there anyway, so I know they were pissed about that.

They asked for a laundry list of items. Any notes I had written, photographs, calendars, recordings, emails, my resume and diplomas. It just went on and on. They went for my medical records, including any psychotherapy that I might have had. My taxes, pension, and 401k information. Everything and anything that had to do with me, they wanted it.

What was even more surprising was that they asked for any documentation backing up whether or not I'd been promoted into a management position, which is crazy since if I had been, I wouldn't have been suing. I guess they were looking for anything to prove my allegations were wrong.

And, they asked for any documents concerning any disciplinary actions that I'd received while I was employed by them. Remember the whole thing about wearing headphones at work? Yeah, that was all they had. One stupid little thing that happened because they had it out for me in the first place.

This is the type of silliness a Black Man has to endure daily, not only at Municipal Hospital but at any other corporate entity in this country.

The following is a summary of the judge's ruling and how the Employment Law Review analyzed that ruling:

Employment Law Review | Employee must authorize current employer to produce limited records for his suit against prior employer

NEWS | Thursday, March 25, 2018

Employee must authorize current employer to produce limited records for his suit against prior employer.

An employee who was allegedly denied post-settlement job opportunities with his former employer after he settled his age, race, and gender discrimination claims must sign a narrowly tailored authorization allowing his present employer to produce certain employment records, including his resume, application, and salary and benefits information, a federal district court in New York ruled, granting the former employer's motion to compel. His claim for damages put the issue of his subsequent employment earnings squarely at issue, and his concerns over the effect the authorization might have on his current employment relationship did not override the employer's entitlement to production of relevant information (*Livingston* v. *Municipal Hospital Systems,* February 9, 2018, Jones, H.).

Twelve years after he started working at Municipal Hospital, the employee settled employment discrimination claims against the company.

After the settlement, he was allegedly denied several job opportunities. He then sued, claiming direct discrimination as well as discrimination in retaliation for his prior claim. He subsequently accepted a job with another company that, he asserted, was for the same position for which he had applied "countless times" at Municipal.

Discovery requests. After engaging in extensive discovery, Municipal sought to have the employee execute an authorization allowing it access to certain of his post-termination employment records as well as more complete discovery responses. For his part, the employee sought additional document production and responses to interrogatories.

Rule 26. Rule 26 of the Federal Rules of Civil Procedure, which sets forth the scope of discovery, has been amended on several occasions in an attempt to strike the proper balance between the need for evidence and the avoidance of undue burden or expense. Pursuant to the most recent amendment, effective December 1, 2015, the scope of discovery is defined to consist of information that is relevant to the parties' "claims and defenses," observed the court, noting that the discretionary authority to allow discovery of "any matter relevant to the subject matter involved in the action" has been eliminated. Further, the rule defines permissible discovery to consist of information that is, in addition to being relevant "to any party's claim or defense," also "proportional to the needs of the case."

Notably absent from Rule 26, observed the court, "is the all too familiar, but never correct, iteration of the permissible scope of discovery as including all matter that is 'reasonably calculated to lead to' the discovery of admissible evidence." This language was intended only to make clear that discovery was not limited by the concept of admissibility, the court explained.

Fishing expedition? Turning to the employer's motion to compel production of the employee's current employment records, the court noted that the employee refused to sign the proposed authorization allowing Municipal to obtain records from his current employer, contending that it should not be allowed to "fish through" his entire personnel file. Further, he argued, asking his current employer to sign any authorization would alert it to this lawsuit, and thereby subject him to possible retaliation.

Agreeing that the wage information was relevant to the issue of mitigation of damages, the employee offered to provide tax information showing his wages and benefits as well as his letter offer of employment, resume, and copies of letters of reference he submitted to his current employer.

There was no question, said the court, as to the discoverability of documents showing wages and benefits earned at his current employer.

Rather, the issue was whether he should be compelled to sign an authorization that might jeopardize his current employment relationship.

Squarely at issue. Explaining that the employee's damages claim put the issue of his subsequent earnings squarely at issue and that his concerns over the authorization's effect on his current employment relationship did not override Municipal's entitlement to production of relevant information, the court determined that Municipal need not be compelled to rely on his statements regarding his offer and benefits. Rather, he should be compelled to execute an appropriate authorization for salary and related benefit information. Moreover, the court pointed out that the scope of the records sought was particularly relevant as he alleged specifically that the position he was offered was "the same position" to which he applied for "countless times" at Municipal.

Narrowly tailored. While Municipal was "certainly entitled to discovery of information as to the nature of the job offered, Plaintiff's qualifications, and his application," the authorization had to be narrowly tailored to authorize "the production of all documents showing Plaintiff's salary, compensation and/or benefits associated with his employment with the Revenue Management Group from beginning till this day, Plaintiff's application filed for his initial employment with Revenue Management Group including his resume, application, and any references or recommendations submitted on his behalf and his offer letter."

Motion to compel complete copies of documents. As to Municipal's assertion that a large number of documents produced by the employee were incomplete because only portions of emails were produced, certain copies were cut off at the bottom, and certain pages produced appeared to be portions of a larger document that was not produced, the court pointed out that issues as to whether or not complete copies of any document are in the possession of a party are matters that the parties ought to be able to resolve on their own. Because the parties here were unable to do so, the court ordered the employee to review his production and produce complete copies of all documents produced to the extent such documents were in his possession, custody, or control.

Employee's motion to compel. Finally, turning to the employee's motion to compel the production of additional documents and responses to interrogatories, the court first found that his request for documents, including a document indicating the racial profile of all managerial and supervisory employees from 2009-2015, was vastly overbroad and beyond the needs of the case, which was limited to alleged failures to promote that post-dated the 2014 settlement agreement.

As to the jobs actually at issue, Municipal produced extensive documents and responses. To the extent possible, however, the court directed it to identify the gender, age, and race of each applicant identified in its responses. Denying the employee's request to access the entire personnel files of all individuals who applied for and received offers for the promotions at issue, the court explained that requiring Municipal to produce full personnel files for each applicant would amount to a disproportional fishing expedition.

It was a very interesting article I discovered purely by chance a couple of years after settling my case. I realized that lawsuits are closely watched, followed, and written about unbeknownst to the participants litigating against each other. I imagine attorneys and judges know about what's going on with their cases and which law journals, reviews, and articles to read. While a regular guy like me is ignorant about the contents of a law review article, I am brilliant regarding research and discovery.

I contacted my attorney to discuss this article and obtain some legal perspective.

This article was used in my post-settlement case to highlight the "weakness in a discovery" rule meant to limit lawyers from going on fishing expeditions and how the judge who handled my case mitigated that weakness on both sides. This was a point I would argue, because I knew exactly which employees got preferential treatment. When my attorney asked my employer about all the women and White men who got promotions, the judge called it fishing. But that wasn't true. These employees were hiding in plain sight. We didn't have to "fish" to find them.

The judge compelled me to authorize the Revenue Management Group to provide Municipal Hospital with my employment information, limited to my position title, salary, and benefits. And for me to complete documents submitted to Municipal demonstrating that I applied to the Revenue Management Group position in the exact same manner as I applied to the Municipal positions. The judge deemed that combination of documents sufficient to support my claim that I was able to secure the same position at Revenue Management Group that Municipal Hospital had denied me over and over, utilizing the same materials in the application process.

On the other hand, the judge ruled that my motion for demographics on every promotion at Municipal from 2009 to 2015 was a gross overreach for the case at hand. So, Municipal was also limited in producing demographic information on employees promoted to the position in question after my original case was settled. To me, it was a Catch-22 decision. When I specifically identified a specific period of time and the specific names of employees, they denied my request. Realizing that my case lingered on for seven years, my employer was able to hide behind this so-called "weakness in the discovery" rule, and they used it to their advantage. I certainly didn't see how the judge mitigated that weakness on both sides. But that's the law. One attorney against ten. Who do you think is going to win?

I did feel some sort of vindication that I kicked my employer's ass, but after all was said and done, what did it really mean. Not much! My employer was out several thousand dollars with no admission of wrongdoing. Meanwhile, I had been gagged and ostracized, and the claims of my case swept under the rug.

All of the legal wrangling back and forth for over seven years and I would have happily settled for a little promotion that paid a few dollars more than I was making. Truly, it was all that I was asking for. When I look back on my career, it's really unbelievable. Eventually, after all my complaining, they finally hired a Black Man who did not know healthcare. I was happy to finally see a Black Man get hired into management, but he was hired for all the wrong reasons. Even the Division of Human Rights investigator said in the Final Investigation Report & Basis Of Determination (Chapter 10), "It is reasonable to believe that the hiring of a Black male into a supervisory position was a *"smoke screen"* designed to mask a discriminatory act."

The reality of this situation was that my employer made it personal. For whatever reason, they were not going to promote any Black men into management. I just happened to be that "upwardly mobile" Black guy who was qualified and in line for a promotion.

So I became a target for them. All my hard work, master's degree, workforce development certification, publishing a healthcare article, and superior work ethic… It all meant "nothing" to my employer.

Like I used to say, a Black Man with a Master's degree was the "kiss of death" at my job. As a Black Man, I knew I had to be better than the competition, but I never thought I'd be fighting *impossible* odds. I was head and shoulders above other candidates who applied for management positions, but I believe that I intimidated the hiring managers.

After several years of job hunting, I decided to confide in a few close friends and family members. The common theme among them that was said to me was, "Miles, you're a six-foot-three, two hundred and forty-five-pound Black Man, plus you're smart and articulate. Of course, you're intimidating." I was shocked to hear that. I mean, I am the nicest guy in the world. I would never actively try to intimidate anyone, especially at work.

An article in Newsday around this same time period lays it all out: "Exacerbating the lack of Black men in management positions and other factors,' experts say, 'are social perceptions of Black men that are often rooted in racial biases.

Many potential employers would rather hire immigrants or women over Black men, who are viewed as 'not as compliant, more demanding, not reliable,' said Levitan, citing a large body of research." (Texeira, 2004).

"'Black male job applicants, particularly if they are tall and muscular, need to be aware that many people immediately are intimidated by them,' said Chuck Hoffman, director of Workforce Development Services at New York City College of Technology in Downtown Brooklyn. 'If they're going to an interview and it's a little

White lady, I tell them, 'I would recommend you lower your voice and be aware,' Hoffman said. 'That's the reality.'" (Texeira, 2004)

This was shocking for me to read about and hear. Although this new revelation was troubling, the longer I thought about it, the more this reality began to make sense to me. All the women who interviewed me and felt that I wouldn't be a "good fit" for their respective departments. Were they intimidated? The White men who ran the Municipal Insurance Exchange, were they intimidated by me? My thinking was, if I was a hiring manager, why wouldn't I want a smart, well-rounded, knowledgeable employee? Who cares what color he is or how tall he is? He'll be a benefit to our department and be an asset to our team.

But it did matter that I was Black. When you look at the staff at the Municipal Insurance Company and the only Black men are in housekeeping positions, you really have to scratch your head.

After all was said and done, my *second* case was settled. We haggled back and forth about money (of course, it's always about money), but we settled the case for an undisclosed amount.

"Racial Equity means the development of policies, practices, and strategic investments to reverse racial disparity trends, eliminate institutional racism, impact structural racism, and ensure that outcome and opportunities for all people are no longer predictable by race." (Law Insider, n.d.)

Unfortunately, in my opinion, "Racial Equity" is something that Municipal Health System will never achieve. I do admit that they have made small improvements in the hiring of African American men. But until Corporate America invites Black men to sit at the proverbial decision-making table, they will never achieve true Racial Equity inside the workplace.

13

The Me Nobody Knows

"I'm forced to be an optimist, I'm forced to believe that we can survive whatever we must survive."

—James Baldwin

Throughout this entire ordeal, I was living a double life. Check that. It was probably a quadruple life if I'm being honest. It wasn't easy. I felt like every day, I was being eaten alive by everything that I was going to have to deal with. My income was minuscule. Every check I got, all the money was spent before I even got to see any of it. I was behind on my bills, and child support was kicking my ass. There seemed to be no hope of me getting ahead at work. I was constantly worried about my kids. My love life was all over the place. On top of that, I had to walk around with a phony mask every day at work. When you're Black and perceived as anything other than content, you get labeled the "Angry Black Man," and with my already precarious position with management, I wasn't trying to make matters worse. But even through all that, most people who worked with me liked and respected me. I spent a lot of time listening to my inner voice, which just kept telling me to keep it together and press on.

And On and On

I still had to endure interview after interview with incompetent H.R. professionals and hiring managers who were clueless. Human Resource professionals skipped over my name consistently. Knucklehead supervisors and managers consulted me about job-related decisions, but when my turn came to be promoted, I didn't get the job. And the toughest thing about all that was that I had to go and work with these racist assholes on a daily basis while remaining civil. There were many times when I just wanted to punch my boss out. Just lay him out cold, but my job and reputation be damned. But I couldn't do it. It wasn't just him that was the problem after all. It was a system that was dead set against me.

So many issues were constantly on my mind. The racist parents who let my son walk home by himself at night, who smiled and spoke to me at the PTA and school night meetings. School board members that refused to support any of the African American initiatives that were presented, the way Black men are treated by the police and in media. The fact that every time someone calls attention to the problems within our community, we're shouted down by White people who would rather believe that there's nothing wrong.

All this shit was welling up inside me. Looking back on things, I really needed counseling from a mental health professional. However, my male ego and pride would not allow me to go down that road. I can think back thirty years ago when my wife had to sit me down one day to talk to me about my feelings and how everything I was experiencing at work was affecting the way I treated her and the kids. It was truly an eye-opener. I listened to her explain how difficult I had become and how disgruntled and upset I was all the time. I was crushed by her words. But there was truth in them. I had become a different man than the one she married. All because of the racism that had its foot on my neck. "As Black male professionals, we do not reveal any sense of anger at work: we focus so much on not bringing or showing our feelings at the office, but a lot of times the office produces so much stress, you bring that back home. It's difficult to keep them both separate." (Wingfield, 2007).

And then, one day, I received a termination letter from my employer. I can't describe the rage I was feeling. After everything I'd put up with, all the bullshit I had to endure, I was being fired?? Seriously? It took all my strength to keep calm and not act out at work. But I'll tell you something. I have never wanted to kick my boss's ass more than when I got that notice. I ended up in the Freedmont Human Resource Director's office, where she calmed me down, rectified the termination, and reinstated me as an employee in good standing.

When I reflect back on these memories, I realize now that despite it all, I have been truly blessed with some incredible women who influenced my life in a myriad of positive ways. For all my anger at the system for opening doors for Black women and not Black men, I don't believe in my heart that Black women are the problem or the issue. The unfortunate dynamic for me as a Black Man is that I live in a society that pits Black men and women against each other. In certain scenarios, Black men get lost in the shuffle and denied opportunities. I'm just one more Black Man who got caught in the crossfire of White supremacy.

In a Forbes magazine article entitled "Working While Black: Stories from Black Corporate America." I read the following words from a brother with whom I really identified.

"I have held executive positions at various blue-chip companies. I have hidden my Black culture all my life because I thought it was the "corporate" thing to do. The stress of being a Black Man in corporate America means we can't have the full range of emotions. We can only be happy—never angry. No mentors, so we just have to figure it out. And by the time that we do, the great opportunities have passed us by, as we weren't part of "the network." (Yuan, 2020).

I see myself as an intelligent guy who has the ability to flourish in the healthcare sector. My communication skills allow me to interact well with all types of people and it just so happens that healthcare is something that I'm passionate about and deeply interested in. Deep down, I'm very competitive and I enjoy setting and achieving goals. In the ever-changing world of healthcare, goals, objectives and planning are always needed to improve the delivery of services. My chances for success should be great and yet, I was stalled for something that I didn't have any control over.

Personal Development

One of the things that I decided to do in the early 90s was hire a personal development coach or success coach. I'd been watching Tony Robbins and these self-help gurus, so I decided to go out on a limb and hire somebody to help me. I wanted to invest in myself and couldn't think of a better way than to allow someone to show me the way. Looking back on this chapter in my life, it's truly one of the best decisions I ever made. My success coach helped me to focus and set goals designed around self-improvement. Throughout my life, it's helped me stay on track in the minefield of my career.

I learned how to live my life in balance. Those were lessons that would follow me for the rest of my life. I categorized those lessons into simple directives and found ways to devote time and energy to them. "You will be more productive over a long period of time and find greater satisfaction in your accomplishments when you establish priorities in all six areas of life: financial and career, physical and health, family and home, mental and educational, spiritual and ethical, and social and cultural." (Meyer, 1994).

It breaks down like this:

- *Finances and Career* – I made an appointment to set up my 403(b)-retirement plan, and through that, I went over my finances to get my credit in order and consolidated some debt. As far as my career was concerned, I kept my resume fresh and updated my LinkedIn profile.

- *Physical and Health* – I scheduled an annual check-up with my primary care physician and renewed my gym membership. That's something I still do to this day.

- *Social and Cultural* – I bought a pair of Knicks basketball tickets and made dinner reservations with my wife. That turned out to be a great idea. I got to let my hair down, relax, and focus on something other than my troubles. It was like giving my psyche a break. It was lovely to enjoy a nice date night with my wife.

- *Spiritual and Ethical* – I feel that it's extremely important to be spiritually grounded in life. My parents had given my brother and me an understanding of God and religion growing up, and I'll admit, in my adult years, I drifted away from that. In the spirit of getting myself together, I reconnected with my local Church and started attending services. I also watched religious programming on television when time did not permit me to attend Church services in person.

- *Family and Home* – I planned a snowboarding weekend with my kids. It was absolutely one of the best weekends of my life. We spent the weekend up at Camelback Mountain Resort relaxing and having fun on the slopes. I cherish those memories with them still today.

- *Mental and Educational Health* - I decided to earn my master's degree in healthcare administration, and I joined a professional healthcare organization that kept me busy. Also, my life coach sessions count towards this area of my life.

The trick to living a balanced life is knowing how to execute these six principles consistently every month or bi-monthly at the least. Once I got into it, I realized that it was a win-win. Every time I dedicated myself to a particular area of my life, it was a great experience. As the years rolled by, this would become more and more challenging for me, obviously. But as my success coach told me time and time again, "Miles, we're always under construction. Tomorrow is the first day of the rest of your life. Just pick up your workbook and start fresh tomorrow."

One of the things that was easiest for me was Mental & Educational Health. I've always been looking for ways to improve myself and get ahead. In that vein, I'm always doing continuing education classes and other things that I feel would help me be a better man with a healthy and well-fed mind. My professional organization sent us to CE training on a regular basis and I got a lot of out them on a personal note. Unfortunately, since I was an African American man working within a racist system at my institution, continuing education and self-improvement courses didn't count for anything there. The message was clear: *"We will **not** promote you, no matter what you do.*

Self-Assessment and Reflection

In May of 2006, when I started grad school, I had to take a "Self-Assessment and Reflection" exercise. It began with the discovery of my "learning style." As it turned out, my learning style is Tactile/Kinesthetic. That means I learn best when physically engaged in hands-on activities. It made sense. Reading over the results of my self-assessment test brought back memories of so many things I took for granted about how I did things.

The funny thing is that I have heard many people comment about my kinesthetic characteristics over time. I can remember my parents scolding me for not listening to the instructions they told me to follow. For example, at the same time, if I was actively doing something in class, it didn't take me long to get it. My classmates would cut class and say things like, "We'll just copy Miles's notes," because if I could write it down, there was a good chance I'd retain the information. I enjoyed working out, playing basketball, and jogging, all things I turned out to be really good at. And my DJ career had gone so well because handling the records and listening to the music to find the right cues for mixing were all things that it just seemed I was wired to do. It all fell in line with a "Tactile/Kinesthetic" learning style.

In short, I learn best by doing. Being physically active in a learning environment is best for me. Because of how my mind works, from the outside looking in, it might seem like I have trouble understanding things. However, the truth is, if the information isn't presented to me in a way that my brain can accept, that makes it a little harder for me to get. Sometimes, the simplest things can be difficult for me to understand.

On the other hand, complex things are sometimes extremely easy for me.

My strengths include being an effective team leader. I work best in a team-oriented environment. I can set and achieve my goals. I have excellent communication skills, can organize and coordinate projects well, and problem-solve. I can give an oral presentation and address a group effectively. I also discovered (unconsciously) that I enjoy writing. The amount of writing required to complete an online Master's degree program is extensive. But it was that experience that developed my writing into a strength.

But then, on the flip side, my weaknesses were also revealed to me. I'm not a very good listener, especially if it's something I'm not interested in. I can become disinterested and mentally check out. I sometimes have a short attention span for issues I cannot control or influence.

Sometimes, my schedule will become overloaded, and time management can be a concern. Meeting deadlines has been a challenge for me; however, I promise myself that I will work on this and improve upon all of my weaknesses.

Don Clifton Strength Finder – 2017

I took one of those Don Clifton Strength Finder exams in 2017. At the time, my director had been so impressed by the book that she bought each of us a copy to read. The results of this test reveal the following:

"LEARNER": What Makes Me Stand Out – Chances are good that you are scholarly, especially when you have an important goal to reach. You are willing to examine relevant topics for extended periods of time. You are determined to satisfy your need for knowledge as well as your desire to make measurable progress. It's very likely that you prefer to register for rigorous courses of study rather than take easy classes. This often satisfies your need to do things that do not come naturally. You trust you can endure the unpleasantness and difficulties that accompany the expansion of your knowledge base, the acquisition of skills, and the conquest of deficiencies.

When I read this about myself, it reminded me of my grad school courses. As an online student, you must become part of a work group. We'd have to write these papers for class, and each workgroup would be assigned a topic. Each group member would have to write a section or chapter of the paper. Long story short, I would never pick a topic to write about. I would always allow the other members of my work group to pick out the topics they wanted or were most comfortable working on, and I always took the last topic or section that the others had left behind. Sometimes, the topics were difficult and challenging; sometimes, they weren't. My thinking was if I let the weaker students select topics they were familiar with, they would require less help when it came time to submit our paper.

For every assigned project, the instructor designated a different team leader. I seemed to always gravitate towards a leadership role in all my classes, regardless of whether I was the team leader or not. Most of the time, my initiative was appreciated. One class I was in included a type "A" personality hospital director. She announced to the entire group that she would research, write, and submit the entire project by herself. I never responded to her; I just researched and wrote my section of the project and submitted it. When the final draft of our project was completed, I noticed that my entire section was attached unedited, precisely the way I submitted it. It's like the saying goes, the pen is mightier than the sword.

The next portion of my test said the following:

"ACHIEVER": What Makes Me Stand Out – *It's very likely that you labor tirelessly when you know your performance and results are being compared to those of other people. You probably find it hard to recall a time when you failed for lack of effort. You are naturally motivated to be the very best – not merely one of the top finishers.*

"FOCUS": What Makes Me Stand Out – *It's very likely that you approach most win-lose situations in a practical and realistic manner. When you are intent on being victorious, you automatically extinguish any sentimental feelings you have toward your rivals. Chances are good that you are unsentimental and not often swayed by emotional arguments or passionate pleas. People are likely to describe you as quite realistic and practical.*

VERNON M. O'GARRA

"FUTURE": What Makes Me Stand Out – Chances are good that you are eager to get started on a project once you realize what you can accomplish in the coming weeks, months, or years. You work very hard to breathe life into your big dreams. These often push and pull you into the future. It's very likely that you gain a certain degree of satisfaction from envisioning what your life and the world might be like in the coming months, years, or decades. Instinctively, you naturally consider what you can accomplish in the coming weeks, months, years, or decades.

You usually get more done when you have established goals.

Those results surprised me. I took it very seriously and immersed myself in the exercises. I was surprised at how accurate this test was. It was me. Reading through the test results (which were much more extensive than the brief summary written here) was like looking into the mirror at myself. Don Clifton was a psychologist who developed an assessment tool that could pinpoint a person's strengths. It was amazing to me how accurate the test results were. Clifton's philosophy: "he was tired of living in a world that revolved around fixing our weaknesses. Society's relentless focus on people's shortcomings had turned into a global obsession. What's more, he had discovered that people have several times more potential for growth when they invest energy in developing their strengths instead of correcting their deficiencies." (Rath, 2007).

These are the principles that have helped me navigate through this pressurized and racialized landscape that I live in. Setting and achieving goals in spite of racism keeps me motivated and focused. Family and friends keep me grounded. Staying physically healthy keeps my body fit and strong. Social and cultural time helps keep my sanity intact.

Working on my spiritual and ethical life has helped me to sustain my faith in God and humanity and maintain a positive mental attitude. All of these factors I rely upon because, in life, the powers that be do not understand racism. They don't believe it exists and, therefore, can't begin to care about your feelings about racism.

That being said, just because I was qualified for a management job didn't mean my employer would promote me. *Miles is not a good fit. We don't like him. We don't need a Black male manager. No one can compel me to hire a Black male manager. We don't want Black men to earn a management salary.* It's all in the mindset and attitudes of my superiors. It's a bitter pill to swallow and nearly impossible to accept.

Living a balanced life has enabled me to survive and avoid a meltdown. We've all seen individuals lose it and have mental breakdowns. It's not a pretty sight! I thank the lord every day for my spiritual understanding, intestinal fortitude, personal success coach, and my family.

14

Victims Of Circumstances

"You may not control all the events that happen to you, but you can decide not to be reduced by them."

–Maya Angelou

Black Women are the most resilient human beings on the face of the earth. Looking back, I've come to understand that some of my past criticisms about Black women came from a place filled with anger and misunderstanding. I was making comparisons that didn't make sense because our experience in this country, especially in corporate America, has been uniquely challenging for Black women. Time and reflection have helped me see things more clearly now.

What shifted my perspective was recognizing that the African American experience is like no other. I had gotten caught up in comparing dynamics between different racial and ethnic groups, but our story is distinctive. The relationship between Black men and women carries a unique historical weight and contemporary complexity that sets it apart.

I've grown to deeply admire how Black women have mastered the game of life and the corporate world. They've figured out how to navigate challenges by developing crucial skills - from code-switching to mastering soft skills, understanding workplace dynamics, and recognizing opportunities. They've learned to read the landscape of the corporate world with remarkable precision and adaptability. Like we say in the hood, "Don't hate the player, hate the game." I broke a cardinal rule by hating on Black women. And for that, I apologize.

Their success isn't just about taking advantage of opportunities. It's about resilience and strategic thinking. "Despite their experiences with microaggressions, stereotype threats, and general career setbacks, Black women detailed their ability to persist toward their professional goals." (Wright, 2024). Black women have learned to utilize every resource available through diversity initiatives or protected class laws. They've turned understanding of the system into meaningful advancement, which deserves respect rather than resentment.

One of the most important things I've learned is that you can't paint all Black women with the same brush. They're as diverse as a deck of cards or, like Forrest Gump would say, a box of chocolates - you never know what you're gonna get. Some will challenge a Black Man, while others will stand by him like solid gold, supporting him through thick and thin.

Sure, it was tough for me watching Black women succeed when I was struggling, especially in the corporate world. However, the experiences and criticisms I encountered were specific to my particular context and circumstances. Over time, I've learned to see past that initial discomfort to recognize and celebrate the achievements of Black women, understanding that their success often comes with its own set of challenges and sacrifices. The broader patterns of discrimination and barriers faced by Black women in corporate America are supported by extensive research and data.

When you examine the comprehensive data about Black women in corporate America, a stark picture emerges of the parallel yet distinct challenges faced by Black professionals in their pursuit of executive leadership positions. The intersection of race, gender, and corporate culture creates a complex landscape that demands careful examination and honest dialogue.

At the end of the day, it's all love. Our deep love for Black women is part of who we are as Black men, even when it gets complicated. These women - our mothers, wives, sisters, partners, and colleagues - have shown incredible strength and wisdom in navigating their paths to success, and that deserves nothing but respect and admiration.

My journey through corporate America has shown me firsthand how systemic barriers can impede professional advancement. Like many Black men, I encountered both overt racism and subtle microaggressions that questioned my competence and belonging. The research on Black women's experiences reveals a troublingly similar pattern, but with an added layer of complexity due to gender bias.

The landscape of corporate America presents a particularly challenging terrain for Black women, who face unique obstacles that stem from the intersection of race and gender. Through the lens of comprehensive research and lived experiences, we can examine how these challenges manifest and persist despite decades of diversity initiatives and calls for change.

The Double Burden: Race and Gender

Black women in corporate America navigate what scholars and professionals often refer to as a "double burden" - the simultaneous experience of racial and gender discrimination. Unlike their White female counterparts or Black male colleagues, Black women must constantly manage both aspects of their identity in professional settings. "The data reveals that for every 100 men promoted to manager, only 58 Black women receive similar advancement opportunities, highlighting a stark disparity in career progression." (Prewitt, 2024)

This disparity becomes even more pronounced when examining the highest echelons of corporate leadership. "With only four Black women having led Fortune 500 companies throughout history, despite comprising nearly 7% of the U.S. workforce" (Prewitt, 2024), the numbers tell a story of systematic exclusion and barriers to advancement.

The "Broken Rung" Phenomenon

One of the most critical barriers Black women face occurs at the very first step up the corporate ladder, "what's known as the "broken rung" phenomenon. This early-career obstacle creates a ripple effect that impacts the entire pipeline of Black female talent in corporate America" (Prewitt, 2024). The challenge isn't merely about individual qualification or merit; it reflects deeper systemic issues in how organizations evaluate and promote talent.

Microaggressions and Psychological Burden

The daily experience of Black women in corporate settings often includes navigating a minefield of microaggressions. These subtle but persistent forms of discrimination manifest in various ways:

- Being mistaken for someone at a lower level (38% report this experience)
- Having their competence questioned (20% compared to 12% of all women)
- Facing scrutiny over their appearance, particularly regarding natural hairstyles
- Experiencing the "angry Black woman" stereotype when expressing normal workplace concerns (Brownlee, 2022).

These microaggressions create a cumulative psychological burden that their colleagues may never fully understand. "Black women often find themselves performing additional emotional labor, carefully moderating their tone and expression to avoid reinforcing negative stereotypes." (Brownlee, 2022).

While corporate America often prides itself on being a meritocracy, the experiences of Black women reveal a different reality. "Despite high levels of ambition (59% of Black women leaders aim for top executive roles), they receive the least managerial support among various demographics." (Brownlee, 2022). This disconnect between ambition and support highlights how traditional notions of meritocracy fail to account for systemic barriers and implicit biases.

The "Glass Cliff" Phenomenon

"When Black women do achieve leadership positions, they often encounter what researchers call the "glass cliff" – being promoted to leadership roles during times of crisis or turmoil." (Ellis, 2022). This phenomenon places them in precarious positions with higher risks of failure and less institutional support than their counterparts might receive in similar roles. The pressure to perform flawlessly while navigating these challenging circumstances creates an additional burden that can lead to burnout and eventual departure from these positions.

Parallel Challenges with Black Men

While Black women face unique challenges, there are notable parallels with the experiences of Black men in corporate America. Both groups encounter:

- Systematic underrepresentation in leadership roles
- Heightened scrutiny of their qualifications and capabilities
- The burden of being "the only one" in many professional settings
- Pressure to code-switch and modify their authentic selves
- Limited access to influential networks and sponsors

However, Black men may benefit from male privilege in certain contexts, while Black women must navigate both racial and gender-based discrimination simultaneously.

The Importance of Mentorship and Sponsorship

The research emphasizes the critical role of mentorship and sponsorship in career advancement. However, Black women often face a "sponsorship gap," ranking low in experiencing meaningful sponsorship and allyship. This deficit becomes particularly significant given that effective sponsorship can be transformative for career progression. For Black women, who often face unique challenges and barriers in the workplace, the support and guidance provided by mentorship and sponsorship relationships can be particularly invaluable. (Akhu, 2024).

The Entrepreneurial Response

Faced with these corporate challenges, many Black women have turned to entrepreneurship as an alternative path. "Black women-owned businesses grew by 50% from 2014 to 2019, reflecting both their entrepreneurial spirit and their desire to create opportunities outside traditional corporate structures." (J.P. Morgan, 2021) However, even in entrepreneurship, they face significant barriers in accessing capital and achieving financial parity with their peers.

Conclusion

The pervasive nature of these challenges points to deeper issues within corporate culture. Despite many organizations' stated commitment to diversity and inclusion, the lived experiences of Black women suggest that corporate America has yet to create truly inclusive environments. The disconnect between perceived and actual allyship highlights how even well-intentioned diversity initiatives can fall short of creating meaningful change.

The journey of Black women in corporate America reflects remarkable resilience and persistent systemic challenges. While individual experiences may vary, the aggregate data and research paint a clear picture of systematic barriers that require intentional and sustained effort to overcome. The path forward requires organizations to move beyond acknowledgment to implement concrete actions that create genuinely inclusive environments where Black women can thrive and advance based on their merits and capabilities. The unique intersection of race and gender creates challenges that demand specific solutions and sustained commitment from corporate leaders. While some experiences may be individual in nature, the broader patterns of discrimination and barriers faced by Black women in corporate America are well-documented and require systematic change to address effectively.

Through all my experiences with Black women - the love, the conflicts, the challenges, and the triumphs - I wouldn't change a thing. These experiences have shaped who I am, teaching me valuable lessons about respect, persistence, and understanding. Researching and writing this chapter has allowed me to grow as a Black Man and obtain valuable wisdom and knowledge. It's been a journey of growth that I've come to appreciate deeply.

15

The Invisible Justice

"Institutionalized racism refers to differential access to the goods, services, and opportunities of society by race and is often normalized and legalized."

–Camara Phyllis Jones

Writing this book has been liberating and cathartic for me, a sort of therapy. Racial discrimination will eat you up inside. At some point in time, you have to let it go. If you can't let it go, you must learn how to live with it and remain functional and productive. Easier said than done. Racism takes a toll on your health, psyche, career growth, and relationships. Most importantly, it's usually invisible to everyone except African Americans or people of the global majority being discriminated against. Filing a lawsuit seems pretty extreme, but it's sometimes the only way to get some semblance of justice against all that stands against us. In my opinion, getting the legal system involved and presenting your argument so that an impartial legal governing body can make a ruling carries a lot of weight. I had both Black and White on my side, and, in the end, they compelled my employer to do the right thing. Unfortunately, this allowed them to use the "settlement" loophole in my case. At least a message was sent. Conduct hiring and promotional practices fairly. Do not exclude Black Men. My hope is that they got these messages loud and clear and didn't dismiss my suits against them as one angry Black Man out of the bunch who dared to complain.

I want to think that's exactly what has happened with Municipal. Over the years since my lawsuits, I've seen more and more Black men wearing suits and ties among their ranks. I don't know if what I did had any change over their internal policies to keep Black men out, but I prefer to think that those lawsuits had something to do with it.

These are the stories and events that have shaped my life. The fact is that growing up in an inherently racist society can shape you into someone you may not want to become. The struggle to remain on the right path has been difficult. I thank God every day for my parents, family members, and all the positive role models I've had in my life who have kept me on the straight and narrow-road to success.

I, along with thousands of other African American men, have decided to make a commitment to take a stand against racial discrimination, especially in the workplace. This commitment will take time, courage, money, and discipline. The repercussions of that commitment can be severe, as it can take a toll on you and your family. When you fight just for the right to be seen for your accomplishments, just for your employer to pass you over repeatedly, or choose people less qualified than you, it can feel like you have no hope of getting through to management. If you're in a situation like mine, management might be actively working to break your spirit. The pressure of enduring that has all the potential of leaking out and contaminating your work life as well as your personal life.

I can recall one time I was so consumed with all the stress of work that it led to what might have been a tragic situation. Driving home from work, some kid cut me off on the road. Instant road rage flared within me, and I chased the guy. Imagine me driving through the streets of New York like some stunt driver. I was so blinded with anger that I had no regard for the police or traffic signals. And heaven help any little old ladies crossing the street. I was completely out of my mind with anger.

Just as I was about to catch up with the kid, he cut me off, and my car sideswiped a school bus. I wasn't hurt, and the damage was minimal. I pulled my car over and got with the driver to exchange information. Luckily, since no one was on the bus but the driver and the damage amounted to a scratch, the bus driver just let it go.

I remember getting back in my car and staying there for a minute to calm down. What the hell had come over me? I had so much anger built up inside me that that kid cutting me off was like lighting a fuse. I just exploded without any regard for anything. As I calmed down and came back to my right mind, I started to think about all the what-ifs. What if I'd caught that driver? What would I have done? What if the police started chasing me? Would I be in some high-speed chase that would have escalated into something worse? What about pedestrians or other cars? Or what if there had been a busload of innocent schoolchildren on their way home or going to a sporting event?

My entire life could have been over in about a million different ways just because I was being consumed from the inside out and didn't realize it. It was like I had temporarily become another person, almost like the temporary insanity defense. But that's what discrimination can do to you. It can drive you crazy. If you go down that road into a discrimination case against your employer, you better be ready. More importantly, you don't have to be involved in a legal case or H.R. dispute to be affected by this type of racial trauma. When Blacks are employed in a racially toxic and biased environment filled with microaggressions like I was, you're exposed to racial trauma on a daily basis, and it affects you.

"Research has shown that Black men who ascribed to a strong work ethic but were unable to actualize the expected male role reported increased stress and health problems and were less likely to engage in health-promoting behaviors." (Archibald, 2019).

I was angry that my strong work ethic did not allow me to actualize the success goals I had set for myself. I was struggling to manage my stress levels, which were off the charts! My experiences as a Black Man don't just end when I punch out of work at the end of the day. It stays with me, lurking inside, waiting to be triggered.

Discrimination Lawsuits are Not for the Weak

The thing about discrimination complaints is that it will likely take an extremely long period of time to get any justice. My case, for example, took me all the way into my retirement years, with the lawyers finally threatening me with even lengthier litigation if I didn't settle. Discrimination cases require an enormous investment of time, money, and patience.

One of the things that really bothered me the most was how personal and hateful my employer and even some of my peers were against me. They knew I was qualified for a management position. Still, they hated me so much that they consistently denied me position after position, even going so far as to hire an underqualified Black Man from outside the organization and make him a supervisor.

When the Division of Human Rights ruled on my behalf and compelled my employer to issue me a settlement check, my employer still denied me the opportunity to advance my career. It was surreal, with hours and hours of research, legal maneuvering, legal fees, six years of back and forth, a second trial, and a settlement in my favor. The journey was much longer than I had ever thought it would be.

As an educated, upwardly mobile Black Man, it's been extremely difficult to work in an environment that touted diversity, non-discrimination, fairness, and equitable treatment for all and yet excluded Black men from their management teams. You can't talk about inclusivity if you're actively keeping out a part of the minority group you claim to uplift. Where's the diversity in that? "Corporations that have publicly condemned structural racism have avoided taking strong antiracist policy stances. Even worse, some corporations continue to profit from practices or policies that exacerbate racial inequity, even as they espouse antiracist rhetoric. (Fletcher, 2024).

This is the problem with Municipal Hospital. They can "talk the talk, but can't walk the walk."

When it was all said and done, I was *still* overlooked for opportunities for advancement. Discrimination still lives in the workplace, and I am living proof of that.

New Job, New Perspective

I eventually got my promotion into management. It's an unbelievable feeling, but it's bittersweet. I apply for an Emergency Room Supervisor position at Municipal's sister hospital a few towns over from us. The job is posted by a company called "Revenue Management Group."

Their expertise is in improving hospital billing and payment systems so hospitals can increase their revenue. They can transform the registration process and deliver a better patient experience.

I'm intrigued by this company, so I apply.

Ironically, quite a few Municipal employees now work for Revenue Management Group. I begin my new job on my mother's birthday, April 11, 2016. What an irony. To share a quick story, after I finally got promoted/hired into a Supervisor position, there was an extremely bright and intelligent Black woman, Sandra, training me. Our director is also a Black woman. They are both extremely knowledgeable, and I have learned quite a bit from them. The thing is, these women are brutal towards me. They were making condescending remarks, short-tempered, and had a disrespectful tone of voice. It's terrible. I, on the other hand, have a very thick skin. I've been through hell and back. With all the racial discrimination from White people, I had just lost my mother a few months earlier, and just being consumed with everyday life, trying to make ends meet.

A failed marriage, child support, IRS problems, wage garnishment, employment discrimination, eviction, and/ or bankruptcy, you name it, I've been through it all. Prima donna Black women are the least of my problems.

These Black women don't faze me in the least, but don't get it twisted; Black women will most certainly try you at some point! So when I get pushed into a corner, "I have to do everything I can not to portray that angry Black Man. That means if they say something to me that reflects that they think I'm an angry Black Man, I can't ever get mad. I have to brush it off, always be the nice guy who's not too threatening or militant, because they'll lose it if they ever see me in that way. And that would have serious repercussions for my job." (Wingfield, 2007).

As a Black Man, you've got to learn how to keep your cool. If you ever get upset, you're Finished. You'll be out the door, fired so fast, it'll make your head spin. I've witnessed too many brothers fall by the wayside because of bullshit. I'm naturally a very cool and laid-back individual, so inside the workplace, I don't let most stuff get to me. That's probably part of my problem with some Black women, usually the ones in power. I don't give a Shit, I can ignore them, but I do my job! Anyway, I finished my training, Sandra, my manager, got a nice promotion (of course), and business as usual, and another Black female manager was brought in. She struggles, and six months into the job, she gets fired.

Well, lucky me, I had been working evenings and nights, and I arrived at work that day, and my director immediately called me into her office and gave me the news. Well, Miles, you want to work days, don't you? I say, of course, and my director says, you're on days, we had to make a staffing change, and the previous manager is no longer with us.

So, here's where things start getting interesting. Now, I'm performing the duties of two people. I am one of the E.R. supervisors and the admitting office supervisor. I asked my director to upgrade my status to manager, but of course, she told me that because of budgetary concerns, they're not going to fill that vacated manager position.

Ok, I didn't think so anyway. I'm experiencing an issue one day, and I think to myself, let me reach out to Sandra. She will know how I should address this problem. I sent her an e-mail, thinking it would be a good idea to network and catch up on things. I asked her if I could discuss the Supervisor position with her and pick her brain about a few things.

To my surprise, I got an e-mail from my director the very next day. It's attached to my e-mail to Sandra. She tells me that there is no need for me to speak with Sandra. Whatever issues you are dealing with, we can solve them in-house.

Don't forget that Sandra has only been gone a few weeks. She trained me and worked there for a few years before our director was hired. Sandra was a knowledgeable resource, or at least I thought she was. She shit all over my request to talk with her. If they had been a couple of Caucasian guys, I would have thought nothing of it. I actually would have expected them to blow me off. But certainly not, two Black women. I'm shocked at these Black women. What Bull-Shit!!! If I were a woman, we would have been able to talk and network, and I would have learned valuable lessons from her. But no, not the Black Man,

Fuck You! It's clear that I'm on my own. I certainly didn't feel comfortable going outside of my network, so I figured I would reach out to Sandra, who I have great respect for, by the way, and what does she do? She insulted me by not only sharing my e-mail, but she didn't even have the professional courtesy to pick up the phone and ask me how she could help me.

That's how these Black women are. They will network and support each other but turn their noses up at Black men who are on their level. I can't believe she did me like that. I hoped that I was an isolated example of this type of treatment, but I wondered.

The Role of Black Women's Networks

"These networks offer spaces for mentorship, sponsorship, peer support, and professional development tailored specifically to Black women's needs and experiences. Research by Dumas and Graham (2012) emphasizes the importance of workplace networks and relationships in providing emotional support, career guidance, and opportunities for advancement.

Black women in corporate America are actively involved in Black women's networks, affinity groups, or Employee Resource Groups within their respective organizations. These groups provide opportunities for networking, mentorship, professional development, and advocacy tailored to Black women's experiences.

Once you have established yourself in your career, pay it forward by mentoring and sponsoring other Black women. Share your knowledge, insights, and networks to help uplift and empower the next generation of Black women leaders." (Akhu, 2024).

This is the type of ecosystem I was looking for. Unfortunately, Black men at my organization didn't have a network. That being said, I was a little surprised at the way some of the women treated me, but like I said,

I have a thick skin. I'm a big boy, I can handle it, no worries. It actually would have caught me off guard if I had gotten help with my career. I was so beaten down and apathetic by this point it was burned into my soul that I was on this journey alone, and on my own, and that's just the way I liked it!

"Even when Black men attempt to portray themselves as non-threatening, affable people, coworkers may still find them too daunting and unapproachable for the inter-office friendships and socializing opportunities that are essential to occupational advancement." (Wingfield, 2007). It was a bitter pill to swallow. I was so pissed off that I left work early that day. It turned out to be a valuable lesson for me. I've always been told to network, network, network.

So that's what I do, build my network, and to my surprise, a Black woman who I considered to be sort of a mentor refuses to meet with me to discuss the "job and career." Not bullshit, a legitimate request for a serious business meeting and she dismissed me. WOW! A brilliant Black female mind but an ignorant mind when it comes to understanding the trials and tribulations of a Black Man building a career in Corporate America.

I get it! To all the Black women out there saying, "Hey, my struggle is just as hard as yours. I've got to look out for myself," it's understood, Black woman, I get it! It's just that I was hoping this Sista would be able to relate to my request to meet with her to network and brainstorm, just as she had done with other women. I guess I was naïve to think I would be treated the same way.

Like I said, two females would have gotten together and talked, strategized, and networked continuously to help each other. Even though I'm not a female, I expected the same level of interaction because we both were Black. This experience shows my ignorance about successful Black women "within the same business or employment sector." I'm sure that if I had reached out to another woman who worked in an industry other than health care, she would have openly agreed to meet with me and network. "Black women, not White men, appear most likely to rely on instrumental network assistance to attain positions of power." "Black men are only about half as likely as White men to be managers as supervisors. Thus, without statistical controls, we conclude that a pattern of increasing inequality exists for Black men, relative to White men." (Elliott, 2004).

The lesson I learned was women who are employed at the same company as you and who are successful will always keep you at arm's length because, in their minds, you are considered a threat to them (even though you are not a threat).

It's a conundrum. All I can say is, put it to the test. If you're a successful, well-educated, upwardly mobile Black Man who works in an industry with high-level senior executives who are Black women, approach one of them and ask for a meeting. See what happens! I will also add that most of the older Black women I approached were always open and receptive. Older women, 50+ yrs, have paid their dues; they have nothing to lose. They always scheduled me on their calendars to talk and mentor me, and it was always a rewarding experience.

The other side of the coin was that the Black women who were my peers, with master's degrees, upwardly mobile, smart, younger, focused, and determined, didn't see me the same way as their older female cohorts. I was different. In the entire hospital where I worked, there were probably less than a dozen or so Black men who had master's degrees, not including clinical staff, out of over four thousand employees. I'm in finance, so I'm basically by myself as the lonely Black Man with a master's degree.

So YES, I finally got promoted into management (in the twilight of my career, I might add), but it was the same bull-shit rat race, just on a higher level.

Performance Management

Performance management is a tool that helps Directors and managers monitor and evaluate their team members' work. It is also a tool that is used to perpetuate racist practices against Black men and, in some instances, Black women. An example of this would be a dozen employees making the same mistake, but only the Black male employee gets written up. The other side of the coin is the White guy who comes in late and is a complete screw-up, never gets written up, and eventually gets promoted.

After working for two years as a supervisor for a staff of approximately twenty-five employees, I still wasn't considered their equal. When I was informed that another manager was leaving, I thought I had a shot at a higher position. The manager and I had worked closely over the past couple of years, and I communicated to him that I was interested in assuming his position when he officially left. He assured me he would mention my name when the topic came up with leadership and that he would be in my corner. That sounded a lot like a glowing recommendation to me. After all, he knew that I did well in my position. I was the kind of supervisor who prided himself in learning/knowing all aspects of the job. The department and this manager had consulted with me on several issues during his tenure because I was proficient in everything concerning not only the Admissions Department but all areas of hospital protocols.

A day or two after he informed me about his leaving, I noticed him with a brand new manager who had just transferred to us from another hospital. I don't think I would have thought anything of it except that she seemed to be very familiar with him. I would often catch them being rather friendly in the hallways, the way old friends tended to be when they met up. Right away, I could see that something was up in the way of his position.

Two weeks later, I went in for my interview for the management position. Sometime after, wouldn't you know it? My director told me that that same young woman (we'll call her 'Jane') was chosen for the position instead of me. I wondered why she was selected when I was clearly the most qualified candidate for the position. I needed to know how they justified hiring somebody who had just transferred from another hospital over someone who'd been working here for four years and basically running the show. I responded. She knows "Jack Shit" about this job. How do you justify selecting her? My director's response? "She can learn the job?" *I beg your pardon.*

I didn't flip out. By that point, this was par for the course for me. Yet another time, I got passed over for someone less qualified than I was. And to add insult to injury, my director asked me to "help her out." Damm! He expects me to train her now.

After Jane had been working for about nine months or so, I came into work one morning to find her shuffling through the death registry log books.

"Hey, Jane," I ask her. "What are you up to?"

"Oh," she says, "We're moving to an electronic format for the deceased records."

"Yes, I heard that was coming down the pike. Let me know what you need, and I'll send it to you."

When I first learned that the death registry process was going electronic, I was excited at the chance to work on the initiative. Unfortunately for me, I was not always privy to information in a timely manner. At my job, along with countless other organizations, there is a chain of command where information is cascaded down through the chain of leadership. So Jane had been informed about this project before I was.

After a day or two, I've learned that our director is waiting for this report. So I asked Jane about it. "Hey, I'm waiting for you to send me the details of the report that you're working on."

She says to me, "Oh, I need to learn this stuff on my own, so I want to do it myself if you don't mind."

My first thought was how weird it was to opt to do something like that on her own. I mean, it was a pretty important project, and I knew she didn't know enough about the subject matter to begin with. Just the same, I didn't push the issue. I stepped back and let her figure it out herself.

So, eventually, she completed the project on her own and circulated the website address and a Go-Live launch date to the admitting team and me. I was told to make sure everyone could log on to the platform and familiarize themselves with the new site, and that was it. Already, I could see problems with this new manager's work.

Jane provided no documentation and no training for the staff. We had to figure everything out for ourselves. There was no follow-up by Jane, nor did she bother to check in to see if we knew our parts to play or had any questions. It was certainly a far cry from what I would have done had I been given that task. During this time, I was supervising three shifts of employees without any help. As you can imagine, the admissions office for a 650-bed hospital was extremely busy.

Thirty days later, the Health Department arrived at Municipal Hospital, and of course, they inspected the death registry and requested a report of hospital expirations. My director ran the report, and several omissions were discovered. Apparently, the system had not been updated or reviewed since implementation.

Upon hearing this, I assembled a group of six reps, and around two hundred records were all corrected by the end of business that day. When asked about it, I explained to my director that the staff lacked training and documentation. The entire project was poorly implemented, and there was no follow-up. I approached Jane about assisting her. She informed me my input was not needed.

Ninety days after that, Jane was promoted to Director of Revenue Cycle at another hospital. Out of around thirty-plus hospitals in the Municipal Hospital Network, 80% of the directors were women. So, I wasn't at all surprised. When Jane let me know that she was officially leaving, I was informed that her colleague (another woman) was replacing her. It's interesting how Jane didn't consider me a possible candidate to manage the department.

After Jane left, the new manager, April Brown, decided that her first order of business was to write me up for "Unsatisfactory Work Performance." Honestly, I really didn't know this woman. I had seen her once or twice at management Zoom meetings, but we really didn't interact. But I'm sure that my reputation preceded me by that point. That's what can happen to someone like me who makes a lot of "noise" in the workplace. Leadership will send someone to assassinate your reputation and try to terminate you.

"The angry Black woman stereotype makes it seem as if Black women only feel and express anger and become angry for little to no reason. This stereotype is brought up often in the workplaces and impacts how Black women interact with others and respond to situations in their daily lives." (Parks, 2023). I am certainly not one who buys into stereotypes, but I couldn't believe this Black woman would allow herself to be used and weaponized against me. I can't say it was a personal attack because she didn't know me, but she definitely made it personal.

April's write-up was about the Department of Health's visit to the hospital. That's right. I was being blamed for the department report revealing the omissions and poorly updated system. She failed to realize that her girlfriend, who gave her the job, was responsible for the reporting problem. I was the one who fixed the problem and prepared an accurate hospital expiration report for our director to give to the Health Department on the same day it was requested.

Shortly thereafter, I received an official notice of "Disciplinary Action" from Human Resources. When she called me into her office about it, the conversation quickly got very heated. I felt not only disrespected but flat-out attacked. I didn't know this woman from a can of paint, and she had all but tried and convicted me. It was a classic case of "Performance Management" being used to burn me. My employer just got the Black woman to do it.

A few hours after that exchange, she sent me an email that basically stated, "I have received a Verbal Warning for Unsatisfactory Work Performance. In line with policies of progressive discipline, you are hereby receiving a Written Warning. Immediate and sustained improvement is expected. Failure to do so may result in further disciplinary action, up to and including termination." I guess no good deed goes unpunished. This whole mess ended up with me meeting with my director, a forty-something White man with about as much backbone as a jellyfish.

"Listen, Miles," the director said, "April is very aggressive. She wants to fire you, so it would behoove you to look for another job."

I was stunned. "Wait, you're our director. You know what happened. How are you just letting this happen? You knew that Jane wasn't qualified to work on the electronic format for the deceased records, and you let her do it anyway. I was the one who cleaned up her mess, and now *I'm* getting called on the carpet for it?" I was hot at that point. Maybe it was the culmination of everything that had happened over the years. Or perhaps it was just the injustice of it all. All I knew was that the discrimination tactics against me had gotten out of control, and I wasn't about to sit back and take it.

"And furthermore," I went on, "does April know that I supervise four shifts, days, evenings, nights, and weekends *by myself*? My phone rings every weekend with an issue and I'm the one who handles it on my own. Does she know that?"

His response? "Hey, I really don't want to get involved in this back-and-forth between you two."

And there it is. The Department Director, who could have squashed this whole matter with the truth about my work performance, had nothing to say in support of me. I told him in no uncertain terms that if I was fired, I would sue them for unlawful termination. The fact of the matter is that it wasn't right, and I wasn't going to let somebody step all over me.

This is a perfect example of institutional subordination. For whatever reason, April had made up her mind about me before even finding out anything about me. She was willing to write me up and damage my record and reputation, prohibiting me from promotion to a senior management position.

There are two very important points I need to make here. One, she is half my age and is dead set on emasculating a Black Man in the twilight of his career. Two, silly me, I was expecting this Black woman to work with me and support me in running the department. I wasn't expecting to be blind-sided and stabbed in the back by her.

"Institutional racism or institutional subordination is 'placing or keeping persons in a position or status of inferiority by means of attitudes, actions, or institutional structures which do not use color itself as the subordinating mechanism, but instead use other mechanisms indirectly related to color.' Institutional racism tends to be less obvious since its application does not exclude other blacks.

Moreover, because institutional subordination is much less conspicuous, intent to discriminate may not be present. If intent is present, it will be shrouded in nonracist trappings." (Bullock & Rodgers, 1976).

Right… Like an allegation of *"Unsatisfactory Work Performance."*

And the Beat Still Goes on….

As I pen this conclusion to my story, several racial discrimination situations keep popping up. In 2022, Miami Dolphin ex-coach Brian Flores filed a class action discrimination suite against the NFL. The thing that really irked me was that former U.S. Attorney General Loretta Lynch, the first African American Woman to hold that office, was hired by the NFL to defend the NFL in the lawsuit. That means that when the case comes to trial, she'll be heading up a dream team of attorneys backed by billionaire financing.

Matthew Ritchie wrote about it in the ABA journal: "Twenty years later, the Rooney Rule has done little to break the NFL glass ceiling that's blocked Black coaches from ascending. But where policy has left a vacuum, litigation is filling the void: The league's lack of head coach diversity is now the subject of a class action lawsuit. Former Miami

Dolphins head coach Brian Flores (now a linebackers coach for the Pittsburgh Steelers) filed suit in February 2022, alleging the NFL and its 32 teams discriminated against Black coaches in the hiring process. Two other coaches joined the lawsuit in April: Ray Horton (retired) and Steve Wilks (who started the 2022 season as defensive passing game coordinator for the Carolina Panthers and was named interim head coach in October). The filing of the suit puts the league's track record of hiring and treatment of Black head coaches under intense scrutiny. In a sport where 70% of the players are Black, there are only three Black head coaches at press time: Mike Tomlin, who's been with the Steelers since 2007; Todd Bowles with the Buccaneers; and Mike McDaniel, who is biracial, with the Dolphins. The Houston Texans fired Lovie Smith in January." (Ritchie, 2023). Over the following two seasons the NFL hires three Black coaches, Demarco Ryans, Antonio Pierce, Raheem Morris and one Hispanic coach, Dave Canales. It's so unfortunate, that it always takes lawsuits to effect change because the dominant society does not have a race equity lens.

This is not the first time Loretta Lynch was on the side of the billionaires. In 2022, she was also hired by McDonald's to defend their discrimination suit brought by Media mogul Byron Allen. The Business Insider reported:

"McDonald's is facing a $10 billion lawsuit from media mogul Byron Allen, who has accused the fast food giant of failing to advertise with Black-owned media. The media mogul said: 'The economic exclusion must stop immediately."

"In a press release on (Sept. 22, 2022) Allen said: 'This is about economic inclusion of African American-owned businesses in the US economy. McDonald's takes billions from African American consumers and gives almost nothing back. The biggest trade deficit in America is the trade deficit between White corporate America and Black America, and McDonald's is guilty of perpetuating this disparity.'

"Loretta Lynch at law firm Paul Weiss, which is acting for McDonald's, told CNN that Allen's claims were "meritless. 'Their complaint is about revenue, not race, and plaintiffs' groundless allegations ignore both McDonald's legitimate business reasons for not investing more on their channels and the company's long-standing business relationships with many other diverse-owned partners,' said Lynch, who was President Obama's attorney-general." (Tabahriti, 2022)

In a world where White billionaires are getting over on people of the global majority every day, I feel that hiring a Black woman to fight their battles against other Black people is deplorable. I can't say I know Ms. Lynch's motives for taking on these cases and I'm not going to make any presumptions. I will say that working against the interests of your own people is a bad look. At the very least, the cases she's taken on are a slap in the face for Black Men trying to rise within these corporations.

In the end, I don't doubt that they'll be settled and Corporate America will again throw money at a situation that requires an overhaul. There seems to be no remedy and no solution to these discrimination suits. Corporate America may or may not get a slap on the wrist and then it's back to business as usual.

But even in the midst of fighting the good fight, there are some wins in our column. I came across this article about Sauntore Thomas, an

African American man who also settled a race discrimination lawsuit. The man received a hefty check for his trouble, and when he went to the bank to try to cash it, the bank teller called the police on him, thinking the checks had to be fake. Thomas was arrested but later released when it was discovered that the checks were real. The twist to the story is that he also ended up suing the bank for discrimination. Stephen Robinson from The Wonkette wrote:

- "It seems that a Black Man can't deposit his settlement checks from a racial discrimination suit without experiencing *more* racial discrimination. Sauntore Thomas opened the Russian nesting doll of racism at a Michigan bank that assumed his checks were funny money and sicced the cops on him."

- "Sauntore Thomas sued TCF Bank for alleged race discrimination (presumably, his third racial discrimination suit will be free). He claims the Livonia branch "mistreated and humiliated him." The bank instigated a fraud investigation and called in four police officers all because he was trying to deposit legitimate checks, which is usually standard bank activity." (Robinson, 2020).

It's insane to me that a person could sue for racial discrimination, go to cash the check and be denied because of his race, only to sue *again* for discrimination. It's the kind of thing that can only happen in a racially biased society.

If They Only Knew

Corporate America doesn't realize it, but they have lessened themselves by discriminating against African American men. When I think about all the Black men who have broken records in sports and entertainment, contributed to nearly every field of study known to man, and collectively made society better in about a million different ways, I take pride. We've spent our entire existence in this country trying to build it up while living under the firm hand of a White racist society.

Could you imagine the contribution African Americans could have made to build our country had we been given an equal chance to join as industry leaders and people in business? Racism has blinded the powers that be to a limitless source of good in the world and we are all suffering because of it.

We can contribute and we are contributing. But imagine a world where everyone's talents were used equally and without obstruction. Imagine if the web of racism was lifted just long enough for all of us to be seen as the brilliant humans that we are.

No Remedy or Solution

The major problem in Corporate America is that there is no real remedy for racially discriminatory behavior against Black men in the workplace. There are, however, a few examples of large monetary awards after many years of litigation to prove a case. Just look at the '2014 FDNY settlement. After a seven-year legal brawl, checks from the FDNY discrimination case are finally being paid out to the plaintiffs of their discriminatory suit and they aren't even part of the $98 million settlement earmarked for lost back pay and benefits.

"The Vulcan Society, the fraternal Blackfirefighters organization that was created in 1940 to combat racism in historically white firehouses, won a momentous battle against employment discrimination when a federal judge ruled that exams administered between 1999 and

2002 barred over a thousand additional Black and Hispanic applicants from consideration for appointment as FDNY firefighters." (Abdul-Aleem, 2009).

It's amazing to me that these racist White men who run the New York Fire Department would rather pay $98 million dollars than hire qualified Black men. It's a sickening realization. FDNY was found guilty of fooling around with the exams given to Blacks to become firefighters. They failed to promote the few Black men who were firefighters into management. What retribution was made for that? Tossing money at the plaintiffs. Real change has yet to be seen.

I personally don't believe that a financial award is really a remedy for discriminatory problems. Given that it keeps happening, it's not really a deterrent. After the guilty parties pay out the monetary awards, policies, and procedures, they return to business as usual. Also, these monetary awards come with no admission of guilt or wrongdoing by the perpetrators.

It's unfortunate because the dominant Caucasian culture in corporate America never gets the message that practicing racism is doing something wrong. Their attitude is, let's just throw some money at this problem and it will go away.

The bottom line is that Corporate America can't govern itself and can't police its own bad behavior. "The Brilliant Asylum is being run by The Ignorant Inmates."

Epilogue

When I think about the way everything had to happen for me just to get the only thing I worked so hard for, I often wonder why it had to be so difficult. How is it that something that I had absolutely no control over (Racism) has been a factor at all in just getting what was fair? I am the type of person who does what he needs to get ahead in life. I am not unaccustomed to working hard or educating myself in whatever way necessary to get to the place that I need to. On paper, I should have gotten everything that I worked for.

The True Cost of Racism

The Nationwide protests over the killing of George Floyd sparked a team of brilliant economic research minds at Citigroup to investigate the economic costs of systemic racism. CitiGroup researchers measured racial gaps for Black Americans, including wages, education, housing, and investment. They concluded that if these key racial gaps had been closed two decades ago, *$16 trillion could have been added to the US economy.*

"Racial inequality has always had an outsized cost, one that was thought to be paid only by underrepresented groups," said Raymond J. McGuire, Vice Chairman of Citigroup and Chairman of Banking, Capital Markets and Advisory at Citi. "What this report underscores is that this tariff is levied on us all, and particularly in the U.S., that cost has a real and tangible impact on our country's economic output. Now, more than ever, we have a responsibility and an opportunity to confront this longstanding societal ill that has plagued Black and brown people in this country for centuries, tally up the economic loss, and as a society, commit to bring greater equity and prosperity to all." (Contify Banking News, 2020).

In my view, this was a monumental report! Systemic racism has harmed our entire country, in addition to Corporate America. It was hard for me to wrap my mind around, why the White leadership in America could not grasp this very fundamental concept. The news media seemed to downplay this Citigroup report. I heard it mentioned here and there, but in my opinion, it should have been shouted from the roof tops. This is the kind of thing I'd been complaining about my whole career. Racial discrimination hurts everyone!!!

Also, there are significant costs attached to litigating cases to fight for civil rights and these legal expenses must be factored into the total cost of racism. There is an organization called, The American Alliance for Equal Rights, whose philosophy is that all race-based initiatives are unlawful and discriminatory against Whites. This is what I consider to be a classic case of reverse discrimination theory. This organization, which provided the impetus behind the landmark Supreme Court decision that overturned race-conscious college admissions, is now suing the Fearless Fund.

The Fearless Fund is the first venture capital fund founded by women of color investing solely in businesses led by women of color. Fearless Fund awards $20,000 grants to Black female-owned businesses and start-ups. It is very important to provide some background and history behind the Fearless Fund.

"The Fearless Fund was founded in 2018 to address the chasm in venture capital for start-ups run by women of color. That year, such businesses received $484 million in investment while Black start-ups overall received $1.7 billion - *One percent (1.0%) of the $131 billion allocated that year."* (Mark, 2024).

"Those percentages have largely held steady, though investment in Black start-ups did see a surge in 2021, to $4.9 billion, after the murder of George Floyd by a Minneapolis police officer prompted a flood of commitments toward the Black community. But by 2023, investment in Black start-ups had shriveled to $705 million, or 0.5 percent, of the $140.4 billion in venture capital awarded that year, according to Crunchbase. It also marked the first time since 2016 that investment in Black start-ups fell below $1 billion." (Mark, 2024).

Understanding this dynamic, it is clear to see that Blacks are being shut out of venture capital money. The mission of The Fearless Fund is to rectify this injustice. With the Venture Capital market projected to hit $550 billion in 2024, according to the Business Research Company, Fearless Fund mission is to direct a larger share of venture capital dollars to women of color. Research shows that White men control 97% of venture capital money, but no one questions that.

The conservative activist driving the lawsuit, Edward Blum, says racial equity is not one-sided. That's why he insists that the fund's grant program for Black women is discriminatory." His philosophy is "The law does not — and must not — permit racial preferences to achieve racial balancing," Blum added. "In other words, the bar must never be raised for some races, and lowered for others, to realize racial proportionality." (Mark, 2024).

"Despite these realities, conservative groups are initiating a wave of attacks on racial-equality programs. About 5 percent of practicing attorneys are Black, yet one of Blum's groups, the American Alliance for Equal Rights, sued law firms to stop their diversity fellowships. In August, it also sued the Fearless Fund, a venture capital firm founded by two Black women, which, through its charitable arm, helps other Black women gain access to funding by giving small grants to businesses that are at least 51 percent owned by Black women. According to the World Economic Forum, Black women receive just 0.34 percent of venture capital funds in the United States. Blum declared the fund to be racially discriminatory.

Another Blum group, Students for Fair Admissions, has now sued the U.S. Military Academy, even though the Supreme Court allowed race conscious admissions to stand in the military. Another organization, Center for Individual Rights (CIR), successfully overturned a decadeslong Small Business Administration (SB) policy that automatically treated so-called minority-owned businesses as eligible for federal contracts for disadvantaged businesses." (Hannah-Jones, 2024)

In my opinion, this is flawed thinking. Blum's argument is based on outdated and flawed legislation. Blacks have been barred from receiving venture capital and other funding since its inception. That's why laws were enacted to ameliorate (make better) this financial injustice against Blacks. The Fearless Fund only had access to less than one percent of venture capital monies that they awarded to Black businesswomen. Mr. Blum thinks this is discrimination against Whites even though White men control 97% of the venture capital funds. I sincerely hope the judges presiding over this case can see through this racially motivated discriminatory practice. I imagine Mr. Blum and the American Alliance for Equal Rights organization will be satisfied when White men control 100% of Venture Capital grants and expenditures.

Another cost of racism is broken promises made by Corporate America. Why make financial commitments and pledge support to fight racism and then renege? The easy answer: a lack of respect for African American people. Several industries throughout Corporate America pledged billions of dollars towards efforts designed to fight racial injustice. These pledges were made in the wake of George Floyd's murder. Many of these industries chose to capitalize on the global protests going on around the world demanding change, but they have come up short.

"Now that we are a few years removed from the massive racial justice protests that gripped the United States, some corporations in the US have backtracked on their antiracist commitments. Their financial pledges to antiracist causes have gone unfulfilled. Their promises to diversify their workforces have not been realized. Other corporate antiracist programs that were priorities in the aftermath of George Floyd's murder are no longer so." (Fletcher, 2024). Yet again, Corporate America, led mainly by White leadership, has failed to fulfill promises made to eradicate racial injustice in our country. The United States of America will need the full support of Caucasian leadership to fight against racial injustice successfully.

Under the directions of The U.S. Department of Agriculture, thousands of Black farmers have applied for the Discrimination Financial Assistance Program (DFAP). This program is made possible by the Inflation Reduction Act, which provided $2.2 billion in funding.

African American and other minority Farmers, ranchers, and forest landowners who experienced discrimination by USDA in its farm loan programs prior to January 1, 2021, are eligible for this program.

The thousands of payouts, totaling $2 billion, follow years of delays and lawsuits that frustrated struggling Black farmers.

"The Biden administration reported on August 7, 2024, that it had started disbursing $2 billion to thousands of farmers who have faced discrimination after years of delays and legal battles thwarted the federal government's efforts to compensate them." (Rappaport, 2024).

Long story short, it's pretty obvious that The United States of America will need the full support of Caucasian leadership to fight against racial injustice successfully.

Combating Racism in the workplace

In my opinion, there are several different approaches to combating racism inside the workplace, in addition to hard work and excellence, which should have been enough. However, most sectors of the country are still obsessed with skin color, so outside-the-box thinking is required.

CEOs / Corporate Boards of Directors / Human Resource Leaders / Hiring Managers

There is enough factual evidence inside Corporate America to prove that discrimination against Black men exists. Boots on the ground Corporate leadership must put an end to this racist trend. Open your eyes, there are qualified African American Men within your respective companies. Hire them! We are talented, intelligent, intuitive leaders who are ready and waiting to contribute our expertise. Do not hold us back any longer!

"Corporations that have publicly condemned structural racism have avoided taking strong antiracist policy stances. Even worse, some corporations continue to profit from practices or policies that exacerbate racial inequity, even as they espouse antiracist rhetoric. If corporate leaders are serious about advancing racial justice and rooting out racism, they must push past their platitudes and empty statements." (Fletcher, 2024).

"Whether they like it or not, corporations are already intimately involved in racial issues, and this relationship will no doubt continue in the future. Racial justice issues are at the core of corporate operations, even if corporate leaders are not consciously considering race. Each day, corporations recruit, hire, compensate, promote, retain, and dismiss employees, and far too frequently, the employees who experience the worst working conditions and receive the lowest wages are employees of color. Corporate boards notoriously lack racial diversity, and these boards often design policies that disparately affect people of color inside and outside of the corporation." (Fletcher, 2024).

I am not asking for a handout. I am not asking for any preferential treatment. I'm simply asking you to follow the same meritocracy model that is used for all other employees. Attention, all CEOs, Corporate Boards of Directors, Human Resource leaders, and Hiring managers: at some point, the resume from a qualified Black Man will come across your desk. You've got to get over this antiquated obsession with skin color and hire that Black Man. It's not only good business, but it will strengthen your respective companies.

Improve Lines of communication. As Black men, we must allow our voices to be heard. Our lines of communication with our respective leadership teams inside the workplace must be improved. They have to hear from us and know that we are capable of leading our teams and running our respective departments. We must be subtle in our approach to improving communication. We don't always get invited to important meetings. We sometimes don't receive important emails or lunch invitations. These are also lines of communication. We must establish a network of influential individuals who will help us and keep us in the loop about what's happening within our organization or industry.

Strengthen alliances with Black women. At some point during your career, you will discover that there are Black women who have achieved a higher level of power and respect inside Corporate America. As difficult as it may be, Black men must approach these very smart and successful Black women and help them to understand better that together, we can support each other, even if it has to be done surreptitiously. Look for influential women who share your values and aspirations, and don't hesitate to explore opportunities for networking, mentorship, and professional development.

Lead by example. Take the initiative to provide leadership and mentorship for our young Black men and boys inside our communities and Churches. Educate them about the pitfalls that lie ahead and prepare them for the struggles they will encounter inside the workplace.

Participate in workplace diversity programs. My experience has been that these programs have been turned into female and immigrant support groups that exclude Black men. Sure, these diversity groups and forums have the one successful token Black guy who is clueless about the struggles of other Black men inside the workplace. Despite this, we must include our voices and inform our employers that we want the same opportunities that other minority groups are afforded. D.E.I. programs and forums are great for voicing opinions in a non-threatening environment. As we all know, diversity programs are under attack. Brilliant innovative minds will be needed to navigate this new and evolving landscape.

Develop A Race Equity Lens. Know your surroundings, and look at the leadership teams in your organization. What is the racial makeup of the team? Is it a leadership team without Black Men? Look at your immediate leadership team—the managers, supervisors, etc. You would think that racism would be done with, but it's not. All I'm saying is understand your surroundings and also the history of your organization. You might be surprised at what you find out. Begin planning an exit strategy if you don't see any changes within your organization.

Combat stereotypes about Black men. "Most Whites haven't spent too much time around Black people, so what they think they know is usually from TV or some other stupid source. So, if they already think most Black guys grow up in the hood and sell drugs and are basically like [popular rapper] 50-cent, [not throwing shade or disrespect at Curtis] but when that assumption occurs, then we have to do everything we can not to portray that. That means that if they say something to me that reflects that they think that about Black men, we can't ever get mad." (Wingfield, 2007). It's just a matter of time before a stereotype situation will occur at work. When it does, you have to address the individual calmly and diplomatically, but make the point that you are a skilled professional to be treated with respect.

Become an Activist. I don't mean that you walk around work shouting Black Lives Matter. I suggest that you get involved. Join an organization and become an active participant. NAACP, National Action Network, Color of Change, National Bar Association, National Black Justice Coalition, One of the Devine Nine – Sororities or Fraternities, National Association of Black Journalists, just to name a few. Maybe even join one of your work-related organizations. If you are committed to your career, get involved in a professional association and be active. We need to show our colleagues that we are leaders. By lending your expertise to an organization, you make that organization become stronger as we work towards dispelling myths about Black men.

Commit to Improving your Health & Wellness. "Research has shown that Black men who ascribed to a strong work ethic but were unable to actualize the expected male role reported increased stress and health problems and were less likely to engage in health-promoting behaviors." (Archibald, 2019). This, along with other factors, is why Black men have the lowest life expectancy of all major ethnic-sex populations in the USA. As Black men, we have to make our personal healthcare a priority by getting regular check-ups and screenings. Without your health, you have nothing. Your health should be non-negotiable.

Seek mental health counseling for yourself. Battling racism and stereotypes inside the workplace will mentally exhaust you. "Black male professionals do not reveal any sense of anger at work: we focus so much on not bringing or showing our feelings at the office, but a lot of times the office produces so much stress, you bring that back home. It's difficult to keep them both separate." (Wingfield, 2007). Once you get over the stigma of talking to a therapist, you will find that counseling will help you better cope with racism, bigotry, and micro-aggressions at work.

Seek Mentorships or Develop Mentorships. "Mentorships and supervision provide Black men with guidance, knowledge transfer, and networking opportunities, all of which are vital for their personal and professional growth. Also, mentorship allows experienced men to share their expertise, industry insights, and practical knowledge with mentees."

"Black business and tech communities may face unique challenges related to systemic racism, bias, or limited access to resources. Mentors who have experienced similar obstacles can offer guidance on navigating these challenges, sharing strategies for success and resilience."

"Finally, through good and effective mentorship, successful Black professionals can break down barriers and inspire younger generations. When aspiring entrepreneurs or technologists see people who look like they do, they achieve success, it encourages them to pursue their dreams and fosters a sense of community and belonging." (DopeBlack, 2023).

Do Not Repeat The Sins of Miles Livingston. Readers of this book can see with objective eyes that maybe I tried a little too hard to advance my career and probably burned some bridges. During that time, I was determined to be the best healthcare professional I could be. I earned a master's degree in healthcare, actively participated in the Healthcare Association and published a healthcare article, attended the Columbia University Workforce Development Program (HITECH), and diligently prepared for all my job interviews. I applied for countless jobs at that time, but it was overkill. I went overboard trying to impress people who had no respect for any of my accomplishments, which ultimately led me to Federal Court to fight a race discrimination case. I certainly would not advise anyone to follow my path.

Sacrifice Yourself. This approach is not recommended for everyone. My employer had pushed me into a corner. I was angry and had nothing to lose. I am an example of what happens to a Black Man who decides to sacrifice himself and fight against racial injustice in the workplace. Literally, I was overcome with hopelessness and felt that I had nothing else to give. I was blackballed, attacked, and shunned by women and White males, humiliated, and my reputation was damaged.

On the other hand, my employer eventually got the message. An African American man became a Finance Director within the Municipal Health System. I do not know this individual, but I noticed that there were a handful of African American men logged onto our monthly leadership zoom meeting in '2023. I looked up his name and noticed that his title said, "Finance Director." I was so happy and proud of this Black Man. Words could not describe it. He was a Brilliant Mind – an educated, knowledgeable, talented, and articulate young healthcare professional worthy of his Directorship. I pray that he has a great career, filled with respect and growth.

During my twenty-year tenure at Municipal Hospital, I only saw one Black male director. I honestly believe that suing Municipal Hospital opened their eyes so they could finally see that qualified African American Men are available to step into leadership positions. Black men that will strengthen the organization if given the opportunity. My sacrifice yielded a destroyed career and a little bit of money. However, the benefit of my sacrifice was that my employer finally heard the voice of one Angry Black Man who was discriminated against. This small voice caused a large Health System to re-evaluate the way human resources process qualified Black male employment applicants.

These are some of the keys to combating race discrimination inside the workplace. Don't be surprised to learn that hatred against Black men still exists. Unfortunately, workplace racism, although it is shrouded in secrecy, is alive and well.

The Harsh Reality

We live in this world that wants us to believe that everything is equal. The White world has been pushing forth this narrative that in America, all you have to do is work hard and educate yourself and eventually, you'll get your flowers. If you stay on the straight and narrow and keep your nose to the grindstone, the American Dream can be yours. It's a narrative that I have believed for most of my life.

Now, even after settlements and being vindicated in my battles with Municipal Hospital, I still struggle to believe that such a narrative truly exists for anyone who isn't rich, White, and male. Even when they say that they want to be diverse, they still look over Black men in the process. I've had to watch as Black women and other women of color get picked over me just because they met more than one criteria they need for their diversity programs.

And none of it is right. The same thing that's holding me back is unjustly pushing others forward and it's all a part of systemic racism. Getting chosen for the color of your skin instead of your merits is just as wrong as being passed over and it needs to stop if we're ever going to get ahead in this country. Whether management chooses to open or close a door to a member of the global majority, our race and/or gender should not be a factor.

I'm not saying that Black women don't have their own struggles in the workplace. They do. What I'm saying is that all of it is a part of a corrupt system and until we recognize what's going on, it's going to continue.

My personal truth discovery during my journey within the workplace was that there was blatant and overt racism practiced against Black men. I've learned that everyone is susceptible to unconscious bias. This bias allows racism to become normalized and invisible. Colleagues from all racial groups have expressed to me that they don't believe racism is the reason for my dilemma. However, they cannot provide me with a credible explanation as to why Black men have been left behind. The question I always ask when complaining about workplace injustice is, "Why are Black men treated so differently"? I'm sure you would agree that basically every employer or organization in the country has this or similar language written into their employment policy manuals.

BRILLIANT MINDS, IGNORANT MINDS

It is the policy of the health system to provide equal employment opportunity and treat all employees equally regardless of age, race, creed/religion, color, sex/gender... etc.

We've all encountered these words at one time or another during our careers. The point I wanted to make to my employer and the Department of Human Rights is this: If it's not race discrimination, then why are Black men not afforded "Equal Employment Opportunities?" Rather than addressing my concerns about racism, my employer chose to through money at me and sweep my situation under the rug. What a travesty. They were cowards who twisted the laws and settled the case to avoid making changes, content with maintaining the status quo.

So, yes, I finally did get a position in management, but I'm here to tell you that it took more than my education and years of experience to do it. I literally had to *make* them see me as their equal.

What I've learned since? The beat goes on. One Sunday evening, as I was sitting down to do a re-read and soft edit prior to submitting this manuscript to the publisher, I came across an article that hit the news alert on my phone. "American Nurses Association Apologizes for Racism, Past and Present." The A.N.A. is the largest and most prestigious nursing organization in the country. Where do you think its members work? Their membership is employed at top hospital networks like the "Municipal Health System." My employer and the same place I've been struggling within a racist system. Imagine that.

The article goes on to say that they have created a "Racial Reckoning Statement" and directed interested parties to the ANA website to read the statement. Of course, I immediately went to the site to read it. I really felt for all the Black nurses that I have worked with over the years. I could relate to some of the shit they had to endure from racist co-workers and bosses.

My employer's Corporate offices are housed in a new state-of-the-art office building with opulent corporate suites, including the Executive Senior Leadership team. The CEO, CFO, CIO, Hospital Administration, Nursing Administration, Human Resources, Chief Compliance Officer, Capital Projects, etc. have offices. You'd think in a place as polished as that would have moved on from racist practices. Well, you'd think wrong. I'm the best example that racism is alive and well and *not* just restricted to the nursing department. The Racial Reckoning Statement is a great spotlight to shine on the system. A nursing survey was performed by an organization called The National Commission to Address Racism in Nursing. "Survey Shows Substantial Racism in Nursing" was the impetus that prompted the Racial Reckoning Statement:

"According to more than 5,600 survey respondents, racist acts are principally perpetuated by colleagues and those in positions of power. 92% of Black Nurses that were surveyed said that they experienced racist acts from: 70% of Leaders, 68% of Patients and 66% of Peers.

One of the nurses stated, "Speaking truth to power takes courage. I have been ostracized for my advocacy and passed over for promotions." "I have felt as if there was no way I would advance my career at some facilities due to my race. This has caused stress, anxiety, and some depression." [ANA, 2021].

Sounds familiar? Personally, I commend the ANA for bringing this racial phenomenon to light. It really took a lot of strength and courage to admit that systemic and structural racism exists within the Nursing field. I've been fighting this racism battle for my entire career, most specifically the last ten years at Municipal Hospital. Yeah, they paid me off, but money doesn't take the place of career success, especially when racism still runs rampant throughout the healthcare sector. At my employer, for example, the Human Resource Department is guilty of steering Black males into lower-paying healthcare occupations.

Since Municipal Hospital was built approximately seventy years ago, not one Black male manager or director has ever been hired or promoted in the Municipal Hospital Revenue Cycle Department. Black doctors had to accept the same treatment as many of the nurses. Black male I.T. professionals were denied access to management positions. Believe me, there are enough racist practices to go around at Municipal.

Even though this was the ANA nurses stepping up to recognize racism, I wholeheartedly applaud them. The sooner you acknowledge and accept there is a problem, the sooner you can address and rectify it. I wonder what it would take for other healthcare organizations to admit to racist behaviors.

The fight still goes on, even for me. I might be in a management position, but I'm stuck in the position of Supervisor. I am under scrutiny every day. My bosses tend to nitpick my every move, maybe because I've been labeled a "troublemaker." Being a Black Man in America means that having the audacity to stand up for yourself is synonymous with being a troublemaker. But in the end, I don't mind. My story is an example of being the type of person who makes "good trouble," the kind of trouble that affects change. Whatever they might think of me, they'll think twice about challenging another Black Man who only wants to get ahead, as his female and White male colleagues do. Maybe they'll learn to view the next Black Man for his work ethic and achievements.

Corporate America doesn't realize it, but they have lessened themselves by discriminating against African American Men. Look at the sports analogy. Regardless of color, there was no doubt that Jackie Robinson, Willie Mays, and Hank Aaron were all outstanding in baseball. Michael Jordan, Bill Russell, and Wilt Chamberlain are outstanding in basketball. Jim Brown, Walter Payton, and Jerry Rice were outstanding in football. Muhammad Ali, Mike Tyson, and Sugar Ray Leonard were outstanding in boxing. Of course, there were many Caucasian men who were just as skilled and talented, but the curse of discrimination was never in their way.

What you have to realize is that for all the sports geniuses in the world, there are equal numbers of intellectual African American men available to make tremendous contributions in business, industry, agriculture, politics, economics, media, education, finance, medicine, and other sectors, but we never get the chance. Racial hatred and bigotry against African Americans, especially men, has slowed the growth and development of our nation.

Could you imagine the contributions African Americans could have made toward building our country if we had been given the chance to join equally as industry leaders and businessmen? Consider the political contributions these men could have made to address America's problems. I might be dreaming, but it's blatantly obvious that Corporate America and the nation as a whole have not progressed to their full potential because of racism.

So, what's the point? Are there incredible White men who made contributions? Absolutely! Are there gifted Women who made contributions? Absolutely! The fact is, what if Black men also wanted to make contributions in Corporate America? They would have been denied the opportunity because of racism. Racism is woven into the DNA of our country, but it is insidiously targeted towards Black Men.

Also, the last comment I will make concerning D.E.I. is that this debate doesn't have to turn into a Black -vs.- White war, or a bi-partisan back-and-forth issue. We have to look at the big picture and fairly judge it.

D.E.I./Affirmative Action individuals, businesses, and/or entities are all top quality. Just because an African American law firm gets a contract does not mean a drop in the quality of work. If a D.E.I. pilot is flying your plane, they are a superior aviator. If a D.E.I. surgeon performs a surgical procedure, the patient will receive excellence in medicine.

When Black Affirmative Action and/or D.E.I. students are granted admission to prestigious institutions, those schools are getting brilliant and gifted minds attending their universities. These students will strengthen our universities. I'm shocked that White leadership in America can't understand this. There is no need to cheapen and criticize D.E.I. programs. Just make sure they are appropriately run and then reap the benefits. There are similarities to Obamacare.

Many detractors complained about the Obama healthcare initiative, but they could not offer any alternatives. The solution was to get on board and improve Obamacare. It was and continues to be a great program.

The same scenario applies to D.E.I. programs. The only reason we have D.E.I. in the first place is that those in power have historically been unable to objectively evaluate excellence without considering skin color. Consequently, the brilliant minds of their time developed Affirmative Action and D.E.I. programs to ensure that Black individuals had access to the same resources and opportunities controlled by Whites in our country.

However, the implementation of these programs has often been flawed. Employers have exploited Title VII protections by hiring Black women and other minorities, but not Black men, under the guise of the "Protected Class" concept. This strategy allows employers to appear diverse within the race-protected category without genuinely addressing the exclusion of Black men. Since there is no specific protected category for Black men, they are often left behind, undermining the spirit and effectiveness of Affirmative Action and D.E.I. programs.

It's simple, really—not rocket science, just common sense. Black men only want the same equality that everyone else enjoys. For those who advocate for Color-Blindness, including some Supreme Court Justices, my response is that you can't suddenly adopt Color-Blindness after 300 years of racial discrimination against Black people in America. We have been irreparably harmed by racism, and steps must be taken to rectify the years of injustice perpetuated against us. These injustices have spilled over into Corporate America, where Black men bear the brunt. We are ready for fair and equitable treatment going forward.

Until then, it's like I said. The beat goes on…

"Get in good trouble, necessary trouble, and help redeem the soul of America."

–Congressman John Lewis.

VERNON M. O'GARRA

Readers Book Club Guide for

BRILLIANT MINDS, IGNORANT MINDS

by Vernon M. O'Garra

Discussion Questions

1. Throughout the manuscript, Miles describes himself and others as having "brilliant minds but ignorant minds." How does this dichotomy manifest in different characters and institutions? What does this reveal about how knowledge and blindness can coexist?

2. Were there any moments where you strongly disagreed with the author? What sparked that reaction? If you could ask the author one question after reading this book, what would it be and why?

3. Have you ever experienced a time when you didn't receive the support you expected from your boss and all your hard work went unappreciated? Did you feel this lack of support was racially motivated? How did you deal with incompetent leadership inside your organization?

4. Miles is concerned that H.R. cannot see his side of the discrimination argument. What is your feeling? Does he have a valid concern?

5. After years of being held back, Miles reaches his boiling point and files a race discrimination complaint against his employer. What do you think about his decision? Do you feel he had been treated fairly? What would you have done if you were in Miles shoes?

6. Do you find irony in the fact that Miles decides to remain employed at Municipal Hospital after receiving a discrimination settlement? Do you think you could remain employed with the same organization after suing them?

7. Miles talks about living a double-life, "The Me Nobody Knows" (Chapter 13). How do you think he is able to hold it all together, throughout all the turmoil in his life?

8. Miles believes that "Networking" is the avenue to follow, to land a management position. However, his Director discourages his approach. Do you think his Director would have advised her female subordinates differently? Why?

9. Deep down inside, Miles was infuriated that a Federal Judge would allow Municipal Hospital to submit redacted emails into evidence. Do you think the Judge made the right decision?

10. Miles believes that D.E.I. programs are not run properly. When set up correctly, D.E.I. programs do not lower standards; they deliver superior African American students, job candidates, and outstanding minority vendors. What are your thoughts about D.E.I. programs?

11. Miles frequently discusses how discrimination is often "invisible" to those not experiencing it. What were some instances where this

invisibility manifested, and how did it complicate his efforts to address workplace discrimination?

12. Miles concedes that his past criticisms of Black women came from "a place filled with anger and misunderstanding." Do you feel his attitude is valid, or does he overreact? How might personal struggles impact our perception of others' success, particularly across gender lines within the same racial group?

13. The author dedicates a chapter in the book to Black women. He references a quote from Maya Angelou: "You may not control all the events that happen to you, but you can decide not to be reduced by them." How does this philosophy manifest in the experiences of Black women in corporate America as described in the chapter?

14. The author details the complex relationship between Black men and Black women in the workplace. How does Miles' perspective on this relationship evolve throughout his journey, and what insights does this offer about intersectionality in professional environments?

15. Miles concludes his story by talking about the True Cost of Racism to validate his argument about ongoing racial injustice in this country. Why do you think he choose to highlight the "True Cost of Racism"? How does this framing shift the conversation about workplace discrimination to broader societal issues?

Additional Reading and References

Akhu, A. (2024, April 17). *Mentorship and Sponsorship: The Importance of Black*

Women's Networks in Career Development. Received from Dr. Akhu Blog: https://www.drakhu.com/blog/mentorship-and-sponsorship-the-importance-of-black-women-s-networks-in-career-development

AL CAMPANIS GETS CAUGHT OFF BASE: [SPORTS FINAL, C EDITION]. . (1987, April 10). *Chicago Tribune*.

Amadou Diallo Killed By Police. (1999, February 4). Retrieved from History.com: www.history.com/this-day-in-history/amadou-diallo-killed-by-police-new-york-city

American Nurses Association. (2021). *Our Racial Reckoning Statement.* Retrieved from NursingWorld.org:

https://www.nursingworld.org/practice-policy/workforce/racism-in-nursing/RacialReckoningStatement/

American Nurses Association. (2022). *Survey Shoes Substantial Racism in Nursing.* Retrieved from Nursingworld.org: https://www.nursingworld.org/practice-policy/workforce/racism-in-nursing/national-commission-to-address-racism-in-nursing

Basler, B. (1982, June 23). Black Man is Killed by Mob in Brooklyn: Attack Called Racial. *The New York Times*, pp. Section A, Page 1. Retrieved from nytimes.com.

Beller, A. H. (1982). Occupational Segregation by Sex: Determinants and Changes.". *Journal of Human Resources*, Vol. 17, no. 3, pp. 371-92.

Boneparth, E. (1960). Black Businessmen and Community Responsibility. *Phylon*, vol. 37, no. 1, pp. 26-43.

Broderick, D. (August, 8 1990). Cherry Fued Sparks Riot at Korean Deli. *New York Post*, p. pg. 12.

Brown, S. M. (2023, December 13). The Forgotten Legacy of the Black Man who blazed a trail for Stephen A. Smith and others to make millions. *Call & Post, All-Ohio edition; Cleveland, Ohio.*, pp. Vol. 10, Issue 50, Pg. 2C.

Bullock, C., & Rodgers, H. (1976). Institutional Racism: Prerequisites, Freezing, and Mapping. *Phylon*, 37(3),212-223.

Campanis, A. (1987, April 6). ABC News. (T. Koppel, Interviewer)

Christopher, R. (2002). Springsteen, Diallo, and the NYC Police: An Intersection of Race, Gender and Class. *Race, Gender, and Class Journal*, pp. Vol. 9 No. 3 pp. 159-174.

Claude, J. (1986). POVERTY PATTERNS FOR BLACK MEN AND WOMEN. *The Black Scholar*, Vol. 17, no. 5, pp. 20-23.

Doane, A. ". (2016). Beyond Color-Blindness: (Re) Theorizing Racial Ideology. *Social Perspectives*, vol. 60, no 5, pp. 975-91.

Dope Black. (2023, June 28). *The Role Of Mentorship In Black Business And Tech Communities.*

Retrieved from Business & Politics: https://dopeblack.org/the-role-of-mentorship-in-black-business-and-tech-communities/?t

Farber, M. (1990, May 7). Black-Korean Who-Pushed-Whom Festers. *New York Times*, pp. Section B, Page 1.

Feagin, J. R., & Ducey, K. (2017). Elite White Men Ruling – Who, What, Where, When and How. *Taylor and Francis*, 71-90.

Herbert, B. (1999, April 4). Beyond the Diallo Case: Herbert Bob. *New York Times*, p. Section 4.

Holmes, S. A. (1996, July 3). Clinton Seeks Money to Halt Church FIres. *The New York Times*, p. A16.

Jet Magazine. (1979, 20 September). Black Promotes Gripes' Economic, Not Racial: BMA. *Jet Magazin*, p. 60.

Jet Magazine. (1979, September 20). New Black Concert Promoters Group Forms. *Jet Magazine*, p. 60.

Kendi, I. X. (2019). *How to be an Anti-Racist.* New York: One World.

Law Insider. (n.d.). *Racial Equity Definition.* Retrieved from LawInsider.org: https://www.lawinsider.com/dictionary/racial-equity

Lawson, T. O. (2023, March 29). *Huggy Bean.* Retrieved from Huggy Bean.com: www.huggybean.com

Lewis, J. (2020, March 1). Speech on Edmund Pettus Bridge Commemorating "Bloody Sunday". Selma, Alabama, USA.

Loewen, J. (2009). Sundown Towns and Counties: Racial Exclusion in the South. *Southern Cultures*, Vol. 15, No. 1, pp.22-47.

Lu, J. (2024, March 20). *Duke School of Medicine denies lowering admissions standards for DEI goals as alleged by Ben Shapiro, Elon Musk.* Retrieved from The Duke Chronicle.com: https://www.dukechronicle.com/article/2024/03/duke-university-health-school-of-medicine-dei-diversity-equity-inclusion-allegations-lowered-admissions-standards-ben-shapiro-elon-musk-congress-dan-bishop-greg-murphy-department-of-surgery

Martin, J. (2014, July 2). *The economy's Troubling Double Standard for Black Men.* Retrieved from The Washington Post: https://www.washingtonpost.com/news/wonk/wp/2014/07/02/the-economys-troubling-double-standard-for-black-men/

MARYAM ABDUL-ALEEM Special to,the AmNews. (2009, Aug 27). Firefighters still fighting discrimination federal class-action lawsuit. New York Amsterdam News (1962-) Retrieved from https://0-www-proquest-com.search.livebrary.com/newspapers/firefighters-still-fighting-discrimination/docview/2663261451/se-2

Maume, D. J. (1999). Occupational Segregation and the Career Mobility of White Men and Women. *Social Forces*, pp. vol. 77, no. 4, , pp. 1433–59.

McCray, V. (2023, October 24). *Federal Lawsuit Alleges Underfunding of Georgia's Three Public HBCUs.* Retrieved from AJC.com: http://www.ajc.com/education/federal-lawsuit-alleges-underfunding-of-georgias-three-public-hbcus/PJDA4JNJSNBGZDXYRDXJS2RJHI/

McIntyre, T. (2022, June). *Occupational Mentorship & the Black Female in the Corporate*

Midsouth. Business Management Research and Applications. A Cross-Disciplinary

Journal, (ISSN 2769-4666). vol. 1, no 2.

Meyer, Paul J. "Effective Personal Productivity." *Leadership Management, Inc.* Lesson 3, 1994, pp. 1-3.

New York Times. (2019, January 6). The Disappearing Boys of Huntington High. *The New York Times Magazine*, pp. 32-45. Retrieved from New York Times Magazine.

Newsday. (1980, December 9). John Lennon Slain By Waiting Gunman : Ex-Beatle John Lennon is Shot to Death in City. *Newsday*, pp. 1-3.

Nix, E. (2017, 16 May). *Tuskegee Experiment: The Infamous Syphilis Study.* Retrieved from History.com:

https://www.history.com/news/the-infamous-40-year-tuskegee-study

Noguera, P. A. (1997). Reconsidering the 'Crisis' Of the Black Male in America. *Social Justice*, 147-64.

O'Garra, V. (2012, November 9-15). Affordable Health Care, A One-Stop Shop. *Long Island Business News*, p. 23.

Oxford English Dictionary. (n.d.). *Ambition Definition.* Retrieved from oed.com.

Paine, T. (1776, April 24). A Response to Cato's Fourth through Seventh Letters.

Paine, T. (1776). To Cato. *The Forester, Pensnsylvania Journal.*

Parker, L. (2003). Critical Race Theory and Its Implications for Methodology and Policy Analysis in Higher Education Desegregation. *Counterpoints*, Vol. 19, pp. 145–80.

Rath, T. (2007). *"Clifton StrengthsFinder."* Gallup Press. Library of Congress Control Number: 2006938575. ISBN: 978-1-59562-015-6

Ritchie, M. (2023). BLACKBALLED? Class action alleges the NFL discriminates against BLACK coaches. *ABA Journal*, Vol 109, number 1, p.46.

Roberts, S. (1985, 8 August). FARRAKHAN SAYS HIS CRITICS ADD 'FUEL TO THE FIRE'. *New York Times.*

Robinson, S. (2020, January 24). *Black Guy Stuck in Racism Infinity Loop When Bank Won't Deposit His Discrimination Settlement Checks.* Retrieved from Wonkette.com: https://www.wonkette.com/p/black-guy-stuck-in-racism-infinity-loop-when-michigan-bank-wont-deposit-his-discrimination-settlement-checks

Rothstein, R. (2015). The Making of Ferguson. *Journal of Affordable Housing & Community Development Law*, 24(2), 165–204.

Rowe, L. (n.d.). *The Leonard Rowe Story.* Retrieved from Theclientkiller.org: http://www.theclientkiller.org/rowe_story.php

Sauter, V. G. (1968). *Nightmare in Detroit.* Regnery.

Sav, G. (1997). Separate and Unequal: State Financing of Historically Black Colleges and Universities. *The Journal of Blacks in Education*, No. 15, pp. 101-04.

Schumacher, E. (1979, August 23). Black Music Promoters Battle Whites' Control of Marketing. *The Register Guard*, p. 6D.

Solomon, A. (2023, December 13). *Enough Is Enough: Supporting Black Women in the*

Workplace from Advocacy to Allyship. Retrieved from A. Solomon Recruits :

https://www.asolomonrecruits.com/enough-is-enough-supporting-black-women-in-the-workplace-from-advocacy-to-allyship-part-1

Suggs, E. (2013, December 14). *The Freedom Fighter: How Atlanta's C.T. Vivian Changed History.* Retrieved from AJC News: www.ajc.com/news/newsmedleystory2195015/wHV8RSPcwkkGrkpvR9779J/

Sullivan, S., & Tuana, N. (2007). *Race and Epistemologies of Ignorance.* New York: State University of New York Press.

Tabahriti, S. (2022, September 28). *Media mogul Byron Allen is suing McDonald's for $10 billion, claiming it overlooks Black-owned media for its advertising.* Retrieved from Business Insider India:https://www.businessinsider.in/retail/news/media-mogul-byron-allen-is-suing-mcdonalds-for-10-billion-claiming-it-overlooks-black-owned-media-for-its-advertising/articleshow/94504426.cms

Taylor, E. (1998). A Primer on Critical Race Theory. *The Journal of Blacks in Higher Education*, 122-24.

Terry, D. (1990, August 28). Dinkins Responds to 2d Boycott of a Korean Store. *The New York Times*, pp. Section B, pg. 1.

About the Author

Vernon Michael O'Garra is a healthcare finance professional and emerging writer based in Long Island, New York. With over two decades of experience in healthcare finance, he brings a unique perspective to his writing, having published thought-provoking commentaries on healthcare policy in various publications.

Vernon has volunteered his time to assist with several healthcare initiatives, including helping countless individuals navigate access to healthcare insurance. He draws inspiration from his African American heritage and his experiences growing up during the heyday of the civil rights movement.

Vernon holds a Master's degree in Healthcare Administration from the University of Phoenix and has contributed significantly to professional healthcare associations. "Brilliant Minds, Ignorant Minds" is his first novel.

VERNON M. O'GARRA